HOLLYWOOD
TRAITORS

HOLLYWOOD TRAITORS

BLACKLISTED SCREENWRITERS
AGENTS OF STALIN, ALLIES OF HITLER

ALLAN H. RYSKIND
EDITOR-AT-LARGE, *HUMAN EVENTS*

REGNERY
HISTORY

Regnery History™ is a trademark of Salem Communications Holding Corporation; Regnery® is a registered trademark of Salem Communications Holding Corporation.

Library of Congress Cataloging-in-Publication data
Ryskind, Allan H.
  Hollywood traitors : blacklisted screenwriters : agents of Stalin, allies of Hitler / Allan H. Ryskind.
    pages cm
  Includes bibliographical references and index.
  1. Motion picture industry--Political aspects--United States--History--20th century. 2. Blacklisting of authors--United States--History--20th century. 3. Screenwriters--Political activity--United States. 4. Communism and motion pictures--United States--History. I. Title.
  PN1993.5.U6R97 2015
  384'.80973--dc23
                         2014028655

ISBN 978-1-62157-206-0

Published in the United States by
Regnery History
An imprint of Regnery Publishing
300 New Jersey Avenue NW
Washington, DC 20001
www.RegneryHistory.com

Manufactured in the United States of America

10 9 8 7 6 5 4 3 2 1

Books are available in quantity for promotional or premium use. For information on discounts and terms, please visit our website: www.Regnery.com.

Distributed to the trade by
Perseus Distribution
250 West 57th Street
New York, NY 10107

CONTENTS

CAST OF CHARACTERS

THE HOLLYWOOD TEN

Alvah Bessie was one of the celebrated ten screenwriters who in 1947 refused to testify before the House Un-American Activities Committee and were blacklisted in Hollywood. Bessie, who fought on the Soviet side in the Spanish Civil war, bragged about inserting pro-Soviet propaganda that was "subversive as all hell" into the 1943 film *Action in the North Atlantic*.

Herbert Biberman attacked U.S. aid to Britain so fiercely during the time of the Hitler-Stalin Pact that an FBI agent suspected Biberman, who was in fact Jewish, of being a Nazi.

Lester Cole boasted in his autobiography about putting "social realities" and his political "feelings" (translation: Red propaganda) into Hollywood films.

Edward Dmytryk, director of many successful movies, including *The Caine Mutiny,* was the only one of the Hollywood Ten ever to renounce Communism completely.

Ring Lardner Jr., one of the best-known Hollywood Ten figures, died in 2000, laden with honors and acclaim for refusing to tell HUAC whether he had ever been a Communist.

John Howard Lawson was known as "the enforcer" of the Communist Party line in Hollywood after he was dispatched from New York by Party headquarters to monitor writers.

Albert Maltz had briefly bucked the Party line—until vicious verbal attacks from his friends and associates brought him back into the fold.

Samuel Ornitz had been active in the "American Peace Mobilization" during the Hitler-Stalin Pact but quickly became a proponent for American entry into the war once Hitler broke the Pact and attacked Russia.

Adrian Scott had been raked over the coals by higher-ups in the Party for toning down the Communist propaganda in the script for *Cornered,* a 1945 film noir.

Dalton Trumbo wrote many excellent films, including *Roman Holiday, Spartacus,* and *Papillon.* He was also a hard-core Party member, a fervent supporter of Stalinist Russia and Kim Il-sung's North Korea, and an apologist for Nazi Germany until Hitler double-crossed Stalin and invaded the Soviet Union. Yet to this day he is regarded as a hero in Hollywood.

OTHER KEY PLAYERS

Laurence Beilenson, attorney for the Screen Writers Guild, was sure that Red-led factionalism was destroying the Guild.

Michael Blankfort lost his Communist friends after his 1952 testimony before HUAC, though he refused to name anyone as a fellow subversive and clearly lied about his strong support of Communism. The unanswered question is why HUAC thanked him for his dubious testimony.

Roy Brewer was the labor leader who almost singlehandedly defeated the Communist effort to take over the Hollywood labor unions.

James Cain, a major Screen Writers Guild supporter, conceded that, while he disliked many of the Guild's enemies, the charge that "we are loaded with Communists…is true."

John Bright created the gangster movie genre and was a founding member of both the Screen Writers Guild and the Hollywood section of the Communist Party USA.

Hugo Butler was the dyed-in-the-wool Stalinist who talked Dalton Trumbo out of his quondam pacifism after Hitler broke the Hitler-Stalin Pact and Stalin suddenly wanted America to join the war.

Richard Collins, screenwriter and prominent CPUSA member from 1938 on, co-wrote *Song of Russia* with fellow Party member Paul Jarrico; actor Robert Taylor felt the film was stuffed with Soviet propaganda and almost turned down his lead role.

John Dewey was a prominent American intellectual, education reformer, and leftist who resigned from the League of American Writers in mid-1939, realizing it was a creature of the Communist Party.

Martin Dies, Democratic U.S. representative from Texas and chairman of the House Un-American Activities Committee in 1938, charged that the Screen Writers Guild was controlled by Communists—but major hearings on Communism in Hollywood were not held until after World War II.

Max Eastman, an early supporter of the "proletarian class struggle," nonetheless could not stomach the absolute subordination of literature to Stalinist politics. His reporting on the literary scene in the Soviet Union produced turmoil in the ranks of the Left, and Eastman later renounced Communism.

Gerhart Eisler had plenty of supporters after his very public exposure as a top Comintern agent. Among them: Hollywood Ten figures Dalton Trumbo and John Howard Lawson. Also: Howard Koch, chief screenwriter for *Casablanca* and *Mission to Moscow*, and E. Y. Harburg, the lyricist for the *Wizard of Oz*. Eisler would flee America and end up as a propagandist for East Germany.

Benjamin Gitlow was a top Communist Party leader and a member of the inner sanctum of the Comintern, the Moscow-based group that controlled

Communist parties in every country where they existed—but he became an influential anti-Communist after a confrontation with Stalin himself.

Dashiell Hammett, the long-time lover of Lillian Hellman, invented the "hard-boiled" detective story genre and provided story lines for *The Thin Man* and *The Maltese Falcon*. He was also head of the League of American Writers, a major Communist front, when it turned on a dime from appeasing to opposing the Nazis after Hitler attacked Russia. David Lang testified that Hammett was part of a "strong writers' front" in Hollywood, including many of the Hollywood Ten figures, who worked to ensure that film content was in accordance with the Communist line.

Lillian Hellman's script for *The North Star* was embarrassing propaganda on behalf of the famine-producing collective farm system Stalin had ruthlessly imposed in the 1930s. But Hellman, who lied in her memoir *Scoundrel Time* when she denied she was ever a Party member, was beyond embarrassment, as her duplicitous testimony before HUAC and her dishonest memoirs and other writings would demonstrate.

Sidney Hook was a prominent American intellectual who initially embraced Communism but became a ferocious critic of its ideology.

Rupert Hughes warned of a plot to turn the Authors League into a kind of Stalinist soviet with power over all the writers in Hollywood.

Paul Jarrico spiced up dialogue for films (including even a Gene Kelly movie, *Thousands Cheer*) with Red propaganda and preened himself on his performance as a "most unfriendly witness" before HUAC in 1951. Yet he eventually conceded that the Party's undeviating backing of Stalin and the Soviet Union was a "disaster."

Dorothy Jones was the former chief film analyst for the Office of War Information who prepared a 205-page paper on Communism and the movies for the liberal Fund for the Republic. Both Jones and the Fund concluded that there was no Communist propaganda in the movies—but her detailed findings showed otherwise.

Gordon Kahn, managing editor of *The Screen Writer*, the SWG's official publication, which poured out Communist propaganda monthly, was identified as a Communist by over a dozen HUAC witnesses. He was also Morrie Ryskind's next-door neighbor.

Elia Kazan was honored in 1999 with a lifetime achievement Oscar for films including *A Streetcar Named Desire, East of Eden,* and *On the Waterfront.* But some in the audience refused to applaud, because Kazan had not only been a friendly witness before HUAC more than fifty years before but even took out an ad in the *New York Times* urging former Communists to testify before HUAC.

Eugene Lyons was a United Press correspondent who spent six years in the Soviet Union, became disillusioned by Soviet Communism, and wrote devastating critiques of Stalin and his pawns in America in the 1930s and early '40s.

Joseph McCarthy was the well-known Red-hunting senator who, despite popular belief, never belonged to HUAC, which was a committee in the House of Representatives (not the Senate) and never investigated Hollywood. His anti-Communist crusade began in 1950, after the Hollywood Ten had already been indicted for contempt of Congress and blacklisted.

Arthur Miller, the celebrated playwright, was never quite sure whether he had applied for Communist Party membership. He lauded blacklisted Communists and Comintern agent Gerhart Eisler and in *The Crucible* attacked those who cooperated with HUAC. His ardor for the Soviet Union cooled in the '60s—his treatment by HUAC, he claimed, had persuaded him to side with Russian dissidents.

Willi Münzenberg was the German Comintern agent responsible for creating Communist-front organizations all over the world, including the Hollywood Anti-Nazi League. But both he and his wife later turned against the Soviet Union.

Clifford Odets wrote the screenplay for *The General Died at Dawn*, starring Gary Cooper, a transparent piece of propaganda against Chiang Kai-shek and in favor of the Communist revolutionaries in China.

Ernest Pascal was the Screen Writers Guild president who ignited a firestorm and nearly destroyed the SWG by making public his strategy for the Guild to control all Hollywood writers and dominate the studios.

Abraham Polonsky was a screenwriter and director who often hosted meetings of a secret cell of the Communist Party at his home. In 1950 he took the Fifth before HUAC rather than testify whether he was a Communist and refused to say whether he would be willing to bear arms to defend the United States.

Ayn Rand, a Russian émigré, had become an ardent anti-Communist because of her experiences growing up in the Soviet Union. The author of *We the Living*, *The Fountainhead*, and *Atlas Shrugged* gave a devastating critique before HUAC of the WWII movie *Song of Russia*, written by two devout Communists: Richard Collins and Paul Jarrico.

Morrie Ryskind, a playwright and screenwriter with several Marx Brothers productions to his credit, in 1944 helped found the Motion Picture Alliance for the Preservation of American Ideals, which confronted the radicals head-on and was instrumental in bringing about the HUAC hearings on Hollywood in 1947. He was my father.

Donald Ogden Stewart worked on such classics as *The Philadelphia Story* and *A Night to Remember*. A key figure in the League of American Writers, he eventually admitted that he was a "revolutionary Socialist" who favored overthrowing the American government by force and violence.

MORRIE RYSKIND: HOLLYWOOD ANTI-COMMUNIST [AND MY FATHER]

Without Morrie Ryskind, *Hollywood Traitors* would never have been written. True, Tom Winter, my long-time colleague and friend at *Human Events*, and Stan Evans, the prominent conservative writer, scholar, and humorist, goaded me into turning my articles on the topic of Communism among the screenwriters in the movie colony into a book. But those articles could never have been written if it hadn't been for my dad's real-life experiences.

His biography is extraordinary. His parents lived the success story of so many Russian Jewish immigrants who had fled the pogroms in Czarist Russia to come to America. Originally living in a somewhat impoverished section in Brooklyn in the late 1890s, Abe and Ida moved a few years later to Washington

Heights, a more upscale neighborhood, where Abe became the proud owner of a stationery store, allowing the family to secure a solid middle-class lifestyle.

Their only son showed sparks of genius early on. On entering grammar school (when such schools had tough standards), he was reading at a sixth-grade level and soon devouring every word in the dictionary. Because of his off-the-charts grade average, he earned a scholarship from the prestigious private high school, Townsend Harris Hall, where he became the class valedictorian. His graduation speech was in *Greek*—tedious for the audience, perhaps, but a towering educational feat even for that era.

He attended the Columbia School of Journalism when it first opened in 1913, quickly making a name for himself in a talented class. Among his classmates were George Sokolsky, who became one of the most popular and influential political columnists in the country and played an important role in the anti-Communist fight in Hollywood, and Max Schuster, who founded the powerful Simon and Schuster publishing house.

With an abundance of wit and humor, Morrie wrote for the major student newspaper, *The Spectator*, and edited the monthly humor magazine, *The Jester*, a job that permitted him to satirize President Nicholas Murray Butler as "Czar Nicholas." But not without consequence. Enraged, Butler tossed my dad out of school six weeks before graduation.

My dad had become an even bigger campus celebrity for his frequent contributions to "The Conning Tower," a widely read literary column by Franklin P. Adams (F. P. A.) in the *Herald Tribune*. He felt a certain pride in appearing in the same space as George S. Kaufman, Dorothy Parker, Robert Benchley, and James Thurber, each of whom would ride to fame on the capacity to make people laugh.

My father's campus writings, light verse (a very popular item in those days), skits, lyrics, and a book of poetry (*Unaccustomed as I Am*) caught the attention of theater and Hollywood bigwigs. So after a hitch with Joseph Pulitzer's *World* as a newsman, he scribbled scenes for famous silent-film star Katherine Mac-Donald and produced public relations magic for Fox Pictures. And then, at the age of twenty-nine, he was suddenly tapped for greatness by George S. Kaufman himself, now a lion of Broadway. Kaufman and Ryskind became an enormously successful writing team.

Kaufman initially asked my dad to join him in crafting material for the irreverent Marx Brothers comedy team. They would write two of the Marx Brothers' very early plays, *The Cocoanuts* (music and lyrics by Irving Berlin) and *Animal Crackers* (music by Harry Ruby; lyrics by Bert Kalmar). They would then team up to write a groundbreaking political comedy, the 1931 Pulitzer Prize–winning musical, *Of Thee I Sing*, with George and Ira Gershwin doing the score and lyrics.

The Marx Brothers plays and *Sing* are still staged all over the country (in fact, the world), and the Marx Brothers films do a brisk business on Netflix and frequently turn up on TV. (Which, in turn, happily allows my sister and me to *still* receive modest royalty checks.)

My dad soon succumbed to the lure of Hollywood, where there was a lucrative living in a ragweed-free zone, and he carved out another stellar career there. He adapted *The Cocoanuts* and *Animal Crackers* for the screen; wrote, with Kaufman, an original Marx Brothers film, *A Night at the Opera* (which revived Groucho's career); and participated in the writing of more than fifty movies, including *Stage Door* and *My Man Godfrey*, two of the twentieth century's most popular films.

Alas, I not only didn't inherit my dad's talent but had no inclination to write fiction in any form. My folks noticed that I seemed to give little thought as to whether I enjoyed a film but placed much greater store on whether the movie depicted actual events—foreshadowing my life as a reporter.

And while I was happy that my dad made a living that permitted me to grow up in a very nice neighborhood (Beverly Hills, *sans* swimming pool and tennis court, however), my passion was for conservative economics and anti-Communism.

I have spent a lifetime as a reporter, editor, and author defending conservative beliefs—which, even at my advanced age, still mirror most of my dad's core views. Although my positions have shifted somewhat and picked up some nuances over the decades, I still believe he was essentially right, particularly for the times he lived in.

Morrie Ryskind began as an anti-war socialist and trended rightward, turning to the Republican Party in 1940 and never looking back. In the postwar period, he would write for such conservative publications as the *Freeman* and *Human Events*, become good friends with Bill Buckley, help him found *National Review* in 1955, and adorn the publication as a frequent contributor. He also wrote a nationally syndicated column that was popular with conservatives in the '60s and '70s.

I learned about my dad's political leanings early on. Though Morrie had voted for FDR in 1936, he became disenchanted with Roosevelt's spending programs and positively irate when he learned that FDR would run for a third term, breaking the hallowed precedent set by George Washington.

Not shy about letting friend and foe alike know where he stood—Richard Nixon would call him "a peppery fellow"—my father decided to use me, at the tender age of six, as his political prop. The Ryskinds had box seats at Gilmore Stadium in Los Angeles, where we would customarily watch the Hollywood Stars, a Triple-A baseball club, play on Sunday afternoon.

In the 1940 election, when FDR ran for term three, my dad saddled me with what I remember as the largest and heaviest political button ever devised—promoting Wendell Willkie, FDR's GOP opponent—and off we went to the game.

I was hardly a husky kid, and my slight frame felt as if it were being pulled toward the ground by the enormous button snapped onto my jacket. I got lots of stares, most of them unfriendly (Hollywood was largely liberal, even then), but I did enjoy the attention. And so did my dad.

Although my dad hardly needed my assistance, I decided early on to defend his politics in arguments with my frequently more liberal peers. From my grammar school days (Elizabeth Taylor was a grade or two ahead of me), my friends recall that I used to carry around a wealth of statistics and notes on little scraps of paper, all proving that my dad was right to denounce FDR's domestic and foreign policies.

When my seventh- and eighth-grade classmates and I were finished playing football or baseball after school hours, I would engage them in political discussions. Triumphantly pulling out these crumpled pieces of paper to flash statistics before their eyes, I would reveal that FDR's wild spending sprees had come to nought—the jobless situation not having improved much after his first two terms in office. (These were stats I had dug up on my own, the inner reporter having already begun to blossom.)

But I was most known for my zealous anti-Communism, including my denunciation of FDR's deal with Stalin in 1945 at Yalta (my view of the conference was largely absorbed from my dad and his friends). All the way through Beverly Hills High, Pomona College, a two-year stint in the U.S. Army, and then UCLA's school of journalism, I would warn my friends and colleagues about the dangers of Soviet Russia and the penetration of Communists in government, the unions, and, yes, Hollywood itself.

Initially, I defended my dad out of a sense of loyalty to the family patriarch. But my views on Communism were also shaped by a growing knowledge of the issue, which could be traced to my father's political activities, my voracious reading on the topic, and my interactions with his very knowledgeable friends and acquaintances who came to our house over the years.

The well-known left-wing intellectual Sidney Hook, who initially embraced Soviet Communism but then became a ferocious and very potent critic of its ideology, dropped in occasionally. So did the Russian émigré Ayn Rand, author of *The Fountainhead* and *Atlas Shrugged* and a star witness at those famous 1947 hearings on Hollywood before the House Un-American Activities Committee (HUAC).

Once I even met Benjamin Gitlow, a top Communist Party leader in the late 1920s, who became a member of the inner sanctum of the Comintern (the Moscow-based group that controlled Communist parties in every country where they existed) and then in 1929 was kicked out of the Party after a confrontational face-to-face meeting with the murderous Joseph Stalin himself. (I still treasure Gitlow's inscription to me in *The Whole of Their Lives*, his enlightening exposé of what it meant to be a Party member.) I had only very brief encounters with some of these anti-Communist celebrities, but meeting such folks greatly stoked my interest in the Soviet Union and Communist subversion.

Freda Utley, the famous anti-Communist author, and Roy Brewer, the labor leader who proved instrumental in crushing the Red effort to control the Hollywood unions in the 1940s, left far more indelible impressions on me. I knew them both, and their extraordinary tales. Brave and knowledgeable, they had dealt directly with the Communists over a long period of time, Freda in Britain and Roy in America.

Freda, who joined the British Communist Party in the 1920s, had married a Russian Communist, Arcadi Berdichevsky. During the period of Stalin's Great Purge of Communist Party members, Arcadi was arrested in Moscow in 1936 for reasons that are still unclear, put in a labor camp, and never seen by Freda again. She wrote several moving accounts of her frantic efforts to find her husband and her massive disillusionment with Communism, including *The Dream We Lost* and *Lost Illusion*. I came to know Freda fairly well, particularly in her later years. In 2005 her son, Jon, a very dear friend, visited the labor camp in which his father had been imprisoned and discovered from the Soviet records that his dad had been executed for leading a protest for better treatment.

Roy Brewer, a tough, no-nonsense labor leader, was one of my dad's closest friends and became a good friend of mine as well. He figures prominently in this book. Roy, a loyal Democrat for much of his life, almost singlehandedly defeated the Communist effort to take over the Hollywood unions—not the talent guilds, but the labor unions comprised of the behind-the-scenes men and women who built the sets, did the camera work, and operated the sound systems.

I also soaked up enormous amounts of anti-Communist literature that poured into our home, including the socialist-inclined *New Leader*, Frank Hanighen's *Human Events* (a paper I would eventually own, with Tom Winter), the *Freeman*, the *Saturday Evening Post*, the *Reader's Digest*, and the *American Mercury*. I would devour congressional reports (which I found far more exciting than Saturday night dates) and the findings put out by the California Un-American Activities Committee.

There were several books that had a major impact on my thinking as well, including Eugene Lyons's *Assignment in Utopia* and *The Red Decade* (my dad knew Lyons well), Manya Gordon's 1941 scholarly *Workers before and after Lenin*, and *Human Events*' 1946 *Blueprint for World Conquest*.

Lyons, a United Press correspondent initially enamored of Stalin, spent six years in the Soviet Union, then wrote devastating critiques of Moscow and Stalin's pawns in America in the 1930s and early '40s. Gordon's work made hash of the fantasy that Communism had created an economic paradise in the USSR.

Blueprint for World Conquest included translations of actual documents published by the Communist International (Comintern), the Stalin-controlled organization that issued instructions to Communist parties around the world. This book, published by *Human Events*, was the brainchild of Henry Regnery, who later established the prestigious Regnery publishing house. *Blueprint* also included an introduction by William Henry Chamberlin, a Russian scholar and ex–Soviet sympathizer who had earned enormous credibility as an expert on the Soviet Union.

My dad's experiences were also crucial to my understanding of what the Hollywood Reds were up to. A strong supporter of the Screen Writers Guild (SWG) when it was founded in the 1930s, he soon became disenchanted with the SWG's far-Left faction.

He vigorously fought that faction, believing the radical writers were far more interested in exploiting the SWG as a vehicle for their far-Left agenda than in resolving differences between management and labor on bread-and-butter issues. So alarmed was my father by the Reds' influence that in 1944 he helped found the Motion Picture Alliance for the Preservation of American Ideals (MPA), which confronted the radicals head-on and was instrumental in bringing about the seminal HUAC hearings on Hollywood in 1947. Among the MPA's members over the years: John Wayne, Robert Taylor, Roy Brewer, Ayn Rand, and Walt Disney. My dad also testified before HUAC as a friendly witness, discussing Communist penetration of the Screen Writers Guild.

In short, I come to this subject with some background and knowledge that cannot be easily dismissed by critics. Anyone interested in this period, even if they disagree with my opinions, will discover important information they were probably not aware of. And I fervently hope that what I have written would have pleased the people who fought the determined Red effort to control the American film industry—especially my dad.

CHAPTER ONE

THE STALINIST TEN

According to liberal legend, richly embroidered by the media, Hollywood was a wonderfully happy town until the year 1947, when something terrible, on the order of the San Francisco earthquake, took place. Ten members of the movie colony—men bursting with innocence and idealism—were suddenly hauled before the wicked House Un-American Activities Committee (HUAC), where they were pilloried for their "progressive" views by publicity-hungry, bigoted, and venal politicians who accused them of being Communists. With a dash of bravado and belligerence, they refused to respond to any questions about their political beliefs, insisting they were protected by the Bill of Rights and, in particular, the First Amendment.

With a wave of "McCarthyite" hysteria sweeping the nation (in point of fact, Joe McCarthy had been in the Senate for less than a year and had yet to surface in the national media), they were indicted and eventually sent to prison for contempt of Congress. The Ten were also "blacklisted"—that is, they were barred from working in the motion picture industry for refusing to cooperate with the Committee. What's more, the HUAC hearings set off yet another wave of anti-Red hysteria in which hundreds of writers, actors, and directors were driven from the entertainment media in violation of their "freedom of thought." For the Dream Factory, the Dark Night of Fascism had descended. Though the memory of those years has faded, the Hollywood community has neither forgotten nor forgiven.

In a lengthy series for the *Los Angeles Times*, Patrick Goldstein claimed that historians now view the institution of the blacklist as a "seismic shift from the progressive ideals of the New Deal to the anti-Communist paranoia of the Cold War." Patrick McGilligan, author of an insightful book, *Tender Comrades: A Backstory of the Hollywood Blacklist*, goes so far as to say that Hollywood during this time suffered a "cultural holocaust."[1]

Liberals and those further to the Left have been monotonously regurgitating this version of events over the years, with even numerous conservatives now embracing a major portion of what has become the consensus history. But there is clearly another side to this story.

The Hollywood Ten, as they became famously known to history, are no longer household names, though Dalton Trumbo has been making a comeback, and Ring Lardner Jr., the last surviving member of the tribe (he died in 2002), is still mentioned as an important "martyr" to HUAC's "inquisition."

Many were talented men who left their mark on politics and film and, contrary to accepted wisdom, often succeeded in putting their Communist convictions into their work. Lardner may be best known for his post-blacklist movie *M*A*S*H*, which was vigorously opposed to the Vietnam War and became the basis for a hugely successful TV series with Alan Alda.

John Howard Lawson enforced the Stalinist line in Hollywood, so it was not surprising that he also penned the 1930s film *Blockade*, which favored the Soviet side during the Spanish Civil War, and *Action in the North Atlantic*, a World War II film starring Humphrey Bogart in which the Russians are shown as the heroes in the rescue of an American supply ship. Alvah Bessie, who fought on the Communist side in Spain, was hired to write a small but highly acclaimed piece of pro-Soviet dialogue for *Action.*

Trumbo is remembered for many excellent films, including *Roman Holiday* (with Gregory Peck and Audrey Hepburn), *Spartacus* (with Kirk Douglas), and *Papillon* (with Steve McQueen and Dustin Hoffman), and he became the first of the Hollywood Ten to break the blacklist in 1960, which meant he was the first of those officially banned from Hollywood to receive screen credit for his work without ever having to name a fellow Red conspirator or say he was sorry for siding with Joseph Stalin and Adolf Hitler against his homeland.

Trumbo is less well known for a script that never made it to the screen: *An American Story,* whose plot outline, in the words of film historian Bernard F. Dick, goes like this: North Korea finally decides "to put an end to the border warfare instigated by South Korea by embarking upon a war of independence in June 1950."[2] (In his papers at the Wisconsin Historical Society, Trumbo says he "dramatized" Kim Il-sung's supposedly righteous war for a group of fellow Communist screenwriters, including at least two Hollywood Ten members.)

Trumbo also seemed to think that Stalin needed a bit of a reputation upgrade. So one finds in his papers a proposed novel, apparently written in the 1950s, in which a wise old Russian defends Stalin's murderous reign as necessary for the supposedly grand achievements of Soviet socialism.

Those celebrating Trumbo today as a sort of saintly curmudgeon do not feel obligated to mention this aspect of his Red ideology, nor do they point to his writings during the Soviet-Nazi Pact, when he was excusing Hitler's conquests. "To the vanquished," he airily dismissed the critics of Nazi brutality, "all conquerors are inhuman." For good measure he demonized Hitler's major enemy, Great Britain, insisting that England was not a democracy, because it had a king, and accused FDR of "treason" and "black treason" for attempting to assist the British in their life-and-death struggle against the despot in Berlin.

Stalin, Hitler, Kim Il-sung? This is a trifecta of barbarous dictators, all supported by Trumbo, whose reputation as a champion of liberty is rising in Hollywood even as I write.

Writers Albert Maltz, Lester Cole, Herbert Biberman, and Samuel Ornitz—each a Hollywood Ten figure—also left their mark in both radical politics and films, as did producer Adrian Scott and famed director Edward Dmytryk.

Several of the Ten have written about their ordeal in well-received autobiographies. All of them—save Dmytryk, the only one to renounce Communism completely—have been celebrated in countless articles, interviews, and TV documentaries. Numerous movies, including *The Majestic*, with Jim Carrey, and *The Front*, starring Woody Allen and the late Zero Mostel, have dramatized the plight of the blacklisted writer, with the "victims" of the 1947 and 1950s hearings customarily elevated to icon status.

Screenwriter Philip Dunne, who organized a star-studded committee including Humphrey Bogart and Lauren Bacall to defend the Ten, tells an informative story in his memoir, *Take Two*. Dunne recalls that his young daughter, while attending a boarding school in Arizona, blurted out: "Daddy, my friends honor you." Why? he wondered in astonishment. "Because you were blacklisted."

Dunne had never been a Communist and was never blacklisted, despite his penchant for radical politics. But his kid's remarks were revealing. "My daughter's friends who paid me this unearned compliment," Dunne writes, "were mostly sons and daughters of doctors, lawyers, writers, professors, and artists from Los Angeles, San Francisco and New York: a fair cross section within the intellectual community." This community, he reflects, had elevated the Hollywood Ten and other blacklistees "to the status of national heroes."[3]

WHITEWASHING THE BLACKLISTED

In truth, they remain heroes—and not only among America's intellectual elite. Some of the accused may have been Communists, it is conceded by some HUAC critics, a proposition hard to deny since every one of the Ten has been revealed to have been a Communist through public confession or incontrovertible evidence. But not all had necessarily joined the *Party*, critics initially contended, and what evidence HUAC produced was allegedly weak or even doctored. As Larry Ceplair and Steven Englund suggest in their classic volume on the screenwriters, *The Inquisition in Hollywood*, there is "reason to believe" that the Communist Party cards of the Ten introduced into the hearing record "were fabrications."[4]

Even if some of the Ten *did* join the Party, they were not "subversives," as the Committee's members alleged, but good Americans who had become CP members out of a zeal to battle such pressing issues as poverty, fascism, and the oppression of the black race. Indeed, they proved their loyalty to this nation during World War II when they joined the military or wrote some of our best war pictures or spent enormous time and energy boosting the war effort on the home front. HUAC, in fact, had no legal—and certainly no moral—authority to subject these well-meaning citizens to the kind of public condemnations they received.

Such is the customary case for the Ten.[5] The truth about the HUAC investigations is quite different. The Hollywood Ten, far from being "radical innocents," far from having just "flirted with Communist ideas," as their sympathizers so frequently insist, had all been committed to a Soviet America. Each had been an active Communist for several years. Each was participating in Communist activities during the year of the 1947 hearings.

Each was pledging loyalty to Stalin and the American Communist Party at the very moment a large segment of the liberal community was vehemently condemning Stalin, kicking Communist Party members out of both labor and liberal organizations, and forming new groups barring CP members from holding office or even joining.[6]

Each had paid dues to the Party, met in secret CP gatherings, embraced CP projects, adorned various CP fronts, and lavished money or time or both on Party projects, and each had been issued a Communist Party USA card or a Communist Political Association card (the Communist Political Association was the name of the Party for fourteen months during WWII). The cards produced by the Committee were not "fabrications," as Ceplair and Englund falsely suggest.[7]

These men, along with hundreds of their comrades in the movie industry, were determined to transform Hollywood into a colony of the Kremlin. Indefatigable, they recruited Party members, taught radicals of all stripes their craft at Marxist "academies," indoctrinated colleagues with their ideology, and schooled fellow writers on how to insert Red propaganda into American films.

They deeply penetrated or aided others in penetrating the screenwriters', directors', and actors' guilds, and they worked feverishly to help fellow Reds seize control of the labor side of Hollywood through Herb Sorrell's Conference of Studio Unions. If they could gain control over the guilds and the unions, they reasoned, they could then compel the producers to meet not only the economic and political demands of the Left, but the "content" demands as well—that Hollywood make radical, pro-Communist films. They never did subdue Hollywood completely, but they wielded enormous influence. And it took a determined anti-Red contingent in Hollywood and the long-scorned House Un-American Activities Committee to finally break their power.

By October of 1947, when the hearings began and the Soviet Union posed an obvious threat to the West, Hollywood's Communists had been active in a subversive party *that was entirely controlled by Moscow, had thoroughly penetrated American society, and was engaged in massive espionage on behalf of the Soviets (including the filching of atomic secrets)*.

The Party they wholeheartedly embraced had placed agents at the highest levels of our government to shift policy in favor of the Soviet empire, was furiously working for the destruction of our economic and political freedoms, and was pledging to overthrow the U.S. government, by force and violence if necessary. Many of the radical writers, including such high-octane screenwriters as Donald Ogden Stewart, for one, eventually admitted as much.

Nothing the Communist Party in America ever did was without direction from the Kremlin. Nothing. When Hitler initially threatened Russia, Hollywood's Party members, under Moscow's orders by way of Party headquarters in New York, were passionately anti-Nazi; when Hitler turned his guns against the West—enabled by his 1939 Pact with Stalin—they devoted the whole of their lives to crippling the capacity of the *anti*-Nazi nations to survive.

Only when the Nazis double-crossed Stalin with their "surprise" invasion of the Soviet Union in 1941 did Hollywood's Reds—with Moscow still cracking the whip—renew their rage against Hitler. They were not honorable anti-fascists or patriotic Americans, as their defenders argue, but loyal Soviet apparatchiks, a fifth column working for Stalin inside our homeland.

None of this appears to bother Hollywood or the Ten's supporters a whit. Nor is it much dwelt upon—though I cite one conspicuous exception below—in the unrelenting apologias. Hollywood cannot get enough of celebrating the "victims" of those 1947 hearings in movies, plays, books, documentaries, skits, oral histories, and public events.

Fifty years after the '47 hearings, Hollywood commemorated the Ten but also other writers, directors, and actors who had allegedly been persecuted by HUAC in the 1950s. At the October 27, 1997, gala at the Academy of Motion Picture Arts and Sciences in Beverly Hills, these men and women received standing ovations from the audience and lavish tributes from those honoring them on stage. Representatives of the various writers', directors', and actors' guilds sponsoring the triumphant occasion made grand apologies for their having been blacklisted. Such celebrities as Billy Crystal, Kevin Spacey, and John Lithgow were eager to lend their special talents to polishing the legend of the Ten and other targets of HUAC as they took part in skits reenacting the supposed horrors they had sustained.

That night at the Samuel Goldwyn Theatre, Stalinist Ten writers including Donald Trumbo, Albert Maltz, and Ring Lardner Jr. were warmly celebrated. So were Communist writers Abraham Polonsky, Paul Jarrico, Bernard Gordon, Bobby Lees, Walter Bernstein, and Frank Tarloff. Stunningly, the president of the Writers Guild of America, West, Daniel Petrie Jr., presented both Jarrico and Lardner with plaques that, Petrie noted, "are engraved with the text of the First Amendment"—an amendment those two were determined to extinguish. None was more lionized on this occasion than Lardner, one of the original Ten who, despite his passing, remains a major poster boy for HUAC's "victims" to this day.

RING LARDNER'S CONFESSIONS

Lardner came from a distinguished line of American writers and was an excellent scriptwriter himself. At the 1997 gala he was allowed to read the statement that he had not been allowed to give before HUAC in 1947 (because he refused to answer the Committee's questions), and at that gala he received not only his distinguished "First Amendment" award but a thundering standing ovation from a crowd of more than a thousand awe-inspired guests, including dozens of Hollywood's finest.

Lardner was romanticized there, as he has been elsewhere, as a man who went to prison for daring to defy a poisonous congressional inquiry. But should all this praise have been heaped upon a devoted Red revolutionary who believed that the violent overthrow of America's economic system was the surest path to a socialist utopia?

We don't need the HUAC "inquisitors" or those hated "informers" to prove Lardner's abiding loyalty to Stalin, though they provided plenty of solid information to underscore the point. We have evidence from the horse's mouth. In *The Lardners*, Ring Lardner Jr.'s very incomplete memoir published nearly thirty years after his HUAC ordeal, he relates how he toed the Soviet line throughout the '30s and '40s.

Lardner discusses his "conversion to Marxism-Leninism" and his "affiliation growing stronger as I learned more facts and analyzed them in the cold light of reason." In the late 1930s, he would go to "a Marxist study group one night" and "a meeting of the newly formed youth unit in the party on another." Whenever he went out by himself in the evening in the 1940s, "it was to attend a Communist meeting of one sort or another."

He claims that "most of the favorable accounts of the Soviet Union confirmed my own observations" and says that though he "frequently asserted the principle that advocating communism for America didn't mean you had to defend everything that happened in Russia, in practice that's what the preponderant majority of arguments came down to."[8] Lardner scrupulously followed Moscow's script. From the special thrill he felt on joining the Communist Party in the '30s through the '47 hearings, he never deviated. Not once.

Screenwriters like Lardner, Lawson, Trumbo, and Maltz became prominent because they were part of the Hollywood Ten, but there were literally scores of other prominent writers in the Red camp, including Lillian Hellman (*Watch on the Rhine* and *The North Star*), Donald Ogden Stewart (*Life with Father* and *The Philadelphia Story*), and Paul Jarrico and Richard Collins (*Song of Russia*).

But did all these screenwriters deserve to be labeled "Stalinists"? Ceplair and Englund, clearly admirers of the Left, honorably conclude,

The initial answer must be "yes." Communist screenwriters defended the Stalinist regime, accepted the Comintern's policies and about-faces, and criticized enemies and allies alike with an infuriating self-righteousness, superiority, and selective memory which eventually alienated all but the staunchest fellow travelers. ["Fellow travelers," though not formally members of the Communist Party, religiously followed the Party line.]

As defenders of the Soviet regime, the screen artist Reds became apologists for crimes of monstrous dimensions, though they claimed to have known nothing about such crimes and indeed shouted down or ignored those who did....

The Hollywood Communists, Ceplair and Englund admit, defended the Soviet Union "unflinchingly, uncritically, inflexibly—and therefore left themselves open to the justifiable suspicion that they not only approved of everything they were defending, but would themselves act in the same way if they were in the same position."[9]

All of which makes one wonder why anyone would be opposed to questioning such folks before a congressional committee concerned with protecting U.S. citizens from Stalin's American agents.

CHAPTER TWO

THE BIRTH OF THE SCREEN WRITERS GUILD

From its birth in 1933, the SWG was virtually certain to turn into a vehicle for radicals. In early February, ten writers gathered in Hollywood to organize a writers' union, "one of sufficient strength," notes Nancy Lynn Schwartz in her sympathetic and authoritative *Hollywood Writers' Wars*, "to be able to back up its demands by shutting off the source of supply of screenplays" to the studios and producers.[1] Far-Left ideologues were present at the initial meeting.

Future Hollywood Ten members John Howard Lawson and Lester Cole were there. As the '30s unfolded, both became important players in the SWG—and devoted Communist Party members. Lawson, dispatched by Party headquarters in New York to California to monitor writers, became known as "the enforcer" of the Party line.

Also attending the founding meeting of the SWG was Samson Raphaelson, who had written *The Jazz Singer*, a Broadway play that Warner Brothers turned into the first talkie. Raphaelson, who also became an official of the Guild, admitted in later years that he had contributed to plenty of Communist causes, insisting, however, that he "never joined the Party." Still, he liked much of what the Communists were doing and thought if the world "was going to go Communist or fascist, I'd rather see it go Communist."[2] Louis Weitzenkorn, once a young editor of the *Socialist Call*, was also present at the initial SWG meeting, as was John Bright, who became a committed Communist, too.

The SWG was originally founded by a mix of Communists and non-Communists, with the laudable purpose of improving the working conditions of the writers. But the radicals, in league with Moscow, had a more revolutionary vision for the Guild. They wanted it to be an all-powerful union that would further Soviet goals. They wanted to be able to strike the industry at the whim of the Guild leaders, to have the power to bring the movie moguls to their knees.

Lawson, "the enforcer," was elected the first president of the Screen Writers Guild on April 6, 1933. Unsurprisingly for a believer in the class struggle, he took a highly confrontational stance from the beginning. "The founding of the guild in 1933," he recalled in later years, "made it inevitable that there be a struggle with big business to control the new forms of communication."[3] Lawson took the position that the *writers*—and ultimately, that would mean the *Guild*—should be in control of the movie industry; he didn't care to work constructively with the men who were risking their fortunes to put a writer's material onto the silver screen.

Lawson hurled Red-tinged invective at the Establishment with relish, used threatening tactics against the studios (including strikes), and championed Communism. In the November 1934 *New Theatre* magazine, he boldly announced his support of the Communist Party—he was one of the few writers to be so open—and singled out Samuel Ornitz's play *In New Kentucky* for praise.

Ornitz, who would also become a Hollywood Ten member, had done a "magnificent job" in presenting the Communist Party's role in a Kentucky labor conflict, wrote Lawson. "As for myself," he proclaimed, "I do not hesitate to say that it is my aim to present the Communist position and to do so in the most specific manner."[4]

Lawson's combative style and left-wing maneuverings so upset some members of the Guild that the non-radical faction—called "the Liberal Group"—nominated a slate of candidates in the 1934 SWG election "in order that the Hollywood writer can get a square deal from producers without resorting to the alleged radical and militant tactics of some of the present guild leaders." The Liberal Group lost, but lines were already being drawn between the far Left and the moderates in Hollywood.

LAWSON ANGERS PRODUCERS AND WRITERS ALIKE

Two years later, in an appearance before the House Patents Committee in March 1936, Lawson let loose a verbal assault on the movie producers, humiliating the writers in the process. He insisted in his testimony that the studios had hired "ignorant" executives who failed to appreciate the talents of the writers and give them "the dignity" they had attained in other fields. Well-known screenwriters "are treated practically as office boys," Lawson said. And the executives were forcing the writers to write movies laced with "indecent allusions."

Even pro-Guild writers were outraged. Sixty-four screen and songwriters—including such high-powered names as Moss Hart, Irving Berlin, and Oscar Hammerstein (the First)—fired off an angry telegram to the Committee repudiating "John Howard Lawson as a spokesman and his statements concerning conditions in Hollywood." "Not one of us," they asserted, "has ever been asked to write a word of smut for the screen." And the claim that "we are treated as office boys is absurd."[5]

Lawson was continually trying to drive wedges between the writers and producers in his effort to create a writers' organization that could bring the studios to heel. SWG activists in 1935, Lawson among them, had secretly teamed up with the Authors League of America and the Dramatists Guild to establish such a mass organization through the tactic of "amalgamation"—that is, the formation of a giant writers' union that could dictate to the Hollywood bosses. At about the same time as the House Patents Committee hearings, Lawson threw another roundhouse punch at the studios, announcing that the SWG Executive Board had, in fact, embraced the amalgamation plan and the Guild members were certain to adopt it.

The SWG alone represented about 75 percent of the creative writers involved in producing Hollywood scripts, and the Authors League and the Dramatists another 15 percent. The proposed new writers' union, which would be legally harbored under the Authors League, would have considerable power. In March of 1936, the SWG's Executive Board paved the way for its members to vote for the amalgamation, "so that one organization," Schwartz notes in *The Hollywood Writers' Wars*, would control "all available manpower and material for writing for the screen."[6]

Lawson's bad-mouthing of both producers and writers had hardly helped the cause. But what really ignited a firestorm against the amalgamation plan was the essay by the new SWG president, Ernest Pascal, in the April 1936 issue of the *Screen Guilds' Magazine*, provocatively titled "ONE Organization for ALL American Writers [emphasis in the original]." In this article, Pascal laid out his strategy to dominate the studios. He urged Guild members to ratify constitutional amendments at the annual meeting on May 2 that would (a) legally meld the SWG into the Authors League; (b) entrust rule over every writer to just thirty-six individuals, twelve each from the SWG, the Authors League, and the Dramatists; (c) embrace the SWG's Article XII, which prohibited members from "signing contracts binding their services or sale of material" to the studios after May 1938 (thus putting the writers in a position to strike after that date); and (d) clear the way for "an absolute Guild Shop"— meaning that only Guild writers could work for the studios—"in two years or sooner."[7]

The writers, waxed an ecstatic Pascal, would be "in the invulnerable position of controlling both material and manpower." The studios, he believed, would then have to cave to the new organization's demands on a host of issues, including control of scripts. The new union, not the studios or individual writers, would be in the driver's seat.

Both the studios and the more moderate writers were excusably alarmed. The SWG Executive Board had been larded with Communists and their fellow travelers—that is, with writers who thoroughly admired Stalin and ecstatically embraced an economic system that ruthlessly confiscated private property— since the Guild's inception. (And, as we shall see, a goodly number of the SWG activists—Lawson, Cole, and Guy Endore—had been involved in the formation of the League of American Writers, affiliated with the International Union of Revolutionary Writers, headquartered in Moscow.)

No wonder those friendly to the industry were appalled at Pascal's article. The April 25 *Motion Picture Herald* berated Pascal for trying to set up a "dictatorship" through a "closed shop" that would enable the writers to trigger an industry-wide strike. Do the screenwriters, asked the *Hollywood Reporter*, really "want to kill the goose that has been hatching all those beautiful golden eggs?"

The *New York American* pointed out that Hollywood writers were already "amply paid," claimed the Guild plan was "a radical, destructive scheme for 'power' and 'control,'" and reported that "the motion picture producers are justly marshaling their forces to defeat the proposal." The paper blamed "Communist radicals" in the Guild for devising the proposal.[8]

The producers, along with allies among the writers, such as James McGuinness and Howard Emmett Rogers, crusaded against the Guild proposal, bombarding the trade papers with anti-Guild ads and personally buttonholing writers on the matter.

On the crucial night of the May 2, 1936, meeting, the hard-line radicals and McGuinness reached a temporary compromise, avoiding a vote on some of the critical issues. But the compromise quickly unraveled, as ultimately there was no squaring the views of the moderate elements with those of the militants who favored an all-powerful radical writers' Guild.

AMALGAMATION FAILS

Within a week of the temporary truce, 10 percent of some nine hundred writers in the SWG had resigned to form a rival organization, the Screen Playwrights (SP). Writer Rupert Hughes, speaking for many of the breakaway writers, informed the *New York World Telegram* that the plan "to amalgamate all writers into one grand national union" smacked of a "soviet" the anti-radicals wanted nothing to do with.[9] Hughes insisted the amalgamation proposal was designed to control writers of all kinds, including novelists and radio writers as well as screenwriters, and would give "gigantic power to a committee, which, in turn, would have a single lady or gentleman in command and actually running things." He warned that it would "set up a group of Stalins in the Authors League."[10]

The newly created SP waged a tough war to defeat the SWG, Article XII, and amalgamation. It won the producers' backing by rapping the Guild's radicalism and pledging "sane negotiations" with the studios. The producers immediately recognized the Screen Playwrights, offered new contracts to many non-SP writers (to keep them out of the SWG or lure them from it), and forcefully told all the writers—on the phone, in the studios, and in trade paper ads—that they would resent their embracing the SWG's amalgamation plan, and especially its closed-shop feature.

The result of all these pressures was continued hemorrhaging of SWG members. What seemed at the time to be the Guild's last meeting was held in a run-down building on Hollywood Boulevard near the Grauman's Chinese Theatre. A forlorn Pascal looked around at the nearly empty room, then proclaimed, "There's no point in going on. We can't even pay the rent."[11]

The Guild, however, only looked dead. The pinkish corpse was poised to return to life.

Much of what we know about the rebirth of the Screen Writers Guild after the "amalgamation" debacle comes from Dick Collins, who was a prominent screenwriter and a Communist Party member from 1938 until early 1950, when he finally informed the FBI of his previous CP activities. He had been subpoenaed to appear before the House Un-American Activities Committee in 1947 as an "unfriendly" witness but never had to testify, because the hearings were abruptly terminated before he was called.

Along with Communist Party member Paul Jarrico, Collins had written wartime films including *Thousands Cheer*, starring Gene Kelly and Kathryn Grayson, and the controversial *Song of Russia*, an 1944 MGM film that actor Robert Taylor had initially balked at starring in because it portrayed Soviet Russia as a country just this side of paradise.

Collins appeared as a friendly witness in April of 1951 before HUAC, where he discussed the SWG's rebirth. He described a group of people, both Communist and non-Communist, who in the 1930s "met under the leadership or guidance of V. J. Jerome," the cultural head of the Communist Party who operated out of national CP headquarters in New York City. "The group," he added, "met for the purpose of reconstituting the Screen Writers Guild.... The group had met before I came. How long I don't know. They met for about three months afterwards. As I remember, these meetings were very long, very drawn out. Tremendous arguments took place in them ... and usually V. J. Jerome won, because he had more energy than anybody else."

Counsel Frank Tavenner then asked about Communist participation in the resuscitation of the Guild:

> **Mr. Tavenner**: Would you say the group was organized because of the efforts of the Communist Party?
> **Mr. Collins**: You mean the Screen Writers Guild?
> **Mr. Tavenner**: Yes.
> **Mr. Collins**: Yes, it was.[12]

THE REBORN GUILD, REDDER THAN BEFORE

The revised Guild held its first open meeting on June 11, 1937, at the Hollywood Athletic Club. It was attended by more than four hundred writers, most of whom had been active in the old Guild. The new Guild tilted even further to the left, with such radicals as Lillian Hellman, Dashiell Hammett, Dorothy Parker, and Donald Ogden Stewart gracing the board.

Laurence Beilenson, who had been the Guild's attorney in its first incarnation, refused to become counsel to the reconstituted SWG, insisting that the Communists had killed the first Guild by forcing the amalgamation issue. (Beilenson had publicly supported amalgamation but had secretly advised against it.) He hated the Red-led factionalism: "It was wrecking my life to stay up every night and listen to all this nonsense. John Howard Lawson was the leader of the communist group on the board. They would try to railroad the meetings."[13]

Jean Butler, wife of Hugo Butler, a Communist, has conceded: "There's no question but that the most devoted early members of the Guild were from the Left—the most passionate, the most devoted, the most directed. They were willing to stay late, whereas the conservatives couldn't abide a meeting that lasted more than two hours."[14]

The reborn Guild swiftly won converts. First off, the SP was far more exclusive than the SWG. To become a Screen Playwrights member, you had to have written three screenplays or had two years' work in a major studio. SWG rules were far more lenient: just two weeks' work gave you voting membership. Hence the new Guild became hugely popular with struggling and less established writers, while the SP continued to lose ground.

The SP members never viewed themselves as union members poised to squeeze blood from the studios but rather as a favored group who, by and large, got along with management despite some serious differences. The Screen Playwrights was verbally pummeled as a "company union"—which it wasn't—but its elitist attitude did cost it with the less well paid writers.

Guild leaders had also learned from the SWG's first encounter with the studios. They knew they had to undo the Guild's 1936 vote to "amalgamate" with the Authors League. On May 4, 1938, the SWG members ratified a new constitution and bylaws under which the Guild would now operate as an autonomous body in California, completely divorced from the Authors League.

And when Franklin Roosevelt's National Labor Relations Board handed down a sweeping decision dealing with the movie industry in June 1938, the SWG was instantly invigorated. Under this historic ruling, the board declared that the movie industry was engaged in interstate commerce and thus subject to the Wagner Act.

Screenwriters were now to be considered "employees," not individual contractors, as the Screen Playwrights had insisted. Furthermore, the board decreed that union elections must be held at the individual studios. This action cleared the way for an SWG triumph. On June 28, 1938, the Guild won a smashing victory over the SP, sweeping each of the fourteen studios where a vote was held. The SP fought a rear-guard action, insisting that, despite the vote, no writer could be forced to join the SWG. Not until 1940 did the studios nullify the Screen Playwrights contracts and sign the Guild contracts. The SWG had finally won the day.

Within a few years, the far Left had propelled itself to control of the most powerful writers' group in Hollywood.

CHAPTER THREE

"COMMUNISM . . . MUST BE FOUGHT FOR"

John Howard Lawson and the other hard-left writers who helped found the Screen Writers Guild had already tipped their hand as to what they wanted for this country in the early 1930s when they formed the League of American Writers, an affiliate of the Moscow-headquartered International Union of Revolutionary Writers. A good idea of the direction the League desired to take its members in can be gleaned from the work of Max Eastman, a respected intellectual on the Left who reported on what was happening to the Russian literary class.

In 1934, Eastman wrote *Artists in Uniform*, charging that the "bureaucratic political machine" in the Soviet Union had begun a systematic effort "to whip all forms of human expression into line behind its organization plans and its dictatorship."

DICTATORSHIP IN THE ARTS

Not only must "all art be propaganda in Soviet Russia," said Eastman, but it must be produced "like any kind of commodity…under the direct control and guidance of the political power." Soviet artists were having to embrace such slogans as "the five-year plan in poetry," "poetic shock troops," "the militant struggle for partyism in the arts," and the "creative duty to the socialist fatherland." Russian artists had abandoned inspiration, he suggested, becoming nothing more than "artists in uniform."

To sharpen his point, Eastman reported on a humorless congress of predominantly young artists and authors, representing twenty-two countries (including America) that had met in Kharkov, the capital of the Soviet Ukraine, in 1930. The assembled participants viewed art and literature, now organized by the Communist Party on a mass scale, as "weapons of the working class in its struggle for power."

"Their mood," said Eastman, "may be summed up in the words of the international secretary, Bela Illes of Hungary, who spoke in a uniform presented to him by the Red Army. Alluding to this formidable costume, he exclaimed: 'Pen in hand, we are soldiers of the great invincible army of the international proletariat.'"

Certain principles were dictated to the conclave by a "juvenile lieutenant of the political bureaucracy named Auerbach," explained Eastman. Among them: Art is a class weapon. Artists are to abandon "individualism." And artistic creation is to be "systematized" and "collectivized" under the "firm guidance of the Communist party."

Eastman's exposé of the Soviet literary scene, with all its absurdities, caused a commotion in the West. His words were particularly wounding to the Left because Eastman was a well-known radical who insisted that he still supported the "proletarian class struggle."[1]

Journalist Eugene Lyons, who had become disillusioned with the Soviet Union during his stint as a Moscow correspondent for the United Press International (UPI), confirmed that the Kharkov Congress had been held under the "aegis of the Russian writers' organization, abbreviated as RAPP, which had for a great many years exercised a ruthless terror in the Soviet cultural fields."

The delegates, Lyons reported, scattered to bring its message of "soldier-artists" to their respective shores—including American delegates especially entranced with the Soviet message. The U.S. contingent, "captained by Michael Gold, a slightly hysterical editor of the *New Masses* [and later the premier *Daily Worker* columnist], went home with what [the contingent] described as a 'Program of Action for the United States, intended to guide every phase of our work.'" According to Lyons, "a large number of...writers and critics promptly put themselves in the RAPP harness and thrilled to the sensation of 'collective reins.'"[2]

THE REVOLUTIONARY "LEAGUE OF AMERICAN WRITERS"

The First American Writers' Congress, held in New York in 1935, clearly partook of the spirit of the Kharkov Congress. In January of that year, a group of prominent American left-wing novelists, playwrights, and screenwriters— including several future members of the Hollywood Ten—issued a revolutionary "call" for the Congress: "The capitalist system crumbles so rapidly before our eyes that, whereas ten years ago scarcely more than a handful of writers were sufficiently far-sighted and courageous to take a stand for proletarian revolution, today hundreds of poets, novelists, dramatists, critics and short-story writers *recognize the necessity of personally helping to accelerate the destruction of capitalism and the establishment of a workers' government....*" The organizers proposed a three-day Congress in April in New York City of "all writers who have achieved some standing in their respective fields; who have clearly indicated their sympathy with the revolutionary cause; *who do not need to be convinced of the decay of capitalism, of the inevitability of the revolution* [emphasis in both quotations added]...."

The Congress was directed to "create the League of American Writers [LAW], affiliated with the International Union of Revolutionary Writers," headquartered in Moscow. The League's main goals would be to "defend the Soviet Union against capitalist aggression," "fight against imperialist war and fascism," strengthen "the revolutionary labor movement," fight against "white chauvinism," show "solidarity with colonial people in the struggles for freedom," battle "the influence of reactionary ideas in American literature," and take up the cause of imprisoned "revolutionary writers and artists, as well as other class-war prisoners throughout the world."

The League "would not occupy the time and energy of its members in administrative tasks," but would "reveal, *through collective discussion*, the most effective ways in which writers, *as writers*, can function in the rapidly developing crisis [emphasis added]."[3] In short, American writers, guided by "collective discussion," were to use their talents to "accelerate" Red revolutionary movements everywhere, but particularly in their own country.

The "call" announcing the Congress and the establishment of the League was signed by numerous American authors, many already well known for their radicalism, such as Erskine Caldwell, Theodore Dreiser, Guy Endore, James Farrell, Granville Hicks, Langston Hughes, Lewis Mumford, John Dos Passos, Lincoln Steffens, and Richard Wright.[4]

Many were Communists, and those who weren't were "fellow travelers," at the very least. Dreiser, for instance, the author of *Sister Carrie* and *An American Tragedy*, was viewed for most of his adult life as a "non-party Bolshevik," and he did not formally join the Communist Party of the United States of America (CPUSA) until 1945. Hicks, the keynote speaker at the Congress, had just become a Party member.

Wright and Hughes would go on to become famous black writers. Richard Wright, who would pen the much-acclaimed *Native Son*, had joined the Party in 1934 and was already writing for such Party publications as the *New Masses*. Langston Hughes, who became a well-known poet, was never a Party member, but he had written a poem for the *New Masses* urging the "Great Mob that knows no fear" to tear the capitalist "limb from limb." Hughes had, no doubt, voiced the sentiments of his fellow writers at the Congress in a lyric he had published in the *Daily Worker* the previous year: "Put one more S in the USA to make it Soviet... Oh, we'll live to see it yet."[5] There was little question about where these literary figures wanted to lead America.

Recognized Communists such as Earl Browder, then chairman of the CPUSA; Michael Gold, who became the *Daily Worker's* most celebrated columnist; and Clarence Hathaway, the paper's editor, were also signatories to the "call" for the Congress, and they would play prominent roles there.

John Howard Lawson and Samuel Ornitz, two Party members who would become part of the Hollywood Ten, were also on board. Lawson became a major Communist Party figure in Hollywood as well as a popular scriptwriter best known for his World War II movies, *Action in the North Atlantic* and *Sahara*, now seen frequently on Turner Classic Movies. He would play a central role at the Congress as a speaker and an organizer. He and Ornitz were founders of the Screen Writers Guild, the most important writers' organization in Hollywood. Another Hollywood Ten member, Albert Maltz, was named as an executive officer of the League of American Writers, the organization the Congress founded in its concluding session.[6]

The major gathering of the Congress took place at the Mecca Temple, New York City, on the night of April 26, 1935. Present as delegates were 216 writers from twenty-six states, plus 150 writers attending as guests, including fraternal delegates from Mexico, Cuba, Germany, and Japan. The hall was packed with four thousand spectators as Granville Hicks, author of *The Great Tradition: An Interpretation of American Literature since the Civil War* and a noted critic, opened the meeting. Hicks, who had recently joined the Communist Party, says in his memoir that he was "exhilarated and awed" by the experience. He also admits that the Congress "was frankly initiated by the Communists and their sympathizers."[7]

Revolutionary greetings came from all parts of the world, with Hicks reading several messages from Soviet well-wishers. Famed Soviet writer Maxim Gorky, author of *The Lower Depths* and by now a thoroughgoing apologist for Stalin's crimes, cabled, "My brotherly greetings to the Congress of American Writers organized for intellectual struggle against fascism and a new, bloody war. We are with you, dear friends."

The aforementioned Soviet-created International Union of Revolutionary Writers issued a more pungent message, urging the American writers to use art as a weapon to bring about a Red revolution: "Today the flower of humanity has rejected the old world and hails the revolution.... In this hour the writer's weapon is his creative work. To conquer, the weapon must be sharp and strong. Sharpen your weapon! Develop the art of revolution! Strengthen the courage and heroism of the masses and their will to victory! May your Congress be the impetus to a wide front of struggle against fascism, against imperialist wars, and for the defense of the Soviet Union, the fatherland of the toilers of the world."[8]

The Soviets had come to power by crushing an eight-month-old democratic regime. They had deliberately starved several million people in the Ukraine. They had compelled their own artists to sing hosannas to the Communist Party or lose their livelihood—and sometimes their lives. But the American literary artists gathered at the Congress clearly viewed the Stalinist regime as a beacon of beneficent light.

Virtually all the major speeches hailed Communism, the Soviet Union, revolution, or a combination thereof. If there was conspicuous dissent, it doesn't appear in the proceedings or the news coverage. The major purpose of the Congress was clear: to persuade those gathered to push for a Communist revolution in America.

"In whatever medium a writer works—fiction, verse, drama, biography, essay, journalism," Harry Ward told the attendees, he must write with the "awareness of the basic fact that capitalist society has reached the stage where it has become an organized system of scarcity and destruction." (Ward was the founding chairman of the American Civil Liberties Union who would later resign that position to protest the ACLU's decision to ban Communists from its membership.) Capitalism is synonymous with fascism, according to Ward, and in its "search for profit it is compelled to doom millions to slow death from undernourishment of body, mind and spirit."[9] The writer must educate the masses that revolution is the cure. No other solution—such as *mending* America's economic system rather than violently wrecking it—should be contemplated.

Moissaye J. Olgin, founding editor of the *Morning Freiheit*, urged the participants to follow the lead of the authors at the First All-Union Congress of Soviet Writers, who, he explained, had turned out literary masterpieces because, under Stalin's inspiration, they now "acknowledge the leadership of the Bolshevik [Communist] Party as the vanguard of everything that is creative in the land of the Soviets." Revolutionary writers in "bourgeois" nations, where socialist victories had not yet been achieved, must, according to Olgin, fight for "the class struggle of the workers, for the dictatorship of the proletariat, for Communism."[10]

Matthew Josephson, an American revolutionary and literary figure, explained that Russians were writing with spirit because "they have won their class revolution and are engaged in championing a new order." But in America, Josephson argued, writers must begin tearing down the old order: "Here there is a good deal of sapping and destroying to be done. Here there is need...for such powerful satire as the Russians used before October 1917 [when Lenin came to power]."[11]

American Communist Party chieftain Earl Browder attempted to reassure the non-Communist revolutionaries among the attendees that the Communists were not attempting to "control" writers, but much of what he said made it clear that, in fact, they were. Browder candidly stated that the Party desired "to arouse consciousness among all writers of the political problems of the day.... We believe the overwhelming bulk of fine writing has political significance. We would like to see all writers conscious of this, therefore able to control and direct the political results of their work."[12]

Browder pointed to the articles in the *New Masses*, a cultural and political weekly largely financed by the Communist Party, as the kind of writing Communists wanted to see flourish. "While not a party organ [in fact, it was a mouthpiece for the Communist Party], the *New Masses* represents the Communist line," he averred.[13] Browder clearly wanted the authors at the Congress to follow "the Communist line," too.

Toward the end of the three-day Congress, Michael Gold, who had enthusiastically embraced the Kharkov Congress in Russia, was introduced as "the best loved American revolutionary writer." He informed the delegates, "Now, comrades, friends and fellow authors, we approach a very serious and historic moment in this Congress. We are about to organize a permanent organization of American writers in order that the work of this Congress may spread during the next year."

WRITERS SING A RED ANTHEM

That permanent organization would be called the League of American Writers. Members of the Congress's "presiding committee" and of its "organizing committee"—controlled by Communists—had already selected the League's general secretary, Waldo Frank, who was approved by the delegates unanimously. Frank had begun his long-winded address to the Congress with this blunt observation: "My premise and the premise of the majority of writers here assembled is that communism must come, and must be fought for."[14]

The Congress's organizers also named seventeen members of the League's Executive Committee, two of whom—John Howard Lawson and Albert Maltz—became Hollywood Ten celebrities. Clifford Odets, Richard Wright, Lincoln Steffens, Michael Blankfort, and James Farrell became part of the National Council. Odets and Wright became prominent Hollywood Communists, and Blankfort was at least a fellow traveler—more likely, a Party member.[15]

Frank, moved by his selection as general secretary, uttered a few thank-yous, adding, "With these words I should like not to end this Congress, but to begin the League of American Writers." When the applause had died down, novelist James Farrell, author of the popular *Studs Lonigan* trilogy, arose and suggested that the Congress conclude the three-day event with a song appropriate for this grand occasion. It was *The Internationale*, a revolutionary song that had been adopted by the Soviets after being sung by anarchists and revolutionaries since radicals established the Paris Commune in 1870. Revolutionaries would often sing this refrain with the left hand raised in a clenched fist: "'Tis the final conflict / Let each stand in his place / The International Soviet / Shall be the human race."[16]

Daily Worker columnist Michael Gold described the "heartening" scene as writers rose from their seats to join in the anthem. John Howard Lawson said he "shared a kind of euphoria" with the other writers as *The Internationale* "was sung with fervor and with deep conviction."[17]

Three of the Hollywood Ten—Lawson, Ornitz, and Maltz—became founding members of the League of American Writers. At least five more joined or were affiliated with it in later years. Other famous writers such as Lillian Hellman, Donald Ogden Stewart, and Dashiell Hammett—all Communists at the time—would become League members. Stewart and Hammett were to lead the organization in the late 1930s and early 1940s.

Thus numerous prominent American writers, including several Hollywood Ten luminaries, joined a Moscow-controlled group devoted to channeling their artistic talents to bring Communist revolution upon this country. The next few years would show just how eager these Hollywood writers were to toe the Soviet line.

CHAPTER FOUR

ANTI-FASCIST, OR PRO-STALIN?

There were three more major American Writers' Congresses, in 1937, '39, and '41. Despite the softer tone of the succeeding "calls" for the Congresses, which expressed opposition to fascism and support for black rights, the bottom-line message was always the same: American writers were *obligated at all times to embrace the Soviet Union and its Stalinist policies and enterprises.* This is what these Congresses—and the League of American Writers, which had been founded at the First Congress—were all about. The Congresses and the League were in Stalin's corner whenever he needed their support.

Scores of prominent literary figures—most of whom had to have been aware of the revolutionary nature of these twin enterprises—eagerly sponsored one or both organizations over the years. Among those who lent their prestige to these organizations' activities: Ernest Hemingway, Lillian Hellman, Carey

McWilliams, S. J. Perelman, Budd Schulberg, Irwin Shaw, Upton Sinclair, Louis Untermeyer, Carl Van Doren, and Orson Welles.

Five of the Hollywood Ten figures—Lawson, Ornitz, Maltz, Cole, and Bessie—were conspicuous supporters of the Congress and the League when both groups, on the signal from Stalin, turned on a dime to a pro-Hitler foreign policy.

THE POPULAR FRONT

The revolutionary nature of the first Congress was obvious. But the other Congresses followed the Soviet line just as closely in substance, if not rhetorically, and the first Congress's call to revolution was never repudiated. The Second American Writers' Congress met in June 1937 in New York City's Carnegie Hall. This was the heyday of the "Popular Front," when Stalin sought alliances with even "bourgeois" and "imperialist" nations to oppose what the Russian despot rightly viewed as the growing threat to Moscow from fascism and Nazism. A major purpose of the 1937 Congress was to help convince the literati to support this critical Soviet goal.

Familiar American authors signed on to the "call" for the 1937 Congress, including Communist hard-liners and pro-Soviet propagandists such as John Howard Lawson, Erskine Caldwell, Langston Hughes, Donald Ogden Stewart, and Ella Winter (Stewart's wife), and softer leftists such as Jean Starr Untermeyer, Archibald MacLeish, and Carl Van Doren.[1]

While less provocative, the rhetoric at the Second Congress was still pro-Soviet and enthusiastically in favor of the latest Stalinist project: the Loyalists' war against the Hitler-backed forces of Franco in Spain. The Congress could still resort to fulminating against American capitalism and the "bankers and industrialists" who would bring fascism to America. "Fascism will be encouraged and financed" by these powerful forces, it claimed, "as an effective means of 'keeping labor in its place.'" And "war will be used" by these men of money to break the laboring class. Under fascist rule the literary class—that is, those attending the Congress—will be censored and "fare no better than labor."[2]

Many of the speeches delivered at the Congress were still ardently pro-Soviet, as well. Walter Duranty, the former Moscow correspondent for the *New York Times* who had somehow overlooked the man-made 1932–33 Soviet famine that took over three million lives (a very conservative figure), was still offering up soothing words about the Soviet Union. "What do the Russians want?" he asked. "They want to cultivate their own garden, continue what they are doing. They want to live as free men. They want to live happily at home. They don't want to invade other people's countries. It's fascism that does that."[3]

The speeches at the Congress were clearly designed to persuade the writers to direct their polemical skills against Hitler and Mussolini and concentrate their efforts on assisting the Loyalist side in Spain, where the great battle against fascism was presumably being played out.

Writers including Hemingway, Archibald MacLeish, Malcolm Cowley, and Martha Gellhorn fiercely advocated the Loyalist cause at the Congress, even as the forces fighting Franco were being taken over by Stalin's henchmen. Gellhorn sang the praises of writers in Spain who were putting down their pens, donning military garb, joining Red military brigades, and placing themselves "at the service of socialism." A writer, she declared, "must also be a man of action now."[4]

MacLeish was in ecstasy about the Loyalist cause, urging writers to plunge into the fight. How, he thundered, can we "not claim the war as ours? How then can we refuse our help to those who fight our battles—to those who truly fight our battles—*now*—*now*, not in some future war—*now, now* in Spain?"[5]

Earl Browder, the general secretary of the Communist Party USA, had sharp words for writers and intellectuals who were at all critical of the Soviet Union, its "alleged" artistic rigidity, the Moscow show trials, or Stalin's intervention in Spain. He sneered that theologian Reinhold Niebuhr, for instance, was for "free-lancing" in the fight against fascism because Niebuhr had condemned Soviet censorship. Browder also condemned the pro-Communist Waldo Frank, the outgoing president of the League of American Writers, for doubting the manufactured evidence produced at the Moscow show trials.

Despite the massive persecution of Soviet writers going on even as he was speaking, Browder disingenuously proclaimed that "Communists are the last to want to regiment the writers." But then he turned around and stressed that the American writers he was addressing must be "disciplined" in the fight against fascism and excoriated those who backed "the Trotskyists and their anarchist allies" rebelling against the Soviet-directed Loyalists in Spain. There should be no "toleration" of "such agents of the fascists," Browder insisted. Creative power effects change "when it is organized, disciplined and directed," he growled. Without such discipline, "the victory of fascism is inevitable."[6]

The point of Browder's remarks was that writers in America and around the world should write movingly, creatively, and effectively in the service of the Soviet political agenda. At the moment, Stalin was demanding resistance to Hitler and Mussolini and absolute allegiance to the Soviet-led faction in Spain.

One significant development at the Second Writers' Congress was the emergence of Donald Ogden Stewart, already a prominent Hollywood screenwriter and Communist activist, as a leader. Stewart is probably best known for winning an Oscar for *The Philadelphia Story*, starring James Stewart and Katharine Hepburn, and for his adaptation for the screen of that warm and humorous play, *Life with Father*, featuring William Powell, Irene Dunne, and Elizabeth Taylor. Waldo Frank, the first head of the League of American Writers, who had claimed that "communism must come, and must be fought for," had now begun to question not Communism itself but Stalin's blood purges—in the pages of the *New Republic*. As a result, he was, in effect, fired by the Communists as head of the League of American Writers. He was replaced by Stewart, who in his autobiography, *By a Stroke of Luck!*, acknowledges his long devotion to Stalinism.

The proceedings of the 1937 Congress report that Stewart was chosen "unanimously" by the Congress's delegates to head the League, but he himself explains that the position was really secured for him by the Communist Party, for which he was "grateful." He did little, he confesses, but contribute "my name and an occasional speech," and in "this, as in other organizations to which I belonged, it was largely the Communists who did the work."[7]

Stewart got off some stunningly revolutionary remarks at the Congress, suggesting that he adhered to the Communist belief that "ninety-five percent of the people in America" lived in "slavery" and that capitalism, now in its death agonies, was "giving birth to fascism."[8]

Stewart lets us know very explicitly what he meant by a writer using "every weapon at his command" to change conditions in America. Like so many members of the Hollywood Ten, Stewart agreed that the violent overthrow of the American government was essential. In his autobiography he plainly states that "I wanted to fight for Socialism in America as the next step toward Abraham Lincoln's speech about the 'revolutionary right of any people to overthrow their government' in their march toward liberty and justice, *and I accepted with it the Marxist doctrine of the need for a 'final conflict' in view of the fact that those in possession of the means of production were not going to surrender them without a fight* [emphasis added]."[9]

ON THE EVE OF THE HITLER-STALIN PACT

The Third American Writers' Congress, held in New York City in June of 1939, followed the same script; it was also designed to please the Communists' masters in Moscow. The Hitler-Stalin Pact was just around the corner, but the organizers of the Congress were kept in the dark about Stalin's maneuverings, and so they were still eager to secure allies for Russia's fight against "fascism." Thus the "call" for the Congress placed special emphasis on getting the United States to cooperate "with other nations and people opposed to fascism—including the Soviet Union, which has been the most consistent defender of peace."[10]

There were "literary" and "history" lectures by various writers, including Communist Joseph Freeman, who informed his colleagues that the French Revolution "was the most liberating event in history" until the Russian Revolution in 1917. Comparing Stalin's murderous rule to the French Revolution's Reign of Terror—and defending both—Freeman chastised the poets William Wordsworth and Samuel Taylor Coleridge for turning against the bloodbaths instigated by Maximilien Robespierre. "Wordsworth and his friends," Freeman argued, were mistaken to be so "horrified...by Robespierre." Why? "Because they did not understand that he was ridding France of traitors and counter-revolutionaries."[11]

The 1939 Congress's major resolutions dealt with the dangers of Hitler and Mussolini and the need for "the closest cooperation" between the United States and the Soviet Union, as well as with Britain and France, to resist fascist aggression.

The delegates embraced the "Thomas Amendment," whose purpose was to make it easier for FDR to assist the forces that menaced Moscow.[12] They expressed their support for writers in exile from Germany and Italy and elected

one of the most eloquent anti-Nazi writers of the era, Nobel Prize winner
Thomas Mann, as honorary president of the League of American Writers.[13]

Well-known writers publicly endorsing the Third Congress or attending it
included pro-Soviet notables such as Hellman, Lawson, Guy Endore, Dorothy
Parker, and S. J. Perelman. Donald Ogden Stewart, Erskine Caldwell, and Albert
Maltz had also signed the "call."

In *The Red Decade*, Eugene Lyons, the United Press's disenchanted former
Moscow correspondent, explained,

> Of the seventy-two signers of this call, at least fourteen were gener-
> ally known to be members of the Communist Party. The others
> were names that had become fixtures on Stalinist manifestoes and
> whitewash documents....
>
> The Congress was largely another communist mass meeting,
> with the usual greetings from the writers of Russia (those not yet
> liquidated, that is), praise of Moscow's "anti-fascist" leadership,
> resolutions embodying every inch of the party line.
>
> The Soviet message, we may note for posterity and the current
> party-liners, said: "The attempt to hide behind neutrality, non-
> intervention or isolationism has become a mockery."[14]

But the "anti-fascist" sentiment of the Congress and the League was soon
to undergo a dramatic change—within a little over two months.

CHAPTER FIVE

THE HOLLYWOOD ANTI-NAZI LEAGUE

O rganized in June 1936, the Hollywood Anti-Nazi League (originally the Hollywood League against Nazism) became one of the most popular anti-fascist groups in the country. Among its major sponsors were such stellar Hollywood celebrities as actor Fredric March, entertainer Eddie Cantor, lyricist Oscar Hammerstein (the Second), and humorist Robert Benchley. Director Ernst Lubitsch, satirist Dorothy Parker, and producer Frank Tuttle also joined.

The most Reverend John J. Cantwell, then Catholic archbishop of Los Angeles, wrote the organization, "I am very glad to be associated with the 'Hollywood League against Nazism,' or with any organization opposing the wicked pretensions of Nazism."

Prince Hubertus zu Loewenstein, the exiled leader of the German (Catholic) Center Party, became a leading figure in the founding of the League. Lowenstein had opposed Nazism from the beginning, had written two anti-Nazi books, and, fearing for his life, in 1933 had fled to Austria, where he founded an anti-Nazi group. Hitler's Germany deprived him of his German citizenship and forced his exile from Austria in 1935. He eventually came to America.

Loewenstein met with a group of literary and film luminaries in Hollywood, including Parker, March, Hammerstein, and Donald Ogden Stewart, who agreed to hold a white-tie-and-tails banquet to raise money for the relief of the victims of Nazism. A one-hundred-dollar-a-plate affair was held at the Victor Hugo Restaurant in Los Angeles in April 1936. The dinner, supported by such Hollywood moguls as Samuel Goldwyn and David Selznick and presided over by Archbishop Cantwell, was a rousing success.

In the wake of this dazzling event, Stewart and others formed the Hollywood Anti-Nazi League. On July 23, five hundred guests attended the official launch at the Wilshire Ebell Theatre, and by autumn the League was sponsoring a mass meeting at the Shrine Auditorium. Some ten thousand people came to hear Cantor, Hammerstein, Parker, actress Gale Sondergaard, the American Legion's John Lechner, and Mayor Frank Shaw denounce fascism.

THE LEFT BLACKLISTS A FILM MAKER

The League took off. At its peak it boasted between four and five thousand members. Communist writers including Ring Lardner Jr., Robert Rossen, and John Bright eagerly joined, but so did anti-Communists such as Herman Mankiewicz and Rupert Hughes. The League pledged to boycott Japanese goods and called for "concerted action by the democratic nations" against "fascist aggressors."[1]

Not at all averse to the principle of boycotting and blacklisting those with extreme political views—a principle loudly decried by the Hollywood Left only when those weapons were used against Communists—the League frankly mobilized its forces to blacklist Leni Riefenstahl, the celebrated German filmmaker who had glorified Hitler in her lavish "documentaries" on Nazi Germany. When MGM signed German actress Louisa Ulrich in 1937, the League protested loudly, with its publication, *Hollywood Now*, portraying her as "a close friend of Propaganda Minister Joseph Goebbels."[2]

The League honored the distinguished German exile Thomas Mann, held a meeting to warn of the fascist danger to Czechoslovakia, demanded collective security as "the basis of our foreign policy," and picketed a local German-American Bund convention.

Despite its popularity among a broad spectrum of the Hollywood movie colony, there were increasing suspicions that the League was under Communist Party control. In a nationwide broadcast in August 1938, Representative Martin Dies, head of the House Un-American Activities Committee, speculated that most of the League's members were not Communists but that it was controlled by Party members. Dies announced that his Committee would come to Hollywood in September "to hold hearings at which members of the film colony will be afforded an opportunity to reply to charges that they were participating in communistic activities."

Dies was immediately assailed by such League members as Lubitsch, March, and Parker. The League then flooded President Roosevelt and Congress with anti-Dies mail. And at a mass meeting in the Philharmonic Auditorium in Los Angeles, the League challenged "the Dies committee to present substantiation of these so-called charges," suggesting that the Dies Committee might be guilty of misusing public money "to aid reactionary fascist interests contrary to the law."[3] Stewart, meanwhile, prepared a radio broadcast in defense of the League, insisting that Dies's real purpose was to undermine "all liberal organizations—all progressive labor movements and all faith in the progressive policies of President Roosevelt."[4] Dies eventually buckled. No hearings were held.

Nevertheless, Dies would prove to be far more accurate than his critics. Communist control of the League should have been obvious early on. The League's first chairman, Donald Ogden Stewart, was already one of the Communist Party's most loyal followers. He would admit in his autobiography that he fully sanctioned the violent overthrow of our government.[5]

The vice president was Marion Spitzer, a key CP leader in the cultural field. And among the thirty-two board members and sponsors were at least ten Communist writers, including Herbert Biberman, John Howard Lawson, and Samuel Ornitz, who would wind up as members of the Hollywood Ten. Ursula Daniels, a Young Communist League member, was the circulation manager of the League publication, the *Anti-Nazi News*, which was later renamed *Hollywood Now*.[6]

The League had won its following by tapping into a mother lode of anti-Nazi sentiment that existed in Hollywood and across the country. But "anti-fascism" wasn't the real motivation of those running the organization. The League featured active Communists, such as Stewart and Herbert Biberman, in whatever project it was pushing at the moment. It enthusiastically championed the government-funded Federal Theater Project, which was saturated with Communists and fellow travelers. And the Spanish Loyalists, whose leadership had become rigidly Stalinist, were the League's dearest cause.

Screenwriter Hy Kraft, a major figure in the League, took the Fifth to avoid testifying before HUAC in 1952 but admitted Communist Party membership in his 1971 autobiography. He recounts how the League supported the left-wing Culbert Olson for governor of California; "fought the deportation of Harry Bridges," the West Coast's Communist labor leader; and blocked efforts to add the name "anti-Communist" to the organization after it had been accused of being a Red front. The League, Kraft boasts, refused to make any "alliances with red-baiters" since, deep down, "you would probably find a Negro-baiter, a Jew-baiter, a labor-baiter and a Franklin Roosevelt hater."[7]

THE LEAGUE LOSES ITS LUSTER

Author Leo Rosten, a tough critic of the anti-Communist representative Dies, notes that when anti-Communist resolutions were introduced by those in the League who wanted to shield the organization from anti-Communist attacks, the League's leaders "reacted promptly; they fought down efforts to put the question to a democratic vote; they raised a hue and cry that the matter of communism was irrelevant; and, using the classic *argumentum ad hominem*, they accused their critics of being everything from 'wreckers' and 'saboteurs' to 'Fascist lackeys.'" They were more determined, Rosten insists, "to hold to the Communist Party line than to further the purpose—anti-Nazi—for which they were organized."[8]

Hence during the League's three years of operations, a number of people initially sympathetic to it became wary of its activities. Only a few months after warmly endorsing the Anti-Nazi League, Archbishop Cantwell insisted through a spokesman that his name should be "withdrawn from the list of sponsors...as he feels that the organization is not what it seems to be and he has no desire to be connected with it."[9]

The famed director Ernst Lubitsch, at one point a major supporter of the League, eventually began telling friends that he was determined to resign since he had become convinced that the League was under Party control.[10] The screenwriter Morrie Ryskind was initially sympathetic to the Loyalist cause in Spain. He might well have been tempted to join the Anti-Nazi League had it not been a Communist front. But when the newspapers proclaimed he was a member, Ryskind, an anti-Communist liberal at the time, immediately issued a strong denial.

The Hollywood Anti-Nazi League was not "taken over" by Communists. It was Red from the outset. Foreign Communists were instrumental in its birth. The true story of the Anti-Nazi League's inception can be gleaned from the liberal Fund for the Republic's 1956 *Report on Blacklisting I: Movies* and from the accounts of left-wing writers like Ceplair and Englund and League insiders such as Stewart and Hy Kraft.

The idea for the Hollywood Anti-Nazi League apparently originated with Willi Münzenberg, the Comintern's extraordinarily effective promoter of Communist-front organizations worldwide. Münzenberg had linked up with the anti-Communist Prince Loewenstein in Paris after Loewenstein was expelled from Austria. Münzenberg had arranged for Loewenstein to meet Otto Katz, Münzenberg's own personal representative in Hollywood. Katz, a member of the German Communist Party since 1922, had moved to Moscow in 1930, was summoned to Paris in 1933 by Münzenberg, and then was dispatched to America as a fund-raiser for the "anti-fascist" underground—that is, Communists loyal to Stalin—in Europe.

In *The Inquisition in Hollywood*, Ceplair and Englund describe Katz as a "charismatic leader and superb fund-raiser" who "helped found the anti-Nazi movement in Hollywood."[11] Hollywood Anti-Nazi League insider Hy Kraft said he met Katz in New York under the name Rudolph Breda. Kraft found Breda (Katz) to be an inspiring figure—his own "personal Che Guevara." Kraft followed the charismatic Katz to Hollywood in the 1930s, "by which time he'd enlisted a number of influential adherents and had prepared the groundwork for the formation of the Hollywood Anti-Nazi League."[12] Katz was admired by Soviet-firsters including League chairman Stewart and Lillian Hellman, who modeled her resistance hero in her play *Watch on the Rhine* after Katz.[13]

The Hollywood Anti-Nazi League was so valuable to the Soviet cause that at one point in 1937 the Communist Party's cultural director, V. J. Jerome (the alias of Isaac Romaine) was dispatched to Hollywood to rescue it financially. "Jerome and John Howard Lawson put the front on a paying basis," according to the 1948 California Un-American Activities Committee.[14]

The reality that the League was a creature of Stalin rather than just a liberal group with a few Red trimmings, as its apologists suggest, emerged with vivid clarity upon the signing of the Hitler-Stalin Pact. Just eight months prior to its signing, the Hollywood Anti-Nazi League had initiated one of its most vigorous campaigns in protest of Nazi aggression. As the liberal Fund for the Republic study reports, in December of 1938 the League "launched the Committee of 56," after which "a declaration of democratic independence" was sent to the president and to Congress, requesting them to bring "such economic pressure to bear against Germany as would force her to reconsider her aggressive attitude towards other nations."[15]

The formal signing of the declaration—in essence a demand for a total economic boycott of Germany—took place at the Beverly Hills studios of Twentieth Century-Fox with considerable fanfare. Among the signers were some of Hollywood's most illustrious names: Joan Crawford, Paul Muni, John Ford, Walter Wanger, Edward G. Robinson, Melvyn Douglas, Rosalind Russell, James Cagney, Jack Warner, Henry Fonda, Bette Davis, Groucho Marx, Ben Hecht, Joan Bennett, and Dick Powell.

A MIRACULOUS TRANSFORMATION

The League continued its spirited anti-Hitlerism for most of 1938. "Committees of 56" were organized in other cities, and it was announced that twenty million signatures to the declaration would be gathered to persuade the Congress to force a complete economic break with Germany. The New York 56ers, the *Daily Worker* noted, would be headed by Dorothy Parker, Sylvia Sidney, Frances Farmer, Dashiell Hammett, John Garfield, and others.[16]

Then came Stalin's stunning about-face, a "peace" agreement with Adolf Hitler in August 1939. Once the Hilter-Stalin Pact was signed, the Anti-Nazi League's campaign against fascism, Hitler, and Nazi aggression was suddenly shelved. "Overnight," notes the Fund study, the Anti-Nazi League "became the Hollywood League for Democratic Action…no longer in favor of 'concerted action' as 'the only effective measure against fascist aggression.' Its New Year's card for 1940 denounced 'the war to lead America to war.'"[17] The fervent Hollywood anti-Nazis had suddenly become appeasers—simply because opposing Hitler no longer served Stalin's purposes.

Hollywood Now, with Stewart's name still prominently displayed on the masthead, would continue to publish after the Anti-Nazi League had changed its name. But its editorial line was now drastically different. Stewart's formerly robustly anti-Nazi publication was now just as energetically *condemning* the American defense buildup, promoting "powerful anti-war" films, and charging that critics of the Soviet invasion of Finland were fanning war flames to a "white heat." *Hollywood Now* also accused America's "war-makers" of using anti-Hitler propaganda "to destroy democracy in the United States."[18]

The line *Hollywood Now* took toward Hitler had changed dramatically. But its attitude toward anyone who exposed and opposed Communists was the same as ever. The paper waged a campaign to get Congress to eliminate the Left's nemesis: Representative Martin Dies's House Un-American Activities Committee. The January 12, 1940, issue carried "An Appeal to Congress" by the Executive Board of the Anti-Nazi League's successor organization, the Hollywood League for Democratic Action. The appeal demanded "that Congress repudiate this Committee and its un-American actions by refusing to grant further appropriations and by denying the Committee an extension of Congressional power."[19]

The September 1939 meeting of the former Anti-Nazi League, held shortly after the Hitler-Stalin Pact was signed in August, showcased the remarkable transformation of the organization. Hitler had already invaded Poland, but that act of aggression did not disturb the former anti-Nazis. The League's anti-Nazism had simply been dropped down the memory hole. A plenipotentiary from Communist headquarters in New York explained to the attendees that the alliance between Russia and Germany was a magnificent contribution to world peace. Those who went along with the new Party line after this meeting, including League president Donald Ogden Stewart and future Hollywood Ten celebrity Herbert Biberman, represented "the crème de la crème of Hollywood Stalinism," notes Gene Lyons, the United Press's former Moscow correspondent.

But the new Party line was not without cost. "Alas," writes Lyons sarcastically, "movie stars upon whom Jerome and Biberman once could count on implicitly [to support Red fronts] now visited Congressman Dies.... Melvyn Douglas accepted the lead in such sacrilegious [that is, anti-Communist] pictures as *Ninotchka* and *He Stayed for Breakfast*, swore off Communist organizations and even began to write for the anti-Stalin *New Leader*."[20]

The much-denounced Congressman Martin Dies, accused of "smearing" the League to undermine the New Deal, had been proved right after all—a fact that Hollywood still refuses to concede.

CHAPTER SIX

THE PRO-HITLER CONGRESS

Three American Writers' Congresses had revealed that their participants were enthusiastic supporters of the Soviet Union, eager to be used as Moscow's pawns. But none of the Congresses, not even the first, was more illuminating as to the abject loyalty of its backers to Stalin's Russia than the Fourth American Writers' Congress, held in New York City, June 6–8, 1941.

For approximately five years, Soviet Russia had loudly beaten the drums for America to lead the world against Adolf Hitler and fascism. Taking its cue from Stalin, the American Communist Party had regularly called for cooperation with the "imperialist" powers in the West, including England and France, to contain and even confront the fascist powers in Europe. "Hands off Poland" was another rallying cry frequently heard on the Left.

Communist Party boss Earl Browder's report to the CP's National Committee in the fall of 1938 was a polemic against American isolationism and "pacifism": "We cannot deny the possibility, even the probability, that only American arms can preserve the Americas from conquest by the Berlin-Tokyo alliance.... It will be necessary to clear away all remnants of the pacifist rubbish of opposing war by surrender to the war makers."[1]

Indeed, most of the Hollywood Ten—six of whom were Jewish—have said they were initially drawn to Communism because of the Soviet stand against fascism. If that claim is true, it's something of a mystery why they chose to stick with the Party after the Hitler-Stalin Pact. For the shrill voices emanating from the June 1941 Fourth American Writers' Congress carried a message stunningly different from the urgent anti-fascist theme that had prevailed at previous Congresses. The speakers and the delegates at the Fourth Congress called for a policy of total isolationism, harshly condemned Great Britain and the West as "imperialists" (Hitler was barely a secondary target), and frantically urged a massive campaign to disarm the United States and cripple its ability to aid *any* nation threatened by the fascist powers that had now conquered virtually all of Europe.

Why had the Writers' Congress so dramatically changed its tune? Just weeks after the previous "anti-fascist" Congress in 1939, Hitler and Stalin had stunned the world by entering into a "friendship" pact, with Stalin giving the Nazi leader the green light to invade Poland, the decisive act that set off World War II. Both England and France had repeatedly warned Berlin's warlord that if his armies marched against his next-door neighbor they would have to wage war against him. Barely eight days after the Hitler-Stalin Pact was signed, Nazi Germany stormed into Poland, and World War II was on.

Stalin had never really objected to Hitler's militarism or butchery; indignant Communist Party condemnation of Nazi aggression had simply been rhetorically useful to Stalin during the time when he saw Hitler as a threat. Now that the two were allies, Stalin rejoiced when Hitler, responding to England's and France's military efforts on behalf of the Poles, sent his legions into Western Europe in 1940 and swept the Continent.

While Hitler's legions were marauding Europe, Stalin, as the Pact required, was lavishing the German war machine with critical raw materials and, as a good-will gesture, unleashing his global fifth columns to subvert, propagandize, and bully countries Hitler had targeted for conquest or was intent on neutralizing so they couldn't furnish aid to the Fuehrer's active enemies. The Soviet dictator got almost as good as he gave, having himself been awarded plenty of plundering rights in the Pact. Stalin had Hitler's support to conquer the eastern half of Poland, seize the Baltic states, invade Finland, and take a slice of Rumania—and the Kremlin's potentate eagerly took advantage of the Fuehrer's generosity.

THE COMINTERN'S PRO-HITLER INSTRUCTIONS

Immediately following the Pact, America's Communists, who had been leading a ferocious charge against Hitler and fascism, were initially in a dither. Many continued to attack Hitler and fascism in the immediate post-Pact period—until they were straightened out by the Soviet-controlled Comintern.

The Comintern's head was George Dimitrov, who nearly five years before had announced the Popular Front strategy—the policy under which the Communists had sought to ally themselves with the Western "imperialist" powers against Hitler. Now Dimitrov sent CPUSA boss Earl Browder the Comintern's new instructions—coded messages sent to a short-wave radio receiver with an attached recorder during prescribed hours in the evening[2]—in keeping with Stalin's spectacular *volte face*. In late September and early October, Browder received two messages from the Comintern boss. The thrust of those messages: *the anti-Nazi strategy must be totally abandoned.* Browder was instructed that Hitler was unknowingly in the process of destroying the "bourgeois" nations in the West—a much-desired goal. The Comintern urged Browder that Communist Party members must act so as to promote this destruction of the capitalist nations.

In the September 1939 message, Dimitrov enthusiastically informed "Comrade Browder" that the war was "driving the capitalist world into a phase of most acute and profound crisis." Thus the fight against fascism was now "secondary," for the main struggle was now "against capitalism," the "bourgeoisie," and the "imperialists" in Western Europe and the United States. In this fight Germany was an ally, not an enemy, of the Soviets.

This is not—as Moscow had previously stressed—a "war of democracy against fascism, but of reactionary imperialist Germany against the reactionary, imperialist states of Britain, France and Poland. Question of who first attacked is of no importance; main thing is it is war for imperialistic domination."

The war, according to Comintern instructions, was "the continuation of the struggle between the rich countries (England, France, USA) which are backbone of capitalist system, and the wronged states (Germany, Italy, Japan) which…are deepening and sharpening the crisis of the capitalist system."

Dimitrov's instructions to American Communists were in keeping with this new interpretation of the world situation. They were to abandon the "United Front and People's Front" strategy against fascism and instead fight a "bold struggle against war." They must "concentrate fire against bourgeois dictatorship of [their] own country," "expose bourgeoisie as war speculators and freebooters," and "hold high the banner of proletarian internationalism."[3]

There were more instructions to Browder from the Comintern in early October 1939. The greatest base of imperialism, the coded message explained, is in "England, France, Germany, USA. Benefit to working class if they are weakened. Hitler without knowing it leads to shattering bourgeoisie."[4]

Hitler, according to the Comintern take on the situation, was doing Stalin a gigantic favor with his war against the West, destroying capitalism and its middle class along the way. Thus Communist Party members were urged to undermine anti-fascist sentiment that might lead America to resist, or aid nations willing to resist, Hitler's murderous regime.

This hard-line policy against the West was followed scrupulously by American Communists during virtually the entire period of the Pact, from August 23, 1939, until June 22, 1941 (though, as noted, there was a bit of confusion at the very beginning). Hitler and the fascist nations (Germany, Italy, and Japan) *were no longer the main enemy.* Instead, the main enemies were Hitler's *targets* in the West, those "bourgeois dictatorship[s]" and "bourgeois democracies," with their "imperialist" and "capitalist" systems. After the Pact was signed, no one—including the supposedly starry-eyed Hollywood idealists—could back the Soviet Union and still honestly consider himself an "anti-fascist."

While committed Communists at the Congresses and in the League of American Writers went along with Stalin's about-face on Hitler, some on the Left had begun to desert these Red Congresses and the League even before the

Soviet-Nazi Pact. Left-wing intellectuals John Dewey and Sidney Hook had resigned from the LAW in mid-1939 because it was a creature of the Communist Party. So had Babette Gross, the wife of the late Willi Münzenberg, who had created Communist fronts all over the world—including in Hollywood— but died disillusioned with Communism.

New Republic editor Malcolm Cowley, who had been a prominent member of the LAW, wrote a major article for his publication in August of 1940, detailing his reasons for abandoning the League. His essay was penned over a year after the Pact, by which time Hitler had dominated Europe. The occasion for his piece was the publication of a small book by Donald Ogden Stewart called *Fighting Words*, including a report of several speeches that had been given at the June 1939 Third American Writers' Congress, which had taken a strong anti-fascist line and had reelected Stewart as head of the League. In reviewing Stewart's work, Cowley lamented that the League hadn't said boo to the Nazis since the Hitler-Stalin Pact of August 1939, less than three months after the Third Writers' Congress had disbanded. Cowley noted that the week Stewart's book appeared, "half a dozen members withdrew from the executive board of the League. In a sense, these resignations were only the latest in a long series that included the honorary president, Thomas Mann, and four of the ten vice-presidents."

Cowley himself had resigned because the League was following the Communist Party line in proclaiming there were no real differences between Adolf Hitler and English prime minister Neville Chamberlain and his successor, Winston Churchill. According to Cowley, the League insisted Americans must "remain neutral not only in deed, but also in thought" and that money spent for defense "is an incitement to war and a means of strengthening the fascists at home."[5]

"ANTI-FASCISTS" DEMONIZE HITLER'S ENEMIES

Yet, while many noted writers fell off the Red bandwagon, at least temporarily, many of the most prominent Hollywood writers still aggressively followed Stalin's lead. In *The Inquisition in Hollywood*, Ceplair and Englund lay out the League's "anti-war" activities during the Pact period. "While the non-Communist Left split several ways on the question of war and intervention," they write, "the Communists in the League of American Writers and the peace mobilizations appeared to launch themselves wholeheartedly into the non-intervention cause.... Keep America out of War committees were formed in all branches of the League of American Writers; an *Anti-War Bibliography* (sixteen pages of anti-war music, drama, poetry, fiction, memoirs, films, art, periodicals, and pamphlets) was published in 1940; liaisons were established between all similarly motivated left-wing groups (Hollywood Peace Forum, Hollywood Peace Council, etc.)."

Rallies were directed and participated in by members of the League's anti-war committees, "one of which, 'America Declares Peace,' reportedly drew eight thousand people to the Olympic auditorium in Los Angeles on April 6, 1940, to see a 'Living Newspaper on Peace,' written by Michael Blankfort, Gordon Kahn and other leftist screenwriters...."[6]

Writers of such stature as Lillian Hellman, Donald Ogden Stewart, Langston Hughes, Dashiell Hammett, and Erskine Caldwell backed the League-sponsored Fourth American Writers' Congress, which savaged the parties resisting Hitler and the nations overwhelmed by his armies as "imperialist" and "fascist." Caldwell, author of *Tobacco Road* and *God's Little Acre*, sent his greetings from Moscow.

Five who would go on to be numbered among the Hollywood Ten, still revered today, had signed the "call" for this Congress, including Lawson, Bessie, Ornitz, Maltz, and Cole. These men, who had prided themselves on their Jewish heritage and their anti-fascism, appear to have had few qualms about siding with Hitler's Nazi Germany, the greatest enemy of the Jewish people in history. (Three other members of the Ten—Biberman, Lardner, and Trumbo—were not listed as sponsors of this Congress but also embraced the Hitler-Stalin Pact. Biberman was Jewish, Lardner's first wife was Jewish, and though not Jewish himself, Trumbo insisted he was a defender of the Jewish people.)

Other "controversial" writers—that is, Communists who were later blacklisted and heralded by Hollywood—who embraced this pro-Hitler Congress were Gordon Kahn, Waldo Salt, Robert Rossen, and Paul Jarrico—a number of whose writings and deeds we will catch up with later.

To this day Hollywood honors the Left for their supposed "anti-fascist" leadership, a claim that is utterly undermined by the events of the Fourth American Writers' Congress, which showcased the luminaries of the Hollywood Left applying all their considerable prestige and polemical skills to oppose any American effort to assist in the fight against Hitler or even to bolster our own emaciated defenses. This appalling spectacle took place against the backdrop of Hitler's swift and brutal conquest of Western Europe and his murderous bombing assaults against England. Since the Hitler-Stalin Pact, the Fuehrer had taken the western half of Poland in September 1939, launched his war against Western Europe in the spring of 1940, conquered Denmark and Norway, overran the Low Countries (Holland, Belgium, and Luxembourg), and then aimed his legions against France.

In four days, May 12 through May 15, 1940, German forces bypassed the highly touted Maginot Line, split the French army, drove all the way to the English Channel, and forced the British Expeditionary Force to evacuate their troops from the Continent at Dunkirk. Paris fell on June 14, and France surrendered just one week later. When France fell, Vyacheslav Molotov, Stalin's minister of foreign affairs, sent Hitler his congratulations.

On July 10, 1940, the Germans began the Battle of Britain, raining death and destruction on the country's major cities and coastal towns. Fascism was on the march, but the supposed "anti-fascists" of the Hollywood Left were lining up with the Fuehrer. They were doing everything they could to make sure that America in no way interfered with Hitler's triumphs.

Though the death camps were in the future, Hitler's anti-Semitism was hardly hidden. Since Hitler had become chancellor in 1933, the Third Reich had been ruthlessly persecuting the Jewish population. In the first year of Hitler's rule alone, as the prominent author William Shirer reminds us, the Jews had been "excluded from public office, the civil service, journalism, radio, farming, teaching, the theater, the films." Soon they would be barred from practicing law or even medicine.

By the time of the 1936 "Nazi Olympics," Shirer reports in *The Rise and Fall of the Third Reich*, Jews had been "excluded either by law or by Nazi terror from public and private employment to such an extent that at least one half of them were without means of livelihood." Shirer notes that the Jews "found it difficult if not impossible to purchase food…. In many communities Jews could not procure milk, even for their young children. Pharmacies would not sell them drugs or medicine. Hotels would not give them a night's lodging. And always, wherever they went, were the taunting signs 'Jews Strictly Forbidden in This Town.'" [7]

More horror was to come on *Kristallnacht*, the Night of Broken Glass. On November 7, 1938, Herschel Grynszpan, a seventeen-year-old German Jewish refugee, shot and killed an official of the German Embassy in Paris, seeking revenge for his father and thousands of other Jews who had shortly before been deported to Poland by boxcar.

Official German documents reveal that Reinhard Heydrich, a top official in the SS and the Gestapo, then organized a pogrom against the German Jewish population as punishment. November 10 "was a night of horror throughout Germany," Shirer writes. "Synagogues, Jewish homes and shops went up in flames and several Jews, men, women and children, were shot or otherwise slain while trying to escape burning to death."

By Heydrich's own account, the preliminary figures of 815 shops destroyed and 171 dwelling houses set on fire "indicate only a fraction of the actual damage so far as arson is concerned…. 119 synagogues were set on fire and another 76 completely destroyed…. 20,000 Jews were arrested. 36 deaths were reported and those seriously injured were also numbered at 36. Those killed and injured are Jews…." Heydrich noted that more than 7,500 Jewish shops had been looted. [8]

AN ORGY OF BRITISH BASHING

This is the reality of the Hitler regime that no longer concerned the "anti-fascist" Congress of Writers in 1941. The Congress was, however, deeply concerned about nations, organizations, and individuals actively *opposed* to the barbarous warlord.

The Fourth Congress had opened at Manhattan Center with a public "anti-war" rally, which became a mighty forum to assail Hitler's foes as tools of imperialism—just as the Comintern's Dimitrov had instructed CPUSA boss

Earl Browder twenty-two months earlier. The *Daily Worker* reported approvingly "[s]ome of the boldest and clearest attacks against the imperialist war" made at that rally: "They feel, as Dashiell Hammett so well put it in his Friday night speech, that the war-makers are out to 'kill all that is good and true and honest in American life.' They fervently agreed, with tremendous applause, when John Howard Lawson, noted playwright, said the same night that: 'Writers and artists recognize the defense of culture as inseparable from the defense of democracy. Writers and artists see this war as a brutal, tragic and corrupt scramble for world markets."[9] From the speeches, no one could have guessed that Nazi aggression, enabled by the Soviets, had caused the war.

The Congress was an orgy of Britain- and America-bashing, punctuated by worshipful praise of Stalinist Russia. The novelist Theodore Dreiser, who would become a Communist Party member in 1945, and whose anti-Semitism was so extreme that the *Daily Worker's* Mike Gold had rebuked him for it, received the "prestigious" Randolph Bourne Memorial Award for "distinguished service to the cause of culture and peace." His most conspicuous "distinguished service" consisted of nearly twenty-two months of venomous attacks against England during the Pact period.[10] The Congress also "loudly cheered mention of the Soviet Union and [CP boss] Earl Browder," noted the *New York Times*, and "booed...the government's aid to Britain program."[11]

Richard Wright, then a young black novelist, stirred the audience by singing hosannas to Moscow. "The Soviet Union and its leaders," he doggedly insisted, despite Stalin's enabling of Hitler's conquest of Western Europe and his own unprovoked attacks on Finland and Poland,

> stand today as living testimony to the profound hatred of war....
>
> The universal demand for peace is the secret weapon of the masses of the common people! It is a weapon which Hitler, Churchill, and Roosevelt fear more than any bomb! ...
>
> Is it not clear that the whole movement toward war in the United States has taken upon its shoulders the task of defeating the progressive moves of the Negro people and the laboring masses throughout the country? ...

Who can deny that the Anglo-American hatred of Negroes is of the same breed of hate which the Nazis mete out to Jews in Germany? ...

Wright equated "the imperialist policy of the United States" to

the imperialist policy of the German High Command! The two policies were so identical that I could not distinguish between them!

Time and again, during the course of this war, I have been struck by the startling similarity of the pronouncements, ideologies, and aims of the two warring camps....

The entire military strategy of this war has been one long process of two powerful imperialist groups of nations to grab and capture raw materials, new markets, or entire nations....[12]

The torrent of Red voices declaring that the West was as malignant as Hitler were, of course, attempting to persuade this country to give not even a drop of aid to Great Britain, the sole nation in Europe still confronting the Nazi warlord.

The American Writers' Congress went on record pledging "ourselves to speak the truth about this criminal war," insisting that it was "a brutal and shameless struggle for the redivision of empire—for profits, territories and markets."

The participants added, "We recognize the obvious identity of aims and methods between the Anglo-American warmakers and their German opponents."[13]

Many patriotic Americans had hoped we could stay out of the European war and opposed U.S. intervention in the conflict, but most of them were not resting their argument on the premise that Hitler's Nazis were no different from the Western democracies that he had crushed. Hollywood's Communist writers displayed not a sliver of shame in making that equivalence.

To demonstrate opposition to the "imperialist war," the Congress voted to send a large delegation of writers to Washington to join in the picketing of the

White House by the American Peace Mobilization (APM), the Communist-led organization that for nine months had been relentlessly bashing FDR's policy of strengthening America's defenses and aiding Great Britain.

But the Fourth Congress had a few more things to wrap up before joining the APM's "anti-war" effort in Washington. It voted *Native Son* the most distinguished American novel published since 1939, the last time the Congress had met. By embracing *Native Son*, the Congress was heaping honors on its author, Richard Wright, who, as we have seen, was a new and passionate anti-American, pro-Soviet voice.[14]

The Congress also supported the Communist-incited CIO machinists who were striking the North American Aviation company in Los Angeles, an important component of America's nascent defense industry.[15]

The assembled writers and artists chose Dashiell Hammett, mystery writer, lover of Communist writer Lillian Hellman, and a committed Communist himself, as the new head of the League of American Writers. The Congress folded its tent on June 8, 1941.

AN EMBARRASSING SWITCH

There is an ironic addendum to this ferociously anti-war Congress. Two weeks later, Hitler invaded Russia. The League of American Writers, through Hammett, its new president, issued an urgent call to all writers and writers' organizations for "immediate and necessary steps in support of Great Britain and the Soviet Union to insure the military defeat of the fascist aggressors."[16]

Hollywood's Communist writers had proved themselves Stalinists to the core through all these Congresses. They were Hitler's enemy when Stalin felt threatened by the rising power of the Third Reich. When Stalin embraced the Fuehrer, they gave a warm hug to the Nazi warlord. When Hitler invaded Russia, the American writers cast off their pacifist pose and began frantically beating the drums for massive aid to England, a policy that they had just weeks before proclaimed would shove America into a bloody and senseless war. Now that their beloved Soviet Union was under attack, they didn't mind a bit if American soldiers were to be tossed onto foreign battlefields—not to defend their own country, but to rescue the Soviet despot they worshipped.

CHAPTER SEVEN

RED AND BROWN
SABOTAGE

"Open-minded Americans have been properly reluctant...to pin the Communist label on any defense strike. In the case of the North American Aviation strike, however, the evidence of Communist inspiration has been mounting to a point where it now leaves little room for doubt." These were not the words of House Un-American Activities Committee chairman Martin Dies, though he certainly shared those sentiments, but the lead editorial in the June 10, 1941, *New York Times.*[1]

During the time the Hitler-Stalin Pact was in force, some twelve thousand aviation workers had gone out on strike in Southern California, and the *Times* had plenty of solid facts to support its conclusion that Communists were behind the strike. Its chief promoters—Elmer Freitag, Lew H. Michener, and Wyndham Mortimer—were all knee-deep in Communist Party activities.

Freitag, the head of Local 683 in Inglewood, which had called the strike, had already acknowledged to the Dies panel in May 1941 that he had registered as a Communist voter just three years previously.[2] Michener, regional director of the UAW at the time of the strike, was a long-time fellow traveler.[3] Mortimer, Michener's close associate and the UAW's representative for the aircraft industry on the West Coast, had joined the Communist Party under the alias "George Baker" as early as 1933.[4] Numerous witnesses before HUAC would identify him as a Party member. Even the *New York Times*' liberal labor reporter referred to him as "a follower of the Communist Party line,"[5] and Benjamin Stolberg, a widely respected labor journalist, informed his readers in the *American Mercury* that Mortimer "has played a large role as a Stalinist agent in American labor for many years. In 1938, he was put in charge of organization in the aircraft industries on the West Coast."[6]

STRIKING TO HELP STALIN—AND HITLER

There were good reasons the Reds were eager to shut down North American: it was the largest military aviation producer in the United States. North American would put thousands of warplanes in the American inventory, and half of the planes it produced were destined for England, now struggling for its very survival against Nazi Germany. The plant's production facilities were so crucial to our defense efforts that the Roosevelt administration had threatened to seize the plant if the strike weren't called off—and, when the strike leaders refused to bend, FDR dispatched federal troops to take over North American.

In a somewhat rare instance of harmony, in this case President Roosevelt, management, and responsible labor leaders were on the same side. None desired to see the strike continue, especially since the issues were in mediation.

Richard Frankensteen, national director of the aviation division of the United Auto Workers, squarely addressed the issue of Communist involvement in the strike before a mass meeting of striking UAW members on June 7. Frankensteen lit into an "irresponsible minority" of North American leaders who were inflaming the situation and complained of "the infamous agitation, the vicious maneuvering of the Communist Party...."

Frankensteen revealed how the local union had called the strike at Inglewood "completely without authorization" from the national UAW and in violation of the local's own agreement to await the findings of the National Mediation Board, a government agency that Frankensteen stressed was "outstandingly fair" in all its dealings with unions belonging to the CIO.[7] Frankensteen called upon the men to return to work and cashiered Mortimer and other Communist agitators from their critical UAW posts.[8]

But Communist sabotage of the American war effort, as shocking as it was, was only part of the story. Mortimer and other Communists in the CIO and the UAW were also working with members of the pro-Nazi German-American Bund to cripple American armaments manufacturers.

During hearings before the Dies panel, Hugh Ben Inzer, elected president of Local 216 of the UAW in May of 1940, testified that shortly after his election he was asked to attend a meeting at CIO headquarters in Los Angeles. The ostensible purpose of the meeting was to share ideas on how to get more folks into the UAW. Most of the attendees were union officials, and some of them—Mortimer, Lew Michener, "Slim" Connelly, and Pettis Perry—were Communists or leading fellow travelers.

But a man named Hans Diebel was also present. He embraced a different philosophy from all the others gathered at union headquarters. Diebel was a Nazi, loyal to Adolf Hitler, and a leader in the German-American Bund. Diebel also owned the Aryan Book Store, which sold Nazi materials and pro-Nazi propaganda. He cooperated with the Communists in distributing their literature to help foster strikes in the defense industry. Apparently Diebel was participating in the Communists' "The Yanks Are Not Coming" program, designed to sabotage the American military buildup and block U.S. assistance to Great Britain.

All of this came out in convincing testimony before Representative Dies's HUAC hearings in May 1941. Inzer testified that he was told Diebel owned a bookstore, was a publisher, and could print literature "to be distributed to the different CIO plants in case we wanted to call a coast-wide strike to effect the negotiations at any plant that they [CIO officials] were working on at the time." Inzer, however, did not learn of Diebel's Nazi background until he and Richard Franklin, another UAW member, looked into Diebel's background on their own.[9]

No group was more supportive of the strikes in the defense industry than America's radical writers, and no group was more supportive of the North American walkout in particular than the men and women who attended the pro-Hitler Fourth American Writers' Congress. That gathering, notes a Dies report, "voted to send a telegram of sympathy to the 'outlaw' strikers who had tied up" the North American plant.[10] The writers had also enthusiastically "cheered a reading of the text" that the strikers had sent to FDR.

Other strikes fit the same pattern—Communist agitators using a genuine labor dispute as an opportunity to shut down production of armaments and cripple the resistance to Hitler and the defense of the United States. The same Wyndham Mortimer who was instrumental in the strike at North American had also been involved in a November 1940 strike at Vultee Aircraft, a plant of four thousand workers in Downey, California, notes Max Kampelman in his highly authoritative *The Communist Party vs. the CIO*. "The original dispute between the company and the union was over wages and that was speedily settled," writes Kampelman. But Mortimer worked his magic for Red mischief, breaking off negotiations and engineering a strike over far less important grievances. Both the War and Justice Departments pressured the union for a settlement, with Attorney General Robert Jackson charging the strike had been Communist inspired.[11]

The most serious Communist-inspired defense strike may have occurred at Milwaukee's Allis-Chalmers Manufacturing Company, which produced equipment for the navy. Though wages, hours, and conditions—the usual matters of dispute—were not at issue, the strike lasted seventy-six days. Harold Christoffel, the head of Local 248 of the UAW—who, according to Kampelman, "had for a number of years been associated with Communist leaders"—played a major role. "Testimony of a former Communist Party member alleged that Christoffel had discussed with the Wisconsin organizer of the Communist Party the strategic value of organizing Allis-Chalmers, a vital navy defense plant, as a way of furthering the anti-war activities of the Communist Party."[12]

During the eight months before the strike, as Benjamin Stolberg of the *American Mercury* reported, Christoffel called seventeen work stoppages "for all sorts of petty and absurd reasons." Finally, in January 1941, the Communists decided to strike the whole plant. Since the law in Wisconsin forbids the calling of strikes without a secret strike ballot, a vote was taken. Later it was disclosed, and admitted by Christoffel, that over 40 per cent of the votes had been faked.

In the end, the Defense Mobilization Board settled the strike by the simple ruling that nobody was to be permitted to agitate during working hours. It was really settled when William Knudsen and Secretary Knox, of the Navy, threatened to proceed against the strike leaders for faking the strike vote.[13]

The House of Representatives Committee on Labor and Education, which included a young John F. Kennedy, came to the same conclusions as Stolberg and Kampelman. "At the direction of the Communist Party and for the purpose of carrying out its programs," said the committee report, "Harry Christoffel called a seventy-six day strike at the Allis-Chalmers plant. In doing this, he used over 2,000 fraudulent ballots and betrayed his country, his employer and his fellow workers."[14]

America's radical writers had given their wholehearted support to the Red-Brown effort to sabotage the American armaments industry. But when Hitler betrayed Stalin and attacked the Soviet Union, the writers turned on a dime. American Communists and their fellow travelers in Hollywood began wildly beating the drums for a massive rearmament program in America and frantically urging the formerly evil, warmongering FDR to lavish as many military weapons as he could possibly spare upon the Soviet Union and even "imperialist" England.

Stalin had changed direction again, and America's radical writers turned with him.

CHAPTER EIGHT

THE AMERICAN PEACE MOBILIZATION GOES TO WAR

When the Fourth American Writers' Congress voted to send a contingent to join the "pickets for peace" at the White House during the Hitler-Stalin Pact, it was teaming up with yet another full-fledged Communist organization. The American Peace Mobilization (APM) was born on September 2, 1940, in Chicago, Illinois. From its inception it was inspired by Communists, saturated with Communists, and run by Communists. The release from prison of the Communist Party's general secretary, Earl Browder, who had been jailed for a passport violation, was one of its major demands.

Determined to block America from assisting victims of Nazi aggression, the APM not only flogged the slogan "The Yanks Are Not Coming," popularized in a pamphlet produced by Communist Party member Mike Quin. But the APM also did everything it could to disarm this country and ease Hitler's path to victory over his foes.

A SUCCESSION OF RED FRONTS

The APM was successor to a string of Communist fronts designed to shape American opinion to conform to Soviet foreign policy. The first major "peace" front established by the Soviets in the United States was the American League against War and Fascism, actually incubated in Amsterdam under the aegis of the Comintern but formally organized in New York City in late September and early October 1933.

The manifesto and program adopted by the League demanded the end to the "increasingly widespread use of the armed forces" against "workers" and "farmers," and the "special terrorizing and suppression of Negroes in their attempts to maintain a decent standard of living." The whole program of the Roosevelt administration, it charged, while sold as a way to establish peace, is "permeated by preparedness for war" and must be opposed "through mass demonstrations, picketing and strikes" as well as through giving "international support to all workers and anti-war fighters against their own imperialist governments."

The documents also called for worldwide support for the Soviet Union, the sole nation "where this basic cause of war [monopolistic capitalism] has been removed." The League pledged "to oppose all attempts to weaken the Soviet Union, whether these take the form of misrepresentation and false propaganda, diplomatic maneuvering or intervention by imperialist governments."[1]

The first national chairman of the American League against War and Fascism was J. B. Matthews, who later became a skillful and scholarly opponent of the Communists. In his famous 1938 memoir, *Odyssey of a Fellow Traveler*, Matthews explained the two purposes behind the League: (1) the Soviets feared we would join with other "imperialist" nations to fight the USSR; and (2) the Communists believed they could trigger an uprising of the masses with a ferocious barrage of anti-administration propaganda.

In pursuit of its goal of stirring up the great unwashed, the Party itself waged an all-out verbal assault on the Roosevelt administration. Party head Earl Browder's full-throated cry against the president, accusing him of "carrying out more thoroughly, more brutally than Hoover, the capitalist attack against the living standards of the masses and the sharpest national chauvinism in foreign relations"[2] was typical.

But by 1935 the Soviet Union had decided that the revolution in America was not imminent after all and that it needed allies to challenge an increasingly threatening Germany and Japan. So the Party softened its revolutionary image, setting up "Popular Fronts" to rally as many Americans as possible behind policies congruent with Moscow's rising fears.

To alter its tainted anti–New Deal image, in 1937 the American League against War and Fascism changed its name to the American League for Peace and Democracy. This "new" group not only supported FDR and his domestic policies but began promoting a "people's boycott" of Japanese goods and agitating for the removal of restrictions on shipping goods to China and the anti-Nazi Loyalists in Spain, now controlled by Stalin.

Of course this anti-Nazi phase of the renamed league would not last long. When Stalin made his Pact with Hitler two years later, the American League for Peace and Democracy became the essentially pro-Nazi American Peace Mobilization. America and the New Deal were the enemies once again, and Hollywood's radical writers, as we shall see shortly, were racing to team up with the newest Communist vehicle for promoting "peace."

The Reds running the APM operation selected the Reverend John B. Thompson of Oklahoma as "chairman." The Communists had chosen a willing pawn. Thompson, though probably never a Communist Party member, was an ardent Soviet apologist into the 1950s. As nominal head of the APM, he signed innumerable Red petitions, joined Communist-front groups, and never appeared to doubt that the Soviet Union was a grand old country.

A thick FBI document on the APM and Thompson depicts him as a "Marxist" who adheres "closely to the CP line in all of his activities." He was quoted as saying from the pulpit of his church in Norman, Oklahoma, in January of 1941 that "Russia enjoys more of freedom" than Oklahoma.[3]

The man who really ran the APM was Frederick Vanderbilt Field, the millionaire Communist who was a descendant of the powerful tycoon Cornelius Vanderbilt. Field funded and participated in dozens of Red causes during his lifetime, including the pro–Chinese Communist faction in the Institute of Pacific Relations (IPR).

He resigned as executive of the IPR in September 1940 to take up the executive secretary position in the APM. Field, who would take the Fifth in 1950 rather than say whether he had ever been a Communist, became a frequent writer for such Red publications as the *New Masses* and the *Daily Worker*. In 1949 he wrote an article for *Political Affairs* in which he referred to "our tasks as American Communists."

But we don't really have to draw any inferences about Field from his writings for Party and left-wing publications, since he confessed his Communist ties and beliefs in great detail in his autobiography, *From Right to Left*. The APM, Field frankly admits, was a "Communist-front organization, which meant that it came into existence through the Communist Party initiative and that many Communists were active in it ... Some time before the APM was formally organized, Earl Browder asked me if I would accept the executive secretaryship if it were offered me."

Field, who said he had "worked with and within" the Party, but never formally joined, told him yes. (Field said he viewed himself as a Communist while the Party viewed him as a "Communist-at-large.")[4]

When the organizing conference for the APM was held in Chicago, with some five thousand delegates from labor unions, farm groups, religious organizations, and others in attendance, Field's name was presented to the delegates without discussion. Field acknowledged that he was "not well known among the delegates" and that he had done no trade union or community organization work, but the vote was "uncontested." The delegates "had evidently been told that I was to have the job."

Just before he was "nominated and unanimously elected," the Party pulled a fast one on Field himself. His fellow Reds quickly moved "someone else.... to the position of administrative secretary. I had never heard of her and had not even been told that there was to be such a position." Clearly, she had been chosen to keep a comradely eye on Field.[5]

Eugene Dennis, a top Party official who got his instructions on the APM from Comintern chief George Dimitrov, discussed the organization's goals in a confidential memorandum to Party officials. ("T. Ryan"—the name Dennis frequently used when conducting Party affairs—was typed at the end of this memo.)

Noting that the APM had been organized "on the initiative of our party," Dennis expressed pleasure that it had "set in motion important mass activities and campaigns" against U.S. defense preparedness and for the "right to strike" in disputes involving "all government and armament contracts."[6] As "Comrade Dimitrov has counseled," he noted, it is "more essential than ever" for Americans to resist FDR's "imperialist" program, "especially the government's 'aid to Britain' policy," and to "strengthen the ties of friendship . . . with the great Land of Socialism [meaning, obviously, the USSR]."[7]

FOLLOWING THE SOVIET SCRIPT

The APM's attitude toward Hitler's bloody conquest of Europe would mirror that of the Fourth American Writers' Congress and the League of American Writers—they were all following the same script. "Behind our backs," according to the APM, "the peace and further prosperity of our land have been bartered for world empire and the imperial ambitions of the lords of Wall Street."

The APM's official March 1941 statement, in the form of a leaflet designed to "clarify" the views of its own members, equated moderate, pro-democratic, and besieged England with murderous, conquering, and totalitarian Nazi Germany. The leaflet laid down the Party line in question-and-answer format.

"But even if we don't approve of England's war [notice who is being blamed for the war Germany started]," one question began, "isn't her side still preferable to Hitler's, and isn't it better to fight and beat Hitler with England than without her?" "No," was the answer. "An English victory will result in the same sort of imperialist, anti-democratic peace as will a Nazi victory."[8]

This grotesque Party line was set by the Comintern and spouted by scores of loyal Communists and fellow travelers, including many on the Hollywood Left. We have seen how the Fourth American Writers' Congress, controlled by Communists and sympathizers, had made exactly the same point: Nazis were no worse than Englishmen.

In his reminiscences, Field was somewhat apologetic about the APM position that "the European war in those early stages was one between rival imperialists, the British Empire and the Nazi Reich." Representative Vito Marcantonio, vice chairman of the APM and a member of the pro-Soviet

American Labor Party, had generously conceded, "While there may be some difference between the tyranny of Hitlerism and that of British imperialism…that difference is one of degree, and the degree is so small as not to warrant anyone justly to say that this is a war between the democratic forces of the world and the Nazi forces of the world."[9]

But no one directed more venom toward England than the APM's 1940 vice chairman, the novelist Theodore Dreiser, a Hollywood darling who formally joined the Party in 1945. In March of 1940, Dreiser found himself in a debate with Philip Dunne, a far-Left Hollywood screenwriter who never brought himself to embrace Stalin's Soviet Union but who would rush to the defense of the Hollywood Ten in 1947. (More about Dunne later.)

"Mr. Dreiser," Dunne wrote in his autobiography, "opened the debate by saying that the British people should be allowed to be engulfed by Hitler because they were a cruel people who hunted foxes." During the Pact period, Dreiser also wrote *America Is Worth Saving*. The APM's Field, who edited the book, conceded it contained "a violent denunciation of the British Empire and all that it stood for."[10] APM was not the primary publisher but was permitted to sell a special edition.

Dreiser, the famous author of such heralded novels as *An American Tragedy* and *Sister Carrie*—each turned into a Hollywood movie—wrote, "The wealthy class of England is splashing around in a stagnant, reeking pond of blood profits." He argued that "if Germany can beat England at the game of mass human torture…then it will have to go some."[11] Dreiser's words were published in January 1941, when Hitler had already swept the Continent and had been blasting London's cities from the air.

On the other hand, Dreiser was euphoric about the economic and social progress—nothing short of miraculous, in his view—taking place in the Soviet Union. Dreiser concluded by saying he could "do no better" than quote from "one of the most courageous and honest Christians of the day in England, who recently visited Russia and compared what he saw with his own country—the Reverend Hewlett Johnson, Dean of Canterbury Cathedral." And what had Johnson seen in Russia? "Nothing strikes the visitor to the Soviet Union more forcibly than the absence of fear.…"[12] Six months later Dreiser won the League of American Writers' Randolph Bourne Memorial Award for his fight for peace.

Most of the Hollywood Ten were up to their necks in the APM movement as sponsors, supporters, or officials. Five of the Ten—Lawson, Bessie, Ornitz, Maltz, and Cole—were on record as favoring the Fourth American Writers' Congress, which voted to join the APM's White House pickets.

Ring Lardner and Dalton Trumbo were APM activists who, according to a quotation from Lardner in a friendly biography of Trumbo, "worked together on American Peace Mobilization."[13] In his novel *The Remarkable Andrew*, published during the Pact period, Trumbo appeared to prefer Nazi Germany to Great Britain.

Lawson and Maltz were listed as "sponsors" in APM literature, while Ornitz, like Lawson, was also a major participant in APM activities. Herbert Biberman was a member of the APM's "National Council." In an APM gathering in Washington in January of the same year, Biberman, according to an FBI summary of his remarks, charged the United States with having become "a colony of the British Empire…Mr. Biberman then charged that Hitler, Roosevelt and Churchill are making a deal for the money markets of the world, and using the lives of millions of men" to achieve this goal.[14]

An FBI informant told of Biberman receiving "a standing ovation" at an APM rally in the Embassy Auditorium in Los Angeles, where he "was more caustic than usual in his tirade against President Roosevelt, Ambassador [Joseph] Kennedy [our envoy to Great Britain] and Great Britain."[15] Another informant, hearing Biberman at a different "peace" group, wondered if he "might not be really a Nazi working within an anti-Nazi organization."[16]

The Hollywood chapter of the League of American Writers was awash in comrades cooperating with the APM. Among those on the chapter's "Peace Committee," which worked with the APM and other "peace" groups, were several other Communist screenwriters, including Paul Jarrico (chairman), Paul Trivers, Bob Lees, and Fred Rinaldo—also members of the radical faction of the Screen Writers Guild.[17]

APM leaflets portrayed England, not Germany, as the major world villain. FDR was viciously caricatured and harshly condemned for permitting the selling of "munitions to Britain" and "lending Britain money—not only money, but everything including the aluminum right out of our kitchen pans.

That's bringing the war right into our homes…." In a leaflet titled "Songs of APM," there's a parody of "Billy Boy" by the singing group The Almanacs, who wonder if "Billy's" too afraid to fight. "Billy" responds, "You can come around to me / when England's a democracy." (Nazi aggression isn't mentioned.)[18]

The APM existed for just nine months, but it put on a whale of an "anti-war" campaign in over two hundred towns and cities, including the nation's capital. The APM fulfilled the Comintern's instructions to a T, furiously fighting every effort to assist anti-Nazi forces anywhere on earth or even to rebuild our own defenses. The group activated ferocious "anti-war" chapters across the country, poured out "peace" pamphlets by the score, and staged mass demonstrations, with the bitterly anti-American Negro singer Paul Robeson frequently the star entertainment.

Hardly a day went by when the *Daily Worker* wasn't publicizing the APM's enormous effort on behalf of "peace" in blazing headlines. Examples include

- "APM Calls Giant American People's Meeting for Peace"
- "APM Launches Crusade to Defeat War Power Bill"
- "APM to Maintain Perpetual 'Peace Vigil' Outside White House to Fight War Drive"
- "Noted Figures Address Washington Parley"
- "Cities, Towns, Hamlets Urged to Begin Tremendous Protest against War Drive"
- "Peace Mobilization Maps Fight on FDR War Bill"
- "Brooklyn Anti-War APM Rally to Hear Quill, Curran Speak"

And there was even more sinister mischief afoot. "From an intimate source," writes Gene Lyons in The Red Decade, "it is learned that decisions for dramatic anti-defense action on American docks, harbors and ships were taken at a secret meeting in a Greenwich Village apartment. The Communist Party commissar for shipping, Roy Hudson, told about 25 leading Communists to prepare for an all-out test of 'our party's strength in the maritime industry.'"

The meeting, Lyons continues, "was attended by the leaders of Communist 'fractions' in such shipyards and ports as Mobile, San Francisco, San Diego, Philadelphia, Boston, New Orleans and New York."[19]

APM members had apparently infiltrated various military posts as well. Special Agent B. E. Sackett was alarmed enough to write FBI director J. Edgar Hoover, presumably in March 1941, that he had been given information "to the effect that the American Peace Mobilization has so-called active cells at several military camps," including at Fort Dix, New Jersey, and Fort Bragg, North Carolina.[20]

Beginning in late 1940, the APM orchestrated an "anti-war" picket line in front of the White House. Representatives of Communist-controlled unions such as the National Maritime Union and the American Communications Association joined the vigils at 1600 Pennsylvania Avenue. Members of all sorts of Communist groups showed up, including folks who had fought for the Loyalists with the Abraham Lincoln Brigade in the Spanish Civil War.

APM executive secretary Field boasted that the "picket line in front of the White House was...maintained without one minute's interruption for 1,029 hours." The protesters suddenly and mysteriously disappeared, not on the day Japan bombed a sovereign America at Pearl Harbor in December 1941, but six months earlier, the weekend the Nazis invaded the country that Hollywood's Red writers had lovingly embraced over their own.

A SOMERSAULT FOR STALIN

The APM, like the League of American Writers and in fact all Party-controlled organizations, turned a fancy somersault when the Nazis rolled into Soviet-controlled territory on June 22, 1941. Eight days later, the APM's national board frantically urged "active support of the Soviet Union as well as of all other forces fighting Nazi Germany." U.S. assistance to Great Britain, formerly anathema, was now a necessity.

With the breaking of the Hitler-Stalin Pact, what the Soviet Union and its fifth column in America feared most was that the United States might adopt a "plague on both your houses" policy or, even worse, assist Germany in its effort to overthrow the Bolshevik regime in the East. The *Daily Worker* was in panic mode when Harry Truman, then a Missouri senator, sardonically announced, "If we see that Germany is winning, we ought to help Russia, and if Russia is winning, we ought to help Germany…." The famous isolationist senator Burton K. Wheeler of Montana caused the paper's editors more heartburn when he demanded that the United States do nothing to assist Moscow. These were the mouthings of "pro-fascists," proclaimed the Communist Party's official publication, pronouncements representing the "Munich capitulations magnified tenfold."[21]

The APM, which only a fortnight before had opposed any actions that could possibly irritate Hitler, was now desperately calling upon Americans to plunge into the European conflict to destroy Nazi Germany. Among its new recommendations:

- "Aid to the people of Great Britain and the Soviet Union and to all people in their fight against Nazi Germany."
- "Aid to the united people of China."
- "Embargo Japan."
- "Expose and isolate those forces which work for a victory of fascism by a policy of appeasement."

"Under the false cloak of isolationism," the APM warned, "certain demagogic leaders are now calling for an appeasement" of Hitler. Other "fascist appeasers" are for "sabotaging aid to the Soviet Union and to genuine antifascist peoples…."[22]

With the Soviets under attack, the APM was no longer eager to keep America's young men from the bloody battlegrounds in Europe and Asia. Its leaders now called for policies certain to draw us into wars they had so recently declared were being fought for the "lords of Wall Street." Now things were different; it was perfectly all right to send young Americans to their doom for the warlord in the Kremlin.

CHAPTER NINE

RED PROPAGANDA IN
FILMS

"**A**s for myself, I do not hesitate to say that it is my aim to present the Communist position and to do so in a specific manner."[1]

So proclaimed John Howard Lawson, "Grand Pooh-Bah" of the Hollywood Red colony, when he was converting to Communism in the early 1930s. Lawson was dispatched to Hollywood in 1937 by Communist Party Central Committee member V. J. Jerome to become the "boss" and the "cultural czar" of Hollywood's Reds. He was probably the most controversial, and rigidly ideological, member of the Ten—even more so than Dalton Trumbo.

Lawson was quoted as urging revolutionary writers and actors to follow his lead in injecting Communist or class struggle ideas into the movies. John Moffitt, the motion picture critic for *Esquire* when the Hollywood Ten hearings got under way in 1947, testified that he had had "several conversations" with Lawson a decade earlier, after Moffitt had joined the Communist-front

Hollywood Anti-Nazi League. During the period Moffitt was a member, Lawson confided to him and others his strategy for softening up the minds of Americans so they could better appreciate Communism.

SNEAKING COMMUNISM INTO THE MOVIES

As Moffitt recalled Lawson's words, the top Hollywood Red urged authors *not* to write "an entire Communist picture. The producers will quickly identify it and it will be killed by the front office." Instead, "try to get five minutes of the Communist doctrine, five minutes of the party line in every script that you write."

Lawson suggested that Communist doctrine be dropped into an expensive scene involving expensive stars, plenty of extras, and lavish sets because "the business manager of the unit, the very watchdog of the treasury, the very servant of capitalism, in order to keep the budget from going too high, will resist the elimination of that scene."

Moffitt left the Hollywood Anti-Nazi League after six months, but a short time later was taken by friends to "what purported to be a school for actors in Hollywood" to hear a lecture. The speaker was Lawson, the cultural commissar himself.

During the course of the evening, Lawson, as Moffitt recalled, stressed to his audience of young actors that it "is your duty to further the class struggle by your performance. If you are nothing more than an extra wearing white flannels on a country club veranda do your best to appear decadent, do your best to be a snob, do your best to create class antagonism. If you are an extra in a tenement street, do your best to look downtrodden, do your best to look a victim of existing society."[2]

Moffitt's testimony appears never to have been challenged by any of the leading apologists for the Hollywood Ten, including Ceplair and Englund, although their book mentions him in another context. The liberal Fund for the Republic's famous 1956 study on Communism and the movies, discussed at length below, never deals with Moffitt's accusations. I have read Lawson's unpublished memoirs but found no reference to Moffitt's claims in them.

Lawson's instructions about what committed radicals should do when they write or perform in movies reveal, at the very least, that dyed-in-the-wool Hollywood Reds were eager to manipulate the films to serve their ideology.

The Left, in fact, was always sneaking propaganda into movie scripts, or trying to, despite liberal protestations to the contrary—the Fund for the Republic study, for instance, asserted that it is "now generally accepted as true that there was no Communist propaganda in films...."[3]

No Communist propaganda in films? That statement defies belief. Several anti-Communist producers, including Jack Warner and Louis B. Mayer, insisted their films were untainted by Communist scriptwriters. But these claims are belied by an enormous amount of contrary evidence, including some uncovered by the Fund itself.

THE FUND FOR THE REPUBLIC STUDY

Report on Blacklisting I: Movies, the 1956 Fund for the Republic–financed study directed by John Cogley of the liberal *Commonweal* magazine, remains one of the most important investigative reports on Communist writers and unions in Hollywood, the fight against them (led by labor leader Roy Brewer, a key member of the anti-Communist Motion Picture Alliance), and the blacklist. Much of this report is informative, well documented, and even balanced, despite a far too critical attitude toward the blacklist—and the inexplicable conclusion that Communist propaganda in films was virtually nonexistent.

Dorothy B. Jones, the former chief film analyst for the Office of War Information, prepared a 205-page paper for the Fund about Communism and the movies, now housed in the Seeley G. Mudd Manuscript Library at Princeton University. A much shorter version of this 1956 paper was appended to the full Fund report. Both documents cut against the Fund's formal findings.

The chief argument from both the Fund and Jones that there was no propaganda in the movies is *not based on the films' actual content* but on dubious criteria laid out by Jones. She relied on the fact that the producers, who weren't Communists, had control of the scripts. But the major criterion should have been whether the final product was filled with propaganda that showered praise on Communism and the Soviet Union, boosted Soviet objectives, or condemned the American way of life. Using this definition of Communist propaganda as a yardstick, the findings of Jones's own investigation demonstrate that

Hollywood's screenwriters relentlessly attempted to put Communist propaganda onto the silver screen and were frequently successful.

What Jones herself concedes in her detailed study of various movies is illuminating. She admits that the Communist screenwriters, Dalton Trumbo in particular, made a deliberate effort to control picture content for political reasons. And she acknowledges that writers introduced material that "paralleled" or was "consistent with" the Party line.

Jones also documents that the industry was well aware of the determination of the radical writers to push propaganda into the finished screen products. Jones cites an intra-office memo compiled by a staff member of the Production Code Administration of the Motion Picture Producers and Distributors of America, which reviewed films prior to production.

"This [Communism]," the memo states, "is a very dangerous subject as screen material. Some Hollywood writers are Communists, and try to inject communistic propaganda speeches into scripts they write. These speeches take the form of condemning the capitalistic system, and wealthy people, or bemoaning the plight of the poor, and suggesting this condition would not exist under communism."[4]

Jones gives many details of how left-wing writers used their writing to promote their ideology. In the early 1930s, she notes, these writers constructed plots showing America's elites as under the thumb of gangsters and corrupt and greedy businessmen. Typical of this genre was the 1934 film *The Man Who Reclaimed His Head*, written by Samuel Ornitz, a future Hollywood Ten member.

The Man Who Reclaimed His Head, starring Claude Rains, tells the story of a French World War I soldier who ghostwrites inspirational anti-war editorials for a famous publisher. The writer goes off to war, and the publisher sells out to the munitions makers and then steals the soldier's wife. In the film, war is presented as a dirty business, "which is the special property of munition moguls whose God is money," Jones reports.

The social, political, and economic ideas expressed in a number of these films written by Hollywood radicals were in keeping "with the line being followed by the Communist party at the time...." The Party was "eager to underscore and to dramatize for all the world to see, any and all of the weaknesses of the American democratic system of government."[5]

PROPAGANDA FOR THE CHICOMS

In 1935, Clifford Odets, "by his own testimony then a member of the Communist Party," according to Jones, wrote the screenplay for *The General Died at Dawn*, a film that astute movie reviewers realized was propaganda for the Chinese Communists—euphemistically called the "people's movement" in the movie—against the "warlord," General Wang, obviously a stand-in for Chiang Kai-shek.

The film was set in Shanghai in 1927, when Chiang had emerged triumphant over the Communists. Studio publicity releases described the movie as "based on the struggle between modern China and the predatory war lord who is laying the country to waste. On the side of oppression is General Wang, ambitious warlord intent upon crushing China under his iron heel. On the other is a growing people's movement. Gary Cooper is in the ranks of this movement." The Odets film was such obvious anti–Chiang Kai-shek propaganda that, according to Jones, Paramount Studio heads, "at the request of the Chinese Nationalist government, did not distribute this picture outside the United States."[6]

Dalton Trumbo was another energetic propagandist for the Communist Party line. Jones notes that a detailed analysis of Trumbo's original screenplay for *We Who Are Young* (MGM, 1940) reveals "that this script's unequivocable condemnation of the American way of life would have served the Communist cause if it had been produced as originally written." The two major figures in the script, William and Margy, are totally destroyed by the cruel and corrupt American economic system. There is little hope for them, or—so the Trumbo script would suggest—for any working man in America.[7]

Lester Cole, another Hollywood Ten figure, revised characters to suit his Marxist beliefs. The original screenplay for *Sinners in Paradise* (Universal, 1938) described a group who were forced to land on a deserted South Sea island, with each individual reacting differently to the situation. Harold Buckley's original script included a beautiful rich girl, Doris Dodd; an amusing but harmless U.S.

senator; and two representatives of large oil companies competing for business in the Far East.

Cole and another writer moved the script in a direction that the Comintern would certainly have approved. "Miss Dodd," says Jones, "had become Thelma Chase, traveling incognito, who was given an unfavorable portrayal and identified as 'heiress to the Chase millions and one of the richest girls in the world...who was going abroad to absent herself from the growing labor troubles at one of her auto plants, which was closed on strike.' The senator was shown to be less amusing and more pompous, and was also shown using his governmental influence in making 'private deals' on war supplies in the Far East." The oilmen in the revised script became munitions salesmen, callously selling armaments that they know will be "'responsible for approximately 100,000 lives.'"

Even the Fund's Jones had to admit that the "script provides an example of what might be called the 'politicalizing' of film content."[8] It's hard to miss, really.

Cole boasts of his own efforts to insert his Red politics into the movies in his autobiography, *Hollywood Red*. He scoffs at the idea that the far Left sought to subvert the industry by "'sneaking in' lines of revolutionary propaganda"— then turns around and trumpets his own small victories in pushing plots and dialogue leftward.

"My politics, pro-union and pro-socialist, were never 'injected' into films," claims Cole. But he admits that "the feelings" associated with those politics "were represented in attitudes of the characters" and that he did insert "social realities" into films "when the subject called for it."[9] That seems like a distinction without a difference. (Cole is also being modest when he describes his views as "pro-union and pro-socialist." In those famous 1947 hearings, HUAC produced a copy of his 1944 Communist Party membership card bearing the number 47226.)

Cole may have been mum when he appeared before HUAC, but he unashamedly concedes his Communist past in his confessional autobiography. He reveals he joined the Communist Party in Hollywood in late 1934 or early 1935, persuaded by Karl Marx's *Communist Manifesto*, that hymn of hate against the middle class. "It was as if I had been brought up on this way of thinking from childhood," he allows. He had not joined some silly "club," Cole brags, but a "Marxist revolutionary party."[10]

He stoutly defends all things Soviet, including the Hitler-Stalin Pact and Stalin's war of aggression against Finland. Cole also makes another astonishing admission: the Federal Bureau of Investigation's files on his Communist activities—which he obtained through the Freedom of Information Act—were dead-on accurate. So were the charges of the so-called "informers." It's all very interesting in light of the huge left-wing effort over the years to discredit both the FBI and the "informers."

Over and over again, Cole relates, "informers" sent in information, listing him as a participant in twenty-odd organizations, such as the League of American Writers, the League against War and Fascism, and on and on. "It is true," he allows. "I was active in them all."[11] Each of these organizations was a thoroughgoing Communist front. In short, when Cole was twisting plots toward Marxist propaganda in the '30s and '40s, he was doing it not as some innocent "man of the Left," but as a hard-core Red working to bring the Communist revolution to America.

When Cole and Nathanael West were asked to write a mystery about a disillusioned corporate lawyer who finds his wife murdered, Cole says he "saw an opportunity for a politically oriented subtext which eventually took over."[12] The movie was *The President's Mystery*, and that subtext was evil corporations depriving farmers and canners of their livelihoods.

According to Cole, "The story developed beautifully once we saw our goal: the desperate farmers and the cannery workers get together, form a cooperative, illegally take over the cannery, and start production on their own.... The conflict, of course, was with the big corporation, which sought to drive them off the property." The workers' defiance of the corporation led to a "fighting, action showdown" and triumph for the farmers and workers.

When Republic Pictures president Herbert Yates saw the film prior to its release, he was outraged, Cole reports, saying, "Put that communist shit on the shelf. We're not releasing it."[13]

Cole claims Yates didn't want to put the film out because it might assist FDR in the 1936 presidential election and Yates was betting on Alf Landon. In fact it was released after the election. The *Hollywood Reporter*, while praising the film, admitted it leaned "a little heavily toward sociological propaganda at times."

Hollywood's liberal apologists may deny it forever, but this episode establishes beyond a shadow of a doubt that left-wing ideologues like Cole energetically tried to tilt film storylines in the direction of Communist propaganda, and were frequently successful.

In 1939, Universal wanted Cole to write a screenplay from Nathaniel Hawthorne's classic *The House of the Seven Gables*. Again, Cole transformed the story to fit his Communist ideology.

> Deep changes in the character relations were required, and I changed one of the principal characters, Holgrave, from one Hawthorne describes as a "radical" with only abstract philosophical tendencies, to an active Abolitionist. *The House of the Seven Gables*, in 1940–41, showed Northern capitalists of 1850 engaged in illegal slave trade; it was a radical bombshell....
>
> When the film was finished and ready for release, the executives at Universal became even more alarmed upon seeing it. They accused [producer Burt] Kelly—and me, of course—of writing radical politics into the film and emphasizing them in the shooting. Their anxiety was caused by the abolitionist's role, and the villainous Northern slave trader.[14]

But despite some executives' objections, Hollywood did release a number of "socially aware" films. In 1937, Cole writes, a "truly revolutionary film appeared: a Warner Bros. production of *The Life of Zola*.... They held nothing back. The power elite and the military were exposed as corrupt tyrants, immoral, deceitful, and willing to go to the most inhuman lengths to preserve the power of the explicitly described ruling class."

Then there was "*Blockade*, written by Lawson, the film of the Spanish people's war against Franco... and then *Juarez*, written by John Huston, which, like the others, pussyfooted nowhere, and showed the revolution in mid-nineteenth century in which the people overthrew the European colonial despots."[15]

Cole's enthusiasm for *Blockade* (1938) was hardly surprising, given his ideology. It had been rewritten by Lawson, known in the industry as a dedicated Communist, from an original screenplay by Clifford Odets. As we shall explore in some detail in the next chapter, the picture was designed to gin up nationwide support for the Stalinist-controlled Loyalists in Spain. Communists hoped the movie might even persuade the U.S. government to loosen the neutrality laws and actively aid the anti-Franco forces, who were under the control of Moscow.

REDS FORM "A STRONG WRITERS' FRONT"

Even the cautious Jones acknowledges that *Blockade* "was in keeping with the Communist Party line" and that the Communists used the film "as the basis for a propaganda campaign which they carried on vigorously through every means at their command."[16] Cole wore his ideology on his sleeve. When he wasn't injecting his own left-wing beliefs into a film, he was cheering on other Communist writers. So long as the scripts were anti-corporation, anti-military, anti–ruling class, anti-capitalist, and of assistance to the Soviet Union, Cole was eager to see them produced. He and his fellow Red writers pushed as many movies as they could in a Marxist, class-warfare direction.

Cole put a line attributed to a famous Red heroine into the mouth of a rabbi resisting Nazi efforts to haul Jewish prisoners to the gas chambers in the screenplay for the 1944 film *None Shall Escape*. Cole says, "I plagiarized. In the course of the speech there was no way to attribute the words I used to their true author. I stole a line made famous by Dolores Ibarruri, known in Spain as *La Pasionaria*, an idolized woman who inspired tens of thousands of Spanish people and the International Brigades in the thirties. Unforgettable was a speech in which she said these words: 'Fight, fight for freedom, for justice. It is far better to die on your feet than to live on your knees.'"[17]

Hollywood Ten historian Bernard Dick says Cole's memory is faulty and that the line never appears in the final film print. But Cole's memory, even if inaccurate, does show that he believed he had salted the script with the famed words of the left-wing revolutionary.

It is telling that Cole chose to reach into the grab bag of Communist heroes—apparently uninspired by the stirring rhetoric of American patriots such as George Washington, Thomas Jefferson, and Patrick Henry.

Communists were determined to sprinkle—and sometimes soak (as in *The General Dies at Dawn* and *Blockade*)—their scripts with Red propaganda. As screenwriter David Lang would testify before the House Un-American Activities Committee on March 24, 1953, he had belonged to a select group of Communist writers in Hollywood "interested in creating a strong writers' front, so that the content of the motion pictures from their point of view could be approved and that many of their ideals and their beliefs could be worked into the motion pictures."[18]

CHAPTER TEN

BLOCKADE: THE PARTY TARGETS SPAIN

No event energized the Left in the late 1930s so much as the civil war in Spain. For them, the drama that unfolded on the Iberian Peninsula was a simple morality play. General Francisco Franco, with assistance from Hitler and Mussolini, initiated a bloody rebellion in July of 1936 against the democratically elected government of the Spanish Republic. Foes of Soviet Russia, always a concern of the Left, were on the march.

When war erupted, dozens of pro–Spanish government groups suddenly sprang into existence in America. Hundreds of banquets and special events were held to raise money for the "anti-fascists" in Spain. Thousands of left-wing Americans even volunteered to slug it out against Franco's military. American celebrities rushed to support the Republic. Ernest Hemingway, the preeminent writer of his time, covered the war, favored the government (also known as the Loyalists), and wrote the masterful *For Whom the Bell Tolls* from his experience.

Playwright Lillian Hellman, among others, based her heroes on those who had fought for the Republic, and Paul Robeson, in a snowy area of Spain, sang Negro spirituals to soldiers who had volunteered to fight against fascism.

Caught up in the zeitgeist, producer Walter Wanger was eager to have Hollywood make a movie in support of the beleaguered Spanish government. Wanger initially brought out a number of people from the Group Theatre in New York to work on the film, including Clifford Odets, a one-time Communist and still a major icon of the Left. When the Odets script proved inadequate, Wanger reassigned the project to a current Communist Party member, the ubiquitous and highly influential John Howard Lawson, the most fervent inhaler of the Stalinist line in Hollywood.

"AN HONEST PICTURE"

The Communist Lawson, who became head of the Hollywood CP in 1937, the same year he began working on the Wanger picture, believed he and Wanger thought alike on various issues, especially on the subject of Spain. "I had never worked with a producer with whom I had such a sympathetic and frank relationship as with Wanger," Lawson explains in his unpublished memoir. "He had reasonably good judgment" and "was genuinely interested in the people's struggle in Spain, and felt that an honest picture about it would create a sensation."[1] By "an honest picture," Lawson meant a film that faithfully reflected the Communist Party line on the Spanish Civil War.

Lawson rewrote the Odets film script, *The River Is Blue*, complaining that it lacked intensity. He attempted to infuse it with cinematic meaning by creating "an image of what it meant to fight against impossible odds, deserted by most of the world, including the United States." He planned to depict the Soviet Union as a sort of modern-day U.S. Cavalry, rescuing the Spanish people at the very zenith of their peril from fascist forces.[2]

To dramatize the plight of the Loyalists, Lawson focused on the economic and weapons tourniquet imposed by the Franco forces. Lawson says, "I suggested a scene—men, women and children, standing on a hill at dawn, below them a starving city, cut off, facing a ring of foreign armies without weapons or food."

But he would also propose another scene, with a more hopeful note: From the sea "comes a ship out of the mist—a Russian ship because no other would risk the blockade. As the ship moves across the water, it is sunk by an Italian submarine. But another Russian vessel succeeds in bringing food to the beleaguered city."[3]

Wanger, Lawson reports, "was enthusiastic. The starving of civilians and especially of children was the heart of the matter. We agreed on a title, which expressed the great international issue, *Blockade*."[4] The script generally followed along the lines outlined by Lawson. But it could not be as explicit in saluting Stalin's USSR as Lawson (and presumably Wanger) would have liked, because of industry rules then governing the production of motion pictures. (Nevertheless, the film version that reached the screen proved a major boost to the Soviet cause in Spain.)

Lawson and Wanger had to work around these rules in order to produce the effect they desired, and it required some nimble maneuvering. To ensure that movies did not offend the public at large or contain material jeopardizing their distribution abroad, the Production Code Administration of the Motion Picture Association Producers and Distributors of America (MPPDA), popularly known as "the Hays Office," after the Presbyterian elder who was the MPPDA's first president, closely monitored potentially provocative screenplays from the earliest stages of preparation.

The Production Code Administration issued warnings and suggestions about the various drafts of the script by both Odets and Lawson. Lawson's "third-draft continuity" aroused concerns. Lawson was gently prodded not to take sides with any of the factions in the civil war and to make sure "that none of the incidents or locations in your story could possibly be tied in with the actual events that have occurred or are occurring in Spain."

Wanger and Lawson mostly complied with the advice from the Code Administration Office, but ignored it in crucial instances. Thus the screen version of *Blockade*, released by United Artists in June of 1938, became, in the words of Dorothy B. Jones, the former chief film analyst for the Office of War Information who analyzed films for the Fund for the Republic's report on blacklisting, "the most controversial of all motion pictures ever to be credited to one of the Hollywood Ten...." A major reason it stirred such controversy: despite the hoops Wanger and Lawson had to jump through to avoid specifically naming the warring parties involved, *Blockade* was not only obviously pro-Loyalist but, as Jones herself concedes, "*clearly in keeping with the Communist Party line* [emphasis added]."[5]

There was another reason *Blockade* was controversial. The Loyalists were not universally admired. The Popular Front coalition that had eked out an electoral victory in 1936—now known as the Loyalist side in the civil war—was saturated with Communists, Socialists, and other radical Leftists who were anti-clerical, anti–free enterprise, anti-military, and anti–middle class and, in many cases, embraced violence. The extremist agenda of the Front and its various components had been obscured by much of the world media, though by no means all of it; famed correspondent H. R. Knickerbocker painted a dark picture of the Loyalists for the Hearst press. By the time *Blockade* came out in 1938, moreover, Stalin had already taken over the bulk of the Loyalist enterprise, as George Orwell and others were arguing.

Thus when *Blockade* finally opened, it was greeted with noisy picketing and furious verbal assaults, especially from the Catholic community. From the movie's beginning, the faction resisting aggression is easily recognizable as the Loyalists. Marco, the hero, played by Henry Fonda, is a peasant who joins the war to fight for his land. In the opening sequence, Marco tells the other peasants, "That's the earth that belongs to us—it's worth fighting for." He tells Norma (Madeleine Carroll), the love interest, "My own land is beautiful...I want to keep it. That's why I fight." Land ownership for the peasants, a pledge loudly proclaimed, and only partly kept, by the Spanish Left and the Loyalists, is a theme that pervades the film.

"In choosing this as the issue, which brought Marco...into the Civil War," says Jones, "the film identifies him...as a Loyalist." Marco, as becomes obvious, is also supported by the Spanish people—that is, the peasants and workers, who the Loyalists loudly proclaimed were their constituency.

Just as "the Loyalists are unmistakably identified in *Blockade*," writes Ms. Jones "...so are the Franco rebels identified and shown as the 'heavies' in the film story." For example, the faction opposing Marco and "the people" is shown to be primarily military, clearly a reference to the Franco side. The central figure, General Vallejo, and the men surrounding him are revealed as traitors to the government, which, an educated audience would know, had come to power in a democratic election won by the Popular Front.

The Franco forces are further identified when Lawson incorporates—in opposition to the Code Administration's warning against replicating current incidents—"some of the most highly publicized events of the Spanish conflict" (Jones's words). The film has the military, for instance, directing the bombing of cities and imposing a blockade, tactics used by Franco and widely condemned in the world press. Toward the end, Lawson's script has a decoy supply ship torpedoed by the rebels, while another unidentified ship, laden with food, gets through the blockade. The rescue ship, however, is not identified as Russian, as Lawson had desired.

The closing lines of the Lawson script became famous. Praised for his service to his country and informed that he can now go on leave, Marco, filled with emotion, turns directly to the screen audience, pleading, "You go on leave to find peace—away from the front but where would you find it? The front is everywhere. Our country has been turned into a battlefield—there's no safety for old people and children—women can't keep their families safe in their houses—they can't be safe in their own fields—the churches and schools and hospitals are targets.... It's not war—war is between soldiers—this is murder...we've got to stop it! Stop the murder of innocent people! The world can stop it! Where is the conscience of the world?"

BIG BOOST FOR A STALINIST SPAIN

Marco's concluding soliloquy becomes, as Ms. Jones writes, "a plea for...collective action against Franco." Hence, Wanger and Lawson managed—despite all the obstacles—to put together a major propaganda movie on behalf of the Soviet-controlled Loyalist regime.

Life magazine was hardly confused by the movie's basic message. In selecting *Blockade* "Picture of the Week" on June 13, 1938, the then highly influential publication opined, "Though Walter Wanger disclaims partiality and had experts eradicate all recognizable insignia, those who know their newspapers will see *Blockade* as a stern indictment of General Franco's war, a passionate polemic for the humble Spaniards fighting for Republican Spain."[6]

It would be more accurate to say that *Blockade* was a propaganda film on behalf of a *Stalinist* Spain, disguised as a passionate polemic on behalf of humble Spaniards. Both the Communists and their opponents saw it that way. When *Blockade* opened at Radio City Music Hall in New York, the theater was surrounded by pickets sponsored by the *Catholic Worker* carrying signs claiming the film contained "war propaganda" and was in "violation" of America's neutrality legislation.

Joseph Lamb, New York State deputy of the Knights of Columbus, fired off a protest letter to Will Hays, president of the Motion Picture Production Administration and author of the Hays Code. "The picture," he maintained, "is historically false and intellectually dishonest. It is a polemic for the Marxist-controlled cause in Spain, which would ruthlessly destroy Christian civilization."[7]

Wanger, disingenuously, continued to maintain that the picture's sole purpose was to portray the terrible results of the bombing and blockading of civilians. But the Communists, as well as the Catholics, viewed the film as a weapon to advance the Loyalist cause.

As Jones reports, "...the Communists attempted to use *Blockade* as the basis for a propaganda campaign which they carried on vigorously through every means at their command.... Through all of their many publications, through the Associated Film Audience, through their many 'front' organizations, the Communists attempted to keep *Blockade* in the headlines and to make explicit much that the film did not say.... *There can be no doubt whatsoever that the picture was utilized as the focal point for a campaign of 'Leftist propaganda,' once it was released* [emphasis added]."[8]

While the *Daily Worker*, the CP's flagship publication, hailed the film's "attack against fascism," the *New Masses*, the Party's cultural outlet, thought it could be used as a tool to repeal legislation barring arms for the Loyalists. "Where we have been searching...for means to remove the shameful neutrality legislation which lets fascism murder Spain," argued the *New Masses*, "we have in Walter Wanger's film *Blockade*...the biggest opportunity" to mobilize public opinion to end the embargo.[9]

The CP front the Associated Film Audience had still another reason for wanting *Blockade* to do well. Its success "is important," argued the association, "for if it succeeds, it will be in the forefront of a great many other progressive films."[10]

When the Communists feared that the protests and the demands for a boycott might harm *Blockade*'s appeal, the Conference on Freedom of the Screen suddenly burst upon the scene, holding its first meeting at the Hollywood Roosevelt Hotel toward the end of July 1938. About 350 people representing a wide range of organizations were on hand. Few noticed that this was another Communist-manipulated enterprise.

Liberal speakers raged against the boycott effort, with Wanger insisting that motion pictures "must be protected…against restrictions of small groups." Director John Ford expressed his own resentment against "the effort of an isolated group to ban the picture *Blockade*."[11]

All this rhetoric, of course, helped serve the Communist aim of transforming *Blockade* from a mere picture showing the evils of war and Franco's war tactics into a major left-wing event designed to promote an important Stalinist objective. In retrospect, Jones concedes, "it is easy to perceive that the Communists undoubtedly provided the steam and energy behind this Conference for the Freedom of the Screen."[12]

Not only were "such Communist front groups as the American Artists Congress, the League for Peace and Democracy, the American Student Union, etc.," sponsoring the gathering, she writes, but "the Hollywood Anti-Nazi League for the Defense of American Democracy was one of the major supporters" of the affair. Not surprisingly, the gathering named Herbert Biberman chairman of a committee to deal with future efforts to inhibit "freedom of the screen." Biberman was a full-blown Communist at the time and in less than a decade would become a famous member of the Hollywood Ten.[13]

LAWSON'S WARPED HISTORY

It is impossible to understand just how grossly Lawson's *Blockade* skewed the history of the Spanish Civil War without knowing some details of that history. Even some moderate leftists were concerned about the Popular Front elected to rule Spain in February and March of 1936. The ruling majority comprised a wide variety of leftist groups—including socialists, Communists, and syndicalists. Many of the leaders in the coalition were actively encouraging violence.

As soon as this victory came, there was great fear that the Left might resort to the methods it had used in the revolt in Asturias in 1934. When Spain's moderate-left government at the time agreed to allow the conservative and pro-Catholic CEDA three minor positions in the cabinet, the Socialist UGT declared a general strike. The strike soon exploded into an armed rebellion in several cities. The miners in Asturias, according to historian Hugh Thomas, with the backing of the "Anarchists, Socialists, Communists and semi-Trotsky-ites of the Workers and Peasants Alliance" (later the POUM), launched some-thing akin to "a full-scale working-class revolution." These different groupings later comprised a major portion of the Popular Front Party that captured the Spanish parliament in 1936.

Manuel Grossi, a leader and private chronicler of the Asturias rebellion, urged actions that, according to Thomas, "implied attacks on the Civil Guard posts, churches, convents, town halls and other key buildings in the villages and towns of the province."[14] Each town or village in Asturias was controlled by a revolutionary committee. Recruitment offices demanded the services of workers between eighteen and forty for "The Red Army." Violence swept through the province, with priests being shot, middle-class women raped, and churches and convents burnt.

Alarmed at these developments, the Madrid government called upon a dedicated forty-year-old military man, General Francisco Franco, to put down the uprising, and he did, brutally. After more than two weeks, Belarmino Tomás, the Socialist leader who had been deeply involved in the insurrection, called upon the rebels to yield.

Addressing his audience as "Comrades, Red soldiers," he lamented that all that could be accomplished now was surrender, but said this "does not mean that we abandon the class struggle. Our surrender today is simply a halt on the route, where we make good our mistakes, preparing for our next battle which must end in the final victory of the exploited...."[15]

The insurrection in Asturias had hardly been forgotten by conservative and even moderate Spanish elements when the Loyalists took power in 1936. The Socialists won the largest number of seats in the Parliament, holding nearly one-third of the total 278 seats captured by the Popular Front majority. That Party, largely dominated by Francisco Largo Caballero, could hardly have instilled confidence in citizens interested in peace and reconciliation. Since 1934, the Socialists had lurched violently leftward. Caballero, egged on by the Communists who flattered him by calling him the "Spanish Lenin," was prophesying a bloody uprising even *after* the 1936 election. He was preaching to wildly cheering crowds that the hour of revolution was near, notes Thomas.

On May 24, Largo Caballero displayed his gift for rhetorical pyrotechnics at Cádiz: "When the Popular Front breaks up, as break up it will, the triumph of the proletariat will be certain. We shall then implant the dictatorship of the proletariat, which does not mean the repression of the proletariat, but of the capitalist and bourgeois classes!"[16] His demagoguery, says historian David Cattell, "made even the moderate elements uneasy."[17]

The *major* flaw in Popular Front or Loyalist rule was not the revolutionary rhetoric of so many of its leading members, however, but its inability to keep order. The scholarly Cattell gives this description of the times: "Burning of convents, the seizure of land and the burning of the landowners' homes and fields became everyday occurrences. In the cities, assassinations and gang warfare went on almost continuously."[18]

Winston Churchill summarized the situation that led to the Franco rebellion this way:

> Many of the ordinary guarantees of civilized society had been liquidated by the Communist pervasion of the decayed Parliamentary Government. Murders began on both sides [by both leftist revolutionaries and fascist elements on the Right] and the Communist pestilence had reached a point where it could take political opponents in the street or from their beds and kill them.
>
> Already, a large number of assassinations had taken place in and around Madrid. The climax was the murder of [Monarchist]

> Señor Sotelo, the Conservative leader.... This crime was the signal
> for the generals of the Army to act. General Franco had a month
> before written a letter to the Spanish War Minister, making it clear
> that if the Spanish Government could not maintain the normal
> securities of law and daily life, the Army would have to intervene.[19]

In short, Franco's core ideology at the time was not fascism, as such, but general law and order, and it's a reasonable supposition that he might not have intervened if the Loyalists had been capable of restoring peace to Spain.

Blockade did not touch on the scandal of the government's inability to keep the peace. Nor was there any hint in the movie as to why even moderates distrusted rule from the Left. Nor did Lawson and Wanger let the viewers know that Stalin and the Comintern had seized control of much of the anti-Franco forces within a comparatively short period of time after the conflict had erupted.

"After the first hectic year of the Spanish civil war, control of the Loyalist government apparatus was unified and systematized in the hands of the Communists and their creatures," the famous American journalist Eugene Lyons wrote in his groundbreaking book, *The Red Decade*.[20]

Walter Krivitsky, one of the earliest defectors from the Soviet secret police, the GPU (which later became the NKVD and then the KGB), underscored the same point in his revelatory 1939 memoir. Krivitsky was chief of Soviet Military Intelligence in Western Europe and, as he writes, "on the inside of every major step taken in the Spanish matter by the Kremlin."

Krivitsky had been instrumental in setting up "business" outposts in Europe to move arms to the Spanish Republic, but Stalin, eager to control Spain on his own terms, decided to assist only those factions loyal to Moscow. He was, as Krivitsky tells us, determined to support with arms and manpower "only those groups in Spain which were ready to accept without reservation his leadership."[21]

Soviet, French, and Italian Communists, many of them to become big names in the pantheon of Red heroes, poured into Madrid. "The able and ruthless leader of the Italian Communist party in exile, [Palmiro] Togliatti...went to Spain using the names 'Alfredo' and 'Ercoli' as the director of tactics of the Spanish Communist party," Thomas reports. He was joined by Jacques Duclos, the French Communist whose famous 1945 essay would cause the American Communist Party to dump its chief, Earl Browder, on the grounds that he had abandoned the class struggle.

Another Comintern leader who wound up in Spain was the Hungarian Erno Gero, who also used several Spanish aliases to help bring Communism to Spain's masses. Thus, Thomas writes, "Stalin was most ably represented in Spain." Soviet funds dispatched to the Loyalists were directed by a committee that included Diaz, La Pasionaria, and Caballero, but was dominated by Togliatti and Maurice Thorez, head of the French Communist Party.[22]

Meanwhile, a huge number of organizations throughout Europe and America, "nominally humanitarian and independent, in fact dominated by Communists," were set up to provide aid to Spain, notes Thomas. These were devised "by the Propaganda Department of the Western European section of the Comintern, under its brilliant German Communist chief, Willi Muenzenberg."[23]

As Moscow began to send military assistance to the Loyalist government, tilting the aid heavily to those who would follow Soviet instructions, the Soviet GPU, or Cheka, as it was called in Spain, came to Madrid to direct the outcome. Though nominally part of the Loyalist Ministry of Interior, the GPU operated independently; had its own trials, prisons, and executions; and rapidly imposed "a reign of terror," as Cattell puts it.[24] Moscow's critics were silenced one way or the other. Somehow, all this escaped the attention of Wanger and Lawson.

THE ROMANCE AND REALITY OF THE RED BRIGADES

Few events have been so romanticized in left-wing history as the International Brigades, composed of thousands of young men who flocked to Spain to fight against Franco. The men who fought have been lionized in song and story as heroes and freedom fighters. But these brigades were not the brainchild of liberal democrats or sincere anti-totalitarians. They, too, were a Stalinist creation.

The French Communist leader Maurice Thorez advised Stalin in September of 1936 that aid to the Republic should be, in historian Thomas's words, in the "form of volunteers raised internationally by foreign Communist parties." These brigades, Thorez felt, would be a propaganda plus for the Soviet Union and could become the nucleus of an international Red Army.

The formation of the International Brigades became the main work of the Stalin-controlled Comintern, which directed Communist parties in various countries to raise a certain number of volunteers. Comintern member Joseph Broz, the future Marshal Tito of Yugoslavia, as Thomas describes the history, was in Paris organizing "the flow of recruits through his so-called 'secret railway,' which provided passports and funds for East European volunteers. Where the volunteer was not a Communist, he was usually well investigated by a NKVD representative and by a Communist doctor."[25]

The allure of the brigades was spelled out by Alvah Bessie, a member of the Hollywood Ten. He felt that joining the Abraham Lincoln Brigade, the American contribution to the International Brigades, was one of the proudest moments in his life. When he appeared before HUAC in 1947, he lashed out at the panel for "believing that support of the Spanish Republic was and is subversive, un-American, and Communist inspired." The greatest honor "I have ever enjoyed," he said, was "to have been a volunteer soldier in the ranks of its International Brigades."[26] Bessie, of course, was still an avid Stalinist when he made these remarks.

Ring Lardner Jr., another famous Hollywood Ten figure, was also an active supporter of the Spanish Republic. His brother, Jim Lardner, joined the Abraham Lincoln Brigade, went to Spain, and was killed in the war. Did Jim Lardner hope to liberate Spain from a terrible totalitarianism, as the Left likes to pretend such men did? Not precisely. He wrote his mother that one of the reasons for joining was that he thought that "communism is probably right." Jim also said he would "come into contact with a lot of Communists, who are very good company and from whom I expect to learn a lot."

According to Ring Lardner's memoir, "At some point that summer [1937], Jim became a Communist himself. Like other Lincolns who took the same step, he joined the Communist Party, not of the United States, but of Spain."[27] The Spanish Party, like Communist parties elsewhere, was hardly a force for liberty.

Blockade was written by a Communist (Lawson), embraced the Communist Party line (as Dorothy Jones acknowledges), and was ballyhooed by the entire CP apparatus in this country for the purpose of achieving a Communist victory in Spain. Communism did not succeed in Spain, and Franco, no Hitlerian stooge,[28] provided important assistance to the Allies during critical periods of World War II.[29] Stalin may have stumbled in Spain, but it was not for lack of support from his devoted friends in Hollywood.

CHAPTER ELEVEN

NINOTCHKA SLIPS THROUGH A RED FILTER

uring the HUAC hearings on Hollywood in 1947, Richard Nixon, then a California congressman, questioned producer Jack Warner and urged him to start making anti-Communist films. With the Soviet Union now our major enemy, he would ask, why couldn't Warner Brothers show the "methods and the evil of totalitarian communism, as you so effectively have pointed out the evils of the totalitarian Nazis?"[1]

Warner said his studio was "preparing" one called *Up until Now*. It's unclear whether Warner Brothers ever made the movie, and it certainly didn't release it under that title.

But Hollywood did release at least one effective anti-Soviet film. Surprising as it may seem, probably the most effective anti-Communist movie ever made was filmed in 1938 by MGM and released the following year. It featured one of the greatest movie stars of all time, Greta Garbo. Ironically, it was directed and scripted by those whose politics tilted to the left.

How did Hollywood come to poke serious fun at a country that so much of movieland's intelligentsia had embraced? That is still something of a mystery. The idea of a satirical assault on Stalin's rule may have been hatched when writer Melchior Lengyel was having lunch at the Brown Derby in Hollywood. Salka Viertel, a close friend and promoter of Garbo, reportedly came to Lengyel's table to inform him that Bernie Hyman, an MGM executive producer, was eager for Garbo to star in a comedy so the studio could promote the film with the slogan "Garbo Laughs," just as the studio had publicized *Anna Christie* with the slogan "Garbo Talks."

Lengyel apparently called Viertel the next day with an interesting idea, then convinced Garbo it would be a perfect vehicle for her. The plot, as Lengyel succinctly described it: "Russian girl saturated with Bolshevist ideals goes to fearful, capitalistic, monopolistic Paris. She meets romance and has an uproarious good time. Capitalism not so bad, after all."[2]

Gottfried Reinhardt was chosen to direct. Viertel and Lengyel were to do the writing. They failed to come up with an acceptable script. Eventually, Ernst Lubitsch[3] became the director, with Billy Wilder,[4] Charles Brackett, and Walter Reisch the writers. The final screenplay, though changed considerably from Lengyel's original story, did not stray far from his summary. But in the movie, the glamorous Bolshevik doesn't just yearn to enjoy the simple pleasures of the West—music, romance, liberty, and an apartment she doesn't have to share— she also decides to flee Soviet tyranny.

The decision to make an effective anti-Soviet film during this time period was remarkable, to say the least. Hollywood was still very much enthralled by Moscow. Screenwriters tended to believe that Soviet Communism was creating a new man to live in an economic system that would end labor exploitation as well as cure depressions such as much of the world was still enduring. Furthermore, many Americans, not only in Hollywood, erroneously believed that Stalin was the only major world leader willing to stand up to Nazi Germany—especially after the West had surrendered Czechoslovakia at Munich in 1938.

A DIRECTOR'S BRUSH WITH TOTALITARIANISM

Maurice Zolotow, in his *Billy Wilder in Hollywood*, suggests that director Ernst Lubitsch was the key to the picture's anti-Soviet slant. Lubitsch reported to the MGM lot on February 8, 1939, and promptly announced that he didn't like the script. He then proceeded to reshape much of the film's story line, as was his wont. The movie credits not only mention Lubitsch as the director but describe the film as a "Lubitsch production."

Hence Lubitsch's attitude toward the Soviet Union is of some interest. Lubitsch, who was Jewish and had been born in Berlin, was of a leftish bent. Nazi Germany had revoked his citizenship in January 1935, along with that of 207 other naturalized Russian and Polish Jews and others deemed "dangerous to the state." As early as 1933, the Nazis had been insulting Lubitsch as an amusing but "low-grade" entertainer. Then in 1940 they had attacked him in *The Eternal Jew*, a vicious anti-Semitic "documentary" produced in 1940, which claims, "The Jew...is interested instinctively in everything abnormal and depraved."[5]

But Lubitsch had learned to distrust the Soviets as well as the Nazis. In 1936, as Zolotow informs his readers, Lubitsch had been invited to visit the Soviet Union, in accord with Moscow's new "Popular Front" policy. He had planned to visit Moscow and Leningrad for eight weeks but stayed for less than three. He stopped off in Vienna to see his friend Walter Reisch, but he clammed up when Reisch asked him why he had shortened his trip so drastically. Lubitsch didn't "speak ten words about what he saw in Russia," according to Reisch. Herman G. Weinberg says in *The Lubitsch Touch*, "I have been unable to find out any details of his Moscow trip."

Zolotow speculates that Lubitsch had become disillusioned on learning that many of his friends in the Russian film industry had been purged, were in jail, or had been murdered. His distrust of Red fronts became pronounced. He informed Garbo's friend Salka Viertel, for instance, who was at least a fellow traveler, that he was getting out of the Hollywood Anti-Nazi League, the hugely successful Communist front that had initially attracted a broad range of individuals, including liberals, conservatives, and radicals.

Viertel says in her memoir, *The Kindness of Strangers*, that one day Lubitsch "told me that he was withdrawing from the Anti-Nazi League because it was dominated by Communists. He advised me to do the same. I begged him to reconsider." But Lubitsch wouldn't bend. "I know it from a reliable source that the Reds are controlling the Anti-Nazi League," Viertel quotes Lubitsch as saying. When Viertel sort of laughed it off, he responded, "I am only warning you. I am getting out."[6] Lubitsch, as we have already seen, turned out to be right.

If the increasingly anti-Soviet Lubitsch controlled the direction of the film, still, according to Zolotow, Billy Wilder, despite his apparent love of Russia—if not of Communism—wrote most of the anti-Soviet jibes. The result was a film that remains a classic. *Ninotchka* was a terrific spoof of Stalin's Moscow laced with biting anti-Soviet satire and combined with a pleasant love story. Ninotchka eventually chooses the charms of the West and her pursuer, Leon, over a drab and stifling tyranny.

AN ANTI-COMMUNIST CLASSIC

Some of the picture's barbs at Moscow are worth recalling. Three Soviet bureaucrats are in Paris to sell the grand duchess's jewels, confiscated by the Communist rulers, in order to raise money for a Soviet government hard up for foreign exchange. The three bureaucrats have chosen to stay at the luxurious Hotel Clarence—in the royal suite, no less—and are having a grand bourgeois time dining, wining, and wenching until Moscow sends an envoy extraordinary to monitor their carryings-on.

They are told to meet the envoy at the railroad station but have been given no clue as to the envoy's identity. The scene at the station is full of anti-Soviet sallies. When the Russians spot someone who "looks like a comrade," they follow him until the "comrade" greets his wife with a full-blown Hitlerian salute! Soon they realize that the real envoy is a dour but handsome woman in a severely tailored outfit—and a true-believing Bolshevik. She (Garbo) introduces herself as "Nina Ivanovna Yakushova, Envoy Extraordinary, acting under direct order of Comrade Commissar Razinin." As Nina Ivanovna, or Ninotchka, shakes their hands, they wince because of her iron grip.

When Kopalski, one of the Russian bureaucrats, says if we'd known Moscow was sending a woman, "we would have greeted you with flowers," a stern Ninotchka replies in a somewhat menacing voice, "Don't make an issue of my womanhood." The Russians are intimidated, even more so as Ninotchka bends down to lift her two very heavy suitcases. When a porter asks to take her bags, she responds with a rebuke: "Why should you carry other people's bags?"

> **Porter**: That's my *business*, madame.
> **Ninotchka**: That's no business... that's a social injustice.
> **Porter**: That depends on the tip.

Ninotchka, unsmiling, walks off with both bags, leaving the porter without his gratuity.

As they walk, Buljanoff, one of the three Russian amigos, asks, "How are things in Moscow?"

Ninotchka responds, "Very good. The last mass trials were a great success. There are going to be fewer but better Russians."

The three comrades continue to exchange troubled glances, and as they go through the hotel lobby, Ninotchka demands to know what she is seeing in a showcase and is informed it's a fancy woman's hat. Shaking her head, she says, "How can such a civilization survive which permits women to put things like that on their heads? It won't be long now, comrades."

When she gets to her room, she finds it too elegant for a Bolshevik. She reluctantly agrees to stay but punctuates the episode by pulling out of her bag a reminder that she is not going to forget her Soviet roots while in Paris. It is a picture of Lenin, which she lovingly puts on the desk. (It eventually lands on her bedside table.)

Ninotchka's demeanor gradually thaws under the spell of Leon, played by Melvyn Douglas, whom she meets by accident. He is eventually able to convince her that there's more to life than Bolshevik slogans. (Leon was almost certainly named after Leon Trotsky, Stalin's ferocious enemy. But this Leon, unlike Trotsky, actually bests the Soviet ruler.)

Ninotchka is initially cool to Leon's advances, unimpressed by his pickup line: "I have been fascinated by your Five-Year Plan for the last fifteen years!" But Leon eventually wins her over, and in her suite they agree to start a new party, with the slogan: "Lovers of the World, Unite!" She is deliriously happy, but she says she must confess her guilt for possessing such bourgeois feelings. In Russia, she notes, "everyone wants to confess and if they don't confess, they make them confess. I am a traitor. When I kissed you, I betrayed the Russian ideal. Leon, I should be stood up against the wall." Leon stands her up against the wall, blindfolds her, then kisses her again.

Life does not remain so sweet. When she temporarily loses the crown jewels, Ninotchka is persuaded by her rival for Leon's affections to return to Moscow rather than be exposed for her carelessness.

But on returning, she is reminded how awful the place really is—with its secret police, "monitors" in the apartment buildings, unbearably small living space, and general joylessness. When she gets a love letter from Leon, she opens it up excitedly, looks at it, and then turns glum. The entire letter is censored. One of the Russians whom she supervised in Paris tells her sympathetically, "Ninotchka, at least they can't censor our memories." In the end, however, she gets out of Russia—through Leon's machinations—and the two are destined to live happily ever after.[7]

Ninotchka completed shooting on July 27, 1939. How would Hollywood and the reviewers react to this humorous but very effective anti-Soviet film? Luckily for Lubitsch and MGM, though not for the world at large, the Soviet Union did an about-face on Nazi Germany. Stalin and Hitler joined in their "non-aggression" Pact, in which each totalitarian blessed the other's designs on various portions of Eastern and Central Europe, on August 23. Under the agreement, Nazi Germany would invade western Poland on September 1, while the Soviet Union would seize the eastern half of the country sixteen days later. Given these developments, even much of Hollywood and America's left-wing intelligentsia suffered a certain temporary disillusionment with their Soviet utopia.

When the world premiere of *Ninotchka* opened at Grauman's Chinese Theatre on October 6, 1939, just over a month after Poland's demise as a nation, there was, as Zolotow relates, "a climate of goodwill toward the political satire of *Ninotchka*. The film was praised to the skies. It deserved the praise, but would not that praise have been tinctured with reservations if the film had appeared before the strange alliance and the invasion of Poland...?"[8]

We'll never know. But it's cheering that for one brief shining moment, Hollywood seemed to be sufficiently aware of just how terrible the Soviet Union was to appreciate an excellent picture that ridiculed Communism and was banned in Communist countries. But even in the immediate aftermath of the Hitler-Stalin Pact and the invasion of Poland, awareness of the flaws of Communism was certainly not unanimous. Billy Wilder's left-wing friends were disenchanted with him for writing *Ninotchka*. And unfortunately Hollywood at large soon reverted to blind enthusiasm for Stalin's Russia. Apparently many Tinseltown luminaries decided to forget what they once had been able to see so clearly in Lubitsch's classic comedy.

CHAPTER TWELVE

RED HEYDAY IN HOLLYWOOD

T he Russians were definitely *personae gratae* in Hollywood in the war years, noted the Hollywood Ten's Alvah Bessie, and "every November 7 they held a magnificent party celebrating the October Revolution at their plush consulate on Los Feliz Boulevard."

There, under "huge portraits of Marx, Engels, Lenin and Stalin," VIPs such as Charlie Chaplin, Olivia de Havilland, and Theodore Dreiser could be seen "drinking vodka with lemon juice and gorging caviar, smoked sturgeon, black bread, and other, more American comestibles." Hollywood producers also joined in the festivities.[1]

Hollywood was clearly having a grand old time with our Soviet allies, and the merry mood was such that Communist and radical writers found it easy enough to penetrate the studios, control the film content, and even fill the scripts with heavy-handed Soviet propaganda. The non-Communist producers went along, having half-convinced themselves that the propaganda they were allowing to appear on the screen was fulfilling a patriotic service.

MARXIST SCHOOL FOR SCREENWRITERS

David Lang, a screenwriter and former Communist himself, described the situation to HUAC in March of 1953. Lang had written such middling films as *Yank on the Burma Road, Northwest Rangers, Cheezit the Cops,* and *People Are Funny* for well-known studios. He testified that there was a cabal of top Communist writers who indoctrinated men and women like himself using classic Communist works, including the teachings of Lenin and Stalin. Those who devoured the lessons were expected to lace their scripts with scenes and dialogue compatible with the Party line.

When he joined the Party in the early 1940s, Lang was initially instructed in Communist ideology by Michael Wilson, who would go on to write such well-known screenplays as *A Place in the Sun* (1951) and *The Bridge on the River Kwai* (1957). (Both scripts won Academy Awards, but Wilson would not receive the honor for the second because he had been blacklisted.)

After Wilson's two-month course and a stint with "a definite cell that worked within the Hollywood section," he was later transferred to a "writers' cell," comprised of those "who wrote mostly for pictures." Organized by CP chief John Howard Lawson and including only Party members, these cells, said Lang, were for the purpose of creating "a strong writers' front" that would, among other tasks, work the Party line into films. The Party then decided to create from these cells so-called "writers' clinics," in which only top-echelon screenwriters were involved. In the clinics, Lang explained, these elite writers would exchange ideas with reliable Party ideologues "about scripts, originals, [and] stories that were in work at the studios." After the discussions, the Red screenwriters would attempt "to improve [from a Party point of view] ...the material and the quality of the scripts," with a heavy emphasis on "class warfare."

At least seven members of the Hollywood Ten appear to have been part of the leadership of these "clinics," including Dalton Trumbo, John Howard Lawson, Lester Cole, Sam Ornitz, Alvah Bessie, Ring Lardner Jr., and Adrian Scott.

Other Communist participants: Paul Jarrico, Richard Collins, Robert Rossen, and Gordon Kahn.

Lang said the Party also encouraged the writers to "become part and parcel of the entire motion picture scene," participating in the guilds and unions and, in fact, "all organizations that had any part of making a motion picture."

Representative Kit Clardy, the Michigan Republican, wanted clarification: "Do I understand from what you have just said, the real purpose [of these writers' cells] was to further the Communist cause in any way you possibly could, in every direction?" Lang replied, "That is quite correct." Clardy asked again, "In the script, in the production and in the outside activities of the members in general, to promote the Communist cause?" "That is right," Lang confirmed.[2]

From Lang's unrefuted testimony, we learn that many of Hollywood Communist screenwriters had an exceptional influence over Hollywood scripts. And with the Soviets and the Americans finally allied against the Nazis in 1941, these writers had a far freer hand with the studios to cheer for Moscow and attempt to refurbish the "anti-fascist" credentials of the Left—somewhat tarnished in the twenty-two months of the Hitler-Stalin Pact. They were highly successful in turning the screen to their ends.

"WE HAVE ALWAYS BEEN AT WAR WITH EASTASIA"

Hollywood historian Bernard Dick, author of *The Star-Spangled Screen: The American World War II Film*, notes that several writers, for instance, began establishing a character's anti-fascist credentials by showing he fought with the anti-Franco forces during the Civil War in Spain. The writers were, of course, pushing the Soviet line that the Communists had always taken the lead against fascism—even though the Hitler-Stalin Pact was a stunning refutation of that falsehood. ("We have always been at war with Eastasia," in the common paraphrase of George Orwell's anti-Stalinist novel *1984*.)

In *Paris Calling*—released just prior to America's entry into World War II—Randolph Scott (as Lieutenant "Nick" Jordan) explains that before he joined the British air force, he "flew in Spain against Franco."

In *Gung Ho!* (1943), when war hero Colonel Evans Carlson (also played by Scott) asks a group of volunteers why they want to become Marine Raiders, a recruit boasts that he "fought in Spain" and wants to fight fascism wherever it exists.

In *The Cross of Lorraine* (also 1943), one prisoner of war criticizes another for advocating political tolerance. "I used to hear that in Spain, too," is the rejoinder, "when the fascists attacked Madrid."[3]

The Fallen Sparrow (1943) takes place in November 1940 and salutes the Communist brigades that fought against Franco in the Spanish Civil War (including the American volunteers' Abraham Lincoln Battalion). These brigades, as we have seen, were controlled by the Soviets. Franco's Spain is portrayed as "Nazi" Spain throughout the film—in line with Soviet propaganda, but not precisely in sync with historical accuracy. The hero, played by John Garfield, is a Spanish Civil War veteran who has been tortured and imprisoned by the Franco government. He is released, realizes that his tormentor has killed his best friend, and discovers that the murderer is a Nazi. He proclaims that fascism will never win, for there will be "brigades forming again" to fight against this terrible tyranny.[4] In this anti-Nazi melodrama, as Bernard Dick calls the film, the Red brigades are thus portrayed as having been in the forefront of the anti-Hitler battle.[5]

The best-known World War II–era anti-fascist film hero who turns out to have fought in Spain is *Casablanca*'s Rick Blaine, played by Humphrey Bogart. Blaine is presented as a hardboiled cynic who doesn't like to talk about his past, but he admits that he fought in Spain for the "sake of an ideal."[6] Howard Koch, who wrote the screenplay for the ultimate pro-Soviet movie, *Mission to Moscow*, is personally credited with giving Rick his "Loyalist" background.[7]

In both large and small ways, radical screenwriters during World War II singled out the Soviet Union for its "fight against fascism," despite its past alliance with Hitler and encouragement of the Fuehrer as he invaded Poland and stormed across Western Europe. Dick reveals that Communist screenwriters, sometimes in obscure ways, would sneak in pro-Soviet sentiments (though other movies turned out to be blatant Stalinist propaganda).[8]

Thousands Cheer (1943) was a patriotic musical extravaganza starring Gene Kelly and Kathryn Grayson, with appearances by Judy Garland, Red Skelton, Bob Crosby, Mickey Rooney, and other well-known entertainers. But the two writers, Paul Jarrico and Richard Collins, were hard-core Hollywood Communists[9] who couldn't help spicing up the show with bits of pink propaganda. A soldier in the barracks, for instance, hopes Kelly can swing him an assignment in Russia. The closing number is by Stalin's showcase composer, Dmitri Shostakovich, with lyrics by E. Y. Harburg, of *Wizard of Oz* fame, who had a scarlet political history as well. Grayson belting out words to a Russian military march seems pretty clearly intended to create the subliminal impression that the anti-Hitler forces around the world are marching into battle under Soviet auspices.[10] In *A Walk in the Sun*, released shortly after the war, Communist writer Millard Lampell has American soldiers singing a ballad to the rhythm of a union song that equates the fight for freedom with the Russian victory at Stalingrad.[11]

All this was relatively small stuff, but the radical screenwriters, taking advantage of the casual indifference of the studio chieftains, also crafted films so packed with pro-Soviet propaganda that the anti-Communist contingent in Hollywood decided to form the Motion Picture Alliance for the Preservation of American Ideals. Films like *The North Star*, *Song of Russia*, and *Mission to Moscow* were among those they found particularly galling.

THE NORTH STAR

Lillian Hellman was a prominent playwright and screenwriter with Broadway hits including *The Children's Hour*, *The Little Foxes*, and *Watch on the Rhine* when she was selected by Samuel Goldwyn to pen *The North Star*, a 1943 war film celebrating heroic Russian resistance to Nazi aggression—or, more precisely, the heroism of a collectivized Soviet village. Hellman, with her impressive writing skills and her left-wing views, was a natural fit for such a film. She was asked to do a pro-Soviet script, notes Dick, by "Harry Hopkins, President Roosevelt's personal adviser and the second most powerful individual in the country. Hopkins…envisioned a cinematic tribute to the beleaguered Soviets, who were now our allies." (Hopkins was an extreme Soviet apologist, and evidence unearthed by the late anti-Communist scholar Herbert Romerstein, disputed in some quarters, suggests he may have been a Soviet agent as well.) The pro-Soviet slant of the movie was no doubt enhanced by the director, Lewis

Milestone, whose sympathy toward Moscow was well known in the industry, and who was a favorite of the Russians.

Hellman did not just *tilt* to port. She had been a Communist Party member, a follower of every twist and turn in the Soviet line from the late thirties, including the period of the Soviet-Nazi Pact. It is quite evident from *The North Star* script that she had embraced Lawson's philosophy: add dollops of Red propaganda wherever you can. Hellman was not only intent on demonstrating the bravery of the Russian people, our allies in the fight against Hitler, but also on celebrating the Soviet Union's alleged virtues, including its supposed ability to create a flourishing economy with wonderfully democratic features.

For a variety of reasons, Hellman thought the film the audiences finally saw was far too sentimental. In November 1943, Viking brought out the "master" script of the movie, which omits much of the technical detail and instructions for the actors but includes some of the material that was left out of the final screen version.[12] Hellman wrote an author's note, and Louis Kronenberger, an ex-lover of Hellman's who was considered a respectable literary critic at the time, wrote a six-page introduction full of flowery praise. Hellman, according to Kronenberger, brilliantly commemorates and illuminates the heroism of the Russian people, starkly contrasting the idyllic life of the inhabitants of a small village before the war with the brutality that came with the Nazi invaders. And Hellman tells the viewer just why the average Russian is so brave. As a worshipful Kronenberger remarks, "Another point: in *The North Star*, from sharing the peacetime life of a highly socialized community, we know what the people are fighting for as well as what they are fighting against."[13] Translation: they are fighting not just to rescue their country from the Nazis but for a Communist way of life.

In the Viking script, "the opening of the film takes place in a small village of a collective farm, near the Soviet-Bessarabian border," complete with happy, bustling people with plenty to eat and a song in their hearts. Hellman places the date when the picture begins on June 20, 1941, about forty-eight hours before the German invasion of the Soviet Union.

The head of the village is a man named Rodion, who is about to ship pigs to market. He tells his wife, Sophia, to remind everyone in the marketplace to help with the loading of the pigs onto the train and to tell them that there will be "supper for all when work is finished." Excited, Rodion's six-year-old daughter, Olga, gets her father's permission to inform everyone she meets about his request on the way to school. Then Hellman laces the script with this bit of not-too-subtle dialogue:

> **Olga** [*proudly, carefully*]: I'll say my father, the elected chairman of our village Soviet, orders everybody—
> **Sophia** [*laughs*]: You'll say no such thing. Your father doesn't "order" anybody. The crops belong to the village.

The exchange continues:

> **Olga**: Oh, all right. I'll say it that way. [*She runs toward door, turns.*] I'll say there will be supper for everybody?
> **Rodion**: Yes.
> **Olga**: I'll say there will be music and singing? I'll say there will be dancing, and I'll say there'll be cider for old people and fruit drinks for children—
> **Rodion**: You might also remember to say there will be work.
> **Olga**: Oh, yes. I'll say that too. *Everybody* must work, I'll say.
> [*She runs out.*][14]

In about a minute or two of dialogue, Hellman suggests that Stalin and Communism have made Russia a slice of Utopia. The villagers, drenched in democracy and the work ethic, produce a cornucopia of food and merriment on collectivized farms. And Hellman is not through with her Mary Poppins picture of Stalin's Russia.

An elderly gentleman, Karp, informs an elderly woman, Anna, that he's now learning to read, which, someone else interjects, "only the children of Grand Dukes" were taught to do before the Revolution. Karp then pulls out a small book from his pocket, and, apparently from memory, recites a passage: "*It was early discovered in our country that the most efficient way of farming was by the collective plan* [emphasis added]." He's not only learning to read, says Karp, but he's becoming "a fine, educated man" at seventy-three.

Then Hellman puts in a description of the village collective store: "It is like most village stores but it has certain items which less general stores do not carry: there are furs, racks of Soviet champagne, accordions and mandolins, leather jackets, two bicycles, bad perfumes, a barrel of herring, wrapped sausages, hams and cheeses, boxes of dried fruits and smoked fish."[15]

What was stunning about the master script that Hellman was so eager to see widely distributed through bookstores across the country is that it was a celebration of one of Stalin's cruelest experiments, the collective farm. Much of the sad story of the collectives had surfaced by the time of World War II, when it was known that literally millions had died of famine in the 1930s after armed brigades had swept down onto a farmer's land to seize his crops for export, or to feed the laboring and urban classes in the cities, or to make life more pleasant for Party members. Then there was the fate of the "kulaks," well-off farmers, thousands of whom were simply liquidated or shipped off to labor camps because they were "rich." But Hellman had no qualms about serving up such fairy tales to her countrymen.

The movie seen on the screen omitted some of the most egregious examples of Hellman's propaganda in the script, but it was still a salute to the Soviet collective. With plenty of first-rate stars to help it along, including Walter Brennan, Dana Andrews, Anne Baxter, Walter Huston, and Dean Jagger, it became a box office success.

The Office of War Information, which worked with Hollywood on films to aid the war effort, hailed the script as a "magnificent job of humanizing the plain people of Russia." But the film was, obviously, an effort to make Soviet Communism—not just the Russian people—look good. Naturally the U.S. Communist press loved it, and so did the Soviets. Several Soviet film writers and directors, many of them laden with Orders of Lenin, gathered to discuss the Hellman film on April 13, 1944. These film experts were overjoyed with the way *The North Star* portrayed the life of the average Russian—although they were aware that even fellow Party members might be incredulous at Hellman's rosy view of life on Russia's collective farms.

Ivan Pyryev, director of such scintillating Soviet films as *Tractor Drivers* and *Secretary of the District Party Committee*, insisted that *The North Star* "creates a stupendous impression," though he conceded that some comrades might be "inclined to think the picture has been touched up" and "does not show things as they really are." But, according to Pyryev, this "seems so only at first glance. When we see the collective farm children flocking to their splendid school, when we see the teachers who instruct these children—we know that this is the real thing, this is life."

Soviet movie critic and writer Oleg Leonidov was "glad to see" that both screenwriter Hellman and director Milestone had "understood the progress—the spiritual, economic and general upsurge that gripped our country, the really happy life which prevailed throughout the land"—until the Nazi invasion. In any case, Leonidov had admired Milestone even before *The North Star* because the director had traveled to the Soviet Union in the 1930s and shown his sympathy for "Soviet life and Soviet literature."[16]

The North Star seemed absurdly pro-Soviet even to some on the Left. Anti-Communist liberal Mary McCarthy slammed the picture as "a tissue of falsehoods woven of every variety of untruth"—citing, in particular, the "idyllic" view of the collective farm and the film's portrayal of Russia as peace-seeking rather than belligerent.[17]

Carl Rollyson, in his balanced biography of Hellman, acknowledges, "*The North Star* is a tendentious film. Lillian Hellman knew she was writing propaganda."[18]

And Clayton Koppes and Gregory Black, in their 1988 *Hollywood Goes to War*, point out another way in which *The North Star* deviates from the actual history of the Nazi invasion of the Soviet Union: "Many Ukrainians, still restive because of the millions of deaths suffered during the forced collectivization of agriculture in the 1930s, at first welcomed the Germans as liberators."[19]

SONG OF RUSSIA

Metro-Goldwyn-Mayer's *Song of Russia* was in some ways an even more utopian portrayal of Stalin's Soviet Union than *The North Star*. Louis B. Mayer, who headed the studio in 1942, was a fervent American patriot who made

Russian-friendly films in the war years because the U.S. government favored them. Mayer would testify before HUAC that he went ahead with *Song of Russia* because it "seemed a good medium of entertainment and at the same time offered an opportunity for a pat on the back for our then ally, Russia."

Mayer vigorously defended the film when testifying before HUAC in 1947, insisting that the final result "was little more than a pleasant musical romance—the story of a boy and girl that, except for the music of Tchaikovsky, might just as well have taken place in Switzerland or England or any other country on the earth." But anyone who knows anything about Russia at the time knows its villages were unlike typical towns in Switzerland or England.

Mayer also informed committee members that he telephoned the secretary of the navy, Frank Knox, to delay Robert Taylor's "pending commission in the Navy" so Taylor could play the lead role. Knox agreed.[20]

Committee members and staffers seriously disagreed with Mayer's benign view of the movie, believing it was crimson to a fault. Mayer acknowledged that Taylor "did not like the story,"[21] and Taylor himself told HUAC that "I objected strenuously to doing *Song of Russia* at the time it was made. I felt that it…did contain Communist propaganda." He said, "I don't think it should have been made," and added, "I don't think it would be made today."[22] Obviously, under the right conditions, Red propaganda *could* get by the patriotic, capitalist studio bosses.

Song of Russia turned out to be far more than just a "pleasant romance." The script was written by our old friends Jarrico and Collins, who had managed to insert small bits of Red propaganda into the Gene Kelly musical *Thousands Cheer*. Hollywood historian Bernard Dick, largely sympathetic to Communist writers (but not to their propaganda), calls *Song of Russia* "a Stalinist tract written by Communist writers."[23] *New York Post* critic Archer Winsten said at the time—and the *Post* was a very liberal paper in the '40s—that the film was so pro-Soviet that it "left some [moviegoers] in pain."[24]

But the most devastating criticism came from Ayn Rand, a Russian émigré who by 1947 had become a screenwriter and authored two important works of fiction, including the anti-Soviet novel *We the Living* and the far more successful anti-collectivist work *The Fountainhead*, which she would help turn into a major Hollywood movie. Her indictment of *Song of Russia* before HUAC has been maliciously distorted by the Left—nowhere more so than in Garry Wills's fawning celebration of long-time Stalinist Lillian Hellman. In his introductory essay to *Scoundrel Time*, Hellman's dissembling polemic against anti-Communists, Wills mocks Rand's criticism, saying she "quickly identified the work's major flaw: it showed Russians smiling"—as if this were the gravamen of her charge.[25]

Of course it wasn't, and Rand's thoughtful criticisms had plenty of supporters. She knew whereof she spoke. Born in St. Petersburg in 1905 as Alissa Rosenbaum, Ayn Rand had lived through the Communist Revolution and witnessed Leninist policies produce economic havoc, periods of famine, loss of individual property rights (her father's pharmacy was confiscated), and a devastating destruction of individual liberty. Hundreds of her teachers and thousands of her fellow students were purged from Petrograd State University because of their "bourgeois" backgrounds; many of them would perish in labor camps. Even the very limited aspects of the free market allowed during the NEP era were beginning to be eliminated as her graduation approached in 1924. Eager to find a way to America, where she could write motion pictures—a dream since her youth—she lied to Soviet officials to obtain a passport, saying she wanted to make a short visit to her relatives in Chicago. She left in 1926, never to return.

When HUAC asked Rand to testify, it assigned her the project of critiquing *Song of Russia*. She did so in authoritative detail.

In the movie, Robert Taylor plays an American who, before the war, goes to Moscow voluntarily to conduct concerts. He meets a little Russian girl who begs him to go to her village to direct concerts there. But first she wants him to show her Moscow. Rand describes how Moscow as portrayed in the movie is nothing like Moscow in reality. "First you see Moscow buildings—big, prosperous-looking, clean buildings, with something like swans or sailboats in the foreground." It's a Moscow that Rand believed never existed. The film shows a luxurious "Russian restaurant with a menu such as never existed in Russia at all and which I doubt even existed before the revolution." In the movie, as Rand pointed out, in stark contrast to the real Russia, there are "no food lines anywhere."

But far worse historical travesties occur:

> You have all read about the program for the collectivization of the
> farms in 1933 at which time the Soviet Government admits that
> 3,000,000 peasants died of starvation....
>
> Now, here is the life of the Soviet village as presented in the
> *Song of Russia*. You see the happy peasants. You see they are meet-
> ing the hero at the station with bands, with beautiful blouses and
> shoes, such as they never wore anywhere....
>
> You see the manicured starlets driving tractors and the happy
> women who come from work singing. You see a peasant at home
> with a close-up of food for which anyone there would have been
> murdered....

When Robert Taylor comments on the abundant feast, the peasant answers, "This is just a simple country table and the food we eat ourselves."

Then, Rand continued, the peasant proceeds to show Taylor how he makes his living. "He shows him his wonderful tractor, it is parked somewhere in his private garage. He shows him the grain in his bin and Taylor says, 'That is wonderful grain.' Now, it is never said that the peasant does not own this tractor or the grain because it is a collective farm. He couldn't have it. It is not his. But the impression he gives to Americans, who wouldn't know any differently, is that certainly it is this peasant's private property, and this is how he lives—he has his own tractor and his own grain."

Robert Stripling, the chief investigator for HUAC, interrupted Rand, puzzled about the film's showing of a priest in the village. Why, yes, said Rand, the priest "was from the beginning in the village scenes, having a position as sort of a constant companion and friend of the peasants, as if religion was a natural accepted part of that life." But in fact, for "a Communist party member to have anything to do with religion means expulsion from the Party.... For a private citizen, that is a nonparty member," she explained, "it was permitted, but it was so frowned upon that people had to keep it secret if they went to church." Your job was in jeopardy if you were "practicing any kind of religion," she noted—but

Taylor and the heroine, naturally, have an elaborate church wedding, followed by a sumptuous banquet and marvelous dancers!

Then comes another historical obscenity. In the midst of a concert, "you see a scene on the border of the USSR.... It shows the USSR sign, and there is a border guard standing. He is listening to the concert. Then there is a scene inside kind of a guardhouse where the guards are listening to the same concert, the beautiful Tchaikovsky music, and they are playing chess."

Then comes the surprise attack. "Suddenly there is a Nazi attack on them. The poor, sweet Russians were unprepared. Now, realize—and that was a great shock to me—that the border that was being shown was the border of [Soviet-occupied] Poland. That was the border of an occupied, destroyed, enslaved country which Hitler and Stalin destroyed together. That was the border being shown to us—just a happy place with people listening to music."

Ms. Rand introduced her powerful critique, which has never received an honest answer from her left-wing critics in all these years, with an interesting observation. "Nobody," she remarked, "has stated just what they mean by propaganda. Now, I use the term to mean that Communist propaganda is anything which gives a good impression of communism as a way of life. Anything that sells people the idea that life in Russia is good and that the people are free and happy would be Communist propaganda."[26]

Song of Russia surely fits that definition. No wonder Richard Collins told HUAC that he and Jarrico, both devout Reds when they worked on the movie, "were pleased with the assignment." He also admitted that the script was influenced "to some degree" by their Communist Party membership.[27]

ACTION IN THE NORTH ATLANTIC

John Howard Lawson followed his own advice when it came to putting propaganda into American movies. He had a decent career as a playwright and a solid reputation as a screenwriter, but he was more a dedicated Red than anything else. Up until his death in 1977, Lawson was still yearning for a Soviet America.

Lawson put his Marxist stamp on various movies when he got the chance. We have already looked in some depth at Lawson's *Blockade*, which, former

Daily Worker editor Howard Rushmore told HUAC in 1947, "gave 100 percent endorsement of Stalin's effort to seize Spain as another foreign colony of the Kremlin."[28]

Lawson's best-known war picture was *Action in the North Atlantic*, starring Humphrey Bogart, which was not just anti-Nazi, but a hymn of praise to the Soviet Union and the Communist-controlled National Maritime Union (NMU). The NMU was headed by Joseph Curran—a rabid Communist in thought and action at the time, if not a Party member—when the picture came out in 1943. Indeed, Bernard F. Dick, in his 1989 book, *Radical Innocence*, says the picture "enabled Lawson to show—indirectly, of course—his support for the Party."[29]

The plot of *Action in the North Atlantic* dramatizes the hazards to a U.S. merchant ship navigating Nazi-infested waters to take needed supplies to the Russians, who emerge as major heroes in the movie.

After successfully battling a Nazi submarine, the American ship appears headed unimpeded toward port, but then the crew hears the roar of engines they fear is coming from Nazi fighters.

But as the planes come out of the clouds, a pilot, his fuselage decorated with a red star, drops out of formation, tipping his wings to the Americans. The ecstatic crew realizes the plane is part of a *Russian* air squadron. Bogart's vessel makes it safely to Russia, courtesy of the crew's bravery, yes, but also because the Soviet air force has clearly been performing valiantly in sweeping the skies of German aircraft.

Dick observes that the supply ship is allowed "to proceed to Murmansk, where the merchant seamen are hailed as 'comrades' and reply in kind to the Russians. The cleverest piece of pro-Soviet propaganda occurs when Dane Clark spots the Soviet planes and cries, 'They're ours!'"[30]

Alvah Bessie, another of the Hollywood Ten, reveals in his autobiography, *Inquisition in Eden*, that he helped craft the very scene Dick is discussing after *Action's* producer, Jerry Wald, asked him to work on the dialogue.

Bessie's description of the scene he supplied to Wald, complete with Clark's jubilating on eyeing the Soviet plane, is reproduced in the picture with only minor alterations. Bessie has a ball talking about it, mixing boasting with sarcasm. "You will have to agree that the piece of business was subversive as all hell, but apparently the audiences did not think so, because it got one of the biggest hands and round of cheers in the entire film."[31]

Of course, that's precisely what one would expect from an excellent piece of movie propaganda: the presentation of a scene that convinces the audience to accept the view of the propagandist. What Lawson and Bessie desired was to get Americans to think well of the Soviets, and they were clearly successful.

Indeed, *Action* was just one of many prominent Hollywood war films written by Communists and their fellow travelers, and although the non-Communist producers okayed these films, often for patriotic reasons during the U.S.-Soviet alliance against Nazi Germany, the Red writers purposefully pushed the scripts in such a direction that these films not only saluted the gallantry of the Russian soldiers battling Hitler's legions but also glorified the Soviet Union, Communism, and Joseph Stalin. No picture, however, glorified Soviet Russia more than *Mission to Moscow*, which is a story in itself.

CHAPTER THIRTEEN

MISSION FOR STALIN

The *Daily Worker*'s most popular columnist, Mike Gold, was transported to a state of ecstasy by the release of *Mission to Moscow* in the spring of 1943:

Here is about the best propaganda picture I have ever seen. But its propaganda consists of simply telling the truth about the Soviet Union. This truth is so new in America that it becomes startling.

Hitler has concocted no greater lie than the enormous structure of anti-Soviet faking and slander erected in America by the professional liars. But *Mission to Moscow* paints a quiet, reasonable, sensible, objective portrait of the Russian scene. It does not lift its voice, or become sensational. It merely relates the historic facts.

Yet what a melodrama is packed into each moment of the film. The eyes open; the heart beats quicker with indignation at the Nazified liars as one realizes that nearly everything said about Russia was a lie…. *Mission to Moscow* cuts the ground from under the feet of these traitors.

The Communist newspaper couldn't get enough of this movie that finally told "the truth" about Moscow. Typical headlines that ran in the *Worker*: "Critics Laud *Mission to Moscow*," "*Mission to Moscow*—A Great Win-the-War Film," and "Hollywood's First Realistic Film about the Soviet Union."[1] Stalin, who apparently thought it was somewhat historically inaccurate, nevertheless believed it was a film that would be useful not only in America, but in the Soviet Union as well. He personally approved its wide distribution in the USSR. Communists everywhere liked—no, loved—*Mission*. No more pro-Soviet film has ever been produced or promoted by a major Hollywood studio—or, possibly, even by a Soviet studio.

The film was based on a bestselling book by President Franklin Delano Roosevelt's former ambassador to Moscow, Joseph Davies, and the president himself played a role in getting it made into a movie. But responsibility also lies with *Mission*'s screenwriter, Howard Koch, an ardent fellow traveler whose Communist wife helped him move the script leftward. Koch, who also hired a pro-Soviet technical adviser to help him with the film, has acknowledged that he deliberately sought to puff the Soviet leaders and lionize their deeds.

Mission to Moscow's remarkable whitewashing of Stalinist Russia—including even the notorious show trials of the 1930s—is a key reason House Committee members were concerned about Red writers' influence over Hollywood. How could any picture have been so slavishly pro-Soviet unless Communists were writing the scripts? It was hardly an unreasonable question, given the number of Red and pro-Soviet writers saturating Tinseltown.

Jack Warner, whose Warner Brothers Studios made the film, was thoroughly grilled on the subject in two hearings before HUAC. Chief Investigator Robert Stripling peppered Warner with questions about the movie. Why did he make such a pro-Soviet film? Why were there so many obvious inaccuracies? Didn't he know it was filled with pro-Soviet lies at the time?

Warner was on the defensive before HUAC when it came to *Mission*. He testified that the Soviets had been treated positively because they had had their backs up against the wall in the war and desperately needed support from the American people. But that didn't explain the celebration of the Soviet system and of Stalin personally in the film.

Warner asserted that he "did not consider the film pro-Communist at the time"—an absurd line of defense, since its pro-Communist slant was so egregious—and that he had relied to a great extent on Davies's account of his diplomatic tour of duty. "I had to take his word that they were the facts," Warner claimed.[2]

What's clear from the record is that the pro-Soviet Davies and his trusted friend, President Roosevelt, teamed up to persuade Warner Brothers to do a movie based on Davies's book and that Jack and Harry Warner were eager to oblige. Davies clearly played a big role getting the movie made and also in ensuring that the message listed wildly to port.

AMBASSADOR DAVIES'S CENTRAL ROLE

Davies, ambassador to Moscow from 1936 to '38, had been a successful corporate lawyer, carried a gold-tipped walking stick, and had a high opinion of himself. (Moscow correspondent Quentin Reynolds expressed sentiments his colleagues shared when he vowed "to puncture the inflated ego of this pompous ass.")

Davies described himself as a political "liberal," a "capitalist," and a man of basic Christian faith,[3] but he was colossally blind when it came to the USSR. After he arrived in Moscow in 1937, the career diplomatic staff, under the acting direction of Loy Henderson and George Kennan, seriously considered "a group resignation" to protest Davies's rank amateurishness, ignorance of Soviet history, and strong tendency to "bend both the mission and its function to the purposes of personal publicity at home."[4]

Davies, who shamelessly shilled for the Soviets, did not go unrewarded. The Soviet leaders allowed him and his wife, Marjorie Merriweather Post, to cart back to the United States fabulously expensive art and jewels, including some from the shop of the master craftsman, Karl Fabergé, acquired at bargain prices. Many of these precious artworks and gems, which had been made for the czars, are currently on display at Hillwood, Post's palatial residence in Washington, D.C.[5]

If Davies's book was a remarkable apologia for Stalin's behavior—and it was—the movie went even further, suggesting that the Caligula in the Kremlin was a candidate for sainthood. To make sure that his view of things would not be diluted, Davies signed a contract with Warner Brothers which guaranteed that "Warner agrees to submit to Owner [Davies] for his approval, a copy of the basic story."[6]

Davies came to view himself as "co-author" of the script and made dozens upon dozens of edits, even dictating some of the dialogue. He insisted that FDR, with whom he was in constant contact, supported his recommendations.

The final script was completed in early 1943, but Davies made significant changes before the print release. Aside from giving his movie wife a larger role, he insisted that there should be a "prologue" at the beginning of the film, with the real Davies informing the world of the importance of the movie and attesting to its historical accuracy.[7]

Davies had proved himself a stout friend of Moscow as ambassador and an even better one after he returned to the United States. To ensure the film's "accuracy," he even invited the Soviet ambassador, Maxim Litvinov, and his English wife, Ivy Low, to his "camp," as he referred to his luxurious home on Lake St. Regis in New York's Adirondack Mountains, so that he could receive advice from a Soviet expert.

"[B]ut how often," wondered David Culbert, who wrote an exhaustive history of *Mission*, "does a Soviet ambassador spend an entire week planning the content of a film in which he is a major character and which will be made by another country?" Just once, apparently.[8]

Davies's care in guiding the film paid off handsomely—for the Soviets, if not for historical truth. Davies unquestionably had the most decisive impact on the film, but screenwriter Howard Koch, the super-duper fellow traveler, inserted his own portside propaganda into the script, as he reveals in his memoir, *As Time Goes By.*

For a variety of reasons, including his desire for a vacation after working on the celebrated film *Casablanca*, Koch was initially reluctant to do *Mission*. But he was persuaded to write the script when Jack Warner told him about a recent dinner with FDR and Davies at the White House. The president wanted the Warners to do a film based on Davies's book to educate the American people on the "truth" about the Soviet Union.

A STABLE OF RED WRITERS AND CONSULTANTS

Like Davies, Koch came to the task with his pro-Soviet credentials in splendid order. Though Koch swore in a 1959 affidavit sent to HUAC that he "had never been a member of the Communist Party," he hewed so closely to the Soviet line that even Ceplair and Englund—who deplore anti-Communist "red baiters" and ex-Communist "stool pigeons"—describe him in *The Inquisition in Hollywood* as one of several "fellow travelers... who were Communists in everything but name."[9]

Even in his affidavit, Koch admits he had been associated with such Red fronts as the National Council of American-Soviet Friendship; the Hollywood Writers Mobilization (when it was chaired by Communist screenwriter Robert Rossen); a committee for the defense of Communist longshoreman Harry Bridges; the National Council of the Arts, Sciences and Professions; the Progressive Party headed by Henry Wallace; and a "fund-raising committee for the *National Guardian*," a well-known Marxist publication.[10]

Koch, disclosing his mindset when he undertook *Mission*, informs the readers of his memoir that he believed the American news media had been "anti-Soviet" since the Russian Revolution, "so their reporting could hardly be considered objective." Demanding what he thought was a fairer viewpoint, he managed to get his "own technical adviser, someone with personal experience in the Soviet Union whose veracity and objectivity I could trust." That advisor, named by reliable FBI informants as a Party member, was Soviet enthusiast Jay Leyda.[11]

At one time an employee of Moscow's International Bureau of Revolutionary Literature, Leyda embraced a number of very pro-Soviet positions in the '30s, supporting Stalin's bloody purges and the Hitler-Stalin Pact. He was also a contributing editor to *New Theater* magazine, which, according to Eugene Lyons, the famous United Press correspondent thoroughly disillusioned by his stint in Moscow in the 1930s, "soon became focal center for a lustily Stalinist faction on Broadway and in Hollywood." The January 1935 issue of the magazine "was an all-Soviet number, carrying this inscription: 'This issue was printed in Moscow by Jay Leyda.'"[12] Even Koch acknowledges that Leyda was "sympathetic to the Soviet system."[13]

Indeed, in declassified documents at the famous Tamiment Library in New York, the FBI refers to "Jay Lincoln Leyda," noting that he "is known to us as a member of the Communist Party." According to a bureau memo labeled "LA 100-30551," in June 1944 "[informants] T-11 and T-12, both of known reliability, advised that Jay Leyda was a member of Group A-3 of Branch A (writers' branch), Northwest Section of the Los Angeles County Communist Party; that he was transferred from New York City, Section C, on July 16, 1943; and that he has been active in various Communist Party front groups in Los Angeles."[14] For good measure, Leyda's wife, Si-Lan Chen, a prominent West Indian dancer whom he had met and married in Russia,[15] also had, in Koch's words, "deep feelings" for the Soviet Union.[16] So much, then, for Koch's claim that he was securing personnel with a sense of objectivity about Stalin's Russia!

The original script for *Mission* had been written by another pro-Soviet radical, Erskine Caldwell, but Koch turned Caldwell's work into something more viewer-friendly. He also stuffed every nook and cranny of the script with bits glorifying the Soviet Union and its leaders.

Koch constantly ran his work by Leyda and his secretary, Anne Green, whom he eventually married, for approval. He credits Green with his approach, and she could hardly have been an impartial observer, either. Two former Communists, Edward Dmytryk of Hollywood Ten fame and Leopold Atlas, have said Green was a Communist in the 1940s. Dmytryk informed me of her Red pedigree at his home in Los Angeles in 1997, and Atlas identified "Anne Green, Howard Koch's wife" as a member of his Hollywood Communist unit in hearings before HUAC.[17]

Green happily described herself to Koch as a "socialist" and raved about Davies's book that "a man as rich as Davies could see so much that was good in a socialist country." Delighted with her insight, Koch decided to dwell on this theme because with it, as he explains in *As Time Goes By*, "we might disarm some who would otherwise be skeptical of any report favorable to the Soviet Union."[18]

"After discussions with her and Jay," Koch says, "I would write the scenes and often rewrite them following their appraisal."[19] (Leyda's papers show that he contributed some fifty pages of detailed suggested changes and edits.)

Koch and Co. clearly had no intention of being "objective." Koch's script was so indulgent toward the Soviets that when production began, Jack and Harry Warner themselves were "having some second thoughts" about the film, according to Koch.

Couldn't the pro-Soviet message be toned down a bit, Harry Warner plaintively asked Koch, and "more sins" be injected "into our characterizations of the Russian leaders? For instance, they probably traded favors, quid pro quo, with their corporations, lining their pockets like many American politicians. Why not show that in a scene?"

Koch wouldn't hear of it, arguing that it was not possible for the Soviet leaders "to amass great fortunes, either honestly or dishonestly, because the means of production were publicly owned and there was no area for private speculation or profit."[20]

In Koch's view, the Soviet system had put an end to greed and corruption. It was a preposterous position, and Harry Warner, he concedes, "was not exactly happy with this explanation." Warner nevertheless acquiesced, and Koch went on to portray *every* important Soviet Stalinist in the film as without blemish. (The only flawed Soviets in the movie were "Trotskyites.")

The Davies-Koch script was not just pro-Soviet but *embarrassingly* pro-Soviet, even for that time period. Davies himself set the overall tone. As the movie begins, the real Davies—not the character, played by Walter Huston—talks directly to the film audience in a prologue, solemnly explaining why the film was made: "While in Russia, I came to have a very high respect for the integrity and the honesty of the Soviet leaders.... I also came back with a firm conviction that these people were sincerely devoted to world peace and that they and their leaders only wanted to live in a decent world as good neighbors...."

Davies's speech conveyed just a hint of what was to come: a full-blown propaganda movie, worthy of Goebbels (without the grandeur). No wonder the American Communists were ecstatic. *Mission* is a passionate love letter to the Soviet Union from an adoring America.

STALIN THE MAGNIFICENT

No known accusation against the beloved—in this case, Stalinist Russia—is left unanswered. Have detractors suggested that the food in Russia not quite up to snuff? Immediately upon arriving on Soviet soil, the Davies group is treated to tasty fishes, smoked ham, and caviar, all quite "*excellent,*" Mrs. Davies exclaims.[21]

Do the Russians lack soaps, oils, and perfumes? Davies's wife, seen admiring a cosmetic shop in Moscow, scotches that notion when she exults, "What an attractive display! That might be in a Fifth Avenue window in New York!" Perhaps the Russian women are dowdy? Another canard—the film portrays them as wholesome and attractive, nay, stylish. Their looks are enhanced by the exquisite taste of Madame Molotov herself, who, we discover, learned her trade in Paris and is known as the "commissar of the cosmetic industry." This kind of chirpy Soviet-boosting dialogue never quits.

But Soviet women are to be admired more than ogled. And they are not only wives and mothers but also doctors and captains of state enterprises—all pre–Gloria Steinem. Visitors are overwhelmed by their competence. Davies's chauffeur, Freddie, spies a plump but attractive girl in the cab of a Soviet locomotive and is dumbfounded when he discovers she's the engineer! Tanya, another plucky Stalinist heroine, is not only lovely, but tough—she jumps out of airplanes for the Russian airborne. Women have never had it so good as in *Mission to Moscow's* Stalinland.

Save for a few disgruntled Trotskyites, who end up publicly confessing their sins against Stalin, the Soviet Union is the sweetest place to live on the face of the globe. The common people work hard but happily and productively. They have plenty of time to sing and dance, skate and ski in this earthly paradise. The military—well, gee, Davies is constantly astounded at its readiness, contrary to what America's "fascists" are saying. Only the "reactionary" elements in the West, apparently, are bad-mouthing Mr. Stalin's Dream House.

The Davies-Koch film came out in 1943, when Stalin's infamies—including the famine, the purge trials, the millions deliberately murdered, the Gulags, the Hitler-Stalin Pact, the carving up of Poland, the absorption of the Baltics, the invasion of Finland, the gross violation of solemn treaties—were all well known, especially to the *cognoscenti*, including Davies. They also had to have been known to Koch, who refers repeatedly to Davies's pro-Soviet book as the basis for the script but who very obviously ignored the few portions of the book that do record some of Stalin's evil deeds.

Mission blithely slides over—nay, *omits*—all the horrors. Indeed, every heavy-handed government tactic, every heinous Soviet policy is enthusiastically embraced or excused on Davies's say-so. The secret police are "protecting" Davies and his entourage. Soviet bugging of embassies must be pardoned because "Moscow is a hotbed of foreign agents." Davies remarks on the show trials, "Based on 20 years of trial experience, I'd be inclined to believe these confessions." The Hitler-Stalin Pact was "forced" on Stalin by the democracies. The invasion of Finland was necessary because the country was run by "Mannerheim, Hitler's friend." *Etcetera, ad nauseam.*

Going by the film, no country has ever been graced by such far-sighted leaders as the Soviet Union under Stalin. They are remarkably warm, friendly, kindhearted, savvy, and almost slavishly pro-American. An avuncular President Kalinin, for instance, tells Davies that Franklin Roosevelt is a "great president" who has shown such marvelous sympathy for the "common man."

These leaders have accomplished political and economic miracles. Ambassador Davies, having taken an allegedly "unguided" trip throughout the country, courtesy of the Soviet government, is asked, "What were your impressions, Mr. Davies?"

"Most of all," Davies responds, "I was amazed at the boldness and imagination behind such a vast industrial development. I can think of no other period in history where so much has been done in so short a time."

Stalin is a statesman of the highest order. When Davies says his goodbyes to President Kalinin as he prepares to leave Moscow in 1938, Stalin unexpectedly appears to pay his respects. Davies is exhilarated and begins to lavish praise on this statesman's achievements.

"I've been deeply impressed by what I've seen," he tells Stalin, "your industrial plants, the development of your natural resources, and the work being done to improve living conditions everywhere in your country. I believe history will record you as a great builder for the benefit of mankind."

A shy and modest Stalin protests, "It is not my achievement, Mr. Davies. Our five-year plans were conceived by Lenin and carried out by the people themselves." Can Stalin be trusted to fulfill his foreign obligations? "The Soviet Union," Stalin reassures Davies, "has never repudiated a treaty obligation."

"Your past record," Davies tells Stalin, "speaks well for the future."[22]

TOTALITARIAN PROPAGANDA FOR MASS CONSUMPTION

When *Mission to Moscow* was released on April 30, 1943, the Communist press was in a state of euphoria. The *Daily Worker* and other Party publications poured out dozens of articles celebrating the fact that the Davies-Koch picture had, at last, vindicated the Party's own assessment of just how magnificent a country the Soviet Union really was.

The Office of War Information (OWI), the U.S. government agency that censored war films, was almost as positive as the Communist press. The official OWI summary of *Mission* said the film "pulls no punches; it answers the propaganda lies of the Axis and its sympathizers with the most powerful propaganda of all: the truth."[23]

But the movie triggered an enormous outpouring of skepticism and criticism from across the political spectrum. Knowledgeable experts on the Soviet Union ridiculed the movie, and Stalin himself was reported to have thought it absurd. A Russian film official told British representatives in Moscow that *Mission* was so "naive" that "it made Russians laugh" at various points.[24] Quentin Reynolds, who saw the movie in Moscow, wrote that the film "portrayed a Russia that none of us had ever seen" and that he and his fellow correspondents "were all frankly embarrassed by the picture."[25]

The former ambassador to Moscow, Charles ("Chip") Bohlen, who had served under Davies when he was ambassador, had little regard for the man, his book, or the movie. Davies, he writes in his memoir, *Witness to History*, had gone to Moscow "sublimely ignorant of even the most elementary realities of the Soviet system and its ideology" and was "determined to maintain a Pollyanna attitude."

Bohlen, who himself had a reputation for being soft on the Soviets, says that Davies took "the Soviet line on everything," except when there was a difference between our government and Moscow. Describing the movie as "incredible," Bohlen points out that Soviet technical experts "helped turn it into one of the most blatantly propagandistic pictures ever screened." Bohlen adds that at a private showing at the Office of Strategic Services, "we recorded sixty-seven factual errors in the picture."[26]

Harsher criticism came from two well-respected liberals. John Dewey and Suzanne La Follette, chairman and secretary, respectively, of the highly regarded international commission of inquiry into the Moscow trials of 1937–38, would excoriate the movie in a lengthy letter to the *New York Times*.[27]

Dewey and La Follette had unimpeachable progressive credentials. Dewey, who had initially been quite taken with the Soviet system, was a well-known professor of philosophy at Columbia University, a former president of both the American Psychological Association and the American Philosophical Association, and the author of numerous books when he wrote his critique of the Davies-Koch movie.

La Follette had been secretary to her cousin, Senator Robert M. La Follette Sr., well known for his liberal and pro-labor outlook. She had also served as an editor of the international relations section of the *Nation* magazine. Dewey and La Follette's thorough and lengthy investigation of the Moscow trials established that they were a judicial and human travesty.

In their indictment of the Davies movie, the two conclude that this was "the first instance in our country of totalitarian propaganda for mass consumption." The film, they added, "falsifies history through distortion, omission or pure invention of facts," something that is "alarming" in a film that is introduced as factual and includes "living historical personalities." It was outrageous, in their view, that Ambassador Davies "personally introduces this dramatization of his mission as the 'truth' about Russia."

LEGITIMIZING THE MOSCOW SHOW TRIALS

Davies's tour of duty as ambassador coincided with the Great Terror, as Robert Conquest has memorably and accurately named the period of 1936–38. Yet the film glides over Stalin's orgy of murder, torture, imprisonment, and deportations as if it never occurred. Literally millions of Communist Party members, professional people, workers, peasants, and military men, along with their children and wives, were subjected to the Terror because Stalin was determined to eliminate as many suspected opponents of his reign as he could.

The movie touches on only one aspect of the Terror, the Moscow trials, in which many of Stalin's former colleagues admitted to conspiring with Leon Trotsky, the Germans, and the Japanese to overthrow the Soviet government. But you would never guess that these public extravaganzas were part of bloody purges—or anything but a triumph of firm but righteous justice. As the highly regarded Dewey Commission and other respected liberal groups and scholars determined at the time, the trials were a tragic farce based on demonstrably fraudulent evidence. That the Soviet secret police framed innocent Russians and extracted "voluntary" confessions through torture and threats has now been confirmed by Russian historians.

Dewey and La Follette point out a number of demonstrable falsifications of fact in the film. Immediately after his arrival in Moscow in January 1937, Davies is shown meeting Karl Radek, Nikolai Bukharin, and G. G. Yagoda at a diplomatic reception in his honor. But this is an event that "could not have taken place"—as Radek had been arrested in September 1936 and was never released, Bukharin was also under arrest at the time, and Yagoda was in disgrace. The film even shows Marshal Tukhachevsky, behaving as if he is obviously guilty, having his day in court when Davies is present. In fact, Tukhachevsky was never tried in public. He was secretly executed in June 1937.

The film portrays the show trials as fair. Davies himself is shown in the courtroom deeply impressed by the conspirators' confessions—with the film leaving no doubt whatsoever that all the defendants are guilty as charged.

In the movie the trials end with Bukharin, obviously contrite, acknowledging his role in the plot, reaffirming his support for Stalin and his policies, and telling Andrei Vyshinsky, the chief prosecutor, "The only pressure [to confess] came from my own conscience." Davies has already cooed his opinion of the notorious prosecutor, "Oh, Mr. Vyshinsky, your legal abilities are known world-wide and are much admired in my country."

MAKING EXCUSES FOR THE HITLER-STALIN PACT

Dewey and La Follette also condemn *Mission* for its grotesque justification of Stalin's pact of aggression with Nazi Germany. They point out that the movie

> represents Stalin as having been driven into Hitler's arms by the Franco-British policy of appeasement. There is no reference to the desperate effort of France and Britain to reach a defensive-alliance with Stalin in 1939, no reference to the presence in Moscow of an Allied military mission vainly waiting to confer with the Soviet General Staff at the very time when the Stalin-Hitler pact was announced. Hitler's armies are shown invading Poland, but not Stalin's.
>
> There is no mention of the Soviet Government's demand for a negotiated peace after Stalin and Hitler had divided Poland, or of Stalin's words after the partition, "Our friendship is cemented with blood," or of Molotov's famous remark that "fascism is just a matter of taste...."

Nor, say Dewey and LaFollette, does the film take note of a most important fact:

> in France, England, and the United States—wherever the Communist International was functioning—the Communist parties systematically sabotaged the Allied cause. One would never know that the most determined and noisy isolationists in this country before June 22, 1941, were in the Communist-led American Peace Mobilization.
>
> One would never know that for months before that date the Communists fomented strikes in our defense industries, calculated

to sabotage our rearmament and our aid to Britain. Communist responsibility for these strikes is a matter of record—*vide* the statements at the time of Attorney General Jackson, high-ranking labor leaders and the entire American press.[28]

Mission to Moscow was nothing more than a monumental twisting of the truth.

DAVIES'S CRIMINAL OMISSIONS

Perhaps the most egregious omission from the film was of the real-life Davies's own characterization of Soviet terror. In his confidential report to Under Secretary of State Cordell Hull on April 1, 1938, Davies wrote,

The Terror here is a horrifying fact. There are many evidences here in Moscow that there is a fear that reaches down into and haunts all sections of the community. No household, however humble, apparently but what lives in constant fear of a nocturnal raid by the secret police (usually between one and three in the early morning). Once the person is taken away, nothing of him or her is known for months—and many times never—thereafter.

Evidences of these conditions come from many sources. They are: statements made to myself or members of the staff from first-hand witnesses; statements based on actual personal observations of members of the staff (as in one instance, the sight of a struggling unfortunate being arrested and torn from his eleven-year-old child on the street in front of the adjoining apartment house at 3:30 a.m.); or statements made by Russian citizens who for some reason or other come to the Embassy in search of aid.

The popular psychology in this situation and the extent of the Terror is again indicated by the fact that, almost daily through the kitchen and servant's quarters, there come reports of whispered and fearful confidences of new arrests, new hardships, new apprehensions, and new fears among their friends. The activities of the secret police have extended and reached down to the arrest of Soviet employees of foreign missions, including our own.[29]

Davies's book reveals he was also very well aware of how unjust the Soviet court system was. In a letter to Senator James Byrnes in February 1937, he wrote,

> My dear Jim: In this Radek Trial, the basic vice in the procedure from our point of view was the subordination of the rights of the individual to the state....
>
> The guarantees of the common law to protect the personal liberty of the individual from possible oppressions of government, such as the right to refuse to testify against oneself, the writ of habeas corpus, the right to require that the state shall prove guilt instead of the accused being required to prove innocence—never impressed me with their beneficence in the public interest as they did in this trial. All of these defendants had been kept incommunicado for weeks and months.[30]

Aware as he was of all of this, it defies understanding how Davies could have endorsed so thoroughly and publicly the guilty verdicts of the Moscow trials. How, knowing the terrible truth about the terror and the travesty of justice, could he actively participate in making a movie that whitewashes all these horrors and positively celebrates the Soviet system of justice?

In a later report to Secretary Hull, dated June 6, 1938, and also published in his memoir, Davies acknowledges that the First Five-Year Plan, which began in 1928, was executed with "utter ruthlessness." In its early phase, "the government was again threatened by the passive revolt of the agricultural districts. This revolt was ruthlessly crushed. The government employed the simple but cruel expedient of taking its requirement of grain from the peasantry, even though it left nothing to them for food or for seed. The result was starvation in many sections. It was variously estimated that during this campaign from two to three million agricultural peasants died."[31]

Such horrific events do not appear in *Mission*. Indeed, as Dewey and La Follette remark, in the movie's "make-believe Russia," the mood "is gay, even festive, and wherever Mr. Davies goes, he encounters a happy confidence in the regime."

There were many other harsh criticisms of the movie as well. Liberals, prominent Socialists, and noted labor leaders, many of whom had been early supporters of the Soviet experiment, signed a letter excoriating *Mission* as a movie that "falsifies history," defends the proven "frame-ups" in the Moscow trials, and embraces Stalin's well-known criminal policies.

Dwight Macdonald, editor of *Partisan Review*, was the author of the letter, which was widely circulated across the nation. Norman Thomas (Socialist Party leader), A. Philip Randolph (the black president of the Brotherhood of Sleeping Car Porters), and George Counts (of Columbia University Teachers College) were among the prominent signers. So were Edmund Wilson (critic and author of *To the Finland Station*) and Sidney Hook (of New York University's Department of Philosophy). Hook had been a devout believer in Communism in the early 1930s. Authors Max Eastman (the disillusioned writer whose article, "Artists in Uniform," had caused such outrage among the Stalinists) and James Farrell (author of *Studs Lonigan*) were also on board. The critique was all the more devastating because it came from the cream of the liberal and pro-labor intelligentsia.[32]

Koch admitted he was not prepared for the "violence of the reactions" to the film, but he had his own explanation. "By this time," he insists, "many politicians were making a career of opposing New Deal policies, including recognition of the Soviet Union; with others, anticommunism was almost a religion."[33]

None of these explanations, however, applied to the liberal and left-wing critics cited above. Nor did they apply to the *New York Times*' movie critic Bosley Crowther. Crowther took issue with Warner Brothers, suggesting that *Mission* lacked "integrity" and had "willfully deranged" the facts in such a way as to undermine faith in future Warner films. Whatever might be said about the USSR, Crowther wrote in a reflection on the film, it was "ridiculous to pretend that Russia has been a paradise of purity."[34]

Even the *Nation* magazine was not charmed by the film. Movie critic James Agee argued in that pro–New Deal, pro-Soviet publication that the "film is almost describable as the first Soviet production to come from a major American studio."[35] The *Nation* editorial was far harsher, accusing the makers of *Mission* of engaging in a "whitewash" of Moscow, a "casual manipulation of history," and "some extraordinary liberties with recorded fact." The film, according to the editorial, "undertakes a complete exculpation of Soviet policies in the years just preceding the war. On the purges, the Russo-German Pact and the first Finnish war, it offers the straight party line."[36]

And even Koch admitted, "We had weighted the picture heavily on the positive side of Soviet accomplishments, since in our opinion the negative aspects had been amply publicized in our press ever since the revolution."[37] Koch, too, knew the truth. He had read Davies's book, but deliberately chose to ignore his devastating reports to Hull and Byrnes.

The letter written by Dwight Macdonald and signed by so many prominent figures on the Left summed up the Davies-Koch enterprise quite aptly:

> The fact is that *Mission to Moscow* is not a record of current history; it is not even a film designed to arouse sympathy for the heroic resistance to Nazi aggression of the Russian people; it is quite simply official propaganda on behalf of the present government of Russia. It corresponds in every detail with what the Kremlin would like the American people to think about its domestic and foreign policies....
>
> A Nazi film devoted to whitewashing the Blood Purge, the Reichstag Fire Trial and similar matters would use no other means than are employed in *Mission to Moscow*.[38]

CHAPTER FOURTEEN

THE GREAT ESCAPE

hen the Hollywood Ten testified before HUAC in October of 1947, they were still active Communists, capable of cheering or defending all of the Soviet Union's criminal conduct over the years, including its latest betrayal: the military conquest of Eastern Europe. None of what the Soviets did seemed—at least on the surface—to bother these men, who are now viewed as martyrs by so much of Hollywood and the world.

But after World War II, the Hollywood Ten found themselves out of sync with some of the most prominent Democratic liberals of the day. Many progressives had begun turning their backs on Communism and the Soviet Union after the war, when our alliance with Stalin was essentially at an end.

In the May 13, 1946, issue of the *New Republic*, James Loeb, national director of the Union for Democratic Action (UDA), issued a historic challenge to the progressive wing of the Democratic Party, urging it to break completely with American Communists.

LIBERAL DISILLUSIONMENT WITH THE FAR LEFT

What had set Loeb off was the April "Win-the-Peace" conference, bally-hooed by the *Daily Worker* as an effort to block the Truman administration's "policy of studied anti-Soviet provocation and drive for world domination."[1] The conference, which set up a permanent organization cochaired by the ostentatiously pro-Soviet singer and actor Paul Robeson, was addressed by left-wing Democratic senators Claude Pepper of Florida and Glen Taylor of Idaho. Pepper was considered so pro-Soviet that he was nicknamed "Red" Pepper by his critics. Taylor would become Henry Wallace's running mate on the pro-Soviet Progressive Party ticket in 1948. Union officials from the CIO adorned the steering committee. Communists and pro-Communists were clearly in charge at the gathering reminiscent of the "Popular Front" days of the 1930s.

The conference concluded with a call urging unrestricted aid for Soviet Russia—but opposing a loan to Great Britain until guarantees were made that the aid would not be "used for the exploitation and the oppression of the colonial peoples."[2]

Loeb argued in his letter to the *New Republic* that progressives couldn't go along with a group that had resolved that current international tensions were the exclusive result, in Loeb's paraphrase, of "the imperialistic, capitalistic, power-mad warmongering of the Western democracies aimed at the destruction of the peace-loving workers' democracy of the Soviet Union." Nor could true progressives agree that "human freedom" was not as important as "economic security."[3]

Loeb said that "democratic progressives of America" must make a critical decision: "whether or not they can or should work within *the same political organizations* [emphasis in the original]" open to "Communists." "I submit," said Loeb, "that if the American progressive movement is to survive and grow, this…decision must be in the negative.…"[4]

Loeb insisted that no "united front" organizations will "long remain united; it will only become a 'front.'" Communists are more "zealous" and more "disciplined" in pursuing a pre-determined goal, he added, and will only exploit "any legitimate differences of opinion" to further their own ends. Hence cooperation was impossible. Loeb also argued for the "practical, political fact that a united front movement, tending inevitably to be less united and more front, cannot in the long run win political power through democratic means."[5]

Loeb's letter set off a furious debate among liberals and leftists, and the upshot was a January 3, 1947, gathering of liberals at the Washington, D.C., Willard Hotel. With noted theologian and UDA chairman Reinhold Niebuhr presiding, they heard Chester Bowles call upon liberals to "organize a progressive front, divorced from Communist influence." The purpose of creating a new organization, said Bowles, was "to establish liberal control of the Democratic party...."

AMERICANS FOR DEMOCRATIC ACTION

The meeting ended with the establishment of the Americans for Democratic Action (ADA). *Louisville Courier Journal* editor Barry Bingham released its statement of principles. Among them: "We reject any association with Communists or sympathizers in the United States as completely as we reject any association with fascists or their sympathizers. Both are hostile to the principles of freedom and democracy on which this Republic has grown great."[6]

At the first ADA conference in March, the group stressed its anti-Communist views. The late president's son, Franklin Delano Roosevelt Jr., denounced those who have "adopted the protective coloration of liberalism" but at heart believe in the "dictatorship of the proletariat." In a nationwide broadcast on April 8, chairman Wilson Wyatt proclaimed that the ADA "rejects...the theory that we must purchase peace through continuous surrender to Soviet pressure."[7] Wyatt put the ADA's weight firmly behind President Truman's program to prevent a Red takeover of Greece and Turkey.

The new organization had attracted the cream of the liberal elite, including Mrs. Eleanor Roosevelt, Mayor Hubert Humphrey of Minneapolis (soon to become a famous liberal Minnesota senator), and UAW president Walter Reuther. Also on board were New Deal historian Arthur Schlesinger Jr.; civil rights lawyer Joseph Rauh Jr.; columnist Marquis Childs; anti-Communist president of the International Ladies' Garment Workers Union (ILGWU) David Dubinsky; and actors Melvyn Douglas and Ronald Reagan.

Many liberals, especially many prominent FDR liberals, had not only awakened to acts of Soviet and American Communist Party treachery, but also had come to believe that liberals, for their own survival, had to make a sharp break with the far Left. Such a move seemed even more imperative after the 1946 elections, when the Republicans swept both houses of Congress—to a large extent by running on the issue that the Democrats had been soft on Communism.

The ADA's birth was symptomatic of the "Great Break" with Communism by a wide range of those on the Left, many of whom had once been considered sympathetic to the Soviet Union. For some time before ADA's founding, in truth, many on the Left had grown weary of Communist tactics.

As early as 1940, the extremely liberal American Civil Liberties Union (ACLU) had decided to expel officials who were Communist Party members. Socialist Norman Thomas and lawyer Morris Ernst, both ACLU members, began urging the organization to distance itself from the Communists during the Soviet-Nazi Pact period. So upset was novelist John Dos Passos with Red influence in the ACLU during this era that he resigned from its national committee.

As a result of the protests from non-Communist liberals, the ACLU in February 1940 held it "inappropriate for any person to serve on the governing committee of the Union or on its staff who is a member of any political organization which supports totalitarian dictatorship in any country." Within this category, said the ACLU, are the "Communist party" of the United States and the "German-American Bund."

In May of the same year, the ACLU Board of Directors, in a highly contentious fight, expelled from its own board Elizabeth Gurley Flynn, one of the ACLU's original members, who had become a CP member in 1937.[8]

The ACLU's actions were unusual for a liberal organization prior to the end of World War II. Still they revealed that even many super-liberals had become, at the very least, wary of Communist participation in their organizations.

Eleanor Roosevelt, FDR's wife, appeared to be one of the most gullible of liberal women when it came to the nature of Communist organizations. She had joined or supported a number of them. But even Mrs. Roosevelt could display a concern about Red tactics, much to the displeasure of the Party. After the war she, too, joined the liberals who were separating themselves from the hard Communist Left. In her April 5, 1946, syndicated column, she wrote: "I happen to think that in the United States people who belong to the Communist party should not be officials or leaders in any group which does not avow itself to be a Communist-controlled organization."[9]

The *Daily Worker*, always solicitous of Mrs. Roosevelt's feelings, gently chided her, remarking that her rationale only made sense "on the grounds that the Communists...are in those [progressive] organizations for ulterior motives." Not so, said the *Worker*, and to accept such reasoning "is to accept a theory engendered by the Rankins and Hooverites to stifle social advance."[10]

UNIONS BEGIN TO SLIP OUT OF RED HANDS

The year 1946 was also a turning point for the heavily Communist-infiltrated Congress of Industrial Organizations (CIO), which had become a bulwark for radical politics. (The American Federation of Labor, or AFL, had always been anti-Communist.) The CIO included such powerful left-wing labor organizations as the National Maritime Workers, the International Longshoremen's and Warehousemen's Union, the United Auto Workers, and the United Steelworkers. Communist-controlled unions represented about 15 percent of the CIO membership.

But at the November 1946 CIO convention in Atlantic City, the anti-Communists launched the beginning of an extended campaign—which eventually proved successful—to end direct Communist influence in the labor federation. They managed to slip into a resolution approved by the CIO's Executive Board a paragraph criticizing "efforts of the Communist Party" to "intervene in the affairs of the CIO."[11]

The head of the CIO, the revered Philip Murray, a reluctant anti-Red, made a statement to the convention urging approval of the resolution on the ground that the CIO "must never be Communistically controlled and inspired." The resolution was approved unanimously.[12]

The CIO Executive Board also unanimously adopted an amendment to Rule Number 81, which stated that local and state industrial union councils "shall take no action or issue statements in conflict with CIO policy."[13]

The amendment proved a major blow to the far Left. Many of the local councils, which included a combination of CIO locals normally in the same state or city, had issued statements and policies pleasing to the radicals and Soviet boosters.

Now the CIO's national office used the amendment to bar the councils not only from issuing pro-Communist resolutions but also from "making gifts or sending delegates" to groups considered by the CIO to be Communist-run.

After the amendment was adopted, John Brophy, director of Industrial Union Councils for the national CIO office, sent a letter to the councils ordering them to sever all ties to the National Negro Congress, cited by Attorney General Francis Biddle in 1943 as "sponsored and supported by the Communist party."[14]

Following the convention, state CIO labor groups and industrial councils all across the country began issuing anti-Communist statements and implementing anti-Communist policies. The Reds were clearly on the run. Walter Reuther, a left-wing Democrat but an anti-Communist, became president of the United Auto Workers in 1946. Joseph Curran of the National Maritime Union, long considered pro-Soviet, sharply broke with the Party line when he successfully ran for reelection in the same year. He exposed the Party's efforts at union control and lambasted the Communists as being "more interested in assuring that the National Maritime Union becomes a stooge union of the Communist party than they are in keeping it an instrument belonging to the rank and file seamen who built it."[15]

Thus when the Hollywood Ten appeared before HUAC in 1947, not only were the majority of Americans opposed to Communism, but so were the majority of American liberals and progressives. The Democratic administration, the two major labor coalitions (the AFL and the CIO), the ACLU, and the numerous and prominent liberals who had formed the ADA had turned against the Soviet Union and its pawn, the American Communist Party. These liberals had managed to save themselves and the popularity of the Democratic Party by abandoning their Red former bedfellows.

Even liberal members of the Screen Writers Guild, where the Communist writers were still exerting considerable political influence when those HUAC hearings began, had begun to hatch a plot to oust the Communists and fellow travelers in their midst.

The Hollywood Ten, however, weren't concerned with the criminal activities of the Soviet Union or how its pawn, the American Communist Party, was goose-stepping along with Moscow. They remained dutifully shackled to the Stalinist camp.

CHAPTER FIFTEEN

THE ANTI-COMMUNISTS WEIGH IN

T he Motion Picture Alliance for the Preservation of American Ideals was unveiled in Beverly Hills, California, on February 4, 1944, with a single purpose: to combat the visibly increasing Communist influence in the movie industry. Hollywood notables who helped launch the MPA, as it came to be known, were producer-director Sam Wood (who became its president); Walt Disney of Disney Studios; James Kevin McGuinness, a major power at MGM; and Pulitzer Prize–winning playwright Morrie Ryskind (coauthor of the original Marx Brothers comedies and the Gershwin musical *Of Thee I Sing*).

The MPA would attract other celebrities into the organization, including such famous actors as John Wayne, Clark Gable, Gary Cooper, Robert Taylor, Adolphe Menjou, and Charles Coburn. Lela Rogers, the mother of Ginger, Fred Astaire's famous dancing partner, joined. So did Ayn Rand, author of *We the Living* and *The Fountainhead*.

Prominent labor leaders were also to climb aboard. None would prove a more formidable opponent to the Communists than Roy Brewer, the powerful International Alliance of Theatrical Stage Employees (IA) figure who would be largely responsible for breaking the grip of the far-Left unions in the movie industry. (Brewer, as we shall see, was able to break the influence of the Conference of Studio Unions, headed by the pro-Communist union chieftain Herbert K. Sorrell. Brewer would also play a major role in "rehabilitating" those in Hollywood with Communist pasts who sincerely wanted to make a clean break with the Party.)

What MPA members especially resented, executive chairman Jim McGuinness informed the liberal *New Leader*, was "a succession of organizations using either Hollywood, or Motion Picture in their names and subsequently being disclosed as Communist fronts." McGuinness named several, including the Hollywood Anti-Nazi League, the Motion Picture Democratic Committee, the Hollywood unit of the League against War and Fascism, and Hollywood's Emergency Peace Committee, which had later become the American Peace Mobilization.[1] Each, as McGuinness charged, was in fact run by Communists.

STEMMING THE CRIMSON TIDE

During the war years, the influence of the pro-Moscow radicals over the movie industry appeared to have grown substantially. Hollywood Reds were active in writing numerous movies glorifying the Soviet economic system and Stalin himself. They had also tilted various "victory" committees toward supporting Stalin's war demands and running relief outfits designed to lavish aid on Russia. And they had continued to deeply penetrate the various Hollywood guilds and unions, including the powerful Screen Writers Guild. The Hollywood Writers Mobilization, founded to supply wartime agencies and public service groups with thousands of writers, was itself largely controlled by Communists and fellow travelers, and after the war it became obvious even to skeptics that it was just another Soviet front.

Thus the MPA's challenge to the Communists drove the Left to fury. Among the most "offending" paragraphs of the MPA's statement of principles, according to an SWG bulletin: "We refuse to permit the effort of Communist, Fascist and other totalitarian-minded groups to pervert this powerful medium into an instrument for the dissemination of un-American ideas and beliefs." The Guild also objected to this MPA principle: "In our special field of motion pictures, we resent the growing impression that this industry is made up of, and dominated by, Communists, radicals, and crackpots."[2]

Somewhat surprisingly, the MPA's birth received applause from an important quarter in Hollywood's Establishment. *Variety*, the highly respected trade publication, gave the MPA a generous welcome (though its warm embrace would not last). "In times like these," wrote *Variety*'s editors, "the formation of the Motion Picture Alliance for the Preservation of American Ideals is most essential and necessary, as well as highly commendable."[3] As *Variety* read the MPA's statement, its primary purpose was to block the "rising tide" of Communism, fascism, and kindred beliefs and to make certain such poisonous views were "expelled from any films or messages that reach the screens of the world from the American production center."

The MPA wasn't treated so benevolently for long. Within a week, noted McGuinness, the MPA was attacked in "an industry-wide whispering campaign"—as fascistic and anti-Semitic. The Hollywood Guilds and Unions, including the very left-wing Screen Writers Guild and the actively pro-Communist Conference of Studio Unions, formed an "Emergency Committee" that began to unleash savage assaults against the anti-Communists. In a spring issue of the *Hollywood Reporter*, the group took out an ad charging the MPA with being soft on fascism (by not devoting enough attention to it) and undermining "the unity of the motion picture industry behind the war effort" by raising the issue of Communism.[4]

Five days later, the Hollywood Guilds and Unions, seventeen groups in all, decided to issue a full-blown jeremiad against the MPA in multiple resolutions, summed up in a pamphlet, "The Truth about Hollywood." Among the contributors assailing the new organization were Mary McCall, head of the Screen Writers Guild; Walter Wanger, who had produced the pro-Soviet movie *Blockade*; and Emmet Lavery, a notorious ally of Hollywood's radicals, soon to replace McCall as the SWG's president. Either directly or through insinuation, the MPA was accused of all manner of sin, including Red-baiting, fascism, anti-Semitism, and virtual treason.

REDS RESPOND WITH SLURS AND ABUSE

Weeks later the Executive Board of the Screen Writers Guild voted "unanimously" in favor of the Hollywood Guilds and Unions' venomous resolutions, singling out for special support the one that read: "the so-called Motion Picture Alliance for the Preservation of American Ideals is potentially a subversive and dangerous organization, which may comfort the enemy; and that all decent, loyal Americans in the industry, who may have been misled into joining it, should promptly withdraw from the organization and publicly disavow it."

Playwright Elmer Rice slammed the MPA with equal ferocity in the November 11 *Saturday Review of Literature*, then one of the most prestigious publications in the country. Rice, though not a Communist, hurled every bit of vicious gossip he could dredge up against the Alliance—without, it turns out, a sliver of proof—and strenuously tried to tar it as an agent of fascism.

Alliance members' public pronouncements, he insisted, were "modeled strictly along orthodox Red-baiting and witch-hunting lines." A careful and exhaustive analysis, he claimed, "has disclosed striking parallels" between the utterances of MPA members and "The America Firsters" and the pro-Nazi "Bundists." One need not "look far below the surface," Rice added, "to discover that the organization and its leading spirits are deeply tinged with isolationism and anti-unionism and—off the record, of course—with strong overtones of anti-Semitism and Jim Crowism."[5]

My father was furious at Rice's assault and wrote a lengthy—and telling—reply in the *Saturday Review of Literature*'s late December issue that effectively challenged the poisonous polemics that had been thrown the MPA's way not only by Rice but by the left-wing guilds and unions as well. As for the charge of anti-Semitism frequently launched against the Alliance, my father pointed out that when he went to its meetings, "I find there other Jewish fellows who, like me, became bar mitzvah at thirteen." And while "we long ago stopped donning phylacteries, none of us spends his spare time looking up anti-Semitic organizations to join." As for the non-Jewish members, "they work with, dine with, drink with, golf with, bowl with, and play bridge with Jews; at least three of them have had the *chutzpah* to marry Jewish girls."

Anti-unionism? Well, Ryskind said, "let's see"—and produced the names of fifteen Alliance members who were also important officials in various unions, including the Teamsters, the International Alliance of Theatrical Stage Employees, the Studio Utility Employees Union, the Lamp Operators, the Motion Picture Internationals' Committee, and so forth.

He conceded that

> Walt Disney's a member, too. And some of our labor boys fought Walt hard and bitterly in the strike at his studios. But they got around the table finally—which I like to think in my own, naïve, isolationist, anti-Semitic, Jim Crow fashion, is the ideal American solution—and ironed things out. The Commies were so sore at the fact that an agreement had been reached that they tried to upset the apple-cart. That's one of the reasons, by the way, that both Walt Disney and the honest labor men who struck against him are now in the MPA, together, fighting the American Sovieteers.

So far as "isolationism" was concerned, he added, he didn't believe that anyone could be so charged with that label except himself. "Most of my fellow MPA members were on the other side of that battle. . . ." But with Pearl Harbor, that "argument ended."[6]

Rice's "rebuttal" in the same issue of the *Saturday Review* was wildly off the charts; he even accused my dad of saying he was "a Communist," a charge no unbiased reader of his essay would ever conclude. Nor would the liberal *SRL* ever have allowed him to make such an unsubstantiated charge.

My father, in fact, had strongly suggested Rice was wholly innocent of what the Reds were up to and should talk to such informed folks as writer John Dos Passos, labor leader David Dubinsky, and Democratic lawmaker Jerry Voorhis of California—each a certified liberal well known for his pro-labor and anti-fascist views. As soon as he conferred with them, Rice should then "humbly go over to the MPA and apply for membership." But my father wanted Rice "to wash his mouth out with soap first," because of the untrue things he had said about his friends in the Alliance.

Rice was not persuaded and was hardly contrite; indeed, in his response he appeared eager to toss more venom. "The MPA leaders," he argued, "are, in the main, men and women who, however guarded they may be in their public utterances, are known in the Hollywood community to be anti-Semitic, anti-Negro, anti-alien and anti-labor; in short, fascists."

Fascists? In using that word in 1944, of course, Rice was basically accusing the MPA folks of being on the same page with our wartime foes Mussolini and Hitler. It was not only an inflammatory statement but an outright lie. He did not present a single fact to support his provocative contention. To get around my father's thorough debunking of Rice's anti-MPA tirade, Rice limply responded: "Mr. Ryskind seems unaware that there are anti-Semitic Jews, anti-labor union leaders and writers who are traitors to the literary craft."[7] Rice, in short, couldn't provide a speck of evidence to support his outlandish assault.

McGuinness's earlier article in the *New Leader* had also been effective in answering the kind of charges Rice was bringing. The MPA, McGuinness had noted, was politically ecumenical. It included "case-hardened" Republicans and "case-hardened" Democrats, with people who have elevated FDR "to at least a junior partnership in Heavenly Days, Inc., and people who have cordially demoted him to a senior membership in the rival firm." There were "New Dealers and anti–New Dealers," a pair "who call themselves Catholic Socialists," and some "who go right on voting for [Socialist] Norman Thomas."[8]

HITLER'S REAL ENABLERS

Despite all evidence to the contrary, the Reds, with more than a sprinkling of liberals in tow, continued to attack Hollywood's anti-Communists as virtual allies of Nazi Germany. But it wasn't the MPA members who for twenty-two months had teamed up with the savage anti-Semite Adolf Hitler, deliberately pushing policies that would help the Nazi warlord crush the Western democracies in Europe back in 1939.

The leftists who attacked the MPA never brought forth information to show that *any* important MPA figure favored the Bund or fascism. As my father had stressed, he had been just about the only major isolationist in the group—which, of course, hardly made him a fascist.

The assault against the MPA, however, was unrelenting. The SWG's August 1 *Guild Bulletin* ran a front-page headline that read "MPA EXPOSED AT MEETING OF 950 GUILD, UNION DELEGATES." The *Bulletin* not only applauded the Hollywood Guilds and Unions' resolution condemning the MPA for being "potentially subversive" but singled out for approval a report by Oliver H. P. Garrett insisting there were clear similarities between the Alliance and "known fascist groups in this country and abroad."[9]

But where was the beef? Certainly not in the *Guild Bulletin*'s description of the Garrett report. None of those attacked in the Garrett "study" was quoted by the *Bulletin* or in the report itself as saying anything favorable about fascism or Nazi Germany or the American Bund.

A key target of Garrett's report was the MPA's Howard Emmett Rogers, but he had been a pre–Pearl Harbor supporter of England in its desperate struggle against Hitler Germany. The *Guild Bulletin*, in fact, could not discover a single pro-fascist remark by Rogers, so it accused him of having opposed the first Screen Writers Guild because it had been "taken over by the Communist element." There was more than a germ of truth in Rogers's charge, but his statement hardly justified the "pro-fascist" label the far Left was yearning to pin on the MPA. Rogers, in fact, turned out to be less than an optimal target for the Guild radicals. Our old friends Ceplair and Englund reveal how the MPA's Rogers, far from being sympathetic to fascism, was a leading backer of the British who had strongly supported their beleaguered nation at a July 1940 forum at the Hollywood Chamber of Commerce. After Communist writers Dalton Trumbo and Theodore Dreiser, along with left-wing author Carey McWilliams, tore into the "perfidy" of Great Britain, Rogers noted that he had scarcely heard a "mention of the perfidy of Adolf Hitler," then unleashing massive bombing raids on the sole European nation still resisting the Nazi warlord.

Rogers then asked whether there was "any nation in the world today so low in the estimation of any man or woman in this hall tonight that he or she would want to see that nation conquered and destroyed by Hitler and Naziism?"[10] Many of the hard-core Communists in the audience and on the stage may actually have desired such a terrible outcome, for that was the not-so-hidden Moscow agenda at the moment. Rhetorically, the Red line was that there was not a dime's worth of difference between Tory England and Nazi Germany, but the policies the Communists pursued were manifestly designed to help Hitler and punish Churchill.

No one seemed more eager to do in the MPA than Dalton Trumbo, editor of *The Screen Writer*, the influential flagship publication of the Screen Writers Guild. His magazine, which he made a cozy place for Communist writers, took constant shots at the anti-Communist organization. So distressed was Trumbo with the MPA's creation that he decided to launch a personal tirade against producer-director Samuel Wood in the maiden issue of *The Screen Writer* (June 1945). He mocked Wood's considerable talents as a director, misrepresented his political views, and claimed Wood was undermining the morale of our armed forces by pointing to Communist influence in Hollywood. Trumbo, a deep-dyed Red screenwriter himself, used his publication to portray both Wood and the MPA as friends and favorites of fascists and anti-Semites, saboteurs of the war effort, and purveyors of "the phony cry of Communism on the screen."[11]

The MPA was able to have the last laugh. Three years after the Alliance's founding, HUAC held its famous hearings on the role of Communists in Hollywood, relying to a large extent on solid information furnished by MPA members. Many of the MPA's leading lights, including Wood, McGuinness, Disney, Taylor, Ryskind, Menjou, Rand, and Brewer, gave important testimony exposing Communist influence among the writers, in the guilds, and in the unions. And those hearings proved catastrophic for the Communists, as the Left concedes.

The Left reviled the MPA, but the effort to portray it as some kind of Hitler-lite organization proved a dud. In the end, the MPA achieved a good part of what it set out to do: drastically reduce the Communist influence in Hollywood.

CHAPTER SIXTEEN

THE COLD WAR BEGINS

T he Hollywood Reds were warriors for peace in the post–World War II era. Or so their apologists continue to insist. If only their foreign policy views had prevailed, there never would have been a Cold War. Scriptwriter Walter Bernstein, a longtime Stalinist who wrote such films as *Fail-Safe* and *The Molly Maguires*, touches on the point in his serious 1976 comedy, *The Front*, which was nominated for an Academy Award.

In the film, a sympathetic left-wing figure tells the Woody Allen character about the congressmen investigating the movie industry, "They're trying to sell the Cold War. They're using the blacklist against anyone who won't buy."[1] But the Hollywood Communists, and the Hollywood Ten in particular, Bernstein fails to inform his audience, *embraced the historic move by Stalin that laid the groundwork for that war.*

Some background is in order. From the time the USSR was invaded by Nazi Germany until Hitler's suicide in April of 1945, the Communist Party was the stoutest supporter of a U.S. victory over the Third Reich. No group could touch the Party when it came to exhibiting "patriotic" fervor. The Party called upon labor to take a "no-strike" pledge during the war; swore that it had severed relations with the Soviet-controlled Communist International (Comintern), which Stalin formally terminated in 1943; transformed itself in 1944 into a non-threatening, "non-Party" organization (the Communist Political Association); and proclaimed a newfound enthusiasm for "the Declaration of Independence, the United States Constitution and its Bill of Rights."

Taking their cue from Stalin, as usual, Hollywood's Reds eagerly threw themselves into the war effort. They joined the U.S. military in droves, rushed into crucial intelligence services (bending our policies toward Soviet goals when they could), enthusiastically assisted and worked for various government agencies—the Office of War Information in particular—in the propaganda war, and wrote popular anti-Axis movies for America's major studios, albeit frequently stuffing their scripts with pro-Soviet propaganda. No group rallied around the flag with more gusto.

Few observers understood that Party members were using their talents to save not the United States but the Soviet homeland. Wherever opportunity arose, whether in Hollywood or in government service, they attempted to shift public opinion not in support of American interests but in favor of Stalin's foreign policy.

During the war, America shoveled $11 billion in aid to the Soviets, opened the "second front" as Stalin had demanded (with the Normandy invasion in June 1944), and made critical concessions to the Soviets at Teheran in November of 1943 and Yalta in February of 1945. Until his death in mid-April of 1945, FDR was delighted that he had apparently achieved a decent postwar relationship with the Kremlin.

THE DUCLOS LETTER

But during these apparently halcyon days of the Russian-American alliance, Stalin decided to make an ominous move. Once Hitler's legions were certain to be crushed—and U.S. assistance was no longer needed—Stalin got the American Communists to do another one of their famous policy flips, almost as stunning as their switch from condemning Hitler to virtually embracing him at the time of the Hitler-Stalin Pact. U.S. Party leaders would suddenly return to uncompromising hostility toward America and capitalism. Stalin was starting a Cold War, and Hollywood's Reds were cheering for his side.

Shortly after his return from Moscow to France in the spring of 1945, Jacques Duclos, a prominent French Communist leader who had been a member of the Presidium of the Executive Committee of the Communist International (Comintern), allowed to be published under his name a scorching attack on Earl Browder in the April issue of *Cahiers du Communisme*, a publication of the French Communist Party.[2]

In this article, Duclos accused Browder, who had headed the Communist Party USA since the early 1930s, of having grossly misinterpreted the 1943 Teheran Conference, attended by Churchill, Stalin, and Roosevelt, when he instructed his fellow comrades that in the postwar period capitalism and Communism might have long periods of peace between them.

The United States had never seemed friendlier toward Russia than at the time of Teheran, where FDR graciously made grand concessions in his first face-to-face meeting with Stalin. FDR accepted Stalin's invitation to move the conference from the American embassy to a villa in the Soviet compound (thus giving a negotiating advantage to the Russians), offered to give the Soviet leader surplus American and British ships after the war, and set the Normandy invasion—Stalin's most important goal, since it would be of immeasurable relief to Russia's armies—for the following spring or early summer.

Still in a charitable mood, Roosevelt said the Soviets should have access to Dairen, a major Manchurian port; he felt certain our Chinese friends wouldn't mind a bit (this access was later used by Moscow to undermine Chiang Kai-shek and the Republic of China).

Historian William Henry Chamberlin notes that "Yugoslavia's fate…was settled at Teheran" as well, with the Big Three deciding to support the Moscow-trained Joseph Broz Tito rather than the pro-Western, anti-Nazi, and anti-Communist Draža Mihailović. Poland's future was also settled at Teheran, writes Chamberlin, for Stalin learned there that "Churchill would co-operate in his scheme for annexing almost half of Poland, and that Roosevelt would offer no opposition."[3]

The conference ended in December of 1943 with the declaration: "We came here with hope and determination. We leave here friends in fact, in spirit and in purpose."[4] And Stalin himself seemed to endorse the friendly spirit of Teheran. Less than a month before the conference, he had proclaimed, "Together with our allies we shall have to liberate the people of Europe from the fascist invaders...grant the liberated peoples of Europe the full right and freedom to decide for themselves the question of their form of government...."[5]

"It is no wonder that Earl Browder, then General Secretary of the American Communist Party, took the Teheran Declaration and Stalin's speeches seriously and proceeded to change the character of his Party to accord with what he believed the Declaration meant," wrote Browder's special friend, Phil Jaffe.[6]

The Duclos letter was designed to blow up this era of good feeling, the chumminess among the Allies, and the wartime alliance itself. In it, Duclos excoriated Browder for reading into the events at Teheran any change in Moscow's long-held view that capitalism and Communism would always be in conflict.

Browder, of course, had not "misread" anything; he had been following Moscow's directives all along. But once Hitler was no longer a threat and the Soviets were in the process of occupying Eastern and Central Europe, Stalin was ready to switch back to a tough policy toward the United States. The Duclos letter was his instrument for signaling yet another turn in the Party line.

The letter listed a long catalogue of Browder's alleged heresies. Duclos insisted that Browder had been wrong to dissolve the Communist Party in 1944, wrong to create the non-Party Communist Political Association to replace it, wrong to suggest that (in Duclos's paraphrase of Browder) "capitalism and socialism had begun to find means of peaceful coexistence," and wrong to argue that (again in Duclos's words) "the principal problems of internal politics of the U.S. must in [the] future be solved exclusively by means of reforms...."

Duclos specifically condemned Browder's purported view that there could be "class peace in the United States" and that nationalization of monopolies constitutes a socialist achievement. "No," Duclos rebuked, "in nationalization it is simply a matter of reforms of a democratic character, *achievement of socialism being impossible to imagine without preliminary conquest of power* [emphasis added]."[7] Confrontation, class warfare, and violence must be the order of the day for Communism to eventually prevail.

ALLIES NO MORE

The Duclos letter set off convulsions among American Communists, who accurately saw it as another dramatic change in the Party line. Stalin was commanding CPUSA members to transform the Party once again into an uncompromisingly anti-American organization.

Communist leaders, virtually all of whom had supported Browder's soft line during the war—simply because Stalin himself had found it useful to pursue a soft line—now gathered in meetings to mortify themselves, outdoing each other in self-blame for not having comprehended Browder's alleged weaknesses and stupidities.

At a special emergency national convention held toward the end of July of 1945, Browder was unanimously removed as president of the Communist Political Association, and the CPA was reconfigured once again as the uncompromising Communist Party. Seven months later, Browder was expelled from that Party.

According to screenwriter Richard Collins, who testified before HUAC in 1951 (he was subpoenaed but never testified in the famous 1947 hearings), this was the incident that prompted him to rethink his Party membership. "This was one of the things which I suppose," said Collins, "was the turning point in my Party life... The situation was that a man who loved Browder on Monday hated him on Thursday. Once the national committee of the Communist Party said he was no good, the chorus filled the room...." That position "seemed absurd."[8]

But where did Hollywood's radical writers—and particularly future members of the Hollywood Ten—generally stand on this crucial issue? Did they stand with the softer Browder line or embrace the unyielding Kremlin *diktat* that presaged the Cold War? The Hollywood writers rushed to betray Browder.

According to Dalton Trumbo, this was a contest between Lenin and Browder, and he chose to believe that "Lenin was right."[9]

Screenwriter Norma Barzman writes in her memoir that at a dinner party at her house, Lester Cole "held his glass high" and said, "Now we can toast the revolution again!" Barzman, an enthusiastic Stalinist for so much of her life, insists Cole said it "jokingly," but nevertheless Cole clearly favored the about-face. (Judging from his letters, Cole remained a hard-liner until his death.)[10]

Alvah Bessie and Ring Lardner Jr., two other members of the Hollywood Ten, also made enlightening remarks on this change in the Party line. In a sympathetic interview in *Tender Comrades*, Bessie claims to have once upbraided Browder himself for his wartime views in the dining car of a train headed toward Hollywood.

"In the course of the conversation," says Bessie,

> I raised some questions with him. I was finding it very difficult to agree with certain ideas that he and the Party were putting out—that there could be such a thing as "progressive capitalism" and that it would be possible to have a peaceful transition from capitalism to Socialism in the United States.
>
> I said, "I can't envisage a situation whereby the capitalists of this country would say, 'Okay, boys, we can't run it anymore, you do it,' and quietly steal away." He said, "Can't you really, Alvah? Can't you really?" I said, "No, I can't... *really.*"[11]

Bessie's remarks should be an eye-opener for those who think the Hollywood Reds were only hoping for a nonviolent transformation of American society. He himself admitted that he adamantly opposed a "peaceful transition" to socialism.

Bessie's encounter with Browder was prior to Browder's ouster, but Ring Lardner Jr. lets us know what occurred afterward. The American CP, writes Lardner (and he includes the Hollywood contingent), "rallied around [hard-liner] William Z. Foster and tossed out Browder, his Association and all his heresies"—his "heresies" being Browder's advocating relative peace between Moscow and Washington.

"The membership of the Hollywood section emerged more or less intact from the ferment," Lardner adds. "We were flattered that the leadership in New York considered us important enough for Foster himself to give us his view of the future and our role in it at a private meeting in a member's home."[12]

The Hollywood radicals' wholesale desertion of Browder reveals that they were not so innocent after all. Apparently they fervently held the view—along with Duclos, Stalin's little messenger—that there could be *no* "peaceful transition" to socialism. They cooperated in Browder's defenestration precisely because he appeared to stand for the opposite point of view.

Lardner's remarks also reveal how closely the Soviet-directed national Party controlled the Hollywood Communists. He could have enlightened us further by disclosing which members attended and precisely what "role" Foster had assigned to them for the future in promoting the violent class struggle and Stalin's foreign policy. But Lardner was apparently content to carry that piece of knowledge to his grave.

Philip Jaffe's book, *The Rise and Fall of American Communism*, is of special interest in this connection. Jaffe was a Communist fellow traveler—a "super fellow traveler" for most of his adult life, in the words of Bertram Wolfe, an anti-Communist historian and, oddly, Jaffe's friend. Jaffe was an intimate of Browder's and was privy to Communist Party internal discussions and memos, largely because of his friendship with the longtime chief of the American CP and his devotion to the Soviet Union.

Jaffe pointed out that Duclos accused Browder not only of proposing "collaboration between Communists and capitalists and toning down the class struggle" but of embracing a foreign policy position toward Europe that had to be an anathema to Stalin. Duclos's letter proclaimed that Browder interpreted the Teheran agreements to mean that the "greatest part of Europe, west of the Soviet Union, will probably be reconstituted [after the war] on a bourgeois democratic basis...."

Duclos's condemnation of this particular Browder heresy, Jaffe reminds the reader, was essential to let CP members in the United States and elsewhere know that Stalin had no intention of yielding his recent conquest of Eastern and Central Europe. Stalin had in fact remarked in a conversation with Yugoslavian Communist Milovan Đjilas in the spring of 1945—the same general time frame when the Duclos letter was published in America—that this "war is not as in the past; whoever occupies territory imposes on it his own social system. Everyone imposes his own system as far as his army can reach." [13]

"DELIBERATE CONFRONTATION WITH THE WEST"

Browder had been snookered by Stalin's wartime policy of seeming to stand with the West. The Soviet dictator had only feigned camaraderie until American help in confronting Hitler was no longer needed. Browder had read the tea leaves wrongly, rather stupidly expecting Stalin to continue the softer policy in the postwar period—at least for a time.

After a learned discussion on the controversy surrounding the Duclos letter, Jaffe concludes that

> the Duclos article was beyond doubt a signal and directive not only to the American Communist party but to all Communist parties to prepare for the new Soviet postwar foreign policy strategy.... That policy was deliberate confrontation with the West.
>
> This was only the beginning of a strategy that developed full blown in both Europe and the Far East in the following three years. *The Duclos article...was simply the first shot fired in the Cold War* [emphasis added]....[14]

Having approved the ejection of Browder, Hollywood's Communist writers were back where they had begun in the 1930s, when so many of them had been drawn to the Kremlin-controlled League of American Writers: supporting a militant Soviet Union working for the violent demise of the United States of America.

CHAPTER SEVENTEEN

SCREENWRITERS EMBRACE A COMINTERN AGENT

O n May 2, 1947, the Civil Rights Congress took out an ad in the *People's Daily World* hailing Gerhart Eisler as a "world renowned anti-fascist fighter framed by the Thomas-Rankin Un-American Committee." What had enraged the CRC was that HUAC had royally embarrassed one of the Left's formidable heroes. Fearing he might flee the country to avoid a scheduled hearing, HUAC prompted federal officials to arrest Eisler at his home in New York on February 4 and send him to Ellis Island for detention as an enemy alien. Two days later, HUAC cited Eisler for contempt because he refused to answer questions about his Communist activities. On the same day, HUAC, in a blockbuster hearing, exposed him as a major Soviet agent. And by May, when the CRC took out its ad, Eisler faced possible conviction and jail time for stonewalling HUAC.

Under the heading "ACT NOW!" the ad urged readers to "call on your congressmen to abolish" the Committee and on President Truman "to effect [Eisler's] immediate release." Hollywood's radical writers eagerly affixed their names in support of the CRC's "Free Eisler" crusade.

Among those listed in the ad: Lester Cole, John Howard Lawson, Albert Maltz, and Dalton Trumbo. In a little less than six months, each was to become a famous member of the Hollywood Ten. Other Communists and super-fellow-traveling screenwriters had also signed the ad, including Michael Blankfort, Guy Endore, and Howard Koch.

Indeed, Reds galore, and not only screenwriters, filled up the sponsor list. LaRue McCormick, who had run for Congress on the Communist ticket, was on board, as were Leo Gallagher and Ben Margolis, members of a well-known Communist law firm (though it wasn't so advertised).

Long-time Red sympathizers such as E. Y. "Yip" Harburg, who had written the lively lyrics for those famous songs in the *Wizard of Oz*, and Herbert K. Sorrell, the pro-Stalinist head of the Conference of Studio Unions, were also ad sponsors.[1]

Clearly, the effort to free the German-born Eisler was a thoroughgoing Red enterprise, and, not surprisingly, Eisler turned out to be a thoroughgoing Communist. According to expert witnesses (including ex-Communist officials), his sister, his first wife, and an FBI surveillance team, he was part of the international Soviet apparatus, traveled the world using aliases, engaged in forgery, regularly visited with foreign Communists, and met with Soviet espionage agents. He had also been giving instructions to the American Communist Party in his position as a somewhat concealed member of the Soviet-run Comintern.

"NUMBER ONE COMMUNIST"

Nor was any of this really in doubt when the Civil Rights Congress sprang to Eisler's defense in early May and Hollywood's "activist" writers eagerly embraced the CRC's latest "humanitarian" project. In October of 1946, Louis Budenz, the ex–managing editor of the *Daily Worker* who was now a Fordham professor and a devout Catholic, had made a sensational and widely publicized speech in Detroit exposing the inner workings of the Communist Party and Eisler as the "Number One Communist" in America.

In testimony before HUAC a month later, again prominently highlighted by the media, Budenz expanded on Eisler's influence, disclosing that one of the *Worker*'s most important writers, "Hans Berger," was really Eisler himself. He also recalled witnessing a dramatic incident in the 1930s when the editor of the *Worker*, Clarence Hathaway, meekly listened while Eisler, using the alias Edwards, excoriated him for over an hour for his supposedly poor performance. According to Budenz's testimony, Eisler was clearly looked upon by the *Worker* editors as an authoritative figure.[2]

Eisler burst into the news again just three months before the Civil Rights Congress took out that ad in the *People's World*. February 6, 1947, proved an exciting day for the man some of the most talented people in Hollywood would insist was "framed." His behavior foreshadowed the tactics employed by the Hollywood Ten in October.

Eisler, who had been subpoenaed by HUAC and came with counsel, was politely asked to "take the stand." Startling the Committee (and possibly also his attorney, Carol Weiss King), he declared, "I am not going to take the stand."

Would he "raise his right hand?"

Eisler: "No."

Before he was to be sworn in, he demanded to be allowed to read a "three-minute" statement. "I came here as a political prisoner," he asserted. "I want to make a few remarks, only three minutes before I be [sic] sworn in, and answer your questions.... It is just three minutes."

Chairman J. Parnell Thomas would not let Eisler alter the rules but said that if his remarks were pertinent to the investigation, he could read them after he had been questioned. Eisler rejected Thomas's offer and was ordered to leave the hearing room.

As the guards led him away, Eisler's attorney left on the press table not the short, three-minute statement he had said he wanted to make but a twenty-page mimeographed screed that, according to the *New York Times*' account, "was a disputatious paper, making virtually no references to the evidence later offered...."[3] It was at this point that HUAC had him cited for contempt.

On the same day, the Committee heard from several other witnesses, including Budenz and Eisler's sister, Ruth Fischer. They testified they had known Eisler as a long-time, dedicated Communist.

Eisler's sister, corroborating Budenz's accusation that Eisler had been a Comintern representative as well, recalled Gerhart's visit to her apartment in France in June of 1933. She said he had just come from Moscow and was on his way to America for the first time. According to Fischer's testimony, Eisler bluntly informed her, "I am going for the Comintern to the United States, and I will change the policy of the Communist Party there completely and entirely." Though she and her brother had become increasingly estranged, she heard from numerous sources later that "Gerhart was carrying out his mission to the United States to the full satisfaction of his boss in Moscow."[4]

HUAC also placed into the hearing record a damning statement by FBI director J. Edgar Hoover detailing Eisler's lengthy and covert Communist activities and introduced important documents, including a forged passport and several of his articles, that helped substantiate the testimony against him.

The hearings brought out other illuminating details. Born in Leipzig, Germany, in 1897, Eisler became an Austrian Communist, then a German CP member. In the late 1920s and early 1930s, he was trained as an international Communist revolutionary in Moscow.

Ex-Communist William O'Dell Nowell, a Georgia-born black man, shed critical light on Eisler's Moscow training. Nowell testified that he himself had in 1929 and 1931 attended the International Lenin School, a project of the Comintern, the Soviet-controlled organization that governed Communist parties in every country where a major CP existed. At the school, Nowell said, he learned "Marxism and Leninism," the "history of the Communist International," "conspiracy," and "sabotage."

Nowell disclosed that he was taught "how to capture a city" and "seize the most vital means of communications, transportation, lighting, water supply and so on, food, of course." When attending the Lenin School, he met up with

Eisler, who had gone through the same courses. He knew Eisler, who went under the aliases "Edwards" and "Gerhart," as a representative of the German Communist Party.[5]

Chief Investigator Robert Stripling introduced documents revealing that Eisler had traveled surreptitiously to America in the 1930s, had adopted several aliases, was working for the Communists in Spain during the Civil War, and had obtained an American passport under another man's name so he could travel to the Soviet Union for instructions and then return to the United States.

"EVASION AND DUPLICITY"

This passport, dated August 31, 1934, would eventually lead to Eisler's undoing before HUAC and before a grand jury. Though Eisler's photograph was on the passport, the hearings demonstrated that it had actually been granted under the name of Samuel Liptzen, a staff writer at *Morning Freiheit*, a Yiddish version of the *Daily Worker*.

The handwriting on the passport application, according to the Treasury Department, was that of Leon Josephson, a hard-core Communist who traveled to Moscow from time to time for his instructions. The signature of the "identifying witness," Bernard A. Hirschfield, was identical to Josephson's. The passport was used by Eisler to travel to Europe, and in 1936 on a trip to Moscow.[6] None of this evidence was ever convincingly disputed.

From 1933 until the late '30s, Eisler was a secret Red operative in America, but he then decided to enter this country through a different method. Using his real name, he came to Ellis Island in June of 1941 as an alleged political refugee from France. In applying for refugee status, as the HUAC documents reveal, he demonstrated himself to be a serial liar.

Eisler swore to the Immigration and Naturalization Service on June 14 that he had never been married—but the hearings revealed that he had already been married twice. He swore he didn't have a sister, even though his anti-Stalinist sibling, Ruth Fischer, was living in New York City. He said he had never been to America previously—another falsehood. When asked if he had "ever been a member of any Communist organization," he answered, "No." Had he ever been "sympathetic to the Communist cause?" "No," he replied again. Two more provable lies.[7]

To bolster its case, HUAC dropped into the hearing record an expurgated but injurious FBI report based on the findings of an FBI surveillance team that had been monitoring Eisler's activities since 1941. A major segment of the report was carried in the February 7, 1947, *New York Times*.

Eisler's denials of his Communist activities to the immigration service, stressed the report, "were obviously false," particularly in view of his "long-term activity as an important international Communist and responsible representative of the Communist International."

Shortly after he entered the United States as a political refugee, the FBI report notes, Eisler "became active in the American Communist movement." By virtue of his role in the Comintern, "he was responsible for and instrumental in the determination of American Communist policy and the control and direction of American Communist operations."

The FBI report also states that since 1941 Eisler had "contributed regular articles to the official press of the Communist Party," including the *Daily Worker* and *Political Affairs*, the official theoretical organ of the CPUSA. According to the report several of his articles, all under pseudonyms, "have been instrumental in formulating or solidifying the Communist Party line with regard to particular subjects."

While Eisler customarily described himself as "unemployed" or a "journalist," the FBI revealed that under the name of Julius Eisman he had been "receiving for a considerable period of time regular monthly checks" from the Joint Anti-Fascist Refugee Committee (JAFRC), "a well-known Communist front organization in New York City."

The FBI report concludes, "The entire pattern of Eisler's activities since his arrival in the United States in June 1941 . . . is one of apparent evasion and duplicity, coupled with clandestine but no less important activity. He has been in constant contact with important Communist functionaries and has frequently been in touch with individuals identified as or strongly suspected of being Soviet espionage agents."[8]

Eisler's role as an important Soviet Communist dictating policy to the American CP was hardly a secret. The *New York Times* had been running front-page stories on his activities for some time. HUAC's February 6 revelations made the lead story the next day, with the *Times* printing Eisler's picture and carrying key portions of the FBI report in a separate box.

There was no way that Hollywood's radical writers could have been unaware of the mountain of evidence against Eisler. Yet less than three months later, they were fiercely defending this international revolutionary and hurling invective at his accusers. Would any patriotic American, whatever his ideology, have taken such a stance?

Eisler's troubles were actually just beginning. Representative Richard Nixon, a newly elected Republican from California, laid out the strong contempt case against him in his maiden speech before the House of Representatives on February 18. The House vote to cite Eisler for contempt was nearly unanimous: 370 to 1, with the lone vote in opposition cast by Representative Vito Marcantonio, a well-known stooge of the Communist Party.

Two months later—a month before the CRC ad in his support was run in the *People's World*—Eisler was indicted for making false statements on his application for his 1945 exit visa, including his failure to state, as the application required, that he had used aliases. The grand jury also found that he had committed perjury when he denied in 1941 that he was a member of the Communist Party.

In June he was convicted of contempt of Congress; in August, he was found guilty of the 1945 exit visa fraud. The Eisler saga, however, was not quite over.

With Eisler out on bail and appealing his convictions, the CRC kept holding rallies at which Communists and fellow travelers kept shouting that he was a victim of a "fascist" plot. No matter how steep the mountain of evidence against him, Hollywood's radical writers stubbornly stuck with this international revolutionary. And Eisler would return the favor.

On November 2, 1947, after the Hollywood Ten were cited for contempt by HUAC for refusing to say whether they were Communist Party members, the CRC held a meeting in support of the Hollywood Ten at the Park Central Hotel in New York.

The CRC's purpose: to urge the House to vote down the Committee's contempt citation and eliminate HUAC altogether. Albert Maltz, one of the Ten, declared to the gathering that if the Committee "could achieve the right to burn films, which is what they are after, the results will be that they will get the right to burn the people who made the films."

Present on the dais were five other members of the Ten—Alvah Bessie, Herbert Biberman, Ring Lardner Jr., John Howard Lawson, and Samuel Ornitz. All turned out to be dedicated Party members. Others on the dais included several Hollywood figures who had been subpoenaed by HUAC but had not testified. Among them: Richard Collins, Lewis Milestone, Larry Parks, Irving Pichel, Robert Rossen, and Waldo Salt. Five of the six turned out to be solid Party members. (Milestone was, at the very least, a fellow traveler.) Also present were two of their Communist attorneys, Ben Margolis and Charles Katz.[9]

In the audience, applauding, as an AP photo in the *New York Times* reveals, was Gerhart Eisler.[10]

Two years later, still never having served a day in jail, Eisler fled the country as a stowaway on the Polish liner *Batory*. While it was docked in Southampton, England, Scotland Yard, at the behest of the United States, had him removed from the ship kicking and screaming. He was set free by the British when a magistrate ruled that his false statements under oath to the immigration service, considered perjury in the United States, did not amount to perjury under British law.

Free to leave, Eisler wound up where his ideology and roots naturally took him—in the German Democratic Republic. There he fronted as a propagandist for Germany's Communist regime. "In later years," as FBI Special Agent Robert Lamphere, who had monitored Eisler's movements for Hoover, informs us, "he was seen teaching at the university in Leipzig; he became chief of the Information Office in East Germany, and in 1962 was named chairman of the East German State Radio Committee."[11]

The Eisler case proved, as if additional proof were needed, that Hollywood's radical screenwriters had a far different agenda from that of *bona fide* liberals earnestly attempting to rescue the less fortunate in American society. In backing an obvious Soviet agent and fraudulently claiming that he had been "framed" by HUAC, they had revealed, beyond a quibble, where their loyalties really lay.

CHAPTER EIGHTEEN

HUAC

When the House Un-American Activities Committee opened its probe of Communism in Hollywood on October 20, 1947, the famous Caucus Room in the Old House Office Building was jam-packed with reporters, spectators, and witnesses. More than four hundred people were on hand to see the historical event, with the hearings promising to be jolted by dramatic exchanges between Committee members and both friendly and unfriendly witnesses.

Just five members of the nine-man Committee (technically a subcommittee) were customarily in attendance: Chairman J. Parnell Thomas (Republican of New Jersey), John McDowell (Pennsylvania Republican), Richard Vail (Illinois Republican), Richard Nixon (Republican from California), and John Wood (Georgia Democrat). Wood, the ranking Democrat on HUAC, would join in the questioning, but he was rarely there at the opening of the sessions.

Nixon had been in Congress for less than twelve months; he would rise to national fame when HUAC triggered the Hiss-Chambers case the following year. His role in the Hollywood hearings, however, was somewhat muted, though he did continually press the studio heads to put out anti-Communist pictures the way they did anti-Nazi films during World War II.

Representative John Rankin (Mississippi Democrat), whose enemies accurately described him as a racist and rabid anti-Semite, was a member of HUAC in 1947 and had been responsible for transforming it into a permanent committee in January of 1945. But the Left's efforts to associate him with the Hollywood hearings are unwarranted; Rankin was not a member of the panel set up to explore Communist influence in the motion picture industry.

Indeed this was largely a Republican extravaganza, with the four GOP members of Congress named above constantly in attendance. Chairman Thomas and Chief Investigator Robert Stripling and Director of Research Benjamin Mandel effectively served as choreographers for the hearings.

Thomas, a World War I veteran first elected to the House in 1936, had become chairman of HUAC after the Republican sweep of the House in 1946. Stripling had been with the Committee since fellow Texan Martin Dies, a Democrat, had first chaired HUAC in 1938. (Stripling would also be the chief investigator in 1948 when the Committee heard Whittaker Chambers and Elizabeth Bentley testify that State Department official Alger Hiss had, in fact, been a Communist Party member.)

Mandel had special expertise on the Communist Party, having been a Communist himself in the 1920s and '30s. Using his code name, Bert Miller, he had issued Whittaker Chambers his Party book, decoratively stamped with a hammer and sickle, in the 1920s. He had also been a business manager of the *Daily Worker*.

The first week of hearings produced front-page stories across the country, revealing the astonishing efforts by the Communists to control the movie industry. Studio heads Jack Warner, Louis B. Mayer, and Walt Disney all told damaging tales. Robert Taylor, Gary Cooper, and Adolphe Menjou, as well as other elite movie stars, also expressed concern about Red infiltration.

Less well-known Hollywood figures, along with recognized experts on Communism, including an ex–*Daily Worker* editor, startled the public with details of Red activity in the Dream Factory. (Oddly enough, Ronald Reagan, then head of the Screen Actors Guild, played only a minor role in the hearings; his testimony was quite low key.)

The gist of the charges leveled by the "friendlies," the cooperative witnesses called during the first week, was evoked by the headlines. "Film Heads Tell House of Reds' 10-Year Fight to Control Hollywood" blazed the Hearst-owned *Los Angeles Examiner*. "Reds 'Took Over' Artists, Staged Tieup, Says Disney" was another *Examiner* headline. "Four Film Actors Hit at Reds in Hollywood" was a front-page story in the *Los Angeles Times*. "Mayer, Warner, Wood, Rand Charge H'wood Red Invasion" blared *Variety*, the widely respected Hollywood trade publication.

The East Coast Establishment publications, always hostile to HUAC, normally ran more sedate headlines, stressing that the studio heads thought the Communist drive to control the industry had been largely checked. But even the *New York Times* carried such front-page stories as "Menjou Testifies Communists Taint the Film Industry: Actor Says 'Mission to Moscow' and 'North Star' Were Films Carrying Propaganda."

HUAC's entire hearings—the transcript runs 549 pages in the Committee's single-volume edition—produced a wealth of information on the Red infiltration of various guilds and unions, and the strike against the industry by Herbert Sorrell's pro-Communist Conference of Studio Unions (CSU). But the main focus of the Committee and the "friendlies" became the writers and the activities of the Screen Writers Guild.

THE FIRST WITNESS: JACK WARNER

The leadoff witness was Jack Warner,[1] in charge of production at the Warner Brothers Studios at Burbank, California. He was accompanied by counsel Paul McNutt, who represented the Motion Picture Association of America, Inc., and who immediately asked for permission to "cross-examine" witnesses— a request that Chairman Thomas quickly and firmly denied. Even many of the "friendly" witnesses from the industry turned out to be extremely wary of the Committee's investigation, concerned about their own reputations—as well as the reputation of the industry.

Warner opened with a statement that seemed designed to reassure the Committee—and the public—that he was one of the toughest anti-Communists around. He was overcompensating for his unimpressive appearance in May, when HUAC had interviewed Warner and other friendlies in a non-public session in Los Angeles, a sort of run-up to the main event. In those May hearings, the voluble Warner had been taken aback when members relentlessly pressed him on why he had produced a film so extraordinarily favorable to the Soviet Union as *Mission to Moscow.*

Warner had flashed his anti-Red credentials in the May session, but now his anti-Communist rhetoric was tougher. His statement stressed that "ideological termites" had infested many good American organizations and that wherever they are, we should "dig them out and get rid of them." Both he and his brother would be happy to contribute to a "pest-removal fund" designed to ship to Russia those who "prefer the communistic system to ours."

Clearly responding to the attacks on *Mission,* Warner said his company was "keenly aware" of its duty "to keep its product free from subversive poisons." And it was his "firm belief that there is not a Warner Brothers picture that can fairly be judged to be…communistic in tone or purpose." *Mission,* he argued vigorously, was made when this country "was fighting for its existence, with Russia as one of our allies." If making *that film* in 1942 "was a subversive activity," he went on, "the American Liberty ships which carried food and guns to Russian allies and the American naval vessels which convoyed them were likeways engaged in subversive activities."

The Committee members, however, never completely bought Warner's assurance that *Mission* was an acceptable Hollywood war movie during our alliance with the Soviets. Stripling questioned Warner sharply and at length, much to Warner's obvious irritation.

In the October hearings, Stripling told Warner he didn't see how his movie was aiding the war effort, as Warner insisted, since it perpetrated a "fraud" about what the Soviet Union was all about. He also confronted Warner with a tough critique of the film by the very liberal Moscow war correspondent, Quentin Reynolds, in his book *The Curtain Rises.*

Warner testified that he had become concerned about Communist infiltration of the movie industry in the late 1930s. Stripling then read a portion of his testimony from May, asking if he still agreed with the position that he had taken then.

> **Mr. Stripling**: Mr. Warner, since you have been in Hollywood has there ever been a period during which you considered that the Communists had infiltrated into your studio?
>
> **Mr. Warner**: Yes. Do you mean by huge numbers, or what?
>
> **Mr. Stripling**: In any degree.
>
> **Mr. Warner**: Yes, there has been a period.
>
> **Mr. Stripling**: When was that?
>
> **Mr. Warner**: Chiefly, I would say about 1936 or 1937. That is the first time I started to notice that type of writing coming into our scenarios. It is being put into scripts to this day in some form or another.
>
> **Mr. Stripling**: In your studio?
>
> **Mr. Warner**: In our studio and every studio, yes.

Warner reaffirmed his testimony but added that he would prefer to say these writers were not necessarily Communists, but "people with un-American leanings." Stripling then read to Warner more of his May testimony, where he had agreed that numerous writers attempting to squeeze propaganda into a film were Communists.

> **Mr. Stripling**: Is that the principal medium, the writers, through which the Communists have sought to inject their Communist propaganda into films?
>
> **Mr. Warner**: Yes, I would say 95 percent.
>
> **Mr. Stripling**: Ninety-five percent is through the writers?
>
> **Mr. Warner**: This is my own personal opinion.

Warner had also informed the Committee in May that he had removed those writers from his studios. "Anyone whom [sic] I thought was a Communist, or read in the papers that he was, I dismissed at the expiration of his contract." Much of his information on writers' radical activities came from the *Hollywood Reporter*, the influential and highly respected trade publication, whose publisher, William Wilkerson, was a strong anti-Communist. Warner had also discovered writers' "Communist" or "un-American" ideology from "their writings and method of presentation of screen plays."

NAMING RED NAMES

In his May appearance, Warner had agreed to cite "the names of people who in my opinion wrote for the screen and tried to inject these ideas, and I personally removed them—according to my best judgment or any of the executives working with me." Whether or not they were all Communists, he said, "I don't know...."

"The first one," he stated, "is Alvah Bessie. Then Gordon Kahn. He is in charge of editing the little journal of the Screen Writers' Guild." Warner then rattled off the names of "Guy Endore, Howard Koch, Ring Lardner, Jr., Emmet Lavery, John Howard Lawson, Albert Maltz, Robert Rossen, Irwin Shaw, Dalton Trumbo, John Wexley."

He singled out Koch and Lawson as particularly persistent in trying to propagandize. Koch, as we have seen, had scripted Warner's controversial *Mission*. Warner also noted that Koch would always come up with some "big message" which Warner had "to take out." Lawson wrote the great World War II hit *Action in the North Atlantic*, which critics also charged as being pro-Soviet. "Naturally," said Warner, "he tried to swing a lot of things in there," though Warner himself didn't think Lawson had been very successful.

Warner said he believed that Communists, generally speaking, believed in overthrowing our government by force and violence, but the writers weren't trying to insert that kind of stuff into the screenplays.

In this colloquy from his October testimony, Warner discusses Red attempts to put Communist propaganda into film scripts:

> **The Chairman:** Don't you think it would be very foolish for a Communist or a Communist sympathizer to attempt to write a script advocating the overthrow of the government by force or violence?

Mr. Warner: ... It would not only be foolish, it would be something they could not get away with in the American motion picture industry or anywhere else.

The Chairman: Exactly. So what would they do? They would put in slanted lines wherever they could and that is what you have been trying to keep out?

Mr. Warner: That is correct.

The Left has denigrated Warner's testimony over the years. In truth it was error-prone and full of bombast. But it did not err in the essentials. In the classic *Hollywood on Trial*, Gordon Kahn, whom Warner identified as a possible Communist, brushes off Warner's attack on himself and the other writers, suggesting Warner relied solely on "hearsay" and trade-paper gossip to discover their politics.[2] Warner did rely on newspaper reportage (not just "gossip") but also on his own personal observations about how the writers were trying to slip pink materials into the scripts.

Kahn did catch Warner in several misstatements, and Warner did retract charges he had made against a few of the writers in the May executive hearings. But not against Kahn. Kahn, managing editor of the official publication of the Screen Writers Guild in 1947, never denied Warner's chief accusation against him: that Kahn himself was a Communist or, as Warner attempted to soften the accusation, that he harbored "un-American" sympathies. Nor could Kahn have honestly denied the charge, since he was in fact a Communist Party member, as over a dozen HUAC witnesses—most of them ex-Communists— would eventually testify.

The truth is, the great majority of the persons Warner accused of attempting to radicalize studio scripts were dyed-in-the wool Stalinists. Nine of those mentioned above—Endore, Lardner, Lawson, Maltz, Rossen, Trumbo, Wexley, Bessie, and Kahn, who included five of the Hollywood Ten—turned out to have been loyal Communist Party members, identified under oath as such by numerous ex-comrades.

Koch never belonged to the Communist Party, but he was so close a follower of the Party line that even Larry Ceplair and Steven Englund admit that

Koch was one of a "small group of fellow travelers...who were Communists in everything but name."[3] In short, Warner was not shooting from the hip.

When Chairman Thomas informed Warner in May that he would not "keep a commie" in any business for "5 seconds," let alone in the movie industry, Warner's immediate response was, "That is my policy and that is my brother's policy." Indeed, he wished to "reiterate the very tenor of Congressman Thomas' feeling as just stated because I could not improve on it."

Warner's claim was supported by two questions that Warner Brothers' employees had to respond to in writing when they were hired: "Are you affiliated with any organization or group that is antagonistic to the principles of our American form of government?" and "Are you a member of any organization, society, group or sect owing allegiance to a foreign government or rule?"

In the October 20 hearings, Warner reconfirmed his anti-Red beliefs but balked at the suggestion—pressed by Representative Vail—that the producers impose the Warner Brothers' policy on the rest of the studios. "I can't, for the life of me, figure where men could get together and try in any form, shape, or manner to deprive a man of a livelihood because of his political beliefs," he said (a position at odds with what he claimed was his own studio's policy). The radicals in Hollywood clung to these words of Warner's as insurance against an industry-wide blacklist, believing that such sentiments from the producers could ultimately prevail.

Those radicals who followed Warner's testimony closely, however, would have discovered several unsettling things. Here was a major producer testifying that the Communists had seriously infiltrated the movie industry, had written some of the most important films Hollywood had ever produced, and were energetically trying to shovel Red propaganda into scripts—though Warner insisted that he, personally, had been able to excise such propaganda before those films reached the screen.

Warner also boasted of removing from his employ anyone he had good reason to suspect was placing "un-American"—that is, Communist—propaganda into movie scripts. Warner did not favor an industry-wide ban on these writers—many had gone to work for other studios—but he obviously saw nothing wrong with any individual producer banning Communists or even sympathizers from his own studio. That kind of blacklisting was in fact Warner Brothers' policy. What if, Red writers and sympathizers must have thought, all the studio heads began to think like Jack, whose studio was considered the most politically progressive in the movie industry?

"THEY WORK FOR ONE PURPOSE"

The next witness was Samuel Grosvenor Wood,[4] who over the years had produced and directed such films as *Kitty Foyle*; *Saratoga Trunk*; *Goodbye, Mr. Chips*; and *For Whom the Bell Tolls*.

Wood said the MPA was born in 1944 out of "self-defense" because the Communist Party and its fellow travelers had made a "definite effort" to seize the unions and the guilds of Hollywood. Wood basically confirmed the thrust of Warner's key complaint: the major trouble in 1947 Hollywood was not the producers or the actors or even most of the unions, but the writers. The following exchange between Stripling and Wood makes the point:

> **Mr. Stripling**: What group in the industry must be watched more carefully than the rest?
> **Mr. Wood**: The writers.
> **Mr. Stripling**: The writers?
> **Mr. Wood**: Yes, sir.
> **Mr. Stripling**: Is it your opinion there are Communist writers in the motion picture industry?
> **Mr. Wood**: Oh, yes. It is not my opinion, I know positively there are.

Stripling then asked if he cared to name any. Wood said he didn't think there were any doubts about Dalton Trumbo and Donald Ogden Stewart. "Is there any question in your mind that John Howard Lawson is a Communist?" Stripling pressed. "If there is," Wood responded, "then I haven't any mind." Wood then told how the Communists and the radicals in the industry pushed their own people into positions of influence, a tale often repeated during the hearings.

"For instance," said Wood, "a man gets a key position in the studio and has charge of the writers. When you, as a director or a producer, are ready for a writer, you ask for a list and this man shows you a list. Well, if he is following the party line, his pets are on the top or the other people aren't on at all."

Wood elaborated: "If there is a particular man in there that has been opposing them, they will leave his name off the list. Then if that man isn't employed for about two months, they go to the head of the studio and say, 'Nobody wants this man….' The head is perfectly honest about it and says, 'Nobody wants to use him, let him go.' So a good American is let out."

Would you say, asked Stripling, that the radicals act like this in all other branches of the industry? Wood answered, "I don't think, in any part of the business, they will use a party who is opposed to their ideas, if they can avoid it, and they can usually avoid it."

They operate "as cliques?" asked Stripling. "Oh, yes; they have their meetings every night," Wood announced. "They act together; they work for one purpose." That purpose, he explained, was to implement the Party line, whatever it might be at any given moment.

L. B. MAYER TAKES THE STAND

Louis B. Mayer[5] was the next witness. Mayer's was the typical success story of so many American immigrants. He was born in Russia of Jewish parentage, came with his parents to Canada, and then migrated to the United States with barely enough funds to buy a sandwich. He made his first fortune in Boston as a distributor for D. W. Griffith's colossal epic on the Civil War, *Birth of a Nation*.

When he appeared before the Committee, he had risen to become the powerful head of Metro-Goldwyn-Mayer, which was turning out between twenty-five and fifty pictures annually. Mayer also was politically conservative, was a close friend of media titan William Randolph Hearst, and thought of himself as a fervent anti-Communist.

Mayer, like Warner, began his testimony with a statement denouncing Communism, defending the motion picture industry, and insisting that he, personally, had "maintained a relentless vigilance against un-American influences" in MGM movies.

Mayer was not opposed to the concept of keeping Communists out of the movie industry. He hoped Congress would establish "a national policy regulating employment of Communists in private industry," since "they should be denied the sanctuary of the freedom they seek to destroy." Three writers Mayer thought might be Communists—Dalton Trumbo, Lester Cole, and Donald Ogden Stewart—had been earning huge salaries at MGM during the 1940s. Mayer was right on all three.

Asked if he thought the studios should continue to employ these individuals, Mayer responded, "I have asked counsel. They claim that unless you can prove they are Communists, they could hold you for damages. Saturday when I arrived here I saw in the papers a case where the high court of New York State just held you could not even say a man was a Communist sympathizer without being liable if you cannot prove it."

Chairman Thomas then asked what proved to be a critical question: "If you were shown the Communist dues cards of any one of these three individuals, then would you continue to employ them?"

Mayer's simple response: "No, sir."

Like Warner's testimony, these words of Mayer's must have sent shivers down the spines of Hollywood's Red writers and their attorneys. A blacklist could easily be established if HUAC had hard evidence of their Communist Party membership. But what evidence did HUAC possess?

AYN RAND AND *SONG OF RUSSIA*

The Committee called as its next witness Ayn Rand.[6] She was working in Hollywood during the hearings, having just completed a movie script for *The Fountainhead* for Warner Brothers.

Rand, who had left Russia in 1926, was something of an expert on her homeland. She had kept in touch with Russian émigrés, her family, and journalists who had covered the Soviet Union since her departure. The Committee had asked her to review *Song of Russia*, which had been made by Mayer's studio.

Mayer, also like Warner, had been on the defensive about having made a pro-Soviet film during the war. *Song of Russia*, starring Robert Taylor, "was made to be friendly," Mayer said, because the Soviet Union was our ally and militarily on the ropes. The final script, he argued, "was little more than a pleasant musical romance...." MGM was hardly in the Soviet camp, he wanted to reassure the panel. In the prewar period, Mayer's studio had "kidded the life out of communism" with *Ninotchka*, starring Greta Garbo and Melvyn Douglas, and *Comrade X*, with Clark Gable and Hedy Lamarr.

Rand, however, was scathing in her criticism, condemning *Song of Russia* as a "lie" shot through with Soviet propaganda. Her powerfully persuasive critique, detailed more fully in chapter 12 above, was echoed by yet another star witness, Robert Taylor, who was the leading man in the movie.

MOFFITT'S DAMNING TESTIMONY

As the week wore on, the witnesses kept up a steady drumbeat against Hollywood's radical writers. John Moffitt[7] was one of the more informative of those who came before the Committee. For fifteen years he had been the motion picture editor of the *Kansas City Star*, and then, in 1945, he became the motion picture critic for *Esquire* magazine, considered a prestige publication. He had also worked for MGM, Paramount, Republic, and Warner Brothers.

Moffit first came to Hollywood in 1930. Seven years later, he and his wife—alarmed by the rise of fascism—joined the Hollywood Anti-Nazi League. Over the next few months, they frequently donated money to the group, which was ostensibly buying ambulances and medical supplies for assistance to the anti-fascist forces in Spain. Then, said Moffitt, he and his wife were invited to the home of the director Frank Tuttle.

"Mr. Herbert Biberman, who had been responsible for my being in the Anti-Nazi League," noted Moffitt, "was there, as was his wife, Miss Gale Sondergaard, an actress. Donald Ogden Stewart was also one of those present." (All three were members of the League, and each turned out to be a Communist Party member. Biberman became one of the Hollywood Ten. Tuttle was a Communist as well.) The purpose of the meeting, Moffitt recalled, "was to raise funds for the *People's World*, a Communist newspaper."

Moffitt said that he and his wife had actually "hated communism" but that he remained in the League a little while longer to discover more about the group. He then testified that Lawson had told him personally, in so many words,

"As a writer, do not try to write an entire Communist picture. The producers will quickly identify it and it will be killed by the front office. As a writer, try to get five minutes of the Communist doctrine, five minutes of the party line in every script that you write."

Moffitt also introduced into the record a column by Trumbo from the May 5, 1946, *Daily Worker* in which Trumbo had bragged that Hollywood Communists had kept "tempting" anti-Communist dramas based on such works as *The Yogi and the Commissar* and Victor Kravchenko's *I Chose Freedom* off the screen.

Moffitt placed into the record the alleged Communist Party card numbers of several radical writers, as ferreted out by the trade publication *Hollywood Reporter*. Among the names he gave Party card numbers for were Ring Lardner Jr., Dalton Trumbo, and Lester Cole—all active members of the Screen Writers Guild who would become members of the Hollywood Ten. (So far as I am aware, Moffitt's very deeply damaging testimony has never been challenged in the major pro-Communist apologias.)

Moffitt then discussed the makeup of the Story Analysts Guild, whose members were to read all material submitted to different motion picture studios and to write synopses of the stories submitted. "Those synopses," said Moffitt, "are placed on file and they are available to producers and associate producers in making decisions of what material they wish to screen."

The experience of many non-Communist writers, Moffitt testified, was that members of the Guild prepare atrocious synopses of their stories. Moffitt said the man who headed the story analyst department at Paramount was believed to be a Communist. Also in that department was "Bernie Gordon, a man whose actions and talk follows [sic] the party line." (In fact, Gordon not only pursued the Party line but was a long-time Party member and admirer of Stalin, whom he finally discovered was imperfect only when Nikita Khrushchev condemned Stalin in 1956, as Gordon himself essentially admitted to me in a 1999 telephone conversation.)

Jack Warner himself had confirmed Moffitt's observations about the Story Analysts Guild. He had pointed out that it was "often difficult to prevent the hiring of certain people due to the fact the majority of employees are hired through unions and through the guilds, some of which are Communist controlled."

"One of the guilds was pretty pink," he added, "and we had to close a complete department in order to get rid of them. The Story Analysts was the name of it."[8]

HOWARD RUSHMORE'S REVELATIONS

From 1936 to 1939, Howard Rushmore[9] was not only a member of the Communist Party but a writer and editor for the *Daily Worker*. His chief job was film critic. He informed the Committee how eagerly the Communist Party had sought to capture the culture.

Back in 1925, Rushmore noted, the *Worker* had published an article by Willi Münzenburg, a member of the Communist International (or Comintern) who was in charge of the Comintern's cultural affairs department. "We must," said Münzenburg, "develop the tremendous cultural possibilities in a revolutionary sense. One of the most pressing tasks confronting the Communist Party in the field of propaganda is the conquest of this supremely important propaganda, until now the monopoly of the ruling class. We must wrest it from them and turn it against them." The article, noted Rushmore, "dealt entirely with the movie industry."

Rushmore said the U.S. Communist Party had faithfully followed this line since Münzenburg's piece. Initially the CP had set up independent production units such as the Film and Photo League and, later, Frontier Films, organized by Party member Herbert Kline, to produce "agitation and propaganda" films, though these entities later tried to reach wider audiences with more popular fare.

The Communists also organized Film Audiences for Democracy, setting up branches throughout the United States, with a very active branch in Hollywood. "A lot of prominent people, some of them certainly not Communists," said Rushmore, "were drawn into this innocent sounding Communist front organization."

He noted that Walter Wanger, the producer, "spoke before the Hollywood branch...and he is quoted in the *Daily Worker* of April 14, 1939, defending the motion picture *Blockade*.... I might add that the Wanger picture, *Blockade*, gave 100 percent endorsement of Stalin's effort to seize Spain as another foreign colony of the Kremlin...."

Rushmore, surprisingly, failed to note that *Blockade* was written by John Howard Lawson, who in less than a week would become the first "unfriendly" witness sworn in by the Thomas panel. Rushmore did have other things to say about Lawson's role in the Communist Party and Hollywood. Rushmore recalled meeting Lawson in 1937 or '38 on the ninth floor of the Communist Party headquarters, 35 East Twelfth Street in New York City, where the "Cultural Commission" of the Party was holding a meeting. The ninth floor was considered "the inner sanctum" for the CP's national officers.

Rushmore gave a short history of the Commission's existence and how it operated, remarking that it had been set up by Alexander Trachtenberg, a member of the Political Bureau of the U.S. Communist Party, after his return from "one of his many trips to Moscow." Trachtenberg or Gerhart Eisler, "the Communist International Representative," would hand the Party line to V. J. Jerome, who was in charge of the Commission (and actually chaired the meeting where Rushmore met Lawson).

Rushmore noted that Jerome, born Isaac Romaine, "is one of the most important leaders of the Communist Party" and "has made many trips to Hollywood." And Lawson himself? "We might call Lawson the top sergeant out in Hollywood," said Rushmore, adding that he "took his orders from Jerome." Lawson was a key Red operative, taking his cues from the Kremlin and the Comintern via Jerome.

Rushmore remarked that Lawson "talked at great length about the party's fund-raising in Hollywood." Jerome had expressed dissatisfaction with donations, but Rushmore said the sum mentioned by Lawson "rather astonished me, it was up in the high figures." Lawson was required to reach a "quota," which was "up in the thousands. I was impressed because at that time the *Daily Worker* salaries were $20 a week—when we got it—and this sounded like big money to me."

Lawson was not the only one sent by the Cultural Commission to Hollywood to carry out Moscow's orders, according to Rushmore: "One writer I know went out there, and I am sure he was sent by the Cultural Commission," said Rushmore, "was Alvah Bessie, whom I met several times at the *Daily Worker*, upon his return from Spain, where he was a commissar in the International Brigade in Spain." (That is, he was fighting for the Stalinist wing in the civil war.) Lawson specifically asked Jerome and other members of the Commission to send out to Hollywood "any new writers, any novelists, who had something published, that had had fairly good reviews, and who were either party members or could be handled by the party.…"

Rushmore also enlightened the members of the Committee with other provocative tidbits. He said he had never visited Hollywood, but many Hollywood radicals had visited the *Daily Worker*, including Clifford Odets, the famed author of two radical plays, *Waiting for Lefty* and *Awake and Sing!* Both plays had greatly inspired America's Communist Left. "I remember one meeting I saw him [Odets] with Harry Jannis. Harry Jannis…was foreign editor at that time of the *Daily Worker*, and often writers and other people would meet with Jannis to get the particular party line on Soviet foreign policy, which they wrote into whatever they might have been writing at the time." (When he testified before HUAC in 1951, Odets admitted he had been a Party member in the 1930s.)

The Communists cultivated and used Hollywood actors extensively for their various causes, but the general Party line, as Rushmore heard it from Jerome, Lawson, and others, "was that stars are, 99 percent of them, political morons.…" Jerome insisted their "only use to the revolution was their bank account." But they treated certain actors, even those they had political contempt for, as "sacred cows," that is, "someone that you would always give favorable publicity to and a lot of it." Charlie Chaplin fell into that category, said Rushmore. And Jerome once "told me to always defend [Edward G.] Robinson, even if he was in a bad picture with a bad performance." Rushmore said he had "no knowledge" of whether Robinson was a Communist, but he "started joining one Communist front after another, perhaps innocently, but after 10 years he is still doing it."

Rushmore had something else significant to say to the Committee. He informed Stripling that the Communist Party "received regular information on the kind of pictures coming out from the various studios and in some cases I know that the actual script, or a copy of it, rather, was sent to the Cultural Commission of the party at 35 East Twelfth Street months before the picture went into production."

Then the Party could decide how to deal with it. "One movie that I remember particularly," he recalled, "was *Our Leading Citizen*, put out by Paramount, and the script … was sent to V. J. Jerome." Jerome disliked the message, so Rushmore reviewed the film and called for a boycott, and the Party ginned up progressive columnists and various front organizations to slam Paramount.

The Party, Rushmore noted, uses "every organization that they control or have influence in, not only the major organizations, the CIO and the AFL, but the Council of American-Soviet Friendship, the old time American League for Peace and Democracy, the American Youth for Democracy; they have factions in such church organizations as Epworth League, they have a faction of ministers under Communist control who can be depended on."

More illuminating testimony was to come.

U.S. ambassador to Moscow Joseph Davies (Walter Huston) meets Joseph Stalin (Manart Kippen, uncredited) in the 1943 Hollywood film *Mission to Moscow*, perhaps the most pro-Soviet movie ever made, even in the Soviet Union. Written by Howard Koch, who had married a Communist, the film portrays Stalin as an extremely kind and wise ruler who has transformed a backward country into an industrial powerhouse. The purges, the invasion of Finland, the Soviet collective farm system, the Hitler-Stalin Pact are all excused or praised. Even the pro-Soviet *Nation* magazine called it a "whitewash." Photo: Warner Brothers

Lauren Bacall and Humphrey Bogart lead a group of motion picture stars in the nation's capital to protest HUAC's 1947 hearings on Communist infiltration of Hollywood. Under studio pressure, Bogart would later apologize for his actions. Photo: Bettmann/CORBIS

Novelist and screenwriter Ayn Rand, a Russian émigré, informs HUAC in 1947 in a detailed critique that the 1944 Hollywood film *Song of Russia*, written by Communist Party members Richard Collins and Paul Jarrico, was loaded with "Communist propaganda." Photo: Bettmann/CORBIS

Prominent playwright and screenwriter Morrie Ryskind testifies before the House Un-American Activities Committee (HUAC) in its tumultuous 1947 hearings on Communist infiltration of the powerful Screen Writers Guild. Ryskind was a major anti-Communist figure in Hollywood. Photo: Bettmann/CORBIS

HUAC chairman J. Parnell Thomas talks with actor Robert Taylor at the 1947 hearings. Taylor testified that he had balked at starring in *Song of Russia*, written by two Red screenwriters, and said it should never have been written or produced. For criticizing three people—each of whom turned out to be a Communist Party member (though he never accused them of being Communists)—the Hollywood Left had Taylor's name removed from Lorimar's Robert Taylor Building in Los Angeles. Photo: Associated Press

Ronald Reagan played a major role in limiting Communist influence in Hollywood; actor Sterling Hayden, a former Communist himself, called Reagan a "one-man battalion" against the Reds. Here he is testifying before HUAC in the 1947 hearings about Red infiltration of the Screen Actors Guild, which had recently elected him president.
Photo: Bettmann/CORBIS/AP Images

Dalton Trumbo, one of the Hollywood Ten famous for refusing to tell HUAC whether they were ever members of the Communist Party, was dismissed from the witness stand in the 1947 hearings when he told Committee members that he would respond to their questions but never did. Trumbo called HUAC's actions "the beginning of an American concentration camp." Photo: Bettmann/CORBIS

Screenwriter Ring Lardner Jr., one of the Hollywood Ten, refused to tell HUAC in 1947 whether he had ever joined the Communist Party. In his memoir, written some thirty years later, he admitted he was a dedicated Red who thoroughly embraced Stalinism. Photo: Bettmann/CORBIS

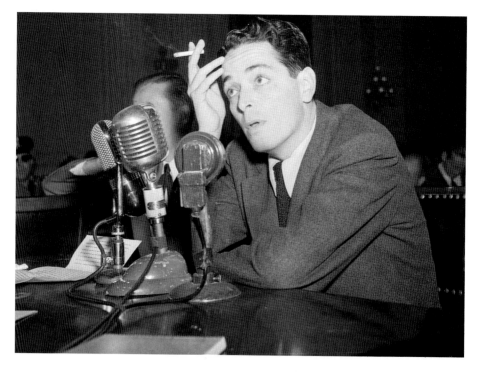

The Hollywood Ten (pictured with their lawyers) pled not guilty on January 9, 1948, to contempt of Congress for refusing to tell HUAC whether they had ever belonged to the Communist Party. Shown as they arrived at the District Building for arraignment in U.S. district court are, from left to right, (first row) director and producer Herbert Biberman, attorney Martin Popper, attorney Robert W. Kenny, and screenwriters Albert Maltz and Lester Cole; (second row) screenwriters Dalton Trumbo, John Howard Lawson, Alvah Bessie, and Samuel Ornitz; (top row) screenwriter Ring Lardner Jr., director Edward Dmytryk, and producer Adrian Scott.

Photo: Bettmann/CORBIS/AP Images

Screenwriter John Howard Lawson, a major figure in the Hollywood Communist community, testifies before HUAC in the 1947 hearings. Many observers believe his strident performance, in which he accused the Committee of using Gestapo tactics, led to the studios imposing the blacklist. Photo: Associated Press

Gerhart Eisler. The overwhelming majority of the Hollywood Ten were enthusiastic supporters of Eisler, a leading Comintern agent who fled the United States in 1949 rather than stand trial for perjury and ended up as a chief propagandist for East Germany. Yip Harburg, the lyricist for the *Wizard of Oz*, claimed Eisler was framed.

Photo: Associated Press

Famous director Edward Dmytryk was the only one of the Hollywood Ten to renounce Communism, Stalin, and the Soviet Union. In his appearance before HUAC in April 1951, Dmytryk said he had become convinced that the Communist Party in America was "treasonable."
Photo: Associated Press

Arthur Miller with his wife Marilyn Monroe. In his appearance before HUAC in June 1956, the playwright told Committee members he could not recall whether he ever applied for membership in the Communist Party.
Photo: Hulton-Deutsch Collection/CORBIS

Playwright Lillian Hellman flatly denied she had ever joined the Communist Party in her 1976 memoir, *Scoundrel Time*, but in April 1952 she had informed her lawyer, Joseph Rauh, "I joined the Communist Party in 1938."
Photo: Bettmann/CORBIS

The Majestic, a 2001 Hollywood film starring Jim Carrey, is an unrelenting attack against HUAC and tosses a bouquet to screenwriter John Howard Lawson, the enforcer of the Communist line in Hollywood.
Photo: Castle Rock Entertainment

CHAPTER NINETEEN

MORE FRIENDLY WITNESSES

The opening week of the HUAC hearings in October 1947 produced plenty of other incriminating information about how the Communists were using the Screen Writers Guild, organizing various front groups, and setting up Marxist centers—such as the famous People's Educational Center in Los Angeles, where Hollywood Reds gathered to teach Communist theory and history to budding young screenwriters. The lawmakers on the Committee would also hear from the current president of the Screen Actors Guild, as well as his two predecessors, who related how they had managed to keep the SAG out of the hands of far-Left and subversive elements. HUAC concentrated, however, on the radical writers.

MORRIE RYSKIND AND THE GUILD

Though a liberal for much of the 1930s, Morrie Ryskind,[1] who had written many successful Hollywood scripts, including for the Marx Brothers, had become upset with the antics of the Communists and other radicals in the Screen Writers Guild. He believed they were far more interested in pushing a leftist agenda than bargaining over bread-and-butter issues, and he had become alarmed at their increasing clout in the motion picture industry during World War II.

He described how both he and his wife had been suckered by some in the Hollywood community into contributing to a couple of innocent-sounding organizations in the 1930s but quickly got out when they discovered the groups were Communist-run. In one case he had thought he was giving money to help defend the Scottsboro boys, black men who had been framed for a vicious crime. But he found out "afterward that the money—they collected an awful lot of money—a good part of that money, went into the hands of the *Daily Worker.*"

He also persuaded friends to contribute to the defense of Tom Mooney because several members of the original jury said new evidence indicated he was innocent. But when my father proudly told John Finerty, Mooney's lawyer, whom he had given the money to, Finerty blurted out, "My God, you have given that money to the Communists. They don't want to get Mooney out of jail. Their whole object is to keep him in jail."

Ryskind felt the Screen Writers Guild, which he had championed early on, had become radicalized. He had joined the Guild's Executive Board in the mid-1930s, believing that writers were just as much entitled to collective bargaining rights as actors. "We had some roughly 15 members on the board," he said, but the radical bloc, though a minority, proved skillful in winning key votes:

> Now, you have got to realize that most of us who are Americans are not used much to political trickery. Here we were, 15, and we thought everybody was in there pitching for the good of the Guild.
>
> We found after a while—we were very naive—that about 7 of the 15 voted together on every doggone question that came up. The question didn't have to be important. Whether the question was whether the next meeting should be on Friday, or whether we

should ask the producers for better terms, it was always the same, with the result that these seven, although they constituted a minority, won every point. The rest, being Americans, would normally divide on any question.

He told how the Communist and pro-Communist members packed Guild meetings and employed all sorts of tactical chicanery to win important votes. So the non-radical majority on the board, just eight of the fifteen members, decided to run their own slate to remove the Reds. "We got out. We electioneered. We campaigned," Ryskind testified. "We had, going into the meeting, a substantial majority—I would say 3 to 1."

But then Lester Cole—"if Lester Cole isn't a Communist, I don't think Mahatma Gandhi is an Indian"—suddenly pleaded with the members not to "split the Guild," for this would play into the hands of the producers. The Reds in the room, some of them not even screenwriters, erupted into cheers for Cole, peeling away many who had originally opposed the radicals. The result was to keep the Communists on the board. Over time, said my father, who had left the Guild in 1942 because it no longer represented his views, the board began tilting even further left. Under President Emmet Lavery, he testified, the Communist faction had gotten stronger, especially since *The Screen Writer*, the official publication of the Guild, had Gordon Kahn as editor.

Asked if he knew Kahn personally, Ryskind responded with some levity: "I do. We don't agree politically. Mr. Kahn happens to be a neighbor of mine. In fact, he bought the house next door to mine. We don't talk; but he is very pleasant to my children; I am pleasant to his; our dogs are very good friends." Asked if he believed Kahn was "a Communist or a fellow traveler," he responded, "Well, this will not increase neighborly relations, but that is my opinion." (My father was erring on the side of caution. Kahn was repeatedly identified over the years as a Communist by those who knew him in the Party.)

FRED NIBLO'S REMARKS

Fred Niblo[2] had lived in Hollywood for two decades when he testified before the Thomas panel. A professional writer, he had worked for many of the major studios, including Warner Brothers, MGM, Columbia, and RKO. For the last half-dozen years or so, he had been a member of the Screen Writers Guild. He strongly believed in the organization and recognized that it had "done some economic good for the working writers," but he was also "convinced that the Screen Writers Guild has been the spark plug and the spearhead of the Communist influence and infiltration in Hollywood."

The Guild had long been under the thumb of "John Howard Lawson and company," Niblo argued. As soon as he became a Guild member, Niblo "found that some of those characters whose names have been mentioned here throughout this testimony were in virtual control of the Guild. They held the offices—not all the offices, but most of them. They were the floor whips, so to speak.... They were the obvious leaders...."

Some curious things happened when Niblo first joined the Guild. He began receiving announcements from "outfits with names such as the League for the Promotion of American-Russian Friendship." As he pointed out before HUAC, four members of the Guild's board in 1941—Lawson, Lester Cole, Donald Ogden Stewart, and Tess Schlesinger—also turned up on the Executive Board of a well-known Communist front, the League of American Writers.

When Niblo, a fervent anti-Communist, was assailed in *The Screen Writer*, the official Guild publication, he was denied the right to respond. The editor at the time was Dalton Trumbo, a thoroughgoing Communist who became a major Hollywood Ten figure. Niblo viewed *The Screen Writer* as a "sort of literary monthly supplement to the *Daily Worker*."

RICHARD MACAULAY'S TESTIMONY

Niblo's testimony was supplemented by that of Richard Macaulay,[3] a screenwriter with MGM who had been an active member of the SWG since its reactivation in 1936. Did the Communists exert control over the Guild? he was asked.

"Yes," said Macaulay. They had some control over the previous Guild, Macaulay explained, but "after we reorganized in 1936, such control became more and more evident."

The Screen Writer, for instance, was run by Dalton Trumbo and Gordon Kahn, whom Macaulay said he absolutely believed were Communists (as indeed turned out to be the case). He noted that the publication had been quite willing to print an anti-capitalist screed by Alvah Bessie, whom Macaulay (also accurately) believed was a Communist, but had refused to run Macaulay's response.

More important, Macaulay stressed that the board meetings were dominated by a group that unleashed "a constant program of intimidation." So fierce was the harassment that, as time went on, "only a very few would get up on the floor of the Guild and attempt to oppose the controlling faction."

Macaulay said there "are some members of the Guild who are booed and hissed the moment they arise—before they open their mouths, on many occasions. This frequently seems to be the result of a well-organized clique. Even if they let you get up without bothering you, before you have proceeded five sentences into your remarks, someone is certainly liable to start hissing you."

Macaulay wasn't hesitant at all about naming names in this group. These are "Communists, and the boys who play along with them." Would he mention them? He said he was "morally certain" that the ones he would name were Communists. "I merely say," he added, "if they habitually consort with bank robbers and the bank on the next street is knocked off, they can't holler if someone blows the whistle."

Macaulay named twenty-eight writers, many of them the same as the other friendly witnesses would mention. All save Howard Koch turned out to be Party members—and Koch was a member in all but name. Among those Macaulay specifically named as Communists were Alvah Bessie, Lester Cole, Ring Lardner Jr., John Howard Lawson, Albert Maltz, Samuel Ornitz, and Dalton Trumbo. Each was a Communist, and each was to become a member of the Hollywood Ten.

OLIVER CARLSON'S CONTRIBUTION

The Committee also brought in Oliver Carlson,[4] a teacher and a recognized expert on Communist propaganda techniques. Carlson knew a lot about the Party because he had been a Party member in his youth. His main contribution was his testimony on how the Communists in the 1920s had decided to capture the film colony and use it for propaganda purposes. A boyhood friend of his,

Eli Jacobson, had been director of the Workers School in New York City, a Communist Party school that taught the "class struggle" to its students. Toward the fall of 1938, Jacobson told Carlson he wanted to break with the Party.

"Then he told me," Carlson related, "how he had been sent to Hollywood under specific instructions from the Central Committee of the Communist Party and that his duties in Hollywood were to conduct classes, and in general, educational propaganda, for the Communist Party among film folk—not among the rank-and-file workers, but, rather, among the elite, so to speak."

Jacobson's other job "was to see to it that many of these important film personalities were softened up so that they would agree to join the various front organizations which the Communist Party was then sponsoring in the Hollywood region." Among the fronts: the League against War and Fascism, the Committee to Boycott the Olympics in Berlin, the Western Writers Congress, and a ton of committees for the defense of Spain. Jacobson, further, had prepared the groundwork for several meetings in Hollywood involving V. J. Jerome, the national CP official who was in charge of directing Communist activities in the film industry.

Jacobson faded from the picture in the late 1930s, but, "along about 1940," Carlson testified, the Communists established the People's Educational Center, a radical school to assist people who wanted to work in the motion picture industry. Carlson entered into the hearing record the school's winter catalogue for 1947.

Sidney Davison, a Communist, headed the Center. On the board of directors was the ubiquitous John Howard Lawson. Also a director: Dorothy Healey, a prominent and open Communist in Southern California. The advisory board included Herbert Sorrell, the far-Left head of the Conference of Studio Unions, which for years had been trying to gain control of the trade unions in Hollywood. Also on the board: Frank Tuttle, a Communist film director; Sondra Gorney, a frequent contributor to the *Daily Worker*; and Robert Lees, a Communist writer.

A variety of Communist and pro-Communist Hollywood writers, directors, and filmmakers taught courses at the school, including the famous director Edward Dmytryk; writers Ben Barzman, Herbert Biberman, and Robert

Lees; and actress Karen Morley. Each in the fullness of time was exposed as a Communist Party member. Both Dmytryk and Biberman wound up as part of the Hollywood Ten.

The school offered a class called "The Soviet Union, a New Civilization." The description for that course suggested that the Soviet economy had blessed its citizens with an abundance of food, shelter, and the good things of life. Another course, "Political Economy," was bluntly described as presenting "the Marxist analysis of capitalist economy." Other subjects taught under the "Political Economy" heading included "Monopoly Capitalism," "Imperialist War," and "Imperialism and Fascism."

An attorney from the Esteman and Pestana law firm was teaching a labor course dealing specifically with the motion picture industry. Esteman and Pestana, Carlson pointed out, "are the official attorneys for the Conference of Studio Unions, Mr. Herbert Sorrell's organization, which has been accused—and I think justly—of being under Communist domination."

Another attorney, from Gallagher, Margolis, and Katz, also gave a course at the People's Educational Center. Two of that law firm's members, noted Carlson, were defending the hostile witnesses who would appear before the Thomas committee during the week of October 27. Carlson didn't mention their names, but the two were Ben Margolis and Charles Katz. Both took the Fifth before HUAC on January 23, 1952, rather than answer questions about their Party membership.

MONTGOMERY, MURPHY, AND REAGAN

The Committee concentrated on the writers, but it was also interested in the Screen Actors Guild, so it subpoenaed two past SAG presidents, Robert Montgomery and George Murphy, and also the SAG's recently elected chief, Ronald Reagan,[5] to testify on October 23. All three had been prominent actors, though Montgomery was now a producer as well.

Each insisted that the SAG, unlike the SWG, was essentially free from Communist control. Montgomery, the first of the three to testify, had been president of the Guild in the years 1935, 1936, and 1937 and, after serving in the U.S. Navy, had been reelected in 1946.

Asked if there were "Communist influence" in the Guild, he said that as far back as 1933, the SAG, like other unions, had "a very militant... well organized, well disciplined" Red group in the Guild, but it amounted to no more than a small minority of the entire membership. Nor did it have any success in dominating Guild policy.

But Montgomery noted that in 1946 there had been a momentous clash between hard leftists and the rest of the SAG members. In the early part of '46, Montgomery introduced a resolution containing three articles before the SAG board. The first two articles passed easily enough, but the third stirred up tremendous opposition. It said, in part, "The Guild in addition states that it has in the past, does in the present, and will in the future rigorously oppose by every power which is within its legal rights, any real Fascist or Communist influence in the motion picture industry or in the ranks of labor."

Whether the opponents of this article were Communist, "I am not qualified to state," said Montgomery. "I only know that they behaved exactly as left-wing groups in various labor unions have behaved in the past and do behave at present." The opposition repeatedly served up "compromise" or "alternative" resolutions, he said, but in all the "compromise resolutions that were offered, the flat statement that we opposed Communism or Fascism was strangely absent."

The resolution was finally adopted with the third article and issued publicly by the delegates of the Screen Actors Guild at the California State Labor Convention in 1946.

The relatively small number of Communists in the industry, Montgomery argued, however, "does not, to me, change the picture as far as their danger is concerned. They are well organized, they are well disciplined. They appear at public meetings tremendously well organized and with a complete program for the evening."

Asked how he felt about Communism generally, Montgomery responded with some fervor, "Mr. Chairman, in common with millions of other men in this country in 1939 and 1940, I gave up my job to fight against a totalitarianism which was called fascism. I am quite willing to give it up again to fight against a totalitarianism called communism." The hearing room burst into applause.

George Murphy was the next witness. He echoed Montgomery's testimony and disclosed how he had helped block a resolution that would have had the

SAG siding with the strike staged by Herb Sorrell's pro-Communist Conference of Studio Unions. He also put forth two recommendations. He urged the U.S. government to label the Communist Party an agency of a foreign power, if it in fact was controlled by Moscow. "I don't think," he added, "that an agent of a foreign government should be allowed to hide under the guise that he is a member of a legal American political party." His second recommendation: U.S. government agencies, with all the knowledge they have of Communism and its conspiratorial ways, should inform the American public about it.

Ronald Reagan was sworn in next. Reagan's testimony was low-key. He had been elected president of the SAG a few months before, to replace Montgomery, who had resigned. The following month he would stand for election for a full term.

His testimony did not stray far from either Montgomery's or Murphy's. There has been a "small clique" in the Guild, he noted, that "has been suspected of more or less following the tactics that we associated with the Communist Party." Yes, they had been "disruptive" at times, but he had no knowledge of whether any were Party members, since he had "no investigative force, or anything, and I do not know."

Reagan admitted to having been hoodwinked a couple of times by some Communist fronts. He recalled that there had been a financial drive to build a badly needed hospital in the Hollywood area. A woman had urged Reagan to sponsor a recital, with all the money for the tickets going to the hospital. The singer, however, would be Paul Robeson, the very fervent pro-Soviet celebrity. Reagan initially balked because of Robeson's crimson views, but thought after all that he would swallow this jagged bone in order to help out with the construction of the much-needed hospital.

The recital, held at the Shrine Auditorium in Los Angeles, turned into a Red propaganda event. The occasion was sponsored by the Joint Anti-Fascist Refugee Committee, a Red front, and not only starred the pro-Soviet Robeson but also featured volunteers who had fought in Spain for the Communist-controlled Abraham Lincoln Brigade.

Reagan appeared rather shy about making any recommendations as to what the government should do about these subversive elements. We should battle the Communists in the political arena, he urged. "So that fundamentally, I would say in opposing those people that the best thing to do is to make democracy work. In the Screen Actors Guild, we make it work by insuring everyone a vote and by keeping everyone informed."

Reagan did leave open the possibility that some government action might be needed "if it is proven that an organization is an agent of a power, a foreign power, or in any way not a legitimate political party."

But that was basically all he had to say. Reagan had taken on the Communists in various organizations in 1946 and 1947, and he played a significant role in undermining Herb Sorrell and his pro-Soviet Conference of Studio Unions, as we shall see. But so far as the 1947 Hollywood hearings are concerned, he declined to figure in a prominent fashion.

The first round of testimony, by mostly friendly witnesses, had not proved that Hollywood was controlled by the Communists. Indeed, both the studio heads and the anti-Communist officials in the Actors Guild had downplayed the influence of the radicals in their midst.

Still, the hearings had established some important points: Party members and their acolytes had deeply penetrated the movie colony, the unions, and the guilds, especially the Screen Writers Guild. Hollywood Communists and radicals appeared to be awash in money and active in dozens of important groups. And despite studio chiefs' attempts to rein in Red material, many of the World War II movies, at least, had been written by Communists and were drenched in Soviet propaganda.

The first week of the HUAC hearings must have had a disquieting impact on those screenwriters who still belonged to the Party. No producer, actor, or writer had actually come out in favor of "blacklisting" the writers, but the heads of two important studios, Warner and Mayer, had averred that they themselves would not hire known Communists. Might the rest of the producers be pressured into the same position? The tenor of the hearings certainly seemed to suggest that the tide of public opinion, in Hollywood as well as in the country at large, had turned against the Reds.

Beginning on October 27, the continuing hearings before HUAC would prove far more explosive. Unfriendly witnesses were about to engage in a Titanic clash with members of the House Un-American Activities Committee.

CHAPTER TWENTY

PHIL DUNNE'S STRANGE CRUSADE

P hil Dunne, the son of famous humorist and short-story writer Peter Finley Dunne, wrote such successful movies for Darryl F. Zanuck as *How Green Was My Valley* and *Pinky*, a picture about a dignified black woman who gives up the love and material comfort that would come at the cost of "passing" in the white world. Dunne was a left-wing activist who in the 1930s happily joined three major Communist-controlled organizations: the Hollywood Anti-Nazi League, the Motion Picture Artists Committee, and the Motion Picture Democratic Committee (MPDC).[1]

So zealous an activist was he that the Communist Party eagerly sought to seduce him into its ranks. But Dunne refused, insisting he was not ready to blindly accept Party dogma and "be spared the agony of thinking my way through difficult issues" on his own.[2]

LIBERAL DON QUIXOTE

And when Stalin allied himself with Hitler in August of 1939, Dunne was outraged at the reaction of his left-wing friends. He battled the pro-Soviet factions in the various groups he belonged to, earning the Communists' wrath. Along with actor Melvyn Douglas—the husband of movie actress Helen Gahagan Douglas, best remembered for losing her Senate contest with Richard Nixon in 1950—he drafted a resolution reaffirming the MPDC's support for Roosevelt's anti-Nazi foreign policy and condemning the Hitler-Stalin Pact.

To the surprise of both Dunne and Douglas, the MPDC's Executive Board approved the resolution without a dissenting vote. But a few weeks later, the board majority executed a *volte face*, rescinding the Dunne-Douglas resolution 10 to 7—"an indication," Dunne writes in his memoir, "of the extent to which the Party had succeeded in infiltrating our executive board." The ten *could* have decided the original resolution was a mistake, Dunne observes sarcastically, but he chose to believe it "more likely that this mass flip-flop was the result of a major policy decision made elsewhere." "Elsewhere," of course, could only mean Party headquarters in New York and, ultimately, Moscow.

After a "savage and protracted struggle," Dunne adds, Douglas resigned, but "I decided to try to salvage a valuable organization by appealing directly to the membership" of about two thousand men and women. When his resolution condemning the Hitler-Stalin Pact lost by an overwhelming margin, Dunne "resigned with regret from the Motion Picture Democratic Committee, as well as from the other popular front organizations which were destroyed in similar fashion by the same wrecking crew, as all over town the industrious Communist tail wagged the lazy liberal dog."[3]

Dunne's anti-Communism was sincere, but he always appeared to have a soft spot for the very totalitarians he opposed. He seemed to enjoy working with them in common causes though he kept having to argue with and, at times, harshly condemn them. Thus when he learned that nineteen Hollywood radicals were to be called before the House Un-American Activities Committee in October of 1947, Dunne sprang to their defense, even though he suspected several of them might be devoted Party members.[4]

Dunne was especially motivated to assist the nineteen unfriendly witnesses (later pared down to the "Hollywood Ten," as we shall see in the next chapter) after he tuned in to the first week of hearings of the friendly witnesses—whom he labeled "right-wing grotesques eager to air their political or private grievances against Communists, fellow travelers, liberals, moderates, or even personal enemies."

COMMITTEE FOR THE FIRST AMENDMENT

In September, Dunne, along with directors William Wyler and John Huston, decided over lunch at Lucey's restaurant in Los Angeles to create what eventually became the Committee for the First Amendment (CFA). All three believed that HUAC was embarked on an assault on civil liberties and that the nineteen—no matter how Red—deserved moral support from the creative side of Hollywood.

Hollywood celebrities flocked to the CFA banner, with the early meetings held in the homes of Wyler and of Ira Gershwin, whose clever and sophisticated lyrics adorned the musical creations of his more famous brother, George. Among those who immediately embraced the CFA were such esteemed Hollywood actors as Humphrey Bogart, Lauren Bacall, Judy Garland, Rita Hayworth, Frank Sinatra, and Danny Kaye.

Both the House Un-American Activities Committee and the California Senate Fact-Finding Committee on Un-American Activities would label the CFA a "Communist front," but this characterization was, in my view, incorrect. Dunne, Wyler, and Huston—none of whom was a Communist—were in charge of both the recruiting and the strategy for the Committee.[5]

Dunne insists they maintained control throughout, with the assistance of an informal steering committee composed of director Anatole Litvak, actor Shepperd Strudwick, writer Julius Epstein, and producers Joseph Sistrom and David Hopkins. According to Dunne, Sistrom was a Republican. Hopkins was the son of Harry Hopkins, FDR's right-hand man.

None of the five, he tells us, was a known Communist Party member or fellow traveler, and there is no evidence to the contrary, although each had decidedly liberal or left-wing views on the subject of the Washington hearings,

Communist infiltration of the movie industry, and internal security matters in general.

Though adamant about not putting his committee into Communist hands, Dunne explains that, naturally, "we couldn't run a security check on all who contributed money or their names to the advertisements we ran in the trade papers, but we...consistently urged anyone who might have had damaging affiliations in the past to stay away from our organization." He informs us that his group also made "every effort to keep any such people off the two radio broadcasts we sponsored and off the [star-studded] plane we charted to fly to Washington and protest the abuses of the House Committee on the spot."

Wyler felt so sure that he and Dunne had kept Communists out of the CFA that he confidently wrote to anti-Communist publisher William Wilkerson of the *Hollywood Reporter* that "no member of our group is a Communist or sympathetic to the totalitarian form of government practiced or advocated by Communist parties in different parts of the world."[6]

"We slipped up just once," Dunne acknowledges, "and this through no fault of our own. On the night before we flew to Washington, Willy Wyler addressed the delegation that had volunteered to make the trip. He said that if anyone aboard that plane was in the slightest degree vulnerable, our entire group and its cause could be discredited." So, he fervently urged the gathering, if "there's anything in your past that could hurt you or us, don't go." Still, two individuals, including the prominent actor Sterling Hayden, chose to ignore Wyler's warning. Both, Dunne acknowledged, were later discovered to have "once and briefly been members of the Communist Party."[7] But this hardly made the CFA a Red front.

Dunne clearly made a good-faith effort to keep his project out of the clutches of the Party. Nevertheless, Dunne's committee and Dunne himself became useful tools for the nineteen unfriendly witnesses—including the overwhelming number of Communists among them—whom HUAC had summoned for hearings.

REDS FIND THE CFA USEFUL

Screenwriter Abraham Polonsky, though not among the nineteen unfriendly witnesses called by HUAC in October 1947, was nevertheless a thoroughgoing Communist who took the Fifth when he testified before HUAC in 1951[8] but who eventually admitted to Party membership.

He recalled attending a founding meeting for the CFA at Gershwin's home. "You could not get into the place. The excitement was intense. Every star was there." According to Polonsky, "We Communists had not created the organization, but we believed in its usefulness and helped to organize its activities."[9]

Hollywood historians Ceplair and Englund examined the rosters of the names of people involved with the various CFA activities. Their research shows that Hollywood figures on the far Left for the most part heeded Dunne's admonition to stay away from the CFA. But at least "sixteen radicals [Ceplair and Englund's term for Communists and fellow travelers] signed the ads."[10]

The CFA took out ads, held news briefings, sponsored radio broadcasts, and famously sent a plane full of Hollywood stars to Washington, D.C., to protest the HUAC hearings. The Committee's central message: the nineteen unfriendly witnesses HUAC had called were protected by the First Amendment from having to respond to *any* questions about Party affiliation.

Dunne was eager to work with the nineteen because these radicals, whom he knew to be both pro-Soviet and pro-Communist, "were our colleagues; most of us had personal friends among them; they were the ones who were suffering a shameless persecution." Once in Washington, Dunne writes, both he and Huston "met privately [more precisely, secretly] with them in order to make sure that nothing our group did would run counter to their own defensive strategy."[11] Dunne was coordinating strategy with the Red-soaked witnesses, though he refused to put it that way.

Then there was the damning advertisement that appeared in the *Washington Post* on October 27, 1947, the day the unfriendly witnesses began their testimony before HUAC. It had all the earmarks of a joint venture between the CFA and the newly dubbed "Hollywood Nineteen," each of whom either had already been or would eventually be exposed as a Party member or fellow traveler.

On the left were excerpts of several editorials denouncing the first week of hearings. Below the excerpts was a strong statement from Dunne's Committee

for the First Amendment signed by over eighty Hollywood stars and personalities, condemning HUAC for its "morally wrong" hearings and its "continuing attempt…to smear the Motion Picture Industry."

In the center of the page, dwarfing these other materials, the "Hollywood
Nineteen" angrily blasted HUAC, pledging to use "every legal means within
our power to abolish this evil thing which calls itself the House Committee on
Un-American Activities."[12]

The two groups almost certainly cooperated in putting out what appeared
to be a joint protest against the hearings and HUAC's existence. No wonder
so many believed Dunne and his crew were fronting for Hollywood's Reds
rather than fighting for the First Amendment.

THE BOGART FLIGHT TO WASHINGTON

Dunne and Co. had done a fabulous job of rounding up high-voltage support to protest the hearings. The plane the CFA charted from Burbank, California, to D.C. carried thirty-five people, twenty-five of them actors and
actresses, including such big names as Humphrey Bogart and his wife, Lauren
Bacall. Gene Kelly, Danny Kaye, Jane Wyatt, June Havoc, Marsha Hunt, and
Richard Conte were also on the flight. In their biography of Bogart, A. M.
Sperber and Eric Lax give a vivid description of the mood on the plane. The
passengers were in high spirits, pulling out flasks of whiskey and belting out
"Galway Bay" and "My Darling Clementine." Comic Kaye emerged from the
cockpit in a pilot's uniform, buttons askew, to ask, "Does anyone have a road
map?" Producer Jules Buck told Sperber and Lax, "We were on a high, high
adventure. It was very good to get the hell out of Hollywood and show them in
Washington that we meant business."

The plane made publicity stops in Kansas City, St. Louis, and Pittsburgh
before landing in Washington, D.C., on the night of October 26 in order to
be on time to give support the next morning to the scheduled lead-off witness, Eric Johnston of the Motion Picture Association, who had been a sharp
critic of the hearings. As the plane winged its way toward D.C., many on the
flight crowded near the cockpit radio to listen to a radio broadcast that more
than a dozen of the stars on the plane had helped record.

HOLLYWOOD FIGHTS BACK

The CFA had persuaded forty-three of Hollywood's brightest celebrities to cut tapes for ABC Radio condemning the hearings in a nationwide broadcast titled *Hollywood Fights Back*. According to Sperber and Lax, the eloquent words of the broadcast had been scripted by veterans of two far-Left groups—the "old Hollywood Democratic Committee and HICCASP." Dunne and Norman Corwin, another far-Left writer, were among the script's editors. Jerome Lawrence, a top radio writer who was outraged at the hearings, put the words in Bogie's mouth.

Americans heard Judy Garland's voice on their radios, recalling her role in the *Wizard of Oz*, saying she didn't think she was in Kansas anymore. "We don't mind being called bad actors," she said, "but we resent being called bad Americans." Bogart, too, slammed the Committee, saying it was "not empowered to dictate what Americans shall think." "Who do you think they're really after?" asked Fredric March. "They're after you." Similar sentiments came across in the voices of others of the Hollywood elite, including Bacall, Kaye, Kelly, Joseph Cotten, Burt Lancaster, Robert Ryan, Robert Young, Lucille Ball, Edward G. Robinson, and John Garfield. Garland brought the program to a close with a warning that concentration camps could be just around the corner and a plea for listeners to write their congressmen.[13]

When the plane arrived in Washington, the weary stars were met by enormous crowds of excited fans who had been standing in the rain to get just a glimpse of their favorite celebrities. The press peppered members of the delegation with questions, but they had been instructed by CFA leaders Dunne and Huston not to answer. The CFA did issue a formal statement, which read, in part, "We do not represent any political group or party whatsoever. We are simply Americans who believe in constitutional democratic government...."

The delegation was persuaded to hold a news conference an hour later at the Statler Hotel. Huston, disingenuously, told the overflow crowd there, "We are not here to attack anybody, neither the House Committee nor the friendly witnesses—nor are we here to defend the hostile witnesses." The CFA was only there to defend the First Amendment and the principle of free speech, he claimed.[14]

That statement was false. Dunne and Huston would secretly coordinate strategy with the nineteen witnesses *just a few hours later*. Under questioning at the Statler, Huston himself conceded that the CFA was determined to see sympathetic lawmakers such as Senator Claude Pepper of Florida and Representative Chet Holifield of California, both Democrats, in order to persuade them to legislate HUAC "out of existence."[15] As Polonsky would later explain, the CFA was quite helpful to the Hollywood Communists who would soon be taking the stand.

In fact, eighteen of the nineteen "unfriendlies" HUAC had subpoenaed would embrace the legal strategy proposed by Dunne's CFA: refuse to answer questions about CP membership on the grounds that posing such questions was contrary to the First Amendment. The nineteenth, German writer Bertolt Brecht, decided before taking the stand to become a cooperative witness.

Ring Lardner Jr. confirms how closely the CFA and the Hollywood unfriendlies worked together on their tactical plans. After hashing it out with their own far-Left and Communist lawyers, writes Lardner in his incomplete memoir, *The Lardners*, the "policy we finally adopted was proposed by Dalton Trumbo and me."[16] (Lardner and Trumbo were hard-core Communists at the time.) We would "refrain from answering questions or cooperating with the committee in any way," says Lardner, "on the grounds that the First Amendment made the whole investigation unconstitutional.... The group and its attorneys...finally agreed on the idea of challenging the committee in this way. And the broader Committee for the First Amendment asserted the same principle in its public relations campaign."[17]

Whatever distance there was between Dunne's CFA and the far-Left witnesses, the public could hardly be blamed for thinking that Dunne's CFA and the Unfriendly Nineteen were cut from the very same bolt of red cloth.

When the hearings opened the next day, Dunne, Huston, and the stars were optimistic. The CFA's crusade had been launched in a blaze of splendid publicity, the radiocast had been well received, the East Coast newspapers were on their side, and Motion Picture Association head Eric Johnston, set to be the first witness on October 27, had been highly critical of the hearings. Johnston had left the impression that he would never support a writers' blacklist and had even taken out a full-page ad in the *Washington Post* the day he was to testify harshly criticizing the first week of hearings.

Even Jack Warner and Louis B. Mayer, the anti-Communist studio heads who had appeared before HUAC the previous week, were known to be less than eager for the Committee investigation. The CFA and its unpaid clients, the Hollywood Nineteen, believed that the mood of the country was swinging against the congressional investigation of Communism in Hollywood. But they were in for an unpleasant surprise.

CHAPTER TWENTY-ONE

THE WRITERS SELF-DESTRUCT

The Washington hearings into Communist influence in the movie industry had opened with a bang on October 20, 1947, and studio moguls'
and Hollywood stars' appearances before the Committee in its jam-
packed House Caucus Room had made huge headlines. The results of the first
week of hearings were indecisive, though, partly because many of the most
important friendly witnesses—especially the studio bosses and the officials of
the Screen Actors Guild—had suggested any Red threat to the industry was
under control.

The week of October 27 would prove far more momentous, setting off a
train of events that would change Hollywood forever: the American people
would see in the newsreels, hear on the radio, and read in the papers about real,
live revolutionary Communists in action—and they would not like what they
saw, heard, or read. The outrageous conduct of the witnesses would impel the

industry to institute what left-wingers and liberals still decry more than half a century later: the so-called "blacklist." Nineteen unfriendly witnesses had originally been subpoenaed, but only eleven of them were actually called to testify before HUAC. Then when Bertolt Brecht, a German writer, decided to cooperate, that left ten uncooperative witnesses who refused to answer the Committee's key questions. They have gone down in history as the Hollywood Ten.

UNFRIENDLY WITNESSES

Hollywood depictions of the 1947 hearings have left the impression of Chairman J. Parnell Thomas furiously wielding his gavel to silence unwanted testimony and ejecting witnesses, *fascisti*-style.

True, Thomas did wield his gavel, and a few of the Ten were forcibly removed from the witness stand. What is customarily omitted from popular accounts of the hearings is that virtually all of Thomas's gaveling and firmness with the unfriendly witnesses was wholly justified because the Ten, in a strategy worked out with lawyers Ben Margolis and Charles Katz (both Communist Party members at the time), Bartley Crum (a radical civil rights attorney), and Robert Kenny (a far-Left Democrat who belonged to the Communist-run National Lawyers Guild), deliberately turned the hearings into guerrilla theater.

Ring Lardner Jr., as we have seen, claimed that the tactic the Hollywood Ten settled on for the hearings was actually "proposed by Dalton Trumbo and me."[1] He maintained that the two of them had "postulated the strategy of not answering the key question, that is, whether they were Communist Party members." Trumbo and Lardner were, of course, hard-core Communists faithfully following the Party line. Thus the strategy of the Ten—pleading the First Amendment, topped with belligerent responses to HUAC members—had been crafted by the most ardent Communists among them. They hoped that the Supreme Court, stocked with FDR appointees, would eventually hold that HUAC had no constitutional right to question their political beliefs.

Eric Johnston, head of the Motion Picture Association of America, was scheduled to be the first witness on October 27. Phil Dunne's Committee for the First Amendment had timed the movie stars' flight to Washington so the stars could be on hand to rally around Johnston, who had been peppering

HUAC with criticisms and had even taken out a full-page ad in the *Washington Post* suggesting that HUAC was engaged in undermining one of "the most precious heritages of our civilization," the concept that "a man is innocent until he is proved guilty."[2]

Chairman Thomas and the Committee, however, made a switch. The lead-off witness was not going to be Johnston, who was sympathetic to the unfriend-lies though anti-Communist himself, but the fervent Communist John Howard Lawson, a major controversial figure in Hollywood, who proved to be the most unfriendly of the unfriendly witnesses. The change would set the tone of the proceedings—and prove to be a disaster for HUAC's opponents.

JOHN HOWARD LAWSON

Lawson, we have seen, was a playwright and screenwriter responsible for *Blockade*, the pro-Communist movie on Spain, and *Action in the North Atlantic*, the patriotic war movie starring Humphrey Bogart with a dash of pro-Soviet propaganda tossed in. He had also been a founder of the Screen Writers Guild, was active in major left-wing and Communist causes, and was in fact the long-time head of the Communist Party in Hollywood. He was known as the chief "enforcer" of the Party line in Hollywood.

Lawson's appearance started inauspiciously enough. His attorneys, Robert Kenny and Bartley Crum, asked Thomas to consider quashing the subpoenas issued to Lawson and eighteen other witnesses "on the ground that the com-mittee is illegal and unconstitutional." They also accused the Committee of trying "to induce the motion-picture producers to create a blacklist, to hire men not on the basis of ability, but on the basis of political beliefs."

Thomas readily agreed to weigh the request, moved the Committee into executive session, then returned saying the panel was operating under Public Law 601 and that Kenny, as a former attorney general of California, should know that "your remedy, if any, is in the courts." Crum then followed up with a provocative question: Would the committee recall the friendly witnesses so they could be cross-examined "in order to show that the witnesses lied"? The request was denied, but the exchanges had been fairly gentlemanly up to this point. Then Lawson took the stand.

Lawson's opening move was to say he had a statement to read. Chairman Thomas, initially agreeable, briefly looked at the first sentence, then insisted the statement was "not pertinent to the inquiry." That first sentence read, "For a week this Committee has conducted an illegal and indecent trial of American citizens, whom the Committee has selected to be publicly pilloried and smeared."[3]

These twenty-six words were rather mild compared to what followed. But Thomas concluded from just the first sentence that Lawson's polemics would contribute nothing to the subject of the hearing at hand: whether Communists had infiltrated and manipulated the movie industry and posed a threat to America. Nor did the statement directly respond to any of the charges made against Lawson or any of the other radicals in the first week of hearings.

Lawson answered a few questions, such as his name and occupation, and seemed quite pleased when Committee chief investigator Robert Stripling later read a list of his picture credits. But mostly he kept up a barrage of anti-Committee insults and self-righteous rhetoric. Asked whether he belonged to the Screen Writers Guild, which was packed with known Communists in key positions, Lawson bellowed that "the raising of any such question in regard to membership, political beliefs, or affiliation is absolutely beyond the powers of this committee." When Thomas politely pleaded with him to "not continue to try to disrupt these hearings," Lawson shot back: "I am not on trial here, Mr. Chairman. This committee is on trial here before the American people."

Lawson did reluctantly admit he had been a member of the SWG since 1933, saying this was "a matter of public record," but then fiercely balked when asked if he had held any office in the Guild. This was also "beyond the purview of the committee" and an "invasion of the right of association under the Bill of Rights of this country." Yet Lawson's position in the Guild had *also* been a "matter of public record." Consistency was not one of his virtues.

Stripling repeated the question, and Lawson again proclaimed that it was "outside the purview of the rights of this committee.... My rights as an American are no less than the responsibilities of this committee of Congress."

Chairman Thomas then provoked laughter by saying, "Now, you are just making a big scene for yourself and getting all 'het up.'"

A much bigger scene was to follow when Stripling posed the question that became the hallmark of the HUAC hearings. "Mr. Lawson," the chief investigator finally asked, "are you now, or have you ever been a member of the Communist Party of the United States?"

Mr. Lawson: In framing my answer to that question, I must emphasize the points that I have raised before. The question of communism is in no way related to this inquiry, which is an attempt to get control of the screen and to invade the basic rights of Americans in all fields.

Mr. McDowell: Now, I must object—

Mr. Stripling: Mr. Chairman—

[*The chairman pounding gavel*]

Mr. Lawson [*continuing*]: Which has been historically denied to any committee of this sort, to invade the rights and privileges and immunity of American citizens, whether they be Protestant, Methodist, Jewish, or Catholic, whether they be Republicans or Democrats or anything else.

The Chairman [*pounding gavel*]: Mr. Lawson, just quiet down again. Mr. Lawson, the most pertinent question that we can ask is whether or not you have ever been a member of the Communist Party. Now, do you care to answer that question?

Mr. Lawson: You are using the old technique, which was used in Hitler Germany in order to create a scare here—

The Chairman [*pounding gavel*]: Oh—

Mr. Lawson: In order to create an entirely false atmosphere in which this hearing is conducted—

[*The chairman pounding gavel*]

Mr. Lawson: In order that you can then smear the motion picture industry, and you can proceed to the press, to any form of communication in this country.

The Chairman: You have learned—

Mr. Lawson: The Bill of Rights was established precisely to prevent the operation of any committee which would invade the basic rights of Americans. Now, if you want to know—

Mr. Stripling: Mr. Chairman, the witness is not answering the question.

Mr. Lawson: If you want to know—

[*The chairman pounding gavel*]

Mr. Lawson: About the perjury that has been committed here and the perjury that is planned—

The Chairman: Mr. Lawson—

Mr. Lawson: You permit me and my attorneys to bring in here the witnesses that testified last week and you permit us to cross-examine these witnesses, and we will show up the whole tissue of lie—

The Chairman [*pounding gavel*]: We are going to get the answer to that question if we have to stay here for a week. Are you a member of the Communist Party, or have you ever been a member of the Communist party?

Mr. Lawson: It is unfortunate and tragic that I have to teach the committee the basic principles of American—

The Chairman [*pounding gavel*]: That is not the question. That is not the question. The question is: Have you ever been a member of the Communist Party?

Mr. Lawson: I am framing my answer in the only way in which any American citizen can frame his answer to a question which absolutely invades his rights.

The Chairman: Then you refuse to answer that question, is that correct?

Mr. Lawson: I have told you that I will offer my beliefs, affiliations, and everything else to the American public and they will know where I stand.

The Chairman [*pounding gavel*]: Excuse the witness—

Mr. Lawson: As they do from what I have written.

> **The Chairman** [*pounding gavel*]: Stand away from the stand—
>
> **Mr. Lawson:** I have written Americanism for many years and I shall continue to fight for the Bill of Rights, which you are trying to destroy.
>
> **The Chairman:** Officers, take this man away from the stand—
>
> [*Applause and boos*][4]

Even reading this in print, it is clear that Lawson, not Thomas, was the major provocateur. After Thomas gaveled the room to order, stressing there would be "[n]o demonstrations, for or against" the witnesses, Committee investigator Louis Russell, a veteran FBI agent, testified he had received a copy of a Party "registration" card issued in Lawson's name for December 10, 1944. The number: 47275. Information on the card, said Russell, included Lawson's name, race, and sex. His address was listed as 4542 Coldwater Canyon in Los Angeles.

The Committee then introduced into the hearing a densely packed, fine-print résumé that takes up eight pages in the printed record of the hearings containing voluminous evidence about Lawson's Communist Party activities. And the résumé was far from complete.

Cited were his writings for the *Daily Worker*, the *New Masses*, and numerous other Communist publications; his unflinching backing of every twist and turn in Stalin's foreign policy since the 1930s (including, of course, a hurrah for the Soviet-Nazi Pact); and his support of dozens of domestic Soviet fronts and causes. Thomas asked a reluctant Stripling to read the entire Lawson résumé into the hearing record for dramatic impact. It proved so extensive that Stripling, fearing that his voice would tire, eventually passed off the chore to investigator Robert Gaston.

While the Committee was exposing Lawson's record in considerable detail, the Red screenwriter was handing out his unread opening statement to reporters. That statement, written in *Pravda*-like prose, argued that he had had "dirt" and "truckloads of filth" heaped upon him in the earlier hearings. But, you "don't argue with dirt.... you try to find out where it comes from. And to stop the evil deluge before it buries you—and others. The immediate source is obvious. The so-called 'evidence' comes from a parade of stool pigeons, neurotics, publicity-seeking clowns, Gestapo agents, paid informers, and a few ignorant and frightened artists."

Having let loose these left-wing thunderbolts, Lawson assailed Thomas as "a petty politician, serving more powerful forces" who are "trying to introduce fascism in this country." They were trying to "trick" the American people into abandoning their liberties by manufacturing "charges against 'reds.'" For good measure, he claimed that "J. Parnell Thomas and the Un-American interests he serves" want to "cut living standards, introduce an economy of poverty, wipe out labor's rights, attack Negroes, Jews and other minorities, drive us into a disastrous and unnecessary war."[5]

Lawson's statement read like a rant from the *Daily Worker*, for which he had been a columnist and contributor. But for all his Red polemics against his accusers, he never refuted—on the stand or in his statement or in subsequent writings—a single, solitary charge that had been leveled against him. Until Stalin's death in 1953, Lawson remained an enthusiastic tool of that murderous Soviet leader, one of whose chief desires was to destroy the United States of America.

DALTON TRUMBO

Dalton Trumbo followed Lawson to the stand as the next hostile witness. Slight, energetic, bespectacled, and sporting a trim mustache, Trumbo came to the hearings with the much-heralded film *Kitty Foyle* and a solid World War II movie, *Thirty Seconds over Tokyo*, under his belt. His *Johnny Got His Gun*, the "pacifist" novel he penned when the Hitler-Stalin Pact was in force, calls for all men in all nations to rise up and murder those who may send them off to war again. (It had been serialized in the *Daily Worker* during the Soviet-Nazi Pact. Following Hitler's invasion of the Soviet Union, Trumbo, like other Communist backers of the Pact, forsook his supposed pacifist ways to urge the United States to save the only nation he truly cared about for most of his life, Stalin's Russia.)

Trumbo's opening gambit was the same as Lawson's. He requested to be allowed to read a statement. His request was denied on the grounds that his statement was "not pertinent to the inquiry," and then Trumbo was asked by Stripling if he was a member of the Screen Writers Guild. Trumbo immediately pounced, insisting he wanted to "introduce statements" by a general in the air force and a municipal judge on his behalf. Informed that he should answer "Yes" or "No" and then give his explanation, Trumbo snapped that "many questions can be answered 'Yes' or 'No' only by a moron or a slave."

Turning the other cheek, Chairman Thomas yielded, saying Trumbo need not answer "Yes" or "No," but that "you should answer the questions." Thomas also agreed to let Trumbo put into the record the testimonials of prominent people who had praised Trumbo's war films.

Stripling then returned to the original question: "Are you a member of the Screen Writers Guild?"

> **Mr. Trumbo**: Mr. Stripling, the rights of American labor to inviolably secret membership lists have been won in this country by a great cost of blood and a great cost in terms of hunger. These rights have become an American tradition. Over the Voice of America we have broadcast to the entire world the freedom of our labor.
>
> **The Chairman**: Are you answering the question or are you making a speech?
>
> **Mr. Trumbo**: Sir, I am truly answering the question.

Trumbo wasn't, of course. He then suggested the Committee members were opposed to the Guild because they were anti-labor, pointing to the fact that some HUAC members favored the Taft-Hartley Act.

After more wrangling, Chairman Thomas posed the question once again: "Are you a member of the Screen Writers Guild?"

> **Mr. Trumbo**: Mr. Chairman, this question is designed to a specific purpose. First—
>
> **The Chairman** [*pounding gavel*]: Do you—
>
> **Mr. Trumbo**: First, to identify me with the Screen Writers Guild; secondly to seek to identify me with the Communist Party and thereby destroy that guild—

The Chairman [*pounding gavel*]: Are you refusing to answer the question?

Mr. Trumbo: I will refuse to answer none of your questions, sir.

The Chairman: Well, you are refusing to answer the question.

Mr. Trumbo: I am, indeed, not refusing to answer the question.

The Chairman: I will ask you the question.

Mr. Trumbo: You ask me.

The Chairman: Are you a member of the Screen Writers Guild?

Mr. Trumbo: I repeat—

The Chairman: Excuse the witness—

Stripling then said he had one more query, which Chairman Thomas asked: "Are you or have you ever been a member of the Communist Party?"

Mr. Trumbo: I believe I have the right to be confronted with any evidence which supports this question. I should like to see what you have.

The Chairman: Oh. Well, you would!

Mr. Trumbo: Yes.

The Chairman: Well, you will, pretty soon. [*Laughter and applause*]

The Chairman [*pounding gavel*]: The witness is excused. Impossible.

Mr. Trumbo: This is the beginning—

The Chairman [*pounding gavel*]: Just a minute—

Mr. Trumbo: Of an American concentration camp.

The Chairman: This is typical Communist tactics. This is typical Communist tactics. [*Pounding gavel*] [*Applause*][6]

Then, as he had done with Lawson, Stripling had Russell read into the record data from a photostatic copy of Trumbo's Communist Party registration card, issued in 1944 with the number 47187. The card, bearing the name "Dalt T," gave the address 620 Beverly Drive in Beverly Hills, California. Other data included Trumbo's sex and occupation and the fact that he was a "club subscriber" to the *Daily Worker*.

Stripling and Gaston then read the six-page dossier on Trumbo's Communist activities into the record.

ALBERT MALTZ

Albert Maltz, who had written such patriotic war movies as *Pride of the Marines* and *The House I Live In* (a much-heralded short film on racial tolerance starring Frank Sinatra), was the next unfriendly to be heard. He was actually allowed to read an opening statement to Committee members—the only hostile witness to do so.

Chairman Thomas may have given permission because of media pressure. Or maybe, scanning it quickly, he viewed it as less tendentious than either Lawson's or Trumbo's. "I am an American," Maltz's statement began on a patriotic note, "and I believe there is no more proud word in the vocabulary of man."

But the Maltz statement soon deteriorated into the familiar Red diatribe, with this sentiment sandwiched in his closing remarks: "I would rather die than be a shabby American, groveling before men whose names are Thomas and Rankin, but who now carry out activities in America like those carried out in Germany by Goebbels and Himmler."

When Maltz was asked if he was a member of the Screen Writers Guild, he trotted out the by-now tired refrain: "Next you are going to ask me what religious group I belong to." When Stripling asked if he was a Communist Party member, Maltz gave an almost identical response. Stripling then repeated the question, and Maltz replied: "I have answered the question, Mr. Quisling"— Quisling being Hitler's handpicked henchman to rule Norway and a byword for cowardly treason.

Chairman Thomas had had enough: "Excuse the witness. No more questions. Typical Communist line." Then Stripling placed Maltz's Communist dossier into the record, including a copy of his Communist Party card.[7]

And so the same predictable routine, with minor variations, was performed by the rest of the hostile witnesses who were to become part of the Hollywood Ten: Alvah Bessie, Samuel Ornitz, Herbert Biberman, Edward Dmytryk, Adrian Scott, Ring Lardner Jr., and, finally, Lester Cole.

RING LARDNER JR.

Ring Lardner Jr.'s appearance before HUAC deserves special mention, for he has been lionized by the Left over the years, and the statement he prepared but was denied the right to present to HUAC in 1947 was read by him fifty years later at an august occasion honoring the "blacklist" victims at the Academy of Motion Picture Arts and Sciences in Beverly Hills. As the eighty-two-year-old Lardner read, the audience listened in reverential awe.

The refusal of the Committee to let him read the statement has frequently been trumpeted by HUAC's foes to show how high-handed the Committee was. Yet the Left passes over this simple fact: Chairman Thomas informed Lardner that he would be permitted to read his statement—just as Maltz had been allowed to read his—but only if Lardner answered the questions put to him by Committee members. Lardner never answered the questions.

Lardner began his testimony before HUAC by saying, "I have a short statement I would like to make."

Chairman Thomas replied, "Mr. Lardner, the committee is unanimous in the fact that after you testify you may read your statement."

Stripling then asked Lardner whether he was a member of the Screen Writers Guild.

Lardner responded, "Mr. Stripling, I want to be cooperative about this, but there are certain limits to my cooperation. I don't want to help you divide or smash this particular guild...."

Thomas pleaded, "Now, Mr. Lardner, don't do like the others, if I were you, or you will never read your statement."

Thomas repeated the question, with Lardner responding, "But I understood you to say that I would be permitted to read the statement, Mr. Chairman."

The Chairman: Yes, after you are finished with the questions and answers—

Mr. Lardner: Yes.

The Chairman: But you certainly haven't answered the questions.

Mr. Lardner: Well, I am going to answer the questions, but I don't think you qualified in any way your statement that I would be allowed to read this statement.

Thomas clearly *had* qualified his statement, but politely remarked, "Then, I will qualify it now. If you refuse to answer the questions, then you will not read your statement."

Then Lardner, like all the rest of the Red witnesses, did his little dance. He kept vowing to "answer the question" but wound up engaging in long-winded evasions and insisting that if he responded, "tomorrow you could ask somebody whether he believed in spiritualism."

Thomas then went through the same rigmarole with Lardner over whether he was a Communist Party member. Round and round the chairman and Lardner went on the issue, with Lardner never answering but still insisting that he would answer the question.

Finally, an exasperated Thomas said, "It is a very simple question. Anybody would be proud to answer it—any real American would be proud to answer the question, 'Are you or have you ever been a member of the Communist party?'..."

Then Lardner got off the famous crack still celebrated in leftist and liberal circles to this day: "It depends on the circumstances, I could answer it, but if I did I would hate myself in the morning."[8]

After this witticism from the witness, Thomas repeatedly told Lardner to "leave the witness chair." Lardner balked, the sergeant-at-arms came to escort him off the witness stand, and then Lardner joked again, "I think I am leaving by force." And so the hearings relentlessly ground on.

But not to the advantage of the Ten, who were far from impressing the public with their antics.

CHAPTER TWENTY-TWO

PORTENTS OF DISASTER

T he witnesses and their supporters may have gained some psychic satisfaction from their blistering assaults and snide attacks on HUAC. But the truth is that their antics eventually sealed their doom. True, there were some on the Left who loved the hard-line tone taken by the witnesses. Samuel Ornitz, one of the Ten, was elated about Lawson's testimony, writing to his wife, Sadie, "I thought Jack was splendid on the stand. He took the first blow for all of us."[1]

Others, however, sensed a looming disaster. Edward Dmytryk, a famous director and the only one of the Ten ever to completely repudiate the Communist Party, recalls that he was "shocked" by Lawson's strident performance, but even more upset with Trumbo's, since he expected better of this smart, unconventional, and witty fellow. The group's behavior "should have been that of underdogs, polite but grievously put upon," Dmytryk writes in his memoir. Lawson's demeanor, he said, "should have been geared to achieve the most favorable reaction possible, especially from the press; instead, he was achieving exactly the opposite." Dmytryk said he actually became embarrassed listening to Lawson, burying himself in his seat as the playwright engaged in his confrontation with Thomas.

"The minutes felt like hours," he remembers. "I didn't dare to look up and around until, to the audible relief of the entire room [in fact, there were some Lawson sympathizers present], Thomas finally begged the police to escort Lawson from the stand. I watched incredulously as he paraded back to his seat with a smug look of triumph on his face."

BELLIGERENCE PROVES A LOSING STRATEGY

Dmytryk rightly believed the Ten's credibility had been undermined by Lawson's antics—and similar performances by many of the others. The testimony, he argued, "was much more devastating on radio and in the newsreels than in the press. It was clear to those who listened that the unfriendly witnesses were behaving as Communists could be expected to behave."[2]

Phil Dunne's reaction was similar. Dunne was always a strange bird, a man of the Left who disliked Communism but seemed to have a mother hen's instinct to care for the liberal Left's more totalitarian offspring. Dunne writes that he desperately tried to persuade the unfriendly witnesses, the original nineteen, to "respectfully" decline to answer questions on First Amendment grounds, and then, outside the Committee room, answer all the queries honestly put to them by reporters. In this way, the witnesses would have revealed themselves as men of honor, objecting only to the government's asking questions they alleged to be unconstitutional. Before the hearing, Dunne and the Communists he was trying to help agreed on the tactic of refusing to answer the Committee's questions. But the belligerent way in which the Reds behaved was something Dunne neither recommended nor endorsed.

But the original nineteen, he notes, "already had settled on their own strategy of pretending to answer the questions while actually evading them and indulging in combative political speeches, a ploy which inevitably—and perhaps deservedly—backfired."

Dunne went so far as to say that while the Ten based their *legal* argument on the First Amendment, there was no evidence that they were ever its public champions, as so many revisionist historians now proclaim. In only a few cases did those words even "fall from their lips. At best, it appeared as an afterthought…." (Neither Lawson nor Trumbo ever specifically pleaded the First Amendment on the stand.)

When Trumbo's lawyers wanted to replay his testimony before a jury in 1948, Dunne told them that he thought this would be disastrous. "What came through," he judged, "was a loud and obstreperous witness obviously evading the questions posed to him by a kindly and fatherly Congressman Thomas."[3]

ERIC JOHNSTON'S BIG SWITCH

The Lawson performance appeared to have had a significant impact on Eric Johnston, head of the Motion Picture Association of America (MPAA). The association represented the major producers in Hollywood, including Warner Brothers, Metro-Goldwyn-Mayer, Twentieth Century-Fox, RKO, Columbia, and International-Universal. Lawson had finished his "testimony," such as it was, in the morning. Johnston spoke in the afternoon.

Johnston introduced a lengthy statement that was sharply critical of the Committee. He said the Committee had given a false impression that Hollywood was "running over with Communists and communism" and challenged them to make public an unpublished subcommittee report that contained the last eight years of "Communist propaganda" films. "Until the list is made public," said Johnston, "the industry stands condemned by unsupported generalizations, and we are denied the opportunity to refute these charges publicly."

Johnston then stressed that he wanted to dwell on an extremely important topic: free speech. "Now, I've been advised by some persons to lay off it. I've been told that if I mentioned it I'd be playing into the hands of Communists.

But nobody has a monopoly on the issue of free speech in this country. I'm not afraid of being right, even if that puts me in with the wrong company."

"You don't need to pass a law to choke off free speech or seriously curtail it," he warned. "Intimidation or coercion will do it just as well. You can't make good and honest motion pictures in an atmosphere of fear." For good measure, Johnston stressed he was also "whole-souledly" against the government telling the motion picture industry, "directly or by coercion, what kind of pictures it ought to make."

From Johnston's initial statement, the hostile witnesses and the Hollywood stars in the hearing room could easily have thought that they had secured a critical ally. Johnston had seemed to line up not precisely with the Communists—he was anything but a Red—but with Phil Dunne and his Committee for the First Amendment, whose argument was that the Constitution protected Communists, as well as Republicans and Birch Society members, from having to give their party affiliation.

During the questioning, however, Johnston was to engage in a colloquy with the Committee's chief investigator, Robert Stripling, that should have made those who had initially thought the MPAA president was rallying to their side deeply uneasy.

> **Mr. Stripling**: Mr. Johnston, you were present this morning when we heard Mr. John Howard Lawson, were you not?
> **Mr. Johnston**: I was.
> **Mr. Stripling**: Did you hear the evidence which was submitted to the committee regarding his Communist affiliations?
> **Mr. Johnston**: I did.
> **Mr. Stripling**: If all of the evidence which was submitted was proved to your satisfaction to be true, would you say Mr. Lawson had any place in the motion-picture industry as a picture writer?
> **Mr. Johnston**: If all of the evidence there is proved to be true, I would not employ Mr. Lawson because I would not employ any

proven or admitted Communist because they are just a disruptive
force and I don't want them around.

This was the most ominous sign to date that things would not necessarily
go right for the hostile witnesses or their supporters. Johnston, like HUAC, Jack
Warner, and L. B. Mayer, apparently put Communists in a somewhat different
category from Republicans, Democrats, Socialists, and Lardner's "spiritualists."
Even those entitled to free speech—so Johnston strongly implied—had no
absolute right to be employed in the movie industry, especially if they were
Communists and agents of the Soviet Union.[4]

The hearings would go on for four more days, the bulk of them taken up
by the ritualistic testimony of the unfriendlies. Two more potentially hostile
witnesses, however, proved of some interest; their testimony would further
undermine the case of the stonewalling Ten.

LAVERY UNDERMINES THE TEN

Emmet Lavery was a lawyer, playwright, and screenwriter. Some of his
best-known works were *The Magnificent Yankee*, a play about Supreme Court
Justice Oliver Wendell Holmes (still seen on Turner Classic Movies) and two
films, *Hitler's Children* and *Behind the Rising Sun*, both produced by RKO.
Lavery had been in Hollywood off and on for more than a decade. When he
appeared before HUAC, he was serving a third term as president of the controversial Screen Writers Guild, an organization several witnesses had claimed
was clearly manipulated, and sometimes controlled, by Hollywood Communists. Many Guild watchers considered Lavery a left-wing pawn, at best, and
expected him to be less than candid in his exchanges with Chairman Thomas.

HUAC, apparently reluctantly, had subpoenaed Lavery to talk about the
SWG and, in Thomas's words, to respond to charges "made against you and
your organization." Chief Investigator Stripling, expecting something less than
full cooperation, initiated his questioning with the hope that Lavery would
answer the question as to whether he was part of the Screen Writers Guild
directly and "without an outburst."

Far from being a recalcitrant witness, however, Lavery appeared eager to talk, saying he had "wanted to volunteer the information that I am both a member and serving my third term as president."

Stripling, recalling the behavior of the Hollywood Ten before the Committee, pressed Lavery: "Do you see anything incriminating in any way for a person answering whether or not he is a member of the Screen Writers Guild?"

Lavery replied, "Well, Mr. Stripling, as one lawyer to another, you know that is something for each individual to decide for himself.... For myself, I am delighted and proud to answer that I am president of the guild, to which I have been greatly devoted."

After a few more exchanges, Lavery interjected, "I have a piece of information that I would like to put in the record on my own motion and on my own volunteering, because I am not sure as a student of constitutional law whether the committee does have the authority to demand it of me, but let me break the suspense immediately and tell you that I am not a Communist. I never have been. I don't intend to be."

Lavery went on to say that he wanted to make another "open confession" and admit that "I am a Democrat who in my youth was a Republican. And if the committee wants to know why I changed from Republican to Democrat—"

When Thomas said, "No, we are not interested in why you changed," the room broke into laughter.

Lavery leapt at the chance to reply to each and every Committee query, at one point insisting, "I would be here whether you gave me a subpoena or not."

With direct responses and a touch of humor, the SWG's president soon had Thomas eating out of his hand. In just a few minutes, Lavery had also undermined the *entire position* of the Ten and the Committee on the First Amendment. These folks were arguing flat out that the Committee could not constitutionally ask any question about the SWG or Communist Party membership. They were also maintaining, as was the SWG itself, that Thomas's panel should go out of existence. Yet here was Lavery, head of the SWG and considered a man of strong leftist sympathies, eagerly and enthusiastically informing the Committee about his association with both groups!

Chairman Thomas, clearly impressed with Lavery's manner, allowed him to testify at length. In an almost garrulous fashion, Lavery defended the Guild and himself against charges of being pro-Communist.

He sharply challenged Jack Warner's claim that he had been fired. (Warner's "own records," Lavery said, would show the separation was at "my request.") And Rupert Hughes's suggestion that Lavery was a "Communist masquerading as a Catholic" was total nonsense, he insisted. Lavery even introduced into the hearing testimony before Senator Jack Tenney's Committee in California in which its hard-line anti-Communist counsel had denied Lavery was a Red. Lavery also hinted that in the upcoming SWG election, he was backing the non-Communist slate. All this seemed very "un-Lavery-like" to those who thought he had been far too friendly with the Hollywood Left.

Thomas was delighted with Lavery's demeanor: "We subpoenaed the other side [meaning, apparently, unfriendlies and potential unfriendlies], and you are the only one to date, however, willing to come here and be very frank. And it is very refreshing."[5]

Thomas and Lavery had become quite friendly during Lavery's testimony, with Thomas thanking Lavery "very much" for his appearance and Lavery cheerily thanking the chairman back. The hostile witnesses would never forgive Lavery for his testimony.

THOMAS BONDS WITH A GERMAN RED

Bertolt Brecht, one of the original nineteen unfriendly witnesses, was the last witness to testify. He was a renowned poet and playwright who had escaped Nazi Germany in 1933 and worked in Hollywood but could barely speak English and needed an interpreter at the hearings.

Brecht's difficulty with the English language produced some of the lighter moments of the hearing. When it was discovered that Brecht needed an interpreter, the Committee found someone it decided to swear in as "Mr. Interpreter," rather than use his real name, for reasons not wholly clear. After vowing to translate German into English and English into German both "diligently and correctly," "Mr. Interpreter" appeared so unable to articulate clearly that Thomas blurted out, "I cannot understand the interpreter any more than I can the witness."

Nevertheless, Stripling did manage to ask Brecht whether he was now or ever had been a "member of the Communist party" of any country.

Brecht answered readily, saying that because his status was different from an American citizen, he would like to respond: "I was not a member or am not a member of any Communist party."

Thomas pressed: "Your answer is, then, that you have never been a member of the Communist party?"

> **Mr. Brecht**: That is correct.
> **Mr. Stripling**: You were not a member of the Communist Party in Germany?
> **Mr. Brecht**: No, I was not.

Brecht readily admitted knowing all sorts of Communists in the United States, and it was clear from the writings introduced into the record by the Committee that he was wholly sympathetic to Communism. Still, Thomas was so delighted with his seemingly forthright responses that he constantly praised his conduct, even sending him from the witness stand with these words: "Thank you very much, Mr. Brecht. You are a good example to the witnesses...."[6]

WHAT HUAC ACCOMPLISHED

The hearings adjourned abruptly on October 30, 1947, at 3:00 in the afternoon. Though for weeks afterward Thomas would insist the Committee was shortly going to resume the investigation, HUAC would not renew its probe of the film industry for a little over three years.

Over a two-week period, HUAC had subpoenaed nineteen unfriendly witnesses, but only eleven of these had been called up to testify. One of these, Bertolt Brecht, had cooperated, denied he was or had ever been a Communist, and would soon leave the United States to live in Communist East Germany. Ten witnesses had taken the First Amendment, either explicitly or implicitly, rather than answer any questions concerning their Communist activities. Each of them was to be cited for contempt by the U.S. House of Representatives.

What had HUAC accomplished? The East Coast Establishment troika of influential newspapers—the *New York Times*, the *New York Herald Tribune*, and the *Washington Post*—had hardly been impressed. All three had laid down a steady barrage of fire against the Committee. Siding with the Hollywood Communists and the Phil Dunne crowd, the *Post* insisted that "we have no doubt that the line of questioning was a grossly improper one for the committee to pursue. It was as improper…as an inquiry into a man's religious affiliation."

The *Post* also claimed it was "offensive" that several witnesses had suggested that "the motion picture industry ought to produce anti-Communist films." (The *Post*, interestingly enough, had never found "offensive" the government's urging the industry to produce *pro*-Stalinist films before or during World War II.)

The *Times*, equally outraged, said it did not believe "that the committee is conducting a fair investigation" and demanded that those charged with Communist activities be given the right of cross-examination. Piling on, the *Herald Tribune* insisted that Thomas, with "blunderbuss and klieg lights," had obscured any real damage the Communists might have done.

Less influential papers also flung insults at the hearings. The *Chicago Sun-Times* echoed the Left, saying the "primary purpose" of "Chairman Thomas and the reactionary Republicans [on his committee]" was to "smear New Dealers and whatever their progressive successors may be called."

True, Committee members and investigators had nodded from time to time. They could be faulted for allowing a friendly witness or two—Jack Warner in particular—to suggest a writer might be a Communist or "un-American" when that was not the case. But false allegations were very few, were quickly corrected, and did no lasting damage to anyone's reputation. On the whole, the Committee had done its job fairly.

Most of the liberal and left-wing criticism, moreover, was simply silly. Few questions could have been more important for a congressional committee to ask than whether American citizens were actually serving as agents of a hostile

foreign government. Nor was it true that the "unfriendlies" were in any meaningful way silenced. They were given abundant chances to respond to respectfully posed questions, but they chose to try to disrupt the proceedings. They
piously proclaimed they would answer questions and then filibustered
instead—all the while aggressively insisting that they were being *denied* the
right of free speech.

Whatever its faults, the HUAC investigation still proved to be one of the
most effective, albeit controversial, probes ever carried out by any committee
of Congress. HUAC had revealed that Hollywood was packed with Communists and fellow travelers, that the guilds and the unions had been heavily
penetrated, and that wartime films, at least, had been saturated with Stalinist
propaganda. Red writers were an elite and powerful group in Hollywood—
many of them working for major studios.

Within weeks, the Hollywood Communists and their fellow travelers were
on the run. No group seemed to be on the ropes more than the nest of radicals
in the Screen Writers Guild, a clique that had been even more subservient to
the Soviet cause than the hearings had revealed.

CHAPTER TWENTY-THREE

THE SCREEN WRITER: RED AS A ROSE

The Screen Writers Guild proved to be the first major HUAC target to undergo an overhaul in the wake of the hearings. The Guild had been preparing to hold its annual leadership election in November, with pro- and anti-Red factions furiously battling for control. A dramatic clash between these two sides seemed inevitable following the war and the rising American resentment against Communism, both foreign and domestic.

The HUAC investigation had badly damaged the SWG's left-wing forces, but the Committee had overlooked a mother lode of material that would have greatly assisted Guild members who believed that nothing but a clean sweep of the Guild's governing board would salvage the organization as a voice of moderation. For reasons not entirely clear, HUAC had failed to focus on the contents of *The Screen Writer*, the Guild's very influential flagship publication, and the ideology of its editors. If they had done so, they would have given a major boost to the non-radical faction. There is no question that the publication was controlled by Hollywood's hard Left.

From June 1945 through December 1947, *The Screen Writer* was in the editorial hands of two devoted Communist Party members, Dalton Trumbo and Gordon Kahn. Trumbo, of course, would become a famous member of the Hollywood Ten; Kahn was identified before HUAC as a Communist by numerous ex-comrades.[1]

Every month these fellows packed *The Screen Writer* with articles and notices in support of the CP line. No trace of anti-Communist or anti-Soviet sentiment would ever stain its pages. Virtually anything hinting of anti-Communism was a target. Giving in to the temptation to produce anti-Communist films was bowing to "anti-Red hysteria," cried *The Screen Writer*. Non-Communist loyalty oaths for union leaders were a violation of First Amendment rights. The House Un-American Activities Committee was a "racist," "fascist" panel, howled the pages of Trumbo's little magazine.

The Motion Picture Alliance (MPA), the *Hollywood Reporter*, and the brilliant journalist Eugene Lyons were all ruthlessly trashed for their opposition to the Soviet Union and the Communist Party line. Under Trumbo and Kahn's special care, *The Screen Writer* became a powerful vehicle for Communist writers to spread Soviet propaganda. Party member Richard Collins, for example, penned a piece suggesting that a 1945 documentary didn't give nearly enough credit to Soviet Russia's wartime effort. "[O]ur Soviet allies," he lamented, "are not mentioned until Stalingrad."[2]

The Hollywood Ten's Alvah Bessie waxed at length about the glories of those "who fought beside the Spanish people"—that is, on the Soviet-controlled side—in the Spanish Civil War. Hollywood, he insisted, had given "only timid and belated tribute" to these men in such highly acclaimed films as *Casablanca*.[3]

Howard Koch, the screenwriter who had made certain that viewers knew the hero of *Casablanca* had fought on the pro-Soviet side in Spain, was also given plenty of space in the Trumbo-Kahn monthly to defend his contribution to the highly controversial *Mission to Moscow*. Koch vehemently insisted that there was no perversion of "basic truth" in the film.[4] Well, not if you believed Stalin was the Messiah and the Soviet Union the New Utopia.

The Screen Writer editorial staff "warmly supported"—Ceplair and Englund's phrase—"Herb Sorrell and his federation," the conspicuously pro-Communist Conference of Studio Unions (CSU) that waged violent strikes against the Warner Studios in Burbank, California.[5] Labor leader Sorrell and his CSU worked closely with Communist writers such as John Howard Lawson; raised money for the Communist publication, the *People's Daily World*; backed Communist labor leader Harry Bridges; supported Communist candidates for public office; and so on.[6] The liberal Fund for the Republic study on movies and blacklisting acknowledges, "The Communists saw [the CSU] as a base for party operations in Hollywood."[7] Apparently *The Screen Writer's* editors were perfectly content with the arrangement.

Much of Trumbo and Kahn's magazine was crammed with little factoids boosting this or that Stalinist event, cause, or author. Do you want to listen to screenwriter John Howard Lawson? The "final sessions of his American Heritage course," notes the March 1946 issue of *The Screen Writer*, will discuss, among other things, "Red-baiting" and "Foreign and Native Fascism." Excerpts of Lawson's "funeral address for the renowned novelist" Theodore Dreiser can be found in the *Book Find News*, according to a brief note in the magazine's April '46 issue. Dreiser, author of *An American Tragedy*, had finally joined the Party in July 1945.[8]

PR FOR COMMUNIST CAUSES

The SWG publication was always advertising some function or lecture—frequently on the topic of the decency of the Soviet Union—being held at the People's Educational Center (PEC) at North Vine in Hollywood. Dozens of Communists flocked to fill the faculty positions of the PEC, which possessed a library donated by the CP-founded Workers School. The PEC not only taught the craft of moviemaking but also held classes on the Russian language, the benefits of Marxism, the economic prosperity of the Soviet Union, and the fascist menace in America.

Future Hollywood Ten members Alvah Bessie and Edward Dmytryk, each a Communist at the time, were listed as teachers in the 1944 prospectus, as were Charles Katz and Ben Margolis of the Communist law firm Katz, Gallagher, and Margolis. (Katz and Margolis, each of whom would take the Fifth before HUAC in 1952 when asked about his CP membership, gave critical legal support to the Ten during the 1947 hearings.)

Nor did you have to be an American Communist to teach: the faculty also included R. Lal Singh, the editor of the Communist *India News*.

During the 1945–47 period, the PEC came under the thumb of director Sidney Davison, described before HUAC by Oliver Carlson, an expert witness on Communism and a former Communist himself, as a current Communist who had been "a member of the Communist party in the New York area." Davison, Carlson added, "was sent out to Hollywood specifically to take over the job of director of this school."[9] The ubiquitous Lawson, a frequent lecturer, wound up on the PEC's Board of Directors.

"Three SWG members," notes the January 1946 issue of *The Screen Writer*, "are listed as instructors in the screenwriting courses announced by the People's Educational Center, 1717 No. Vine St., Hollywood. Robert Lees, Ben Barzman and Melvin Levy will teach Screenwriting I, II and III...."

Lees took the Fifth Amendment before HUAC in 1951 but boasted of his CP membership in a film honoring the Hollywood blacklist shown at a 1997 ceremony in Beverly Hills that I attended. Barzman's wife detailed her husband's life as a CP member in *Tender Comrades* and *The Red and the Blacklist*. Melvin Levy was identified as a Party member before HUAC in May 1953 by Robert Rossen, a major Red figure in Hollywood for about a decade.

Left-wing historians Ceplair and Englund appear enthusiastic about Trumbo and Kahn's radical agenda, reporting that the "left-wing editors and contributors to *The Screen Writer* defiantly returned the fire of the anti-Communists."[10] But *The Screen Writer* also advanced the views of Stalinist writers, pro-Communist and Communist groups, and fervent apologists of the Soviet Union's predatory postwar foreign policy.

Take the activities of the Communist-dominated Hollywood Writers Mobilization (HWM), often publicized by Trumbo and Kahn as the war was winding down and in the immediate postwar period. Designed to encourage writers to sell war propaganda for government and volunteer organizations, HWM was headed by Communist screenwriter and director Robert Rossen during most of the war years. Under his leadership, the HWM eagerly promoted pro-Soviet causes. Its newsletter, *Communiqué*, was soaked in Red propaganda and was increasingly recognized by liberals as a pro-Soviet operation.

The Screen Writer's July 1945 issue excitedly notes the launch of a new HWM publication, *Hollywood Quarterly*, which would "represent a mature approach" to the creative and technological problems of the screen and radio. Not mentioned was that it would also take a *Communist* approach, with its editorial board loaded with radicals such as Lawson, its pages filled by Red writers, and its contents lauding Hollywood's pro-Stalinist films, as we shall see in more detail below.

The Screen Writer also had a penchant for skewering anti-Communists as dangerous bigots and warmongers while painting the Soviet Union as a decent and benign power threatened by a rising anti-Red tide in America. The rhetorical abuse of Eugene Lyons is a case in point.

For many years, Lyons had been a Soviet sympathizer, having worked for the Soviet news agency TASS prior to covering Moscow for the United Press from 1927 to 1933. But in 1937, disillusioned with Communism, he wrote *Assignment in Utopia*, a devastating critique of Stalin's Russia, and in 1941 compounded his sin by writing *The Red Decade*, a powerful indictment of America's pro-Soviet elite. In the postwar period, Lyons would frequently give lectures under the auspices of the Motion Picture Alliance on the nature of the Soviet threat.

Trumbo and Kahn had screenwriter Alfred Hayes write a little hatchet piece on Lyons in the June 1947 issue of *The Screen Writer*.[11] Hayes referred to the noted journalist as "one of the [nation's] most persistent Russia-phobes"—as if it were absurd for Lyons to be deeply disturbed about Stalin's swallowing of Eastern Europe, his installation of Red regimes in Asia, his aggressive acts against Western Europe, and the deep penetration of his fifth column in virtually all areas of American society.

Hayes wrote that he had sat in on an anti-Soviet speech that Lyons was making to "provincials from Bel Air and Pasadena" recently and had not been enlightened. Lyons's anti-Communist theme had a "desolately stale odor about it," said Hayes. That the Soviets have curtailed some freedoms in art, literature, and science is an old story, but it is also "standard history" in the birthing of "revolutionary states." Besides, revolutions also bring about "the release of new artistic energies," so it was silly for Lyons to be alarmed.

Then Hayes "judiciously" equated Stalin's suppression of much of the Soviet intellectual class—involving the murder and harsh imprisonment of thousands—with the Breen office in Hollywood forbidding Hayes to put "elementary sexual facts" onto the screen and forcing him to revise his scripts to "eliminate or soften a few elemental political truths."

Hayes sneered at Lyons's claim that Hollywood was deeply penetrated by Communists—even as Communist Trumbo and Communist Kahn were filling the official publication of the Screen Writers Guild with Communist writers and Communist propaganda, including Hayes's own pro-Communist writings!

The Screen Writer had been launched in June 1945 with a ferocious attack by Communist Trumbo on anti-Communist producer-director Samuel Wood, who had been associated with such hits as *Saratoga Trunk*; *Goodbye, Mr. Chips*; *For Whom the Bell Tolls*; and *Kings Row*. Trumbo clearly hated Wood and even wrote a nasty bit of doggerel about him after his death that can be seen in Trumbo's papers at the Wisconsin Historical Society. Obviously, what had caused Trumbo to erupt on this occasion was that Wood was a founder and the first president of the anti-Communist Motion Picture Alliance for the Preservation of American Ideals (the MPA). Trumbo couldn't contain his fury at the anti-Communist Wood and nimbly fabricated his facts as he went along. He maliciously wrote, for instance, that Wood's MPA had undermined U.S. troop morale when it charged that Hollywood's entire war effort was "the work of Communists, crackpots and radicals." Neither Wood nor the MPA had done any such thing, but Communist Trumbo never thought twice about ignoring the truth to score a polemical point.[12]

TRUMBO MEETS FIVE SOUL MATES

While Trumbo falsely accused the MPA of engaging in activities akin to treason, he apparently thought it was especially patriotic to insinuate pro-Soviet material, and possibly also manufactured incidents, into his "Notes on a Summer Vacation" in the September 1945 issue of The Screen Writer. Though not a newspaperman by trade, Trumbo was covering the tail end of combat operations in the Pacific for The Screen Writer, interviewing doctors, chaplains, and military men in general.

The Americans he "randomly" interviews are surprisingly concerned about the unfair shake Stalin is getting from the media. Five doctors at a hospital in Guam, for example, are all of the same mind: not only hungry for news, but quite upset about the anti-Soviet sentiment that seems to be on the rise in American publications.

One of the doctors asks, "Well, why don't you fellows on the papers do something about the anti-Russian campaign they're putting on?" Trumbo explains that "most newspapermen [as distinct, apparently, from their capitalist publishers] don't agree with the anti-Russian campaign any more" than the doctor.

All five of the doctors, we are supposed to believe, "dislike Time and Readers' Digest" because of their anti-Soviet tilt. The doctors share "one copy of In Fact," an ardently pro-Soviet publication written by an ardent Stalinist—a fact Trumbo neglects to mention.[13] "Another's wife," he writes, "clips and sends them Drew Pearson's column." (Pearson, considered soft on the Soviets, had two former Communists on his staff in the 1940s; one had been a writer for the Daily Worker.)[14] Skeptics of Stalin are nowhere to be found in Trumbo's extensive "Summer Vacation" encounters.

"Fresh from the states, I am less a human being to [the doctors] than a source of news," Trumbo says. "I answer their questions as best I can for over an hour." One can only imagine the "news" that Dalton conveyed to his ideological soul mates.

CONTENTED SOVIET SCREENWRITERS

Nothing proves The Screen Writer was a Soviet propaganda instrument more clearly than its carrying a fourteen-page interview with "the noted Soviet writer" Konstantin Simonov. What *The Screen Writer* actually published in its June 1946 issue were Simonov's comments at a seminar chaired by Communist Trumbo and sponsored by the far-Left Screen Writers Guild and the Communist-controlled Hollywood Writers Mobilization.

Simonov went on at length about the glories of being a screenwriter in Stalin's USSR. He suggested that a Russian author had critical control over his script, that he frequently chose his own director, and that he had a large say in any changes that were made to the script. According to Simonov, as soon as the script goes into production, "the director has the right to introduce changes only with the agreement of the author." From Simonov's account, Soviet writers were blessed with exceptional freedom and job security—better working conditions, a reader could infer, than here in America.

What's conspicuous about this extraordinary piece is that there were apparently no skeptics among the Americans questioning Simonov. America's radical screenwriters were always in high dudgeon about the political constraints they were under when writing scripts for the studios, but somehow it never occurred to any of them to raise a question or two about a Russian writer's political freedom.

Not a single question on the iron control Stalin and his bureaucracy had over Soviet writers and their material was addressed to Simonov. No one apparently thought to ask about the jailing and execution of artists and writers who had displeased the despot who ruled Russia.[15]

Soviet control of writers was hardly an obscure subject. Many stories had appeared in the American press about the topic. Recall that even Alfred Hayes, in his hatchet piece for *The Screen Writer*, would chastise Gene Lyons for dishing up the "stale" story of Soviet control of writers and artists in his lectures to Pasadenans. Lyons knew a lot about the subject, of course. (As Lyons would note in his illuminating *The Red Decade*, "a number of the leading Soviet novelists, poets, playwrights and cinema scenarists were among my Moscow friends. I can attest personally that they lived in a state of continuous fear" that the "artistic inquisition would pounce on them for some word or gesture and crush them forever." These men "squelched their creative impulses" in order to toe the Stalinist line.)[16]

Historian Louis Fischer, a Soviet apologist for much of his adult life, had written as early as November 17, 1932, in the *New York Herald Tribune* that the Party-approved Russian Association of Proletarian Writers, known as RAPP, terrorized authors. "If RAPP frowned on a writer," noted Fischer, "his career was crippled. It persecuted the fellow-travelers... with a bitterness and relentlessness which merely indicated that it had no respect for art.... RAPP drove brilliant literary figures into silence.... Literature and the cinema and theatre, too, were paralyzed by the reign of RAPP...."

RAPP was succeeded by the Soviet Writers' Union, controlled by Aleksandr Shcherbakov, a representative of the Communist Party's Central Committee. The Union was founded at the First Congress of Soviet Writers, which bowed to Stalin's every whim. The great Russian writer and social critic Maxim Gorky, who had become a willing Stalin pawn and had been put in charge of all Russian culture, directed the Congress to embrace the code of "socialist realism," a literary style designed to force writers to promote Stalinism in a language easily understood by the "proletariat."

Writers at this 1934 Congress condemned their contemporaries for straying from Gorky's literary rules. With bizarre irrelevance, delegates also took time from literary matters to brag how children were now eagerly turning their parents over to revolutionary tribunals for being "class enemies." From the main platform of the Congress, the literary giant Fyodor Dostoevsky was denounced as a "traitor."

Indeed, the delegates at this Writers' Congress decided to take sycophancy to new highs—or lows, depending on your point of view—with one delegate claiming, "Comrade Stalin is a mighty genius of the working class," while another called him "the most beloved of all leaders of any epoch and any people."[17]

Hailing the Union's newly formed ideological and literary straitjacket and singing hosannas to the wonders of Stalin didn't necessarily shield you from pain, persecution, and physical destruction, however. For supposedly failing to write in accordance with the Party's rules on "socialist realism" and committing other Red heresies, some "2000 members of the writers' union were arrested, deported to camps or executed" during the late 1930s and very early

'40s, reports Nicolas Werth in the highly acclaimed *The Black Book of Communism*, published by Harvard University.

"Among the most famous victims," Werth says,

> were Isaac Babel, author of *The Red Cavalry* and *Odessa Tales*, who was shot on 27 January 1940; the writers Boris Pilnyak, Yury Olesha, Panteleimon Romanov; and the poets Nikolai Klyuev; Nikolai Zabolotsky; Osip Mandelstam (who died in a Siberian transit camp on 26 December 1938); Gurgen Maari; and Titsian Tabidze. Many musicians were also arrested, including the composer Andrei Zhelyaev and the conductor E. Mikoladze, as were famous figures from the theater, such as the great director Vsevolod Meyerhold, whose theater was closed early in 1938 on the ground that it was "foreign to Soviet art." Having refused to make a public act of contrition, Meyerhold was arrested in June 1939, tortured, and executed on 2 February 1940.[18]

Soviet oppression of writers was common knowledge in 1945 when the Simonov interview was published, but *The Screen Writer* chose to overlook such Stalinist peccadilloes. Instead, *The Screen Writer*'s editors and Simonov's "interrogators" decided to give Simonov a free pass—and allow readers to believe that, deep down, Russian screenwriters had basically the same benefits and freedoms as American screenwriters, maybe more.

Was it any wonder that plenty of objective observers—not only the anti-Red targets of the Left—were concerned about the radicals in the Screen Writers Guild, whose major publication was in the hands of two fanatical Communists? Non-Communist liberals had become deeply troubled, and those within the Guild were chafing at the influence of the radicals. The HUAC hearings had only exacerbated their concerns.

THE SWG TURNS AGAINST THE HARDCORE LEFT

After the HUAC hearings, the media were paying attention to the Communist influence in the SWG, with damaging stories appearing in such anti-Red outlets as the *Hollywood Reporter*, the *Chicago Tribune*, the Hearst press, and the Scripps-Howard newspapers.

The testimony of the unfriendlies had proved so harmful to the Left that motion picture owners and executives felt they would have to move quickly to stem the bad publicity, with some now appearing to favor a remedy they had previously viewed as unthinkable: blocking uncooperative witnesses from working in the industry. Could the Screen Writers Guild ignore the rising pressure to "do something" about the Communists in their midst?

The more moderate elements thought something effective would have to be done. The anti-Red faction in the Guild was by no means right wing but rather made up largely of Rooseveltian liberals who, along with a majority of liberals in the Democratic Party, had become weary of teaming up with Communists in various causes only to see the Communists subvert and discredit those causes.

They did not like being lumped in with folks who appeared more loyal to Moscow than to the United States, and many of them—while despising the "Thomas Committee"—were appalled at the performances of the Hollywood Ten. Furthermore, they believed the Guild should be far more concerned with the welfare of the writers than with radical politics.

There had been apprehension about the pro-Communist element in the SWG for some time. The so-called "Lester Cole faction" or the "Trumbo team" in the Guild was always prodding the SWG to move leftward: to back Soviet foreign policy, support domestic Red causes, promote Communist penetration of unions, hire radical lawyers, subsidize left-wing groups, and engage in massive protests to stir up strife rather than to resolve labor problems. The anti-radicals, in truth, had scores of complaints against the far-Left faction, with *The Screen Writer* being just one of their more prominent grievances.

MULTIPLE GRIEVANCES AGAINST THE RADICAL FACTION

At the prodding of its far-Left faction, for instance, the SWG had poured thousands of dollars annually into the Hollywood Writers Mobilization (HWM), founded in 1941 by Guild members John Howard Lawson and Robert

Rossen. The purpose of the HWM was to channel writers into various patriotic groups to help out with the war effort. Both founders were Party members at the time and, as the liberal Fund for the Republic study states, "Numerous ex-Communists have testified that the organization...was Communist dominated."[19]

Indeed, Rossen himself would acknowledge the fact when he voluntarily testified before HUAC in May of 1953. Rossen, one of the original Hollywood Nineteen, over his lifetime would write such films as *A Walk in the Sun* and direct such major movies as *Body and Soul*, *All the King's Men*, *The Brave Bulls*, and *The Hustler*. He testified that he joined the Party in 1937 and dropped out a decade later. He proved to be one of its most committed members, taking instructions from future Hollywood Ten members Herbert Biberman and Lawson. Rossen vigorously backed the Hitler-Stalin Pact, launched campaigns to free Party boss Earl Browder, and manipulated the HWM toward Communist ends.

He chaired the Hollywood Writers Mobilization from 1941 to 1944 when its steering committee was groaning with Reds. A 1944–45 list of officers unearthed by Committee counsel included a slew of Communists whom Rossen personally identified to HUAC.

Among the familiar names: Lester Cole, Richard Collins, Edward Dmytryk, and John Howard Lawson. Sidney Buchman, Meta Reis, Melvin Levy, and other lesser-known Communists were also on board. Pauline Lauber Finn, another Communist identified by Rossen, was in the important executive secretary position.[20]

During World War II, the HWM enlisted over three thousand writers of all ideological stripes to help the government and volunteer agencies sell the war effort, but under the leadership of Rossen, the HWM also encouraged pro-Soviet radiocasts, pro-Russian publications, and pro-Moscow celebrations.

One of the HWM's most spectacular "salute Moscow" productions included the Western premiere of Dmitri Shostakovich's Seventh (War) Symphony performed before a "sell-out audience at the Shrine Auditorium on October 9, 1942," as Ceplair and Englund point out.[21]

Correspondence between the HWM and various pro-Red groups established "a close pattern of cooperation between every known important

Communist front organization in the state of California," noted the state's Committee on Un-American Activities.[22]

The HWM launched the far-Left *Hollywood Quarterly* and published *Communiqué*, a newsletter saturated with pro-Soviet propaganda. The first issue of the *Hollywood Quarterly* came out in October 1945. The magazine was more subdued than the SWG's *Screen Writer*, even though, as Ceplair and Englund write, "John Howard Lawson and Abraham Polonsky were on the editorial board [although not at the same time] and Sylvia Jarrico was managing [but listed as 'assistant'] editor...."[23] All were *bona fide* Communists.

Despite the muted tone, the tilt of the *Hollywood Quarterly* was obvious. In its lead-off issue, non-Communist Dorothy B. Jones, who served as chief of the film review and analysis section of the Office of War Information during World War II (and would contribute to the Fund for the Republic's report on Communism in the movies), gives a thumbs-up to several pro-Soviet wartime films, including Hellman's *The North Star* and Koch's *Mission to Moscow*. Koch's outlandish celebration of Stalin and Communism in *Mission* didn't stop Jones from arguing that it "was an extremely useful document... because it gave the first fundamentally sympathetic screen portrayal of the Russian allies, who, for decades, had been ridiculed and maligned on the screen and in the press of this country."[24]

Communist writers Ring Lardner Jr., Lester Cole, and Abraham Polonsky decorated the pages of the *Quarterly*, while Jay Leyda, the pro-Soviet technical expert on Koch's *Mission*, monopolized several issues.

HWM's newsletter, *Communiqué* portrayed "Stalin Prize" winners favorably and referred to journalistic critics of the USSR as "political stooges" of the "press lords." The media tagged Hollywood as the "red citadel," *Communiqué* complained, because they are "as yet unable to smash the unions or prostitute its brains." Those who desired a "soft peace for Japan," or thought we should get along with Spain's anti-Communist ruler, Francisco Franco, or suspected Red infiltration of America's institutions were all lampooned in articles and cartoons.

The publication was awash in items celebrating hard-core Communist writers, with Lawson, Hellman, Jarrico, and Collins frequently being saluted. The editors couldn't wait to trumpet the good news when the Soviet Writers Union hailed the pro-Stalinist Hollywood film *Song of Russia* for showing the supposed magnificence of prewar Moscow, "with its fine streets and squares," "beautiful subways and parks," and a visit to a collective farm. To see this film, according to the Writers Union, is to acquire "a thorough understanding of the soul of the Russian people and the reason for their unparalleled stanchness in this war."[25]

While cutting the Guild-backed HWM some slack for its ardent pro-Soviet policies during the war, the liberal Fund for the Republic study notes that in the postwar years, the HWM became "no different from any other front— espousing the cause of the 'people's democracies,' etc."[26] And, as we have seen, *The Screen Writer*, the Guild's own flagship publication, was jam-packed with radical writers airing pro-Soviet and pro-Communist propaganda.

"WE ARE LOADED WITH COMMUNISTS"

The Guild's Executive Board had also been infested with Communists and their camp followers for several years. Nineteen forty-six may have been the high-water mark for the SWG radicals. Of the sixteen board members that year, six were Communist Party members (either identified under oath by ex-comrades or self-confessed), one fellow traveler, and another in their pocket.

Two Communists held important Guild offices in 1946: Vice President Lester Cole and Secretary Maurice Rapf. Treasurer Harold Buchman was, at the very least, a faithful fellow traveler. Untitled board members Richard Collins, Gordon Kahn, and Robert Rossen were also in the Party. Howard Koch, a notorious fellow traveler, was on the board, as was Philip Dunne, a non-Communist who, we have seen, frequently managed to rally to the side of his more reddish colleagues on a whole host of issues, especially those which Dunne somehow felt infringed on Communist liberties.[27] William Pomerance, the executive secretary in 1946, was another Communist Party member. He would take the Fifth Amendment in February 1952 when HUAC asked him about his Party membership.[28]

SWG stalwart James Cain would admit the Communist problem in a leaflet he dispatched to Guild members as part of the campaign to toss out the Communist-dominated leadership. Vocal anti-Communists like California senator Jack Tenney and the HUAC chairman, Representative Parnell Thomas, he wrote, were reprehensible, but they say that "we are loaded with Communists, and whether we like it or not, this charge is true. As we are now constituted, the Party line is more important to certain members commanding a majority of the Executive Board than the interests of the membership and leftist propaganda more important to *The Screen Writer* than material of interest to writers."[29]

Cain's blast was devastating, and only a clean sweep of the SWG's current officers could change the direction of the Guild and what outsiders might think of it. But could that happen? That $64,000 question would soon be answered.

CHAPTER TWENTY-FOUR

EMMET LAVERY'S CRITICAL TURNAROUND

WG president Emmet Lavery had long been a target of the Right, especially of William (Billy) Wilkerson at the relentlessly anti-Communist trade publication, the *Hollywood Reporter*. A founder of that powerful publication, Wilkerson was one of the first prominent newspaper publishers to flag the Red infiltration of Hollywood, zeroing in on the writers with a special zest. His front-page editorials caused convulsions in the movie industry and helped inspire the '47 HUAC hearings. In the summer of 1946, Wilkerson was running front-page editorials topped by alarming, big-print headlines: "RED BEACH-HEAD," "HYWD's RED COMMISSARS!," "MORE RED COMMISSARS."

In these assaults he detailed the lengthy Communist activities of the radical screenwriters, including the customary suspects: Lawson, Ring Lardner Jr., Dalton Trumbo, Lester Cole, and so forth. He even listed what purported to be Communist Party card numbers of powerful figures in the SWG. The Guild's treasurer, Harold Buchman, Wilkerson wrote, should answer these questions: "Are you a Communist? Are you a member of the party's Northwest Section [composed of motion picture people], and do you hold Communist Party Card No. 468027?"

To Dick Collins, Wilkerson posed three queries: "Are you a Communist? Do you belong to the Northwest Section of the Communist Party? Are you the holder of Communist party book No. 11148?" He used this same line of attack on numerous others. Wilkerson would grandly challenge those he named as Communists to respond to his detailed charges. None did.

Wilkerson also sank his teeth into Emmet Lavery on multiple occasions. In three front-page articles on the SWG president in August and September 1946, he speculated whether the SWG leader was a "dupe" or a "dope" and asked why, if Lavery was the devout Catholic he claimed to be, he "allowed himself to become an ally and apologist of men who are reputed to have long Communist records and who do not even deny that they are Communists?"

During the war and even afterward, Wilkerson noted, Lavery had been associated with a number of Red-controlled and heavily Red-infiltrated organizations, including the "pro-Soviet Writers Congress," the "Communist-inspired Mobilization for Democracy," and the "Hollywood Writers Mobilization."

Several names appearing on the literature for Lavery's losing congressional race in 1946, Wilkerson revealed, were hard-core radicals, including Lawson, Trumbo, Lardner, Cole, Bessie, and Maltz (all to become Hollywood Ten celebrities). How come, Wilkerson wondered, this supposedly religious man was always climbing into bed with the anti-religious Left?[1]

Lavery was one of the few screenwriters to reply directly to Wilkerson's attacks. In his response, which appeared on August 29 and covered two full pages of the *Hollywood Reporter*, Lavery categorically denied he had ever been a Communist. But he was far from critical of the Communist efforts to infiltrate Hollywood.

Indeed he lavished praise on many of the left-wing and even Communist-front organizations he had joined and headed, commending the Hollywood

Writers Mobilization, for instance, for its war effort and "giving the industry one of its finest achievements," the Communist-riddled *Hollywood Quarterly*. Lavery also showered specific praise on the Guild's house organ, *The Screen Writer*,[2] which, as we have seen, was a Red propaganda organ run by obvious Communists Trumbo and Kahn.

With all his left-wing baggage and his public avowal that there was no Communist problem in the SWG, anti-Communists found it difficult to believe that the Guild would ever turn over a new leaf with Lavery in charge.

AN UNLIKELY ANTI-COMMUNIST

Yet Lavery, amazingly enough, would emerge as the central figure in the coalition determined to oust the "Marxists" and "near-Marxists"—Lavery's own terms for the pro-Communist faction in the Guild. And he would adroitly exploit the HUAC hearings to push the non-Red slate of candidates for office in the SWG. It was not precisely a Saul-on-the-road-to-Damascus scenario— Lavery remained a left-liberal all of his life—but there were resemblances.

Born in Poughkeepsie, New York, in 1902, Emmet Lavery seemed destined to be an attorney. He received a law degree from Fordham University, worked as a court reporter, and practiced the legal craft for a while in his hometown. Somewhere along the line, he decided to become a writer for the stage and screen.

Among the best-known films he wrote over the course of his lifetime were *The Magnificent Yankee*, an award-winning picture lauding the life of Supreme Court Justice Oliver Wendell Holmes; *Hitler's Children*; and *The Court-Martial of Billy Mitchell*, the general who risked his career to champion the development of American airpower. He would also write an anti-Communist film, *Guilty of Treason*, exposing the Soviet takeover of Hungary and the fraudulent trial of Hungary's Cardinal Mindszenty, but anti-Communism was still in the future for Lavery when he was elected head of the Screen Writers Guild in 1944. At that time, the liberal Lavery clearly had a reputation of making cow eyes at the far Left, as Wilkerson charged. He had also developed a special antipathy toward outspoken anti-Communists, partly because he had tangled frequently with the state senator Jack Tenney, who headed the California Committee on

Un-American Activities, and with conservative screenwriters who viewed him as, at the very least, soft on Communism.

Writer-director Rupert Hughes was so furious with Lavery that he would tell the House Un-American Activities Committee: "Lavery is a good Catholic, he says, but I say a man whose views are Communist, whose friends are Communists, and whose work is communistic is a Communist. I would say that if a wolf wears sheep's clothing that man is a wolf."[3]

In 1947, Lavery also had a major dust-up with Lela Rogers, mother of Ginger and one of HUAC's friendly witnesses. In a radio debate, she accused Lavery of having written a play that followed the Communist Party line, partly because it portrayed the House of Representatives as stunningly corrupt.

The play, *The Gentleman from Athens*, which had not reached Broadway when Rogers made her assessment, may not have followed the CP line in its final incarnation, but it did have a distinctly leftish flavor to it. Starring Anthony Quinn, it featured a corrupt businessman turned high-minded lawmaker whose popular crusade for world government is blocked by unsavory congressmen, including a renowned anti-Communist. Stalin's Soviet Union is portrayed as a rather benign nation, no better or worse than America. The play ran for just seven performances, and Lavery managed to successfully sue Rogers on the grounds that her remark had killed audience attendance.[4]

Despite his well-earned left-wing reputation, Lavery, in a stunning turnaround, would become a major hero of the "All-Guilders," the liberal slate determined to oust the Red faction in the 1947 elections. The SWG president had publicly mocked and justifiably angered the anti-Communists who were warning about subversives in his Guild, but behind the scenes he began to maneuver successfully against the pro-Communist crowd shortly after WWII came to a conclusion.

The far Left, as Lavery himself admitted in various memoranda, made his presidency difficult. He would complain that he had "a sharply divided board through all of my three years ['45, '46, and '47] as president" and that much of his time was spent in "a running battle with the Trumbo team."[5]

Lavery's early victories over the pro-Red faction were not inconsequential, but they were largely defensive in nature. He had, for instance, managed to persuade the board on more than one occasion to resist those eager to push the SWG into backing the pro-Communist Conference of Studio Unions.[6]

He had helped lead a successful move to cut off funds to the HWM[7] as it moved more sharply leftward, and he blocked the Guild from hiring as its counsel National Lawyers Guild member Robert Kenny, who was representing many of the subpoenaed HUAC "unfriendlies" at the time. "At my request," Lavery would boast, "the Board rejected…suggestion from Lester Cole [that the SWG hire Kenny]."[8]

ANTI-COMMUNIST AFFIDAVITS—TO SIGN OR NOT TO SIGN?

Lavery proved most effective in battling the pro-Red crowd in the months running up to the Guild's November '47 balloting. The steps taken then were crucial in clarifying the key issue before the Guild: *Did it or did it not wish to be viewed as Communist-controlled or Communist-influenced? Were the SWG candidates willing to sign non-Communist affidavits to protect the members' legal rights?*

Lavery's blunt telegram to the Guild's Executive Board on September 9, 1947, forced the members to confront this huge problem, which would be highlighted by HUAC in its Hollywood hearings the next month. Ironically, the Republican Congress's passage of the Taft-Hartley Act—which liberals, including Lavery, had deplored as harshly anti-union—handed Lavery the key weapon he needed to club the SWG's far-Left faction.

Under the law, union officials had to sign non-Communist affidavits or they could lose their standing before the all-important National Labor Relations Board. Using this provision as a hook, Lavery sent a telegram to each SWG board member "to join me immediately in filing with National Labor Relations Board (NLRB) certificate of non-Communist affiliation."

A federal district court judge in Fort Worth, Texas, he noted, had already upheld the section of the law "requiring these affidavits and has denied a CIO union the right to appeal to the National Labor Relations Board on the ground that it has not complied with the law."

Lavery had adamantly opposed Taft-Hartley and sought its repeal. He seemed to lament that the procedure he was suggesting "imposes conditions on board members that we do not require" of other members. Still, he insisted on the requirement, on the ground that he was protecting the legal rights of Guild members. "I feel confident," he stressed, "that every officer and every member of the board will place unity and safety of Guild above every other consideration and join me in giving widest possible publicity to our action."[9]

Lavery had clearly tossed down the gauntlet to the current board members and those running for office in the November election: agree to sign the anti-Communist affidavit or be viewed as betraying the security of the Guild.

Initially the SWG's Executive Board ducked the issue, turning down Lavery's request nine to five on the basis that it was "not one of immediate concern to this Guild because the Guild is not involved in any action before the National Labor Relations Board." The issue did not die here, however, as it would become central to the campaign of the anti-Communist All-Guild slate. Determined to put the far-Left candidates in an uncomfortable box, Lavery then drafted an article for *The Screen Writer*, concentrating on the need for Guild officers and board members to sign the affidavits.

With the hotly contested November 19 election about a month away, the All-Guilders used the Lavery draft, which was never published, as a virtual campaign brochure. Lavery had promised to pull no punches when he wrote it, and a careful reading, noted the All-Guilders' cover letter to SWG members, "shows that he kept his word."

Lavery's article said that he couldn't "compel my brother officers to file these affidavits" with the NLRB, but that he had already "filed . . . with the office of the Guild my own affidavit of non-Communist affiliation, so that it may be immediately available" to the NLRB when needed. He said he had been "joined in this action by nine other Board members" and listed their names to isolate the non-signers.[10]

In short, though the board had not voted to make this "loyalty test" official policy, a board majority of ten had voluntarily agreed to sign the affidavits, supporting Lavery's contention that to refuse to take the oath could jeopardize the Guild's legal rights.

The Lavery piece also dealt with other matters, especially the turmoil in the SWG, produced largely, in Lavery's eyes, by its far-Left faction. "Marxists" and "near-Marxists," Lavery wrote, "have carefully cultivated the idea that they are the very heart and nerve center of the liberal tradition in America. It is an amazing and, at times, an effective myth, but nothing could be further from the truth, especially in the Screen Writers Guild. They are not good leaders and they are not responsible leaders. They improvise from one moment to the next and they change their position as frequently as the party line changes its orientation."

These left-wing members repeatedly placed the SWG in jeopardy by pushing for an extremist agenda, Lavery argued. They were wrong in repeatedly trying to involve the Guild's Board in "the second of the two disastrous Hollywood strikes [by Herbert Sorrell's pro-Communist and pro-violence Conference of Studio Unions]," wrong to involve the Guild in causes "obliquely when our membership had consistently refused to participate directly," and wrong to repeatedly urge the screenwriters to take on dangerous risks that could easily have caused the Guild to lose "our Minimum Basic Agreement with the producers."

They had hurt the Guild by failing to "worry about [the agreement's] no-strike" provisions and by pressing it to lend thousands of dollars to a pro-extremist local union. They were foolish to hurl epithets such as "stooges of management" against opponents in answer to rational arguments during SWG meetings—and even more foolish to "encourage mass demonstrations" when simpler, more effective, and far less provocative forms of protest were at hand.

Republicans and Democrats in the Guild, Lavery explained, "seldom if ever function as united political groups," but the "extreme Left does so function and always has. Not admittedly, for this is frowned on by our Constitution, but none the less persistently and continuously."[11]

All of this was heavenly manna to the All-Guilders, and they circulated Lavery's critiques widely. Nor was Lavery through hurling harpoons at the far Left. Few things so angered Lavery's left-wing critics as his October 29 appearance before HUAC. There he cheerily testified that he was a proud member of the Guild and was definitely not a Communist, thus undercutting the very heart of the Hollywood Ten's legal argument: that HUAC had no constitutional right to pose either of those questions to the witnesses.[12]

Indeed, Lavery poured salt into the wounds of the unfriendlies by insisting that his major concern was not that these recalcitrant witnesses were being interrogated but that they might come off as "political martyrs," thus harming the chances of the anti-Red faction in the SWG's upcoming election![13]

Four furious members who had been on the SWG Executive Board—Lester Cole, Ring Lardner Jr., Richard Collins, and Gordon Kahn, Communists all—condemned Lavery for his alleged betrayal. Dalton Trumbo would assail his conduct, without naming him, in his polemic *The Time of the Toad: A Study of Inquisition in America*.[14]

In *The Screen Writer*'s November 1947 issue, the last to reach Guild members before the election, the All-Guild ticket ran a political ad that stressed, "Every [All-Guild] Candidate should he or she be elected and if and when it becomes necessary to order that the SWG obtain NLRB representation, can and will sign the non-Communist affidavit required by the Taft-Hartley Act."[15]

In the same issue, the candidates on the "Independent," or pro-Red, slate, which included such crimson comrades as Hugo Butler, Gordon Kahn, and Lester Cole, deplored "the eagerness with which certain SWG members have seized upon this dangerous weapon [the non-Communist affidavit] for election purposes" and vowed that they would "not NOW sign" the affidavit [emphasis in the original].

ANTI-COMMUNIST LANDSLIDE

The election campaign was in full swing following the hearings. "COMMUNIST ISSUE SPLITS SWG" ran the banner headline in the *Hollywood Reporter* on November 4, just fifteen days before the election and with ballots already in the mail to the Guild's voting members. "One group is fiercely opposed to the non-Red affidavits," reported the *Reporter*, while the other "doesn't mind non-Red pledges and is 'against political issues that have no direct relation to writers' problems.'" A potent slogan of the second group, it noted, was "Get the Guild Back to Writers and Writing!"[16]

The anti-Communist All-Guild slate repeatedly rapped the "Lester Cole faction" for refusing to say whether it would ever take the non-Red pledge. The NLRB would no longer confer any union privileges on the Guild unless its officers signed the oath, the All-Guilders pointed out, so how could the pro-Red faction guarantee protection to Guild members? To its chagrin—and great detriment—the pro-Red faction could never adequately answer the question.

On November 19, the date of the annual election, more than six hundred writers crowded into the California Room of the Roosevelt Hotel in Los Angeles to discover the results. The outcome: a landslide for the All-Guild slate. The All-Guilders swept fourteen of fifteen Executive Board seats, including every top position. Of 886 eligible voters, 720 had cast ballots.[17]

The "Marxists" and "near-Marxists," to use Lavery's terms, had been decisively beaten. *The Screen Writer* was no longer controlled by Trumbo and Kahn. Lester Cole was badly defeated in his run for a position on the Executive Board. The Guild was now in the hands of what might be called the "soft left" and Roosevelt-Truman liberals; the hard-core Reds and their allies had been swept away.

The liberal Lavery and his supporters in the Guild played an important role in the win. Behind the scenes, HUAC's friendly witnesses Fred Niblo and Richard Macaulay proved extremely helpful as well. But the victory also belonged to the anti-Communists in the Motion Picture Alliance and the much-maligned House Un-American Activities Committee, which, through its determination to hold hearings, had exposed the heavy Red infiltration in the movie industry and compelled the soft left, the more moderate liberals, and even the producers to finally confront the Communists in their midst.

CHAPTER TWENTY-FIVE

THE BLACKLIST BEGINS

The SWG election outcome had the far Left reeling. But this was just a whiff of things to come. Five days later the full House took up the issue of whether to approve the HUAC contempt citations. HUAC's subcommittee had run the hearings, the full Committee had unanimously cited the Ten for contempt, and now the whole House was debating whether to uphold HUAC's verdict.

The first name brought up by Parnell Thomas was Albert Maltz. With obvious relish, HUAC's chairman had the House clerk read the representatives much of Maltz's combative exchanges with the Committee, including the writer's branding of Chief Investigator Robert Stripling a "Quisling," after the notorious Hitlerite and Norwegian traitor.

HUAC'S CASE FOR CONTEMPT

Then Thomas and the Committee members laid out what would be their case against each of the Ten. Over numerous years, Thomas argued, these men had engaged in "Communist activities," possessed Party cards, and been loyal agents of a foreign enemy of the United States. Hence there was no more "pertinent question" than the one they refused to answer: *Were they now or had they ever been Communist Party members?*

Nor had HUAC been unfair to any of the Ten, Thomas insisted. Each had had counsel, and there wasn't a single "unfriendly" who had not been given a chance to respond fully to the questions posed. Far from engaging in smears and innuendo, the Committee—with the aid of skilled former FBI investigators and its research director, Benjamin Mandel, himself a former Communist—had placed an abundance of hard evidence into the hearing record confirming the Communist loyalties of each, including photostatic copies of their Communist membership cards.

Thomas also placed into the *Congressional Record* numerous documents establishing the Committee's legal right to question the witnesses. He cited Public Law 601 and House Resolution 5 of the Eightieth Congress, "from which," he said, "we derive our authority" to conduct these investigations.

He read United States Code, title 2, section 192, which provides that any person summoned before any committee of the House "who, having appeared, refuses to answer any question pertinent to the question under inquiry, shall be deemed guilty of a misdemeanor, punishable by a fine of not more than $1,000 nor less than $100, and imprisonment in a common jail for not less than one month nor more than 12 months."

NOT YOUR ORDINARY POLITICAL PARTY

Thomas, Republican representative Richard Vail of Illinois, and other members also skillfully hammered home the point that the Communist Party was *not* like any other legal political party. Nor was it treated as such by the U.S. government. Applicants for federal employment had to answer this question: "Do you advocate or have you ever advocated or are you now or have you ever been a member of any organization that advocates the overthrow of the Government of the United States by force or violence?"

The Communist Party, according to the federal government, clearly fit into that category. FDR's attorney general, Francis Biddle, had concluded on May 28, 1942, that the "Communist Party of the United States of America, from the time of its inception to the present time, is an organization that writes, circulates, distributes, prints, publishes and displays printed matter advising, advocating or teaching the overthrow by force and violence of the Government of the United States." Equally important, according to Thomas, was that the Party was controlled by Moscow. "To say that a committee of the Congress," Thomas emphasized, "cannot inquire into the subversive affiliation—the treasonable affiliation, if you please—of an individual is ridiculous."

The House members listening to him at that very moment, he stressed, had been called into "special session to appropriate billions of dollars to stop the floodtide of communism from sweeping all of Europe." Surely it would be a curious "paradox if the Congress of the United States is to appropriate upward of $20 billion to stop communism in Europe if the same Congress cannot inquire into the activities of a Communist conspirator in the United States, whose first allegiance is to a foreign government!"

Since the 1930s, the House had given HUAC the right to subpoena subversives, including Communists and fascists, and the House had supported the Committee on previous contempt cases. Just earlier in the year, noted Thomas, "our committee reported to you on the contempt of Gerhart Eisler, Eugene Dennis and Leon Josephson, all Communists. You referred these three cases to the United States Attorney and a conviction was obtained in all three...."[1]

THE REDS' DEFENDERS

Whatever one may have thought of their judgment during the hearings, Thomas and fellow HUAC members had made a convincing case for contempt. But Maltz and his codefendants still had some passionate supporters. California Democratic representative Chet Holifield's attack against the HUAC investigation typified the liberal point of view. Holifield admitted he had voted to cite Eisler and others for contempt because "I thought [those cases were] clear cut." He did not deny that Maltz had failed to respond to HUAC's questions but insisted a larger issue was involved: the "wave of fear" that he believed was sweeping the nation. "Fear begets fear, suspicion begets suspicion and hysteria begets mob action," Holifield said. "The result of fear, suspicion and hysteria is the unwise and un-American denial of civil liberties."

To illustrate his point, he then waved about a Montrose, California, community newspaper, which reported that a group of armed men, some carrying guns and wearing veterans' uniforms, had entered a private home and broken up a meeting held by local Democrats. There was no indication from his presentation that the HUAC hearings had stirred the mob, but Holifield suggested that this episode indicated we might well be on the "verge of storm trooper incidents throughout America...."

"If we are to sit in judgment as to the loyalty of every man or a group whose opinions we oppose, who will be next?... We are wading into a quicksand which will engulf our liberties. We are invading the field of thought and opinion, of political conviction.... We can stem the tide of hysteria now. Tomorrow may be too late."[2]

Holifield had to know that HUAC was not "invading the field of thought and opinion" but accurately disclosing membership in a subversive organization controlled by an enemy nation and designed to turn America into a Communist country—a country devoid of the very civil liberties the Californian was championing with such emotion.

The Hollywood Ten's loyalties to Moscow, the hearings had proved, were clear—their Communist Party cards as well as extensive records of their Communist Party activities having been introduced into the hearing record. Yet the California lawmaker, undoubtedly under pressure from the liberal Hollywood community influential in his district, distorted the issue, pretending that HUAC's members were in the business of judging "those whose opinions we oppose."

HOUSE VOTES OVERWHELMINGLY FOR CONTEMPT

Holifield's rant went for naught. The result of the vote was not even close. By a 347-to-17 roll-call vote (a twenty-to-one margin), the House upheld

HUAC's contempt citation against Maltz.[3] The size of the majority was stunning given the sharp critique of HUAC coming from the Establishment press, the support of Dunne's Committee for the First Amendment for the Hollywood Ten, the stout support of Hollywood's most illustrious celebrities, and the vigorous arguments of the liberal-left legal community. Parnell Thomas and his Committee had clearly won a huge victory.

The rest of the votes were somewhat anti-climactic, but there was still a great deal of debate to come. Next HUAC chairman Thomas brought up the name of Dalton Trumbo and reprised Trumbo's Maltz-like performance. Thomas had the clerk read Trumbo's tendentious "testimony" before the House in which Trumbo, too, had promised to respond to the questions but never did.

The outcome was not in doubt, but a few hardy souls would rise to Trumbo's and the Ten's defense. Two New Yorkers, Republican representative Jacob Javits, who would become a famous liberal Republican senator, and Democrat Emanuel Celler, already well known for his left-wing views, opposed the contempt resolution against Trumbo and assailed HUAC.

Javits claimed the Committee had conducted itself badly, especially at a time "when there is so much hysteria about Communists" in our midst. He chastised the panel for some of the questions it put before the Ten, even the question of Communist Party membership, as not in accordance with "Anglo-Saxon justice that a man must be proved guilty of something before he is called upon to deny it." As a result of these hearings, Javits was introducing legislation that would eliminate HUAC.

Javits, of course, was ignoring the difference between a Committee investigation and a criminal trial. He was also ignoring the incontrovertible evidence of Party membership that HUAC had placed into the record.

Representative Celler said he opposed the contempt citation because of the "conduct of the committee in general" which "at times was most unfair." He especially condemned the Committee's allowing the charges of the friendly witnesses to cascade through the airwaves and into the printed media before the accused had a chance to rebut them.

Yet both Javits and Celler, in the course of their defense of the unfriendlies, undermined the core of the Ten's legal case. Despite his objections to HUAC and the manner in which the members posed questions to the Ten, Javits felt impelled to acknowledge that "the men here under consideration should have answered the questions" and that "they appear to be in contempt according to the record and the law."[4]

Celler, while deploring the Committee's behavior and opposing the resolution, conceded the same strategic point as Javits when he said: "I think that the committee had ample power to ask these questions as to whether a man was a member of the Screen Writers Guild, or whether he was a member of the Communist Party."[5]

The House then voted 240 to 16, with the names of House members not recorded, to confirm HUAC's contempt citation against Trumbo.[6] The contempt citations of the other eight were upheld by a simple voice vote.

STUDIOS MOVE AGAINST THE TEN

Some three weeks after the October hearings, Motion Picture Association of America (MPAA) president Eric Johnston, addressing the Picture Pioneers' annual dinner in New York, vigorously defended the industry he represented and reiterated some of the things he had said before HUAC on October 27. Despite abundant evidence to the contrary, he insisted that the Thomas panel had not proved that a single picture had been tainted with "subversive propaganda," and he pledged that no such picture would ever appear on the silver screen.

Johnston also reiterated his determination to "fight forever" for the free speech guarantees in the First Amendment and against the Hearst newspaper campaign for movie censorship. He warned that what Hearst desired would not only affect the movies but end freedom of the press as well. "Freedom of speech is not a selective phrase.... It is either free speech for all American institutions and individuals or it's freedom for none—and nobody," he declared.

Still, the meat of Johnston's speech was a powerful attack against the Hollywood Ten. Johnston insisted that these men, through their bellicose behavior and their failure to respond to the questions posed, had unnecessarily spread an embarrassing cloud over the entire movie industry. Patriotic groups such as the American Legion and various Catholic organizations had already taken a bead on Hollywood's far-Left elements. And Johnston was determined to head off the possible threat that a disenchanted public might decide to boycott movies produced by an industry thought to be infested with militant Communists. Profits, in truth, had already dropped 30 percent from the previous year.

The Ten had performed disgracefully, Johnston charged, so the studios were now ready to take matters into their own hands. Because of the MPAA's defense of the industry, he stressed, people

> have completely misunderstood our position, and some still do. They thought we were defending those 10 men because they are connected with our industry. I don't want to leave the slightest doubt on this point.
>
> We did not defend them. We do not defend them now. On the contrary, we believe that they have done a tremendous disservice to the industry, which has given them so much in material rewards and the opportunity to exercise their talents. Their refusal to stand up and be counted for whatever they are could only result in a confusion of the issues before the committee—and it did.

Johnston said he believed that the Ten's actions hurt the cause of democracy immeasurably. "I believe they played into the hands of extremists who are all too willing to confuse the honest progressive with the dishonest Red. And they fed fuel to the fires of hysteria."

He stressed that "the difference between the position we took before the committee and the line those 10 men followed is as broad as the back side of a barn." The movie executives had criticized "the committee's procedure," but "we didn't challenge the right of the committee to investigate alleged Communistic influence in Hollywood or anywhere else."

Just to be sure no one would mistake the movie studios' position, Johnston proclaimed that the Communist is "a fool and a faker at one and the same time. I think he's disruptive and disloyal, and he'd be dangerous, if he dared to be. I think he's a foreign agent, real or potential, owing his first allegiance to a foreign government.... There is no place in Hollywood for anyone who is subversive or disloyal to this country."

While the government must adopt "a national policy with respect to the employment of Communists in private industry," he said, labor and management "must not shirk their responsibilities by waiting for government to act. The motion picture industry, like every other industry, must therefore take positive steps to meet this problem, and do so promptly."[7]

WALDORF STATEMENT INSTITUTES THE BLACKLIST

Less than a week later, Johnston and fellow movie executives would take those "positive steps." On November 24, the very day the House would approve the contempt citations against the Ten, fifty members of the Motion Picture Association of America, the Association of Motion Picture Producers, and the Society of Independent Motion Picture Producers convened in the Waldorf-Astoria in New York City.

MPAA president Johnston and counsel Paul McNutt, each of whom had harshly condemned HUAC during the hearings, were present. Also on hand were former secretary of state James F. Byrnes, another MPAA counsel; producer Louis B. Mayer; Dore Schary of RKO-Radio; and Walter Wanger, who had produced *Blockade*, the Lawson film taking the Communist side in the Spanish Civil War.

After two days of deliberations, on November 25, Johnston issued a statement announcing the momentous decision reached by the gathering. In the name of the Association of Motion Picture Producers, the statement deplored

> the action of the ten Hollywood men who have been cited for contempt by the House of Representatives. We do not desire to pre-judge their legal rights, but their actions have been a disservice to their employers and have impaired their usefulness to the industry.
>
> We will forthwith discharge or suspend without compensation those in our employ, and we will not reemploy any of the ten until such time as he is acquitted or has purged himself of contempt and declares under oath that he is not a Communist.

On the broader issue of alleged subversive and disloyal elements in Hollywood, our members are likewise prepared to take positive actions.

We will not knowingly employ a Communist or a member of any party or group which advocates the overthrow of the government of the United States by force or by any illegal or unconstitutional methods [emphasis added].[8]

Implementation of this anti-Communist policy was entrusted to a committee of five chaired by Louis B. Mayer. Other members included Joseph Schenck, Henry Ginsberg, Dore Schary, and Walter Wanger. The committee was carefully selected, noted the *Hollywood Reporter*, "to include all shades of American political opinion."[9]

This was the blacklist. The official exclusion of Communists from the movie business had begun.

CHAPTER TWENTY-SIX

GAME, SET, MATCH

hairman Parnell Thomas and HUAC had clearly triumphed. Prodded by the hearings, the SWG had cleaned house. Various other guilds would also pass tough resolutions barring Communists from high-ranking positions. And even liberal studio executives such as RKO's Schary were falling all over themselves pledging never to hire known Communist Party members.

The Screen Actors Guild had already vanquished the radicals a year before the 1947 hearings. But in the wake of the Thomas probe, the SAG under Ronald Reagan overwhelmingly passed a resolution on November 16 requiring officers, board and committee members, and executive employees to sign non-Communist affidavits, a measure even more sweeping than Taft-Hartley required.

By December 1, Hollywood's money people had also revealed their apprehension about the public's reaction to the revelations about Communism in Hollywood. Anti-Communist, veteran, and religious organizations were now threatening boycotts of pictures written by Communist writers and starring Communist actors. All of the Ten—including even those who had been under contract—had been fired from the studios or labeled unemployable by the movie industry.

BOGART BACKS DOWN

Phil Dunne's Committee for the First Amendment was on its last legs, and even the enormously famous Humphrey Bogart, who had played a starring role in the CFA, was being pushed into recanting his Washington appearance in support of the unfriendly witnesses before HUAC. Bogart's situation, vividly portrayed in Sperber and Lax's *Bogart*, was typical of the predicament of high-minded liberals and leftists who were reluctant to reject the Communists in their midst.

Bogart, a box office sensation at the time, was no Communist. But much of the public believed his lead role in the CFA extravaganza was equivalent to supporting Reds in Hollywood. It did not help his reputation that the *Daily Worker* was treating him like a hero.

Bogart kept publicly defending his position after the hearings had concluded. In a CFA-sponsored radiocast following the hearings, Bogart was still slashing at the Committee, likening HUAC to the kind of political weapon employed in fascist countries. "It *can* happen here," he said in his November 2 broadcast, alluding to a highly popular Sinclair Lewis novel depicting fascism coming to the United States.

What the CFA delegation saw in Washington, he insisted, was the

> police tak[ing] citizens from the stand like *criminals....* We saw the gavel of the committee chairman cutting off the words of free Americans.
>
> The sound of that gavel, Mr. Thomas, rings across America! Because every time your gavel struck, it hit the First Amendment to the Constitution of the United States.

The voice was Bogart's, but the words were those of the very liberal Jerome Lawrence, a top radio writer who had bought the far-Left line about the HUAC hearings.

In the November 23 issue of the *New York Herald Tribune*—just a day before the movie executives would meet in the Waldorf-Astoria to move against the Ten—Bogart was defending the Ten and his support of them once again. "Our object," Bogart said, "was to exert our influence in defense of a principle—a principle that no man should be forced to tell what political party he belongs to."

No one was more concerned about the public's reaction to Bogart's role in this true-life drama than Jack Warner, since "Bogie" had been starring in Warner Brothers' films since the 1930s. Among his most notable pictures: *The Maltese Falcon* (1941), *Casablanca* (1942), *Action in the North Atlantic* (1943), and *Dark Passage* (1947).

In the wake of the hearings, film fans were beginning to sour on Warner's huge moneymaker. Fox theaters reported being deluged with letters urging them to block the showing of Bogart films, and box office receipts for *Dark Passage* were plummeting. Jack Warner, livid at Bogart's seeming indifference to the rising tide of public opinion against him, dispatched frantic messages to his own staff to get Bogart to pull in his horns. Among his desperate pleas: "GET THIS MAN TO MAKE A RETRACTION."

Bogart's situation was perilous. "Publicity head Alex Evelove," Sperber and Lax report in *Bogart*, "had offered to screen *The Treasure of the Sierra Madre* for *Cosmopolitan*, a flagship publication of the Hearst empire, and had been flatly turned down; the new Hearst policy was to give no breaks to Bogart or anyone else who had gone to Washington in opposition to HUAC."

Other powerful people in the industry also pleaded with Bogart to back off from defending his Washington trip. Impresario Ed Sullivan, who had a powerful newspaper column, told Bogart privately that he was beginning to alienate "*Americans*.... the public is beginning to think you're a Red. Get that through your skull, Bogie!"

Bogart finally caved. On December 3, Humphrey Bogart, with his wife Lauren Bacall beside him, held a press conference in Chicago attended by the

Associated Press, the United Press, and the International News Service. Reading a prepared statement, Bogart said he had gone to Washington "because I thought fellow Americans were being deprived of their Constitutional rights, and for that reason alone. That the trip was ill-advised, even foolish, I am very ready to admit. At the time, it seemed the right thing to do. I have absolutely no use for Communism nor for anyone who serves that philosophy, I am an American. And very likely, like a good many of you, sometimes a foolish and impetuous American."

Leftists and liberals were stunned and dismayed by the apology; backers of the Hollywood Ten had considered Bogart and Bacall heroes for their stand against the HUAC hearings. The *Washington Post* editorialized that Bogart should be "ashamed" of his switch, and Representative Holifield, one of the few House members who had opposed the contempt citations against the Ten, wrote an "open letter" to Bogart suggesting he had, unfortunately, bowed to outside pressure.[1]

More bad news was on the way. The guilds were still ostensibly opposed to "blacklisting," but they did nothing to assist the Ten in fighting the contempt charges. SWG president Emmet Lavery, as we have seen, would boast that the Screen Writers Guild's policy was to refuse help to those who were cited for contempt. And in January 1948, SWG members "defeated—333 to 224—a resolution presented by left-winger Hugo Butler calling on the Guild to fight for the reinstatement of the three fired writers and to provide them with legal counsel in their breach of contract suits against the studios," according to Ceplair and Englund.[2]

GUILTY OF CONTEMPT

Meanwhile, Lawson's and Trumbo's legal cases were wending their way through the judicial system. On April 19, 1948, a federal jury found the two guilty of contempt for refusing to respond to HUAC's questions. Each was sentenced to a year in jail and fined $1,000, and the District of Columbia's Circuit Court of Appeals affirmed the convictions on June 13, 1949.

Justice Bennett C. Clark dismissed every substantive argument presented by the defendants' lawyers. Clark insisted that their rights had been thoroughly protected during the jury trials and before HUAC, the Committee and its subcommittee had been properly constituted, and the questions posed by the members had been pertinent and constitutional.

The Supreme Court, Clark pointed out, had repeatedly ruled that there is no absolute right of free speech or to remain silent, even under the First Amendment. And given the threat posed by the Soviet Union and the influence of motion pictures, Clark added, "it is hard to envisage how there could be any more pertinent question" than whether these defendants had now or had ever been Communist Party members.

Clark then stressed, "So that there may be no mistakes or misunderstanding…we expressly hold herein that the House Committee on Un-American Activities, or a properly appointed subcommittee thereof, has the *power* to inquire whether a witness subpoenaed by it is or is not a member of the Communist Party or a believer in communism and that this power carries with it necessarily the power to effect criminal punishment for failure or refusal to answer that question…."[3]

Despite this crushing blow, the Ten and their lawyers still managed to hang on to hope. They had somehow convinced themselves that at least five of the Supreme Court Justices—Hugo Black, William O. Douglas, Wiley Rutledge, Frank Murphy, and Robert Jackson—would put HUAC in its place. But this theory, which they had held onto from the outset of their ordeal, was never to be tested. When Rutledge and Murphy died, the more conservative Tom Clark and Sherwood Minton were appointed to replace them on the Court.

In the end, with only Black and Douglas dissenting, the Supreme Court let stand the Appeals Court's decision on April 10, 1950. On June 11, Lawson and Trumbo entered jail in Ashland, Kentucky. The other eight, who had agreed not to appeal their cases if Lawson and Trumbo lost their appeals, were then given swift trials and sentenced. Within three years of the hearings, all of the Hollywood Ten would be serving time in a federal prison.

HUAC, though bruised by elite opinion, had won the support of the American people and a victory over Hollywood Communists, fellow travelers, and the important liberals who supported them. The moviemakers were not only blacklisting Communists, but at least for a while, the studios were actually creating anti-Communist pictures. *Variety* reported in 1948 that anti-Communist films have "become the hottest to hit the screen this year."

CHAPTER TWENTY-SEVEN

HERB SORRELL AND
THE CSU STRIKE

The Communist Party working in Hollywood wanted control over everything that moved on wheels—sound trucks, camera platforms, transportation of equipment and personnel to and from locations, and even the tray dollies in the cafeterias. They soon moved Communist units into those unions having jurisdiction over carpenters, painters, musicians, grips, and electricians. To control these trade unions was to control the motion picture industry.

—*Tenth Report* (1959), **California Un-American Activities Committee**

HUAC had won a decisive victory over the Red guilds in 1947, and against the Communist writers in particular. But as the war was coming to a close, another effort to control Hollywood was being waged by the men on the Left. As the 1956 Fund for the Republic study has documented, the Left hoped to bring the movie moguls to their knees by securing control of the trade unions, which included the craftsmen and technical folks that the better paid actors, directors, producers, and writers so depended on.

The Communist writers played a supportive but important role in this unionization effort. The fight was led by Herb Sorrell and his Conference of Studio Unions (CSU), which waged two furious strikes in 1945 and 1946 to bring the producers to heel. Sorrell himself was suspected of being a Communist Party member, and his CSU just barely deviated from the CP line during World War II—and then for just about eight weeks. Hollywood's Communist and left-wing writers, including several of the Hollywood Ten, would rally around Sorrell, but only after Moscow itself had given its blessing.

CSU VS. IA

The CSU, which had appeared in Hollywood shortly after WWII began, amounted to an unofficial association of largely left-wing unions within the American Federation of Labor (AFL). Sorrell was determined to vastly increase the CSU's membership by raiding workers from its major rival, the International Alliance of Theatrical Stage Employees (commonly known as the IA). Many sensible observers feared that Sorrell's tactics were part of a Communist effort "to control the motion picture industry."

The IA had a total of about sixty-five thousand members, with fifteen thousand of them in Hollywood. The majority of those fifteen thousand included projectionists, sound men, property men, set decorators, and scene shifters (or grips). The CSU had about nine thousand workers in Hollywood, some of them in the same line of work, and some in jobs considered more prestigious, such as cartoonists and story analysts. The Communists, who had a strong position in the CSU, viewed Sorrell as their ticket to power over the industry.

Sorrell and his CSU were eager to challenge the IA in a big way in 1944, with Sorrell's end goal a stranglehold on Hollywood labor. His purpose was to make the CSU powerful enough to dictate terms to the studios. Sorrell believed that if the thousands of men and women who actually filmed the stars, built the sets, and worked behind the scenes would strike on his say-so, the studios would be forced to heed his demands.

In October, Sorrell made a major move. He demanded from the producers immediate recognition of his own group of set decorators, a part of his Painters Union, which, in turn, was a major component of the umbrella CSU. The IA, however, had long been asking the producers to recognize *its* group of set decorators.

The IA appealed to the members of the War Labor Board after one of its key officials ruled in favor of Sorrell. And at the end of February 1945, the producers asked the National Labor Relations Board to determine which of the two rival set decorators' unions should be recognized. Then on March 12, with both governmental bodies still considering the issue, Sorrell's Painters Union suddenly struck.

But something unusual happened. Four of the CSU unions—the Screen Publicists, the Office Employees, the Screen Cartoonists, and the Story Analysts—failed to honor the picket line and went to work.[1] According to Sorrell himself, these unions were "influenced by the Communists." Despite the support Sorrell customarily had from the far Left, Sorrell explained, "when the strike started in March 1945, the Communists bitterly opposed the actions since it did not conform to their slogan of no-strike-during-wartime. A few Communists started a back-to-work movement which nearly wrecked the strike...."

Sorrell's defiance of the Party line in calling the strike produced a flurry of attacks from the Party and its publications. The *Daily People's World* (*PW*), the West Coast Party newspaper, scored Sorrell in an editorial titled "A Good Guy Gone Wrong." With the Soviet Union still needing America's help to defeat Nazi Germany, the U.S. Communist Party didn't want to encourage American labor to divert its attention from winning the war. Sorrell, however, was determined to grab a huge slice of workers from the IA.[2]

ROY BREWER TO THE RESCUE

Into the midst of this battle, as the Fund report notes, charged Roy Martin Brewer. A tough, balding IA labor leader, Brewer arrived in Hollywood on

March 12, the day the Sorrell strike began. Just thirty-six years old, a former IA executive and ex-president of the Nebraska Federation of Labor, he had come to Hollywood to direct labor strategy for the IA against its far-Left nemesis. He was concerned because Sorrell was "making hay" out of the IA's sordid past, including the racketeering convictions of its former president George Browne and Browne's personal representative in Hollywood, Willie Bioff.

Brewer's reputation, however, was untarnished. And he had the skills to take on Sorrell. The IA's president, Richard Walsh, had used the "no-strike-during-wartime" slogan—the position of American labor in general, as well as of the CP—to put pressure on Sorrell to yield on the jurisdictional dispute issue. And Walsh maintained that he wouldn't permit his workers to engage in the kind of militant clashes that the CSU had with management. Brewer, however, exploited a different angle. Under his aegis, the IA began unleashing a barrage of bulletins aimed at Sorrell, bringing up his support of the Communist Party— and its support of him—in the past.

By late April, the IA bulletins were noting not only the length of the strike and the man-hours and wages lost, but its presumed Communist instigation. The strike was said to have been designed long ago "by a certain political party for one reason: To Take Over and Control Organized Labor in the Motion Picture Industry." Sorrell was also accused of being "sympathetic and definitely interested in the communistic idea."[3] While the Party had not initially endorsed the strike—in reality it was vigorously opposing Sorrell's action—the bulletins exposed Sorrell for his "Communist associations," his support of the Party line in 1940 when he condemned FDR as a "warmonger," and his swift change of heart about the president after Hitler invaded the Soviet Union the next year.

Sorrell's personal embrace of a score of Communist causes was unearthed, including his backing of Communist labor leader Harry Bridges,[4] his support of avowed Communist state senatorial candidate LaRue McCormick, and his open sponsorship of the *Daily People's World*.[5] (The July 24, 1944, issue had run a blurb saying, "Both Sorrell and Lawson are supporting the [paper's] current $75,000 Victory Expansion Drive.") Brewer also convincingly argued that the Communists had long been interested in controlling Hollywood's labor unions and that Sorrell had long been considered a useful instrument for their goals. Brewer had plenty of evidence to back his claim.

In the late 1930s, Sorrell, along with Jeff Kibre and disgruntled "IA Progressives," had established the United Studio Technicians Guild (USTG). Sorrell was so close to the Communists at the time that he was viewed as a Party member himself, and, indeed, there is some evidence that he joined the Party in 1936 under the name Herb Stewart.[6] Kibre himself was a known Communist; he had been identified as a Party member by former comrades, and he amiably acknowledged he was one of those "Reds" in a letter to CP functionary Bob Reed.[7]

The CSU was considered the heir apparent of the Red-tinged USTG with good reason. When the CSU was formed in 1941, Sorrell, the pro-Communist founder of the USTG, was its president. The legal attorneys for the CSU strikers were a battery of Communist lawyers including Charles Katz and Ben Margolis, who later became attorneys for the Hollywood Ten. Sorrell's own attorney was a Red. Several officers of the unions that affiliated with the CSU were, in the words of the Fund study, "subsequently named before congressional committees as members of the Communist Party."[8]

Not just Sorrell but the CSU itself had, up until the strike, faithfully followed the CP line on a whole range of issues. The Fund for the Republic study would point out, "At no time in its history, prior to the 1945 strike, did the Conference of Studio Unions diverge from the Communist Party line."[9]

Although Brewer was wrong when he suggested the CP initiated the strike, he was right that the Party and Sorrell had been acting in tandem for most of the CSU's existence. And Brewer's charges against Sorrell began to resonate with the public and the producers when they saw that Sorrell and the American CP were working together again in July.

The major reason for the Communist turnabout in support of the strike? Moscow, no longer needing American help to crush Nazi Germany, felt free to renew class warfare tactics, condemn American foreign policy, and ramp up its war of subversion. As we have seen, this drastic change in the Party line was signaled with the publication in May 1945 of the letter by French Communist Jacques Duclos scolding American Party leader Earl Browder for abandoning revolutionary tactics. With Stalin switching to a hard line against America, the CP, as the Fund reports, "now marshalled its forces to support Sorrell and [the] CSU."[10] With the Party back on his side, Sorrell was emboldened; he was now in a far stronger position to continue his strike.

THE WRITERS TAKE THEIR STAND

Where did the radical writers stand in what was to become a historic struggle between the pro-Communist CSU and the anti-Communist IA? With the Communist Party.

The writers had not initially sided with the CSU. When the strike began in March of '45, the Executive Board of the Screen Writers Guild (SWG)—heavily influenced by the Left—took out an ad in the March 16 *Daily Variety* urging the CSU strikers to return to work. The ad chastised many of the parties involved, but singled out the CSU with this criticism: "We do not believe that the Conference of Studio Unions was justified in calling the present strike and violating the National Wartime No-Strike Pledge." The ad took the same line that would be consistently taken by the producers: that the CSU's jurisdictional dispute "was still under judication [sic] by the Government and would not have been jeopardized by waiting for a final review...."[11] Communists John Howard Lawson and William Pomerance, both important Guild members, staunchly defended the ad against Guild dissenters.

But after Moscow signaled in May through the Duclos letter that a tougher policy toward the United States was in the offing, Lawson and Pomerance switched sides, with Pomerance now arguing that "new developments" demanded that the SWG actively back the strike.[12] The Hollywood leftists, "led as always by the screenwriters," as CSU sympathizers Ceplair and Englund put it, began to weigh in heavily on the side of Sorrell. The four left-wing unions that had initially opposed the strike were now mounting the picket lines. By mid-summer, the Party was revving up massive support for the strike it had adamantly opposed.

The July 24 *Daily People's World* revealed how completely the Party had forgiven Sorrell by running this front-page headline: "SUPPORT THE STRIKE OF THE FILM UNIONS!" The loss of the strike, the *People's World* informed its readers, would have "disastrous consequences" for organized labor and would boost the goals of "reactionary forces." Abandoning the Party's own "no-strike pledge," the *People's World* now insisted "that the strike must be supported and must be won."[13]

Now that it was on board with Sorrell's strike, the *PW*'s campaign was relentless in its support. Hardly a day went by from July 24, 1945, until the strike ended in late October that the paper wasn't sounding the tocsin for the strikers' cause. The paper raked the studios and the IA over the coals, called law enforcement authorities keeping the picket lines open "goons" and "fascists," smothered its news pages and editorials with pro-strike opinion, and ran notices on "How to Help the Film Strikers." Other Communist organizations, including the National Lawyers Guild, the *Daily Worker*, and the Hollywood Independent Citizens Committee of Arts, Sciences and Professions (HICCASP), jumped onto the bandwagon as well.

With the Party firmly in Sorrell's corner, the Hollywood writers were ready to swarm to his cause. Future Hollywood Ten members flocked to the CSU's assistance. They would be especially eager to support him during Sorrell's last-ditch October effort to win the strike, a massive and violent show of force against Warner Bros., as we shall see. The Left would work itself into a frenzy against Warners' treatment of the strikers, even though Sorrell and Co. were clearly responsible for the mayhem.

The writers took the lead in championing the strikers even when their actions were patently illegal. Communist Lester Cole appeared before the SWG Board and urged it to call a membership meeting to vote on a resolution condemning Warners for violating "the civil liberties of the strikers" and promising that the writers would "not work at Warner Bros. until a specific settlement between the striking groups and the studio has been reached." Cole's motion was only narrowly defeated. A second motion, to provide legal assistance to writers arrested while picketing at Warners, was also beaten back.[14]

But the radical writers would come to the aid of the CSU, even if a closely divided SWG would never officially back the strike. Lawson took to the picket lines and was arrested. Other Communist and left-wing writers pretended to be picket-line "observers" but were essentially collecting any information to hamper law enforcement efforts intent on keeping the studios open, as required by the courts.

Among the Communist observers were SWG members John Wexley, Frank Tuttle, Robert Rossen, William Pomerance, and Dalton Trumbo. *Mission to Moscow*'s Howard Koch, a pro-Soviet writer who invariably backed Communist causes, also joined the "observer" team. Guild members Ring Lardner Jr., Sheridan Gibney, Ernest Pascal, and others sponsored an art auction to aid the strikers. (Lardner was a Party member, but Gibney and Pascal were not.) Meanwhile, at a mass demonstration in support of the CSU, Dalton Trumbo delivered a sizzling polemic against the producers for backing the allegedly corrupt and undemocratic IA.[15] Trumbo, editor of the SWG's flagship publication, *The Screen Writer*, also made certain that the monthly reflected his bias and supported Sorrell's strike.

TARGET: WARNER BROS.

Sorrell had unleashed his strike against the Hollywood studios in March of '45. But as the strike dragged on, he was hardly making headway in persuading the studios to give sole jurisdiction of the set decorators to the CSU. Nor had he been able to gravely injure the studios financially. So with growing support from the Left, Sorrell decided on a more audacious tactic: he would continue the strike against all the studios but would engage in a massive show of force against just one, the liberal Warner Bros. Studio in Burbank. If he could break Warners, he figured, the other studios would fall in line.

The move against Warners would gain Sorrell some traction. Sorrell's threat was hardly subtle: Warner Bros. must recognize his set decorators, or thousands of other workers that were part of his CSU would picket the Burbank studio and block the entrances to replacements from the IA or from anywhere else. If violence erupted, so be it. The mass picketing was initiated on October 5, reportedly as a result of a meeting at Hollywood Legion Stadium addressed by Sorrell and others.

According to the *Los Angeles Times*, a rank-and-filer at that meeting had asserted that "if we had 1,000 pickets at Warners in the morning, they couldn't open the studio. Let's do it."[16] Sorrell himself was quoted in a court complaint later filed by the producers as telling law enforcement officials, "We have been nice too long. We have decided to shut down the studio and win this strike." When the police said they were required to protect those entering studio gates, Sorrell was reported to have responded, "[I]f you do what you say, there will be some men killed."[17]

By early morning on the fifth, there were nearly eight hundred pickets. "The first incident," reported the *Los Angeles Times*, "occurred when a studio policeman attempted to drive into the plant. His car was overturned in front of the gate. A few minutes later, the same was done to cars of two other employees."[18]

As tensions grew and violent clashes became more frequent, Chief of Police Elmer Adams, heading Burbank's force of fifty-four officers, requested and received assistance from both the Glendale and Los Angeles police departments to quell the rioting and keep the studio open. Los Angeles County sheriff Eugene Biscailuz also lent assistance.

When the law enforcement authorities arrived, they initially separated the CSU strikers from the IA replacement workers. But at noon, Blayney Matthews, chief of police for the studios, forced his way through the picket line—he was punched in the face running the gauntlet—and then, when he reached the Warners premises, ordered the studio firemen to hose down the pickets. When the pickets attempted to rush the firemen, studio police hurled tear-gas bombs and followed up with more hosing. The pickets finally dispersed.

The violent disturbances raging sporadically at the main employees' entrance of the Burbank studio were "precipitated by mass picketing by the striking Conference of Studio Unions," the *Los Angeles Times* reported. Sorrell's role in the melee appeared clear enough to law enforcement authorities: he and eight aides were arrested by Burbank police on suspicion of violating the anti-rioting section of the state code.[19]

Some of Brewer's IA replacement workers engaged in violent acts to get into the blocked studio, but the cause of the violence was clearly Sorrell's shutting down the main studio entrance. The next day the strikers massed again, in defiance of an explicit court order. The *Times* noted that the CSU had "blatantly" disregarded a Superior Court ruling to limit its pickets at all entrances.

Hundreds of unionists jeered the reading of Judge Joseph W. Vickers's order by a deputy sheriff and continued "to jam solidly" the Olive Avenue gateway. The *Times'* report continues,

> At 1:30 P.M., Dep. Sheriff Frank Reap read Judge Vickers' order over a loud speaker. It called for the unions to restrict their pickets to four at the main gate, two at the administration publicity office, casting office and music department entrances and three at the north gate and laboratory entrance.
>
> As soon as Reap began reading, the pickets began booing. It was impossible to hear what the deputy was saying despite the amplification of his words.
>
> A few minutes later a copy of the temporary restraining order was served on Herbert Sorrell, president of the Conference of Studio Unions.... [Sorrell ignored the order.] The sardine-packed picket line of some 600 demonstrators presenting a solid human barricade across the gateway remained unchanged.[20]

Sorrell's violent and lawless tactics continued for weeks, with headlines telling the tale: "UNIONISTS DEFY COURT ON FILM PICKET LIMIT," "HUNDREDS BATTLE AT WARNER BROS. STUDIO, 40 PERSONS TREATED FOR INJURIES IN CLASHES," "RIOTING RENEWED IN STUDIO STRIKE," and so forth.

Those who wanted to work were mercilessly beaten if they tried to enter the studios. When police cleared the picket lines, many who went to work had to sleep overnight at the studio, fearing roaming squads of Sorrell toughs would attack anyone leaving for home. News accounts bolstered the studio's claim that several employees had been "badly beaten as they went to their cars, while others have had their cars stopped on lonely roads, where they have been assaulted."

Warners also made the claim—unrefuted, so far as I have been able to determine—that Sorrell's pickets engaged in numerous menacing acts toward Warner Brothers' workers such as taking down their license plate numbers, phoning them at work and at home, and photographing them as they approached the studio. Implicit in all these tactics were threats of physical harm, but explicit threats of violence were also made. Real physical harm, as we have seen, was also meted out. "And all this," noted Warners, "in an industry which is 100% unionized."

Sorrell appeared to thrive in the heated atmosphere. Less than a week after the action against Warners, *Daily Variety* reported that Sorrell intended to extend his mass-picketing tactic to the Universal and Republic Studios, "declaring both of them may be closed down before the end of the week."[21]

Sorrell's inflammatory tactics had energized the Left and many sympathetic liberals as well. Red writers like Cole and Trumbo were making plenty of noise with their anti–Warner Brothers tirades. Sorrell, however, had not won the support of any of the studios, which instead assailed his strikers for engaging in inexcusable violence. Two of the most important guilds, the anti-Communist Screen Actors Guild and even the Red-soaked Screen Writers Guild, failed to rally to Sorrell's side, though many of the SWG members did. (As we shall see, Ronald Reagan, SAG vice president at the time, would tangle directly with Sorrell the next year—and come to the conclusion that the union boss was both deceitful and under undue Communist influence.)

The AFL itself had never officially backed Sorrell. In fact, its president, William Green, had condemned Sorrell early on for his "violation of the no-strike pledge" that was AFL policy. Green insisted he "cease and desist" using the AFL's name in connection with "your strike" and demanded that he "terminate immediately the unjustified strike in which you are engaged."[22]

SETTLEMENT BREEDS NEW STRIKE

Nevertheless, Sorrell seemingly secured a big win on October 10. By a slim margin, the NLRB handed down a ruling that would enable Sorrell's set designers to defeat the IA's jurisdictional challenge. Even this victory, however, did not end the strike, since many other disputes had emerged. Nor did it end the violence. Sorrell himself now insisted the jurisdictional issue was just a "side show," a small part of what he was fighting for. So he conducted more massive and illegal picketing at Warners and other studios on the grounds that this would force them to come to terms quickly. Headlines provoked by Sorrell's actions again flooded the papers: "PICKETS CONTINUE WARNER BROS. SIEGE," "OFFICERS SWING CLUBS TO BREAK PICKET LINES," "POLICE BATTLE PICKETS AGAIN IN FILM STRIKE," "SCORES HURT IN STUDIO STRIKE."

All these clashes had been triggered by Sorrell's egging his men on to violate various restraining orders limiting the number of pickets at various studios, not just Warners. On October 24 the *Los Angeles Times* reported a grim "mob scene at the gates of Paramount Studio" as non-striking workers were seriously hurt braving the picket line. "Scores were injured," the *Times* noted, "some seriously, including a policeman slugged and trampled as he attempted to give safe-conduct to workers battling their way to their jobs." Mediator Eric Johnston, who had spent a hectic week attempting to settle the seven-month dispute, finally admitted failure.

At the end of October, however, the AFL Executive Council meeting in Cincinnati laid down the law, forcing a strike settlement. With all the disputing sides agreeing to abide by its conditions, the council ordered an immediate end to the strike, with final disposition of a series of other disputes, including the most intractable area of jurisdiction, left to three executive council members, or "arbitrators"—the so-called Three Wise Men.

On December 25, the three handed down a decision which ruled, among other things, that the IA lost jurisdiction over the Set Decorators, but the CSU-backed Carpenters lost jurisdiction to the IA over who would erect the sets in the studios—a ruling that would pave the way for a Carpenters-CSU brawl with the IA in little less than a year.

So ended the first important CSU strike. But Sorrell's determination to destroy Brewer and his IA had not been softened. The next year would produce more Red fireworks, largely fueled by Sorrell's radical union. But the upshot would resemble Pickett's Charge more than the landing at Normandy. And Ronald Reagan would play a crucial role in Sorrell's defeat.

CHAPTER TWENTY-EIGHT

REAGAN OUTWITS THE REDS

The strike was "over," but nothing much had been settled. The NLRB had made its ruling, but that same ruling would have come down without the strike. The strikers, out of work for eight months, were to return to their jobs, but without any pay increase or improvement in working conditions—or even certainty they could get their old jobs back. Some of the significant promises Sorrell had made to strikers to entice them to return to work turned out to be false. Moreover, dozens of issues, including the jurisdictional ones, would still have to be worked out by the arbitrators.

Despite their NLRB "win," Sorrell and his CSU were hardly popular, not only because the strikes had dented studio profits but also because of the violence they had unleashed. So it was Brewer of the rival IA, not Sorrell of the CSU, who was beginning to make real headway in the movie industry. As the Fund for the Republic study notes, "Brewer was working with the producers now, trying to convince them that it was to their interest to deal with him rather than with Sorrell. He was lining up support within the AFL. He had become active in community work and Democratic Party politics. He was gaining influence and prestige in the MPA; the anti-Communists were full of admiration for his success in whittling away at Sorrell's prestige."[1]

Sorrell suffered another blow in July of 1946 when he was put on trial by the Los Angeles Central Labor Council for being a Communist. Though Sorrell was never convicted by the Council, the trial exposed his radical leanings, and the Council condemned him for his actions.

A "CLARIFICATION" MUDDIES THE WATERS

Sorrell may have been temporarily thrown off stride, but he was still primed for revenge against Brewer. Desperate to make another stab at defeating the anti-Communist labor leader, the CSU helped launch a second major strike in the summer of '46. The seeds of the strike were sown when the Carpenters Union, backed by the CSU, insisted that its men were entitled to regain jurisdiction over the set-erection jobs that had been awarded to the IA in the 1945 strike settlement. The Carpenters Union based its demands on an August 1946 "clarification" of the '45 settlement, which became a subject of a raging dispute.

The IA insisted that the December '45 settlement, accepted by national AFL leaders, could not have been clearer: Brewer's folks were entitled to construct and erect the movie sets. No "clarification," it maintained, could change this basic truth. The producers agreed. And so, eventually, did the three AFL arbitrators, the "Wise Men" who had handed down both the 1945 ruling and the controversial "clarification."

But meanwhile, seizing on the "clarification," the Carpenters and the CSU ordered their members to stop work on sets built by Brewer's IA. The studios discharged those who refused to work on these "hot sets," requesting the IA to furnish replacements. Sorrell then delivered an ultimatum to the producers: rehire the 1,500 workers who had been fired, or face another ferocious strike.

When the producers refused, Sorrell's aggressively radical CSU issued a strike call in late September at a six-thousand-member mass meeting at the American Legion Stadium in Los Angeles. The next day the CSU began forming picket lines at seven major studios. It was, as Yogi Berra liked to say, *déjà vu* all over again.

Virtually all non-CSU union members were willing to cross those picket lines since they considered this a jurisdictional strike, not a strike for wages. They were also growing tired of Sorrell's tactics. The non-CSU unions, in short, were on the side of the producers, whose spokesman, Byron Price, observed, "This is a jurisdictional strike. The issue is so recognized by the AFL. Phoney talk about a lockout will not change the situation. Only a few hours ago, the studios informed Sorrell that the Carpenters and others could come back if they would do the work assigned to them, which they had refused to do for purely jurisdictional reasons."

Just as in the first strike, mass picketing, mass arrests, and plenty of violence were regular occurrences, with the CSU and Sorrell stoking the fires. Sorrell could not seem to open his mouth without hurling incendiary threats against the studios.

The Communists and their supporters in the various guilds and unions were also heavily involved in this new strike. The Screen Writers Guild and the Screen Actors Guild maintained their neutrality, though the Left continued to work feverishly to get both Guilds to back Sorrell. If either or both had backed the radical labor leader, that might have been just the rocket boost Sorrell needed to defeat Brewer. The SWG's very liberal president, Emmet Lavery, kept his Guild neutral in this new strike, with the SWG ruling that the writers would abide by the no-strike clause in their contracts.

RONALD REAGAN'S CRUCIAL ROLE

Ronald Reagan would play the lead role in persuading the Screen Actors Guild to reject Sorrell's arguments and thus help deal a crippling blow to the pro-Communist labor leader and his Red allies in Hollywood. (Reagan's skillful handling of the matter would also get him elected SAG president in 1947.)

Reagan was what he would call "a hemophilic liberal" in the immediate postwar period, but he soon had his eyes opened to the tactics of the Communist Party and the workings of the Left in the guilds and in the unions. He joined several nice-sounding organizations but quit them when he realized they were controlled by Party members. One of these was the Hollywood Independent Citizens Committee of Arts, Sciences and Professions (HICCASP), a Red front that was conspicuously supporting Sorrell.

HICCASP was a home to movie celebrities, many of whom Reagan respected, and when originally asked, he was honored to fill a vacancy on its board. He later attended a HICCASP meeting crowded with left-wingers, and all was harmony until Jimmy Roosevelt—son of the late FDR—introduced a proposal to have the board sign a declaration repudiating Communism.

That set off a Kilkenny brawl, and Reagan jumped in to back Roosevelt. He was then subjected to a string of epithets and boos. As Reagan describes things in *Where's the Rest of Me?*, "Dalton Trumbo, the writer, was very vociferous [in opposition]. Most vehement of all, however, was John Howard Lawson. He persisted in waving a long finger under my nose and telling me off."[2]

Reagan and others gathered later at the apartment of actress Olivia de Havilland, known for her roles in *Gone with the Wind*, *The Adventures of Robin Hood*, and other successful pictures. "Olivia," writes Reagan, "had suspected that perhaps HICCASP was being infiltrated when she had been given a Trumbo-written speech to deliver." She had refused to give it, because it was "so full of Communist-oriented tidbits." (Trumbo admits in his personal papers that he was livid when de Havilland dumped his speech.) The gathering at de Havilland's decided to draft a very reasonable-sounding anti-Communist statement, which repudiated Communism, but only in this country, perhaps in an effort to attract a few more votes in the left-leaning organization.

The resolution read, "We reaffirm our belief in free enterprise and the democratic system and repudiate communism as desirable for the United States." A few nights later, the authors of the declaration met with those who had opposed Roosevelt's effort to get HICCASP to denounce Communism.

Lawson, as Reagan tells it, was furious, insisting HICCASP would never adopt such a statement, though he assured Reagan—falsely, as it turns out—that he, personally, was not a Communist. When de Havilland presented the declaration to a HICCASP executive committee, she was the only one to back it. "I resigned from the board by telegram that night," writes Reagan. "So did some others. Very shortly, HICCASP gave its last groan and expired as an organization."[3]

Reagan had helped torpedo a major Hollywood organization backing Sorrell. He was to deal a more direct blow to the CSU when he became the Screen Actors Guild's chief fact-gatherer on the epic Sorrell-Brewer struggle. The key questions before the SAG were these: *Should it back Sorrell's pickets? Was this just a jurisdictional strike, as the producers claimed, or was it a legitimate strike over wages and other matters as well, as Sorrell's CSU maintained?*

Many members had long had twinges of sympathy for the strikers. They had little knowledge about the strike, and they may have been persuaded by the propaganda being pushed by Sorrell, the Hollywood Communists, and the Communist Party itself. But, largely on Reagan's recommendation, the SAG volunteered to act as a dispassionate observer between the two unyielding sides. Reagan became the indefatigable point man in the SAG investigation. He held marathon meetings and telephone conversations with all the major players, including Sorrell and Brewer, the Carpenters Union president Bill Hutcheson, and the three AFL arbitrators who were determining the meaning of the sometimes-confusing December 1945 strike settlement. The bottom line for Reagan, after a lengthy investigation: the CSU had gone on strike because it misinterpreted—perhaps deliberately—the August 1946 "clarification" issued by the labor arbitrators as transferring jurisdiction over set erections to the Carpenters Union. Reagan had other issues with Sorrell, but this was by far the most critical.

Reagan's view had been crystallized in his attempt to pin down what the "clarification" really meant in a meeting he and a group of well-known actors had with the three labor arbitrators. Along with such stars as Walter Pidgeon, Dick Powell, Robert Taylor, and Gene Kelly, Reagan tirelessly questioned the arbitrators in a room at the Morrison Hotel in Chicago at the time of the AFL's national convention in October.

To a man, the AFL arbitrators claimed they had never wavered from their December 1945 directive awarding set-erection to Brewer's IA. They admitted that their issuance of the clarification "was a mistake." They had issued it on the urging of Carpenters Union president Bill Hutcheson, but they had only intended to clear up any misunderstanding of the '45 directive, not to undermine that directive's decision entitling the IA stagehands to build and erect movie sets. Hutcheson, they stressed, had known their intentions at the time. Gene Kelly, a left-wing friend of Sorrell, asked the three officials whether they meant the IA had control over both the "construction" and the "erection" of a set on a movie stage. The arbitrators gave a resounding "yes."

That meeting turned out to be pivotal in persuading Reagan and the others to side against Sorrell. The "Wise Men" had authoritatively restated their position that the IA should be in charge of building and assembling movie sets. Sorrell was informed of what the arbitrators had reaffirmed, but he still continued the strike. According to Reagan, Sorrell had backed the strike in the face of clear warnings that his "men could be replaced—and in the face of CSU agreements that there would be no work stoppage because of jurisdictional quarrels." Wages and improved working conditions, Reagan concluded, had *not* been a central point to the dispute.

Reagan had soaked up the complicated information on the dispute like a sponge. When folks wanted an impartial explanation, Reagan was the "go-to" guy who could make headway even with those on the Left. Actor William Holden, for instance, asked Reagan to attend a meeting at Ida Lupino's where the Left was planning to propagandize actors on behalf of the CSU. Ida herself was an innocent, but the large gathering was chaired by actor Sterling Hayden, who years later disclosed an interesting piece of information before HUAC: he had been a secret Communist at the time and had been attempting to manipulate the attendees on behalf of Sorrell.

The meeting began with laurels heaped on Sorrell and much bad-mouthing of Brewer—and with the SAG itself getting knocked about for playing peacemaker instead of teaming up with the CSU against Brewer's IA. When Reagan was eventually given the floor by Hayden, he countered the pro-Sorrell faction for about forty minutes, then took questions. Reagan was booed and subjected to name-calling, but he had made a solid case for SAG neutrality, even prompting actor John Garfield, a Communist fellow traveler, to tell the crowd to listen to Reagan, since he knew more about the subject than many of his fellow comrades. (For speaking out so boldly on behalf of Reagan, Garfield was bawled out at the event by his Red friends.)

Reagan's mastery of the subject was critical in keeping the SAG out of Sorrell's clutches. The Guild swung behind the actor's position: that the SAG must stay out of the Sorrell-Brewer contest since it was strictly a jurisdictional dispute. Reagan had managed to convince the Guild that Sorrell had not told the truth on several occasions—including his claim that the arbitrators had told him personally something far different from what the arbitrators themselves told the SAG representatives at the Morrison they had said to Sorrell.

Reagan could bask in his victory at an SAG membership meeting at the Hollywood Legion Stadium on October 2, 1946. The meeting was a star-studded affair, with such big names as Frank Sinatra, Henry Fonda, and Robert Mitchum on hand. Not only was Reagan honored as the keynote speaker, but those present exulted at the SAG Executive Board's decision—heavily influenced by Reagan—urging its members to cross the picket lines.[4]

Every speaker who opposed backing Sorrell was "enthusiastically cheered," noted the *Hollywood Reporter*, "showing conclusively that the sentiment of the majority of the Guild members supported the board's recommendation."[5]

HAYDEN HAILS REAGAN

Reagan's role as the Communists' prickly hair shirt would later be confirmed by actor Sterling Hayden, the actor who had faced off with Reagan at the meeting at Ida Lupino's. In his appearance before HUAC in 1951, Hayden would freely admit his past Communist Party activities. A handsome bear of a man and a genuine war hero, he had joined the Marines early in WWII, fought with the Communist Partisans in Yugoslavia against the Nazis, and performed daring exploits behind enemy lines with the Office of Strategic Services, the forerunner of the Central Intelligence Agency. He became a devoted supporter of Communists both here and abroad, and after the war he formally joined the Party for six months, from June 1946 to mid-December of the same year.

Hayden's HUAC testimony was a tribute to Reagan's capacity to take on Hollywood's Communists. Hayden revealed that he had joined a secret cell of the Party that included Hollywood writers Robert Lees and Abraham Polonsky and that his cell, ranging from ten to upward of twenty people, frequently met in Polonsky's home. Hayden was instructed by the cell's leaders to contact a group of Sorrell-friendly actors and actresses "to swing the Screen Actors Guild in favor of Sorrell's CSU."[6]

How had the tactic fared? "I am sure, as a matter of fact," Hayden replied, "the move was very unsuccessful. It ran into the board of directors of the Screen Actors Guild, and particularly into Ronald Reagan, who was a one-man battalion against this thing. He was very vocal and clear thinking on it. I don't think many people realized how complex [the problem] was. I know I didn't. There was very little headway made."[7]

The Screen Actors Guild tried several times to help settle the dispute. In one last attempt, the SAG selected Joseph Keenan of the national AFL staff to serve as a mediator. According to the Fund study, Guild officials believed Keenan's attempts failed because "the CSU lawyers constantly raised new issues or backed away from the consequences of already settled questions. In any case, the actions of the CSU attorneys convinced the actors' group that the CSU was not seriously interested in settling the strike."[8]

The CSU was on the ropes when its members, weary of the fruitless strike and its burdens, began to return to work with IA union cards. When the IA won a decisive NLRB election in 1949, the strike finally came to an end.

Brewer and Reagan blamed the Communists and the far Left for the endless disruptions, and it is difficult to dispute their assessment. The SAG's Reagan, like the SWG's Lavery, lamented that the Reds never appeared to want a reasonable solution to problems but were forever fomenting chaos and strife to help them gain control of the movie industry.

In November 1950 the National Executive Board of the AFL's Painters Union declared that Sorrell "had willfully and knowingly associated with groups subservient to the Communist Party line." He was ordered not to hold any union office for five years and not to attend any union meetings during that period. In February 1952, Sorrell's local union was dissolved, and he dropped out of all union activities.[9]

CHAPTER TWENTY-NINE

THE SILENCING OF ALBERT MALTZ

ollywood's leading liberals topped off the October 1997 celebration of the Ten and other blacklisted artists by presenting plaques engraved with the First Amendment to Ring Lardner and Paul Jarrico. Lardner, as we have seen, was a member of the Hollywood Ten who relied on the First Amendment in refusing to say before HUAC in 1947 whether he was a Communist. Jarrico was not a member of the Ten, but he, too, had been a Communist. He had ducked behind the Fifth Amendment—not the First—when in 1951 he refused to respond to questions about his hard-core Communist Party activities. He took the Fifth when asked if Richard Collins, his screenwriter collaborator, had accurately testified that he had been a Party member—and then once more when asked if the Party was dedicated to overthrowing the American government by force and violence.[1]

Despite the devoted Communist Party activities of both these men, Dan Petrie Jr. of the Writers Guild of America stressed that this special First Amendment award was "in recognition of your devotion to those words and to your 50-year struggle to uphold them, for yourself and all Americans."[2] Petrie's words inspired a standing ovation for these longtime Stalinists. But the Joe Stalin whom Lardner and Jarrico had so faithfully served for so much of their lives hardly stood for "free speech" and "artistic creativity," phrases that supporters of the Hollywood Stalinists have embraced with such fervor over the years. Indeed, Stalin was famous for murdering and imprisoning virtually anyone, particularly writers, not inclined toward his brand of totalitarian Communism.

The Communist Party USA, Stalin's major vehicle in the United States, never much cared for First Amendment rights either, although the CP loudly championed those rights in defense of Communists engaged in espionage and other forms of subversion. In fact the CP was perfectly willing to compel Hollywood writers to rewrite books and scripts if they didn't scrupulously toe the Party line.

PARTY CHIEFTAINS BULLY SCHULBERG

The famous director Elia Kazan (*A Streetcar Named Desire, On the Waterfront*), who was a Party member in the 1930s, tells how the comrades tried to force Budd Schulberg to alter his novel, *What Makes Sammy Run?*, the story of an ambitious and ruthless Hollywood heel. Hollywood Ten member John Howard Lawson, the CP's enforcer of the Party line, became the "point man in the attack," writes Kazan, with heavy pressure put on Schulberg's wife and "the man who was his closest friend."

Schulberg himself discussed his plight in hearings before HUAC in May of 1951. Schulberg said that in 1937 he joined a Marxist society that by 1940 had turned into a Communist Party group. Those who joined became big-name writers and directors and, with one exception, never turned on the Party. Among those in the group: Richard Collins, Paul Jarrico, Ring Lardner Jr., Waldo Salt, Lester Cole, and Herbert Biberman.

When Schulberg informed the group in 1939 that he was going to write *What Makes Sammy Run?* on the basis of previously published articles, their reaction "was not favorable." His writings were deemed too individualistic for the "progressive [read Communist] forces in Hollywood." He was advised his project "should either be abandoned or discussed with some higher authority than the group before I began to work on it." Richard Collins (*Song of Russia, Thousands Cheer*) urged him to see Lawson.

So, said Schulberg, "I went to see Lawson." The upshot was that Schulberg was supposed to write something along the lines of the "proletarian novel," a book "about factories, about strikes, about opposition to capitalists and so forth." Looking back, Schulberg remarks, "I think it was very similar to what the writers in the Soviet Union were being told at the same time. They were being told that anything that helped the 5-year plan...was a good book."[3]

Schulberg chucked the advice of stalwart Party members, moved to Vermont, and wrote his novel without Party scrutiny. He came back to Hollywood in February or March of 1940, though his book wouldn't be published for another year. When he returned, Collins upbraided him for having failed to submit his manuscript to Lawson.

Schulberg says he viewed himself as out of the group and the Party, but he felt the ideological tug of his ex-comrades to the extent that he did consult Lawson, who urged him to submit his manuscript to the group for monitoring. With nothing resolved, he was then sent to V. J. Jerome, Lawson's boss and a National Committee member of the Communist Party. Schulberg met Jerome in an apartment on Hollywood Boulevard.

"I didn't do much talking," Schulberg recalls. "I remember being told that my entire attitude was wrong; that I was wrong about writing, wrong about this book, wrong about the party, wrong about the so-called peace movement at that particular time [during the Hitler-Stalin Pact, which Schulberg opposed]. I gathered from the conversation, in no uncertain terms, that I was wrong." When he left, "I felt maybe, almost for the first time, that this was to me the real face of the party.... I had talked to someone rigid and dictatorial who was trying to tell me how to live my life...I didn't want to have anything more to do with them."

Schulberg never submitted his novel for CP review. He insisted that he had, at least intellectually, left the Party when he went to Vermont—although it may have taken the Jerome incident to cement his decision to give up his Party membership. Schulberg was still a man of the Left, however, and when his book came out in March of 1941, the CP was obviously puzzled as to how to treat both the novel and Schulberg.

Initially, Charles Glenn lauded Schulberg in his April 7 *Daily Worker* review for having written a "bold and daring work" and claimed that he "must be considered an important 'comer.'" But after a pummeling by Party ideologues, Glenn switched his view. He disclosed to *Worker* readers some two weeks later that "[o]n the basis of quite lengthy discussion on the book [meaning a harangue by CP ideologues], I've done a little reevaluating.... To say I felt more than a trifle silly when these weaknesses [in the Schulberg book] were called to my attention is putting it a bit mildly." Schulberg's novel was now terribly flawed. It was of a piece with the "rather smelly campaigns" movie executives were staging to sell "Bundles for Britain"—which "progressive" Hollywood deplored during the Hitler-Stalin Pact.

After his ideological drubbing, Glenn wondered how Schulberg's "conscience" had allowed him "to show only the dirt and the filth" embraced by Wall Street "capitalists" and failed to promote the fight for the guilds and the Stalinist "pro-peace" line with Hitler. (Schulberg had long opposed the Pact, and he even discussed this grand heresy with the Communist group he had once belonged to, according to his testimony before HUAC in 1951.) For Schulberg's failure as a Red propagandist, the Communist Party had directed Glenn to savage Schulberg's "conscience." The panning, however, did not persuade Schulberg to rejoin the Party.[4]

LAWSON GOES AFTER DMYTRYK

Browbeating writers to toe the Communist Party line was standard operating procedure for the Hollywood Reds. Director Edward Dmytryk, the sole member of the Ten ever to wholeheartedly repudiate the Party, revealed that Lawson reprimanded both him and producer Adrian Scott in the summer of 1945 for removing "anti-fascist" scenes from the melodrama *Cornered*, in which Dick Powell plays a Canadian pilot who tracks down the Nazi killer of his French bride in Argentina. Lawson's ire, as described in Dmytryk's HUAC testimony and his memoir, *Odd Man Out*, was caused by Dmytryk and Scott's hiring a rewrite man, John Paxton, to redo much of John Wexley's original script. Paxton left much of Wexley's agitprop on the cutting-room floor, and Wexley demanded that the omissions be reinserted into the picture—even though the film had been completed and the studio was in the process of making prints to send to the theaters. Squeezing Wexley's propaganda back into the film was clearly impossible, but Dmytryk and Scott were raked over the coals in several Communist sessions for having failed to keep Wexley's material in the movie.

What Dmytryk specifically objected to was not Wexley's message but the fact that Wexley wrote "long speeches, propaganda—they were all anti-Nazi and anti-Fascist, but went to extremes in following the party line on the nose." This sort of speechifying just didn't make for good drama, Dmytryk pointed out, so they needed a rewrite man to rescue the film from utter boredom.

Both Dmytryk and Scott, who also became one of the Ten, were put through the wringer by Lawson and other Party comrades in several meetings. They were confronted by Lawson, Richard Collins, and other Communist screenwriters who agreed with Wexley's complaints. The whole attack, Dmytryk said, boiled down to this: that by removing the material by Wexley, "we were making a pro-Nazi picture instead of an anti-Nazi picture." (Anyone who sees *Cornered* on video can confirm that it is by no means a *pro*-Nazi film.)

Dmytryk and Scott refused to admit the accuracy of the charges and were supported by Albert Maltz (another Hollywood Ten member) and Ben Barzman, but the all-important Lawson sided with Wexley. He was the "'high lama' of the Communist Party at that time," Dmytryk testified. "If there was a switch in the Party line, he explained it. If there were any decisions to be made, they went to John Howard Lawson. If there was any conflict within the Communist Party, he was the one who settled it."

Nevertheless, Scott and Dmytryk wouldn't budge. Scott, says Dmytryk, "was anxious to pursue the matter in the hope of arriving at a reconciliation with the party. He arranged a luncheon meeting with Lawson at the Gotham Deli. It was cold, unpleasant, and unsatisfactory. Lawson was unfriendly and uncommunicative, offering no explanation for his behavior. For him, there was no possible compromise on the matter, or, more particularly, on the principles involved. His final words were, 'For the time being consider yourselves out of the party. When you decide that you can accept party discipline, we'll explore the situation further.' Wearing his usual, mirthless smile, he left us."[5]

Despite Lawson's reproach, the Party did not immediately drop Dmytryk from its membership rolls, nor did Dmytryk precisely resign from the Party at that time. He appeared, in his words, to "drift away" from Communism. He remained "active in what are now called Communist Party fronts.... I was still teaching at the People's Education Center until 1947. I was on the board of the Arts, Sciences and Professions Council and I was a member of the 'Hollywood Ten.'" Dmytryk's final break with Communism did not come until he left prison in 1950. But that clash with Lawson began the long process that eventually inspired him to turn against his former comrades.[6]

THE MALTZ EPISODE

The most famous incident of this kind involved Albert Maltz, another Hollywood Ten member. A short-story writer, novelist, and screenwriter, Maltz stirred up a furor on the Left in an article published in the February 12, 1946, *New Masses*, an official weekly publication of the Communist Party. In a carefully hedged piece, Maltz wrote that "much of leftwing artistic activity" had stifled creativity because writers on the Left had too narrowly interpreted the phrase "art as a weapon." Somehow these four words had been converted from a "profound analytic, historical insight" into a vulgar slogan that has come to mean that "Art should be a weapon as a leaflet is a weapon," serving "immediate political ends." The result of this phrase's misuse, he argued, was that even a "thin" literary work, so long as it followed the CP line, would "be reviewed warmly."

Works that are "rich in human insight" but don't follow the Party line closely enough or are written by Trotskyites "will be indicted severely, mauled or beheaded." Yet many of these works contain passages favorable to downtrodden workers or, as in John Steinbeck's case, even passages favorable to revolutionaries. Maltz's mild suggestion touched off a firestorm. He was pilloried in article upon article in the *New Masses*, the *Daily Worker*, and other official Communist Party publications.

The *Daily Worker*'s literary critic, Samuel Sillen, launched a series of abusive attacks, charging that Maltz was undermining class warfare, the core of

Communism, and Lenin himself. The *Worker's* most popular columnist, Mike Gold, opined that Maltz had directed a "veiled attack on the Communist move-ment" and laid "a new basis for conciliating Trotskyism...." He charged Maltz with lining up with Red "renegades" and "rats" like Max Eastman and Eugene Lyons, "who have been campaigning with endless lies and slanders for war on the Soviet Union." Indeed, said Gold, Maltz "seems to have let the luxury and phony atmosphere of Hollywood at last poison him."[7]

Heavy-duty criticism also came from novelist Howard Fast and Commu-nist Party biggie William Foster, the man who had been instrumental in depos-ing "soft-liner" Earl Browder as head of the CP. And John Howard Lawson, the Party's omnipresent enforcer in Hollywood, condemned Maltz for sabotaging the "class struggle" and thus rejecting "the contemporary responsibility of the artist. He also rejects, less explicitly but nonetheless sweepingly, the fundamen-tal principles of Marxism."[8]

Maltz had been so politically incorrect that he was compelled to go on "trial" in two face-to-face encounters with several comrades. Former Communist Leo-pold Atlas, whom Lawson had drawn into the Communist Political Association (the temporary successor to the Party for fourteen months), vividly described Maltz's plight to the House Un-American Activities Committee in 1953.

Maltz, said Atlas, had evidently committed some "great heresy," and an "execution squad, shipped in from the East, came marching in." When Maltz made an effort to defend himself, "almost instantly all sorts of howls went up to protest against it." A few in the group, including Atlas, made "small attempts to speak" in Maltz's favor, but "we were literally shouted down...the wolves were loose and you should have seen them. It was a spectacle for all time."

From one corner "Alvah Bessie, with bitter vituperation and venom, rose up and denounced Maltz. From another corner Herbert Biberman rose and spouted elaborate mouthfuls of nothing, his every accent dripping with hatred. Others, from every part of the room, jumped in on the kill." The merits of the article aside, said Atlas, "this spectacle was appalling to me...Maltz, I knew, was an associate of theirs of long standing. He was at that time a person of some literary stature and, as I then believed, a man of considerable personal integrity. The least one might have accorded him, even in disagreement, was some mea-sure of understanding, some measure of consideration, but not they. They worked over him with every verbal fang and claw at their command; every ax and bludgeon, and they had plenty. They evidently were past masters at this sort of intellectual cannibalism."

Maltz refused to break, so the meeting was finally adjourned in the wee hours of the morning to be reconvened a week later, again at Abraham Polonsky's home. Atlas says he was fully resolved that if Maltz walked out on his inquisitors, "I would be the first to follow him out." But at the next meeting, he relates, "they completely broke him." This "hyena attack…continued with a rising snarl of triumph, and made him crawl and recant. This entire episode is an extremely distasteful thing for me to recall. I remember feeling a deep anguish for him as a human being, that his closest friends for years, or at least associates, would treat him so shamefully, so uncharitably, so wolfishly. Whatever the cause, his friends had no right, in all decency, to humiliate and break him in this fashion. Or if they did, they were not his friends."[9]

Maltz not only abjectly apologized at the meeting but groveled in print as well. In an article appearing in the April 9 *New Masses*, Maltz, imitating victims of the Moscow purge trials, publicly clawed himself bloody for being guilty of "revisionism." He had, he confessed, "distorted Marxism, turning half-truths into total untruths, splitting ideology from its class base, denying the existence of class struggle in society, converting Marxism from a science of society and struggle into apologetics for monopoly exploitations." And so on. He even assailed those, like Atlas, who thought he had been too harshly criticized, explaining to his more squeamish defenders that he had made "fundamentalist errors" and hence "sharp discussion was required."[10]

The Maltz episode, widely publicized in the major Establishment media at the time, revealed beyond a quibble what it really meant to be a Hollywood Red. There could be no First Amendment rights beyond some very narrow parameters laid down by the American CP. Only in a land of fantasy would Lardner and Jarrico, largely unrepentant Reds who had supported such Party behavior and had never, ever deviated from the Party line themselves during Stalin's reign, be considered First Amendment heroes.

CHAPTER THIRTY

DALTON TRUMBO, COMMUNIST CONFORMIST

Dalton Trumbo was not only one of the more prominent members of the Hollywood Ten but one of the liveliest. He was slight, mustachioed, and extremely witty. Few could be in his presence without admiring his energy, quickness of mind, and above all his tenacity. His courting of Cleo Fincher proved he was a man to be reckoned with.

He met her at McDonnell's (not McDonald's), a Los Angeles drive-in, proposed to her that night, pursued her for more than a year before lining up a formal date, and then, when she wedded her longtime steady instead of him, hired a private detective to prove the two had not been legally married. As Trumbo had guessed, her husband, called just "Hal" by biographer Bruce Cook, had not been legally divorced when the wedding ceremony took place.

Trumbo, with the polygamous "husband" now publicly vowing to "kill him," ran off with Cleo to another town, his driver packing heat for self-defense against the infuriated Hal. Cleo successfully filed for an annulment, Trumbo wedded her at his mother's apartment in 1938, and the two remained married until his death nearly forty years later.

He was a writer of novels, plays, and more than a score of motion pictures during his lifetime, including such successful movies as *Kitty Foyle*, *Thirty Seconds over Tokyo*, *Roman Holiday*, *Exodus*, *Spartacus*, and *Papillon*. Stars including Gregory Peck, Kirk Douglas, Audrey Hepburn, and Steve McQueen graced his films, and by 1945 he commanded top dollar from the major studios.

SCREENWRITING UNDER AN ALIAS

After spending ten months in jail for refusing to respond to HUAC's question as to whether he had ever been a Communist, Trumbo emerged in 1951 as a leader of a group of blacklisted writers initially located in Mexico, then in L.A., who eked out a living by composing scripts for Hollywood under assumed names. Using such aliases as Sam Jackson, Peter Finch, and Robert Rich, Trumbo penned twelve scripts in a year and a half after returning to the United States, selling his work to independent producers of low-budget pictures.

By 1956, he had made enough to repay his debts and was helping other comrades, such as Albert Maltz, secure pseudonymous script-writing jobs in Hollywood. According to Cook, he had become a "one-man clearing house" for information on writing gigs, "passing on to others work he couldn't handle."

Trumbo's most celebrated script during this period, *The Brave One*, received unusual attention. The movie, about a courageous bull whose life is spared, had been nominated for Best Motion Picture Story of 1956. On Oscar night, 1957, actress Deborah Kerr dramatically announced that the winning scriptwriter is "Robert Rich!" The audience appeared puzzled; no one seemed to know who Rich was.

Jesse Lasky Jr., vice president of the Screen Writers Guild, had no real clue either, but accepted the award for his "friend," excusing his absence on the grounds that his wife was about to give birth. As was quickly discovered, Robert Rich, honored writer, SWG member, prospective father, and the man Lasky had called his "friend," did not even exist! The word got out that Rich was really Dalton Trumbo.

All of this turned into something of a mini-scandal for the SWG and those involved in handing out the Oscars. And no one was more delighted with the awkwardness he had caused Hollywood than Trumbo, who would neither confirm nor deny that he was the real author.

Trumbo relished the high irony. Screenwriters ostensibly banished from the film industry because they had been accurately accused of being Moscow's willing pawns were still writing for the movies under the table. (Albeit for less pay and under phony names. In 1975, Hollywood finally awarded Trumbo the Oscar he had won nineteen years earlier.)[1]

Blacklisted writers were not only in great demand at this time—they came both talented and cheap, since they couldn't write under their own names—but were easily picking up honors. The next year the Frenchman Pierre Boulle, who could barely speak English, let alone write it, won the Academy Award for adapting for the screen his own novel, *The Bridge over the River Kwai*. Insiders knew that the script had actually been written by two blacklisted writers, Michael Wilson and Carl Foreman. Two years later, Nathan E. Douglas shared an Oscar for Best Original Screenplay with Harold Smith for *The Defiant Ones*. "Douglas" turned out to be Nedrick Young, who had never recanted his Communist Party membership.

BREAKING THE BLACKLIST

Trumbo won the honor of being the first blacklisted writer to see his real name in the film credits. He got the momentous break he had long been seeking in 1960, largely courtesy of director Otto Preminger. Preminger had been eager to film Leon Uris's novel *Exodus* and had already hired the actors. Production was set for April.

By the first of January, the script had already been worked on by Leon Uris himself and by blacklisted writer Albert Maltz. Preminger thought their products unusable, so in desperation he turned to Trumbo, who—after marathon sessions with Preminger himself—furnished him with an acceptable story. Preminger then decided to cause a stir: he leaked to the *New York Times* that the blacklisted Trumbo was doing his film and would receive credit.

The *Times* story caused a bit of an uproar but sparked no great outrage from the public. Trumbo, the media revealed, had also been working for Kirk Douglas's firm, Bryna Productions, for some time and was currently rewriting a script based on Communist Howard Fast's novel *Spartacus* for Douglas. He had signed on to do the movie, however, under the pseudonym Sam Jackson, and Douglas himself was nervous about giving Trumbo screen credit. But when *Spartacus* came out in October, Trumbo's name was up on the big screen for all the public to see. Preminger's leak had forced Douglas to do what he had wanted to do anyway. *Exodus*, which hit the box office in December, carried Trumbo's name as well, just as Preminger had promised.

Despite HUAC, the 1947 Waldorf Declaration, and the blacklist, Trumbo would receive screen credits for what proved to be two successful films. Left-wing Hollywood was ecstatic: Trumbo had been vindicated. He had returned to writing movies under his own name without ever having to admit he had been a Communist or to point fingers at comrades.

The blacklist had been conspicuously broken, and Dalton Trumbo, hero to the downtrodden Reds, went on to make millions and live grandly. He has been lionized in liberal and left-wing circles ever since.[2]

There has been a renewed interest in his life and works in recent years, sparked by an entertaining and sometimes touching tribute to Trumbo by his son Christopher. Christopher scripted a two-man playlet, with one actor playing Trumbo sitting behind a desk reading Trumbo's real-life letters to family, friends, enemies, and tormentors (some of them demanding money owed). Another actor, playing Christopher, puts the letters in context for the audience. The letters, spiced with Trumbo's wit and flair, are often charming, sometimes sad, and frequently uproariously funny. Christopher says he wrote the script "to honor the First Amendment and to remember the victims of the McCarthy Era."[3]

Trumbo: Red, White, and Blacklisted toured the country to rave reviews, as famous actors clamored to read his literary gems. Alec Baldwin, Steve Martin, Brian Dennehy, Richard Dreyfuss, Paul Newman, F. Murray Abraham, Tim Robbins, and other notables were given lead roles. All of them made it obvious that they shared the sentiments expressed in Dennehy's heartfelt remark: "As far as I'm concerned, Trumbo was an American hero."[4]

In 2008 a worshipful Christopher put together *Trumbo*, a "documentary" based loosely on the play, but transforming Dalton into a modern-day Dreyfus, stuffed with Old Testament wisdom and profound thoughts on liberty. The film also drew liberal accolades, with Kenneth Turan, the critic for the *Los Angeles Times*, portraying the writer as "a contrarian" who "believed passionately in the Constitution and the Bill of Rights." More than a dozen Trumbo idolaters were featured in the documentary, including Michael Douglas, Kirk Douglas, Dustin Hoffman, Donald Sutherland, and Liam Neeson.

The Trumbo legend—of a feisty, funny, independent spirit who bucked Red hunters and the Hollywood studios—lives on. Yet few of the Hollywood writers served Stalin so faithfully. So far as Moscow was concerned, Trumbo, though he sold the Party line with zest, wit, and imagination, was for years a stolid Communist conformist. There appeared to be no corkscrew twist in the Soviet line he wouldn't embrace.

He was anti-Nazi when Stalin demanded it, virulently anti-British (and virtually pro-Nazi) when the Soviets made their Pact with Hitler, an extreme advocate for unilateral disarmament after Stalin had blessed Hitler's war against the West, and a bellowing warmonger when Stalin was betrayed by his good friend in Berlin. During the Cold War, Stalin had no more trustworthy ally.

His public record, his papers at the Wisconsin Historical Society, the documents produced by the House Un-American Activities Committee, and the hundreds of FBI documents on Trumbo's Communist record reveal a man who greatly admired the Soviet Union for its determination to make socialism work. They also reveal Trumbo's venomous hatred of those who attacked Stalin's bloody enterprise. Anyone anti-Soviet, Trumbo was quick to imply, was a Nazi at heart.

EQUATING ANTI-COMMUNISM WITH NAZISM

Trumbo's papers show that he despised Winston Churchill because of Churchill's "clear record of hostility and intervention and plotting against the

Soviet Union." Trumbo saw Churchill's famous 1946 speech at Fulton, Missouri, warning that the Soviets had dropped an "Iron Curtain" across much of Europe, not as a vivid description of objective facts but as a cry for a new "fascist" alliance against the USSR—along the lines of the "anti-Comintern pact joining Germany, Italy and Japan." "Mr. Churchill," he wrote, "now proposes the Second Anti-Comintern of the English speaking peoples of the world and their imperial possessions. So let us therefore not be surprised at the frantic drive for a war against the Soviet Union."[5] All this was Communist claptrap, of course.

Churchill's remarks were aimed at Soviet imperialism and its conquest of Eastern Europe, something Trumbo deliberately ignored. There wasn't any "drive for a war" by the West. If anything, the West was still in a conciliatory mood as far as Moscow was concerned. The Western nations were also in the process of yielding their "imperialist possessions," with the United States taking the lead by first giving independence to the Philippines and second pressuring its wartime allies to end colonialism. (India, Britain's prized possession, would become totally independent in just two years.)

But Trumbo didn't care much for truth. He far more enjoyed directing vicious barbs at the West and anti-Communists, especially when his beloved Soviet Union was taking it on the chin. He relished branding anti-Communism as Hitlerian and accusing those who preached it of being in bed with the Fuehrer. Of course, it was a well-known Communist tactic to tar every anti-Communist with the fascist label, and Trumbo was deeply devoted to this kind of polemic.

"By numerical count of the indices to *Mein Kampf* and to Hitler's Collected Speeches," he said in a talk to the Executive Council of the Hollywood Independent Citizens Committee of the Arts, Sciences and Professions,

> anti-Communism is the first objective of fascism. It was Hitler's argument that the existence of Communism created the need for fascism.
>
> It was his program to expose Communists, to isolate them from all organizational life, and to destroy them. This program was successful. I therefore propose that in our discussion of the menace

of fascism, we seek to determine to what extent anti-Communism
has infected America, and to determine the sources of that infec-
tion....[6]

Reflecting concern that Stalin was beginning to get something of a bad rap
after World War II, Trumbo had in mind a novel that would defend Stalin's
great struggle on behalf of socialism, his papers at the Wisconsin Historical
Society disclose. In the story Trumbo was planning, a wise elderly Russian
believes that those who love the Soviet Union should quietly serve Stalin, for
even to speak out in opposition might "divide and betray not only Russia, but
socialism itself, which, however imperfectly, the SU preserves, maintains and
develops."[7]

When a totalitarian North Korea, armed with Soviet weapons and advisors,
savagely attacked South Korea in 1950, Trumbo immediately rallied to the
Soviet–North Korean side with both a screenplay and a bit of vicious anti-
American and anti-Christian doggerel.

Trumbo camouflaged his Communist record for the longest time, inform-
ing those who inquired that his political views were none of anyone's business.
Precisely when he joined the Party is unclear, but he was its earnest supporter
during the 1930s, '40s, and early '50s. The much-maligned House Un-American
Activities Committee nicely nailed Trumbo's extensive record of support for
Communist causes when he appeared before that group on October 28, 1947.

Trumbo had refused to answer whether he had ever been a Party member,
but the Committee put into the hearing record six single-spaced pages covering Trumbo's Red history. This evidence has never been refuted. HUAC's
memorandum disclosed his Party card, his support of dozens of known Communist and Soviet fronts, his pamphlets and speeches on behalf of known
comrades, and his unwavering support of the Soviet Union.

For much of his life, Trumbo never admitted his Party membership publicly, but he came clean, sort of, to his biographer Bruce Cook some twenty-six
years after the 1947 hearings. He said he had joined the Party in late 1943 (some
ex-CP members said it was many years before), that his "very best friends were
Communists," and that "I might as well have been a Communist 10 years

earlier...."[8] He also acknowledged in an unpublished memo in his private papers that he "reaffiliated with the party in 1954," and then, "In the spring of 1956, I left the party for good."[9]

Los Angeles Communist Party chairman Dorothy Healey recalled that Trumbo was doing heavy lifting for the Party even in the period for which he didn't admit Party membership, at least as early as 1938. He was one of several Hollywood activists, she informed Ceplair and Englund, who "did whatever they were asked."[10] Despite all the grief it may have caused him—jail, blacklisting, and loss of income—Trumbo maintained to Cook that "I've never regretted it [joining the Party]. As a matter of fact, it's possible to say I would have regretted not having done it...."[11]

Trumbo's puppy-dog loyalty to the Party and Moscow was at its most abject during the Hitler-Stalin Pact period (August 23, 1939, to June 22, 1941). In the same month as the signing of the Pact, Trumbo submitted to MGM an original screenplay, *To Own the World*, which painted the U.S. economic system in colors Stalinists would have thoroughly enjoyed. The studio turned down the first two scripts but purchased the third revision, now called *We Who Are Young*, figuring the still heavily anti-American overtones of the writing would have to be muted.

The basic plot involves William and Margy, two young people who work as clerks for an accounting firm, marry, and believe the world is full of hope. But all their hope is snuffed out. Through no fault of their own, they wind up scared and penniless, with no way out—all because of America's crushing, nay, hellish, economic system.

In her *Fund for the Republic* analysis, Dorothy Jones acknowledges that even Trumbo's *third* revision was saturated with Communist propaganda. "The men who run American business and industry are shown as inhuman, mercenary, or as downright crooked," Jones observed.

> On every hand the average man must cope with merciless racketeers who try to extort from him his money (if he has any), and his labor. The only jobs he can find are those which no honest, self-respecting man would consider....

This is, indeed, a picture of America which would meet with the approval of the Communist Party.

The original Trumbo screenplay, even in its third revision, would not only have "served as Communist propaganda" when it was written, but "it would probably today [1956] be showing behind the Iron Curtain."

MGM changed the tone of the Trumbo screenplay considerably. What had "been intended as Communist propaganda" wound up being condemned by the critics as "sentimental hokum," according to Jones. Still, the Party must have been impressed. Trumbo had revealed his tenacity in trying to put a full-blown Red propaganda film into the theaters during the Hitler-Stalin Pact period.[12]

HITLER'S ENABLER

Indeed, despite Trumbo's repeated condemnation of fascism over his lifetime, few embraced the Soviet-Nazi wedding with more exuberance. Under Moscow's orders, the American CP—which had been heatedly demanding that America unite with England, France, and Russia in opposition to Hitler—suddenly did its infamous U-turn in the summer of 1939. When Stalin cut his deal with Germany, the CP launched heavy-duty mud-slinging against those who wanted to assist England and other countries squarely facing the Nazi menace. The CPUSA had also suddenly become violently opposed to any rebuilding of our own military. Eager to show Hitler his *bona fides*, Stalin ordered his fifth columns worldwide to help emasculate any and all possible resistance to the Nazi dictator. Trumbo proved a very willing accomplice in attempting to ease Hitler's burden of conquest.

Before the Pact, Trumbo was viewed as anti-fascist and a hearty supporter of the Soviet-controlled Loyalists in Spain. Trumbo played up this part of his record, and so does his son. But once Moscow teamed up with Berlin, Trumbo quickly became one of Hitler's most enthusiastic enablers, apologizing for German aggression and proposing policies that would make it easier for the Nazi warlord to vanquish the democratic West—precisely the policies that Stalin had ordered his fifth columns to pursue.

Trumbo suddenly became an extreme anti-interventionist, perhaps even a "pacifist," to use Ring Lardner's term, during the Hitler-Soviet embrace. His *Johnny Got His Gun* fit nicely into the Soviet strategy of spreading a radical form of pacifism in Western countries just as Hitler's hordes were poised for conquest.[13]

U.S. Communists embraced *Johnny* to persuade America to disarm, appease Hitler at all costs, and refuse to aid "imperialist" nations like England, a policy they said could lead to the kind of horrors Trumbo had depicted in his novel. The *Daily Worker* started serializing the book in March of 1940—just a month before Hitler unleashed his blitzkrieg in Europe.[14] "Every page of *Johnny* is a passionate indictment of imperialist war," ran a blurb in the *Worker* hyping the upcoming excerpts of the book. Trumbo's slim volume became a rallying cry for the freshly minted anti-interventionist Left. It was stocked in Communist bookstores and circulated extensively by the Party's major "anti-war" group, the Communist-controlled American Peace Mobilization—of which Trumbo was an active member.

Johnny, revived by Trumbo during the Vietnam conflict (and quoted favorably by then-senator John Kerry in the '90s), has been widely viewed as a powerful cry against war, but the plot is also a cry for a massive revolution against the governing classes. The protagonist, Joe Bonham, a World War I veteran, has lost all of his limbs; he's deaf, dumb, blind, and without a sense of smell. His face, covered by a mask, barely exists. His only form of communication is to pound his head against a pillow, tapping out his thoughts in Morse code.

At the book's conclusion, Joe sounds like a Red revolutionary, hoping for an uprising by masses of humanity across the globe. Issuing a stern warning about the future, Joe urges the world's soldiers to turn their guns on those who order them into battle. The pitifully crippled hero wants the planet's ruling classes to know,

> If you make a war, if there are guns to be aimed, if there are bullets to be fired, if there are men to be killed, they will not be us.... It will be you.
>
> It will be you—you who urge us on to battle, you who incite us against ourselves, you who would have one cobbler kill another

cobbler, you who would have one man who works kill another man who works.... We will use the guns you force upon us, we will use them to defend our very lives, and the menace to our lives does not lie on the other side of a nomansland that was set apart without our consent, it lies within our own boundaries here and now....[15]

Urging soldiers to kill those who might involve them in a possible war to resist Hitler's murderous legions must have been as pleasing to the Fuehrer as it was to Stalin, his enthusiastic partner in plunder. Nor was Trumbo through shilling for Stalin's plan to give aid and comfort to the Nazi warlord. *The Remarkable Andrew*, published in 1941—but before Hitler's double cross of Stalin in June—included a breezily written but still serious argument against assisting England in her effort to stop Hitler's conquering legions.

The hero of Trumbo's novel, the ghost of Andrew Jackson, is at times mildly anti-German but always ferociously anti-British. Indeed, England is frequently portrayed as far more antagonistic to America's interests than Nazi Germany—the favorite theme of Stalin and the Soviet-controlled Communist Party in the United States.

Andrew Long, a bookkeeper in Shale City, Colorado, is framed for embezzling funds by some of the town's most respected citizens, who are, naturally, Republicans and men and women of faith. Long is rescued from his predicament by Jackson's ghost, clearly a mouthpiece for Trumbo. When "Old Hickory" gets into a conversation with Long about the conflict overseas, the wise but ancient and ghostly patriot encourages him to embrace Jackson's own anti-British sentiments. He didn't approve of the British much when he vanquished the Redcoats during the Battle of New Orleans, and, from what Long is saying, these Redcoats don't seem to be worth a hill of beans now.

England is watching out for England, not us, Jackson informs Long, and we had to watch them "like hawks" when Jackson was president. And what's all this nonsense about the British fighting for "democracy" when they're still ruled by a king? When Jackson is first told that the Germans and British are fighting again, he exults: "And may they blast each other from the face of the earth!"

This was in precise accord with the Party's pitch to its members and followers in the West—that the Soviet Union had no dog in the fight between imperialists. In truth, the Party's full-throated anti-interventionism was designed to assist Hitler's Germany. Germany, Trumbo argues, has a right to wage war on England because England declared war on Germany first. (There is no mention of the cause, the Nazi invasion of Poland.) When Long plaintively laments that the Germans are "inhuman," Jackson unsympathetically responds, "To the vanquished, all conquerors are inhuman."

Jackson pitches most of his vitriol at England, but he also argues that those who wish to combat the German idea of a totalitarian state should content themselves with improving American democracy. There's no need to annoy the Nazi leader. "Has Germany given us any offense?" he asks. "Stopped our mails? Interfered with our shipping? Impressed our seamen? Unlawfully imprisoned our citizens?" No, Andrew Long assures him. Then, says Jackson, we have no cause to get involved. Jackson even bluntly accuses FDR of "treason" for sending planes and ships to Great Britain and "black treason" for providing guns, since we might need these weapons ourselves someday.[16]

During the Pact period, when Soviet strategy was to appease Hitler at every turn, Trumbo appeared to be obsessed by a desire to prevent young Americans from being sent to foreign battlefields. He engaged in a whirlwind of "anti-war" activity, speaking ably and often for an extreme isolationist foreign policy. He decried the draft, opposed aiding friendly nations, and fought efforts to rebuild our military. What was happening in Europe, he argued, was not worth the life of a single American boy.

He stoutly supported the Communist-inspired strike at North American Aviation (a strike explicitly backed by the Communist Party and designed to cripple America's defense efforts).[17] He produced anti-war skits based on *The Remarkable Andrew*, with Andy Jackson's ghost hurling those charges of "treason, treason, I tell you" against FDR.

When patriotic members of Local 1421 of the CIO's United Electrical Workers demanded that the group open its meetings with a pledge to the American flag, radical members balked. So a compromise was reached: the flag pledge would be recited, but it would be followed by the "peace pledge" written by Trumbo. The Trumbo pledge read, in part, "We do not beg for peace like slaves. We do not plead for it like serfs. We command it."[18]

Trumbo's ferocious anti-interventionism, bordering on extreme pacifism, and his fiercely anti-British posture went only so far, however. Trumbo uttered not a peep of protest against Hitler's brutally aggressive policies during the Pact period, from his conquest of Poland in September 1939, to his devouring of most of the Western European countries in the spring and summer of 1940, to his raining death and destruction on London for a six-week period in the fall of the same year. Nor did this supposed champion of the Jewish people reveal any obvious distaste for Hitler's poisonous anti-Semitism.

But when Hitler betrayed Stalin and launched his massive invasion of the Soviet Union on June 22, 1941, ah, now he had gone too far! Trumbo, like so many of his Red friends, didn't take long to abandon his "deeply held" anti-interventionist views. We now needed to aid Russia, of course. But Trumbo also suddenly saw the need to assist the formerly "imperialist" England as a gallant ally in the fight.[19]

Say what you will about the America First organization, the vast majority of its members were sincerely convinced that an isolationist foreign policy would protect Americans from the terrible conflict abroad. They had perceived that our intervention in World War I was a huge mistake, resulting in a great loss of American lives and the rise of Adolf Hitler and Joseph Stalin. They didn't want the U.S. to make the same mistake twice.

For Trumbo and the American Communists, however, fanatical cries for an isolationist foreign policy were nothing more than a shrewd tactic solely designed to please Moscow, which had proved all too eager to help its totalitarian ally, Adolf Hitler, achieve his aim of brutalizing and vanquishing the Christian and democratic West. And it's a pretty good bet that Trumbo and his "anti-fascist" comrades would never have turned against the Fuehrer if he hadn't betrayed his friend in the Kremlin.

CHAPTER THIRTY-ONE

FROM PACIFIST TO HOLY WARRIOR

E ven Trumbo's friends acknowledged he changed his "nonintervention-ist" and "pacifist" views after the Soviet Union was attacked. Fellow Hollywood Ten member Ring Lardner Jr. says that Hugo Butler, another dyed-in-the-wool Stalinist, had worked Trumbo over after Hitler's stab in the back, and "Hugo said [Trumbo] saw things our way. Gradually, Dalton became increasingly less pacifist in his approach."[1]

Trumbo himself admitted that he became firmly interventionist after Hitler's double cross of Stalin. When interviewed by two FBI agents on January 8, 1944, Trumbo, according to the agents, explained that he had "retained this pacifist view until June 22, 1941"—the very day Hitler had attacked the Soviet Union.[2]

Once his precious Soviet Union was in danger, Trumbo was no longer opposed to policies that could fling American "cobblers" and "the man who works" into harm's way. Now that Hitler was marching east instead of west, Trumbo was not opposed to having Americans risk their lives on foreign battlefields. He was no longer afraid of young American boys tasting the murderous ways of war that he had so powerfully opposed in *Johnny Got His Gun*. Japan's December 7, 1941, attack on *America* would bring many patriotic America Firsters around to a pro-interventionist point of view. But it was the potential destruction of the country he obviously loved the most—Stalin's Russia—that had changed Trumbo's mind six months earlier.

BEATING THE WAR DRUMS

Trumbo became eager for the fight, casualties be damned. He wrote several wartime scripts, including *Tender Comrade* (starring Ginger Rogers and Robert Ryan), *A Guy Named Joe* (with Spencer Tracy and Irene Dunne), and *Thirty Seconds over Tokyo* (with Van Johnson). The ex-pacifist now couldn't get enough of a war he had supposedly hated.

So eager was Trumbo now to join the war that he whipped up a six-page article—distributed by a Red-controlled group, the Citizens for Victory Committee—urging American citizens to petition FDR to quickly shove Americans into the European front to rescue Russia. Along with other comrades, he joined the Artists' Front to Win the War, another Red front eager to plunge Americans into bloody battles for Moscow's sake. (Others of Hollywood Ten fame—Alvah Bessie, Ring Lardner Jr., John Howard Lawson, and Albert Maltz, all violently anti-war during the Pact—graced the sponsors' list as well.)

The Artists' Front made its major debut at a mass meeting at Carnegie Hall in New York City on October 16, 1942.[3] Comedian Charlie Chaplin, named honorary chairman, came all the way from Hollywood to inform the crowd how pleased he was with Stalin and Communism. A thrilled Edith Anderson reported Chaplin's remarks to readers of the *Daily Worker*.

Addressing his speech to the "comrades" in the crowd—"and I do mean comrades," he emphasized—Chaplin extolled President Roosevelt as "the man who released Browder," the CP's general secretary, from jail and made supportive remarks about Communist labor leader Harry Bridges. "Stalin knows what he's talking about" when he asks us to open a second front, "so let us have it now," stressed Chaplin.

"I want to clarify the air," he said. "Communists used to be a big bugaboo. Who, what are the Communists? We are beginning to understand that they are ordinary people like ourselves, who love beauty, who love life…. They don't eat their young…. They say communism may spread out all over the world. And I say—so what?" He continued, "We do know that you cannot stop human progress."

Edith Anderson describes how the "great man left the platform," waving affectionately, with the audience rising to their feet and cheering "as if their life depended on that cheering and waving." Chaplin returned, holding up two fingers in a "V" sign. "V for Victory," he said, and, then, counting his two fingers, insisted they stood "for a Second Front."[4] America's generals wouldn't be ready to launch that second front until June of 1944, but Chaplin, along with Trumbo and his Red friends, wanted American soldiers, ready or not, to storm the European Continent to save Stalin's hide.

In 1945, Trumbo became editor of *The Screen Writer*, the official publication of the heavily Communist-infiltrated and frequently Communist-manipulated Screen Writers Guild. Under his leadership, as we have seen, the magazine became a propaganda organ for the Hollywood Communists, its pages filled with denunciations of anti-Communists and saturated with support for Communist writers and radical causes. In his "Notes on a Summer Vacation," appearing in the September 1945 issue, Trumbo described his brief career as a war correspondent in the Pacific.

Besides, as we have seen, interviewing a surprisingly pro-Stalin group of doctors serving in the Pacific, Trumbo sneaks in his Communist views about a variety of subjects, including Russia and Red union boss Harry Bridges. But much of the piece is devoted to the thrill of being near or in the combat zone. From the Yontan airfield in Okinawa, Trumbo went along on a B-25 combat mission, with each plane, as he reported, "carrying three 500-pound general purpose bombs." The B-25s, with Corsair escorts, were assigned "to bomb Ronchi airfield, which lies up the coast of Kyushu." Cloud cover prevented his plane from reaching its primary target, but the crewmembers "plant[ed] our whole load on Wan airstrip and scoot[ed] for home." Trumbo reveals no regrets; this supposed "pacifist" seems to have thoroughly romanticized the killing experience. He has no doubts about America's involvement in the war or the need to kill the enemy (he calls them "Japs") or the necessity of placing American soldiers in harm's way.[5]

NORTH KOREA: A "MODEL" FOR ASIA

Trumbo's infatuation with U.S. policy conspicuously cooled when Stalin switched signals just as the war was winding to a close. When the Duclos letter in April 1945 condemned Earl Browder's wartime speeches and essays in favor of peaceful collaboration between socialism and capitalism, the Communist Party read the attack as an order from Stalin to oust Browder as boss of the CP and return to the hard line against America and the West, as we have seen. The CP did just that and put in Browder's place William Foster and Eugene Dennis, who obediently echoed the new Duclos line.

Where did Dalton Trumbo stand? He lined up against Browder's belief in a promise of future peaceful relations between Moscow and Washington. Hugo Butler's wife, Jean, tells of a vigorous discussion between Butler and Trumbo, with Trumbo saying: "It comes down to this, if Lenin was right, then Browder was wrong—and vice versa. I prefer to believe that Lenin was right."[6]

The truth is that Trumbo preferred "to believe that Lenin was right" for much of his adult life. Nothing so underscores his love for Leninism, Stalinism, and Communism in general as an unpublished movie script discovered in his papers at the Wisconsin Historical Society.

"This is not by me," Trumbo lightheartedly scribbled onto a piece of paper covering the 145-page screen treatment. Then he boyishly confessed: "Ah, yes it is! For $2,000 I dramatized a local child-custody case for a group composed of Paul Jarrico, Adrian Scott, Herbert Biberman, et.al. It was naturally never made. Dalton Trumbo."

There was a good reason it was never made. Trumbo apparently wrote the storyline for this anti-American film during the Korean War, and it reveals just how deeply committed he was to Communist totalitarianism—no matter how cruel, savage, and ruthless its manifestations in the real world. The script also discloses the depths of his anti-American feelings. The film was titled *An American Story* and clearly is not about a child-custody case, but Trumbo's view of America and the Korean War.

The heroine is Catherine Bonham, who is about to have her children taken away from her because of her political views. Bonham, like Andrew Jackson in *The Remarkable Andrew*, is the voice of Trumbo. In the trial for the children's custody, her ex-husband's lawyer reads a letter before the jury in which Catherine has informed her two children that North Korea's swift and brutal invasion of South Korea in June 1950 was completely justifiable, for this "is Korea's fight for independence, just as we had to fight for our own independence in 1776."

No Communist cliché or absurdity is avoided. America, insists Bonham, "is supporting fascism everywhere," including "Germany, Japan,...and Rhee in Korea." Fascism is also invading the United States because the government is killing FEPC civil rights legislation and "public housing" while passing "a bill like the Mundt-Nixon Act which is designed to muzzle free speech and throw into prison all who express even the slightest disagreement with official policy"—folks like "the Hollywood Ten," says Bonham.

Then Trumbo's heroine sings of the revolution to come. She lovingly informs her children, "The people at the head of our more and more fascist-like government are trying desperately to stop the peoples of the world from coming into their own and really owning their own countries. But bombs will never kill an idea. The people all over the world will one day come into their own. Many will suffer and die fighting for this goal, but we will win. Never doubt it."[7]

This is Soviet Communist ideology in its rawest form, topped off with an enthusiastic prediction of a massive, violent Red uprising across the globe. Virtually nothing Bonham says even borders on the truth. The history is quite clear: North Korea, awash in Soviet arms and ruled by a brutal dictator imposed by Joseph Stalin, suddenly invaded South Korea in June of 1950, nearly pushing the defense forces of this lightly armed nation into the sea. The General Assembly of the United Nations, which had recognized South Korea in 1949 as a government "based on elections which were a valid expression of the free will" of the electorate, labeled North Korea as the aggressor.

At the Geneva armistice conference in 1954, Syngman Rhee's South Korean government proposed that free elections to create a united, independent, and democratic Korea be held under UN supervision. Kim Il-sung's North Korea flatly rejected what became known as the "Geneva formula." Most of the civilized world, including some fifty nations in the UN's General Assembly, recognized that North Korea's invasion was indefensible—but not Trumbo.

His papers contain a malicious poem titled "Korean Christmas," which makes the United States and Christianity—not the atheist North Korean invaders—the murderers of innocent Korean children. It goes, in part, like this:

> Have we hurt you, little boy?
> Ah,...we have
> We've hurt you terribly
> We've killed you
> Hear, then, little corpse...it had to be
> Poor consolation, yet it had to be
> The Christian ethic was at stake
> And western culture and the American way
> And so, in the midst of pure and holy strife,
> We had to take your little eastern life.[8]

No hint that North Korea had initiated the slaughter, no word that nearly one million North Koreans had fled Kim Il-sung's utopia, no mention that we were defending a democratically elected government and a country recognized as legitimate by most of the world.

Trumbo's support of Communism and his loathing of America are nowhere more apparent than in *An American Story*. His heroine's argument that the United States is supporting fascism in Germany and Japan—when we had just *crushed* fascism in Germany and Japan and paved the way for democratic governments there—is the product of a malevolent imagination, a malevolent *Communist* imagination.

Trumbo frequently suggests in his writings that he is fighting for individual freedom, anti-colonialism, and civil rights. But the only nations and movements that he ever enthusiastically tips his hat to are brutal, totalitarian, and Communist—including that barbarous regime in North Korea.

Dalton Trumbo, in truth, never met an argument so outlandish that he was not willing to embrace, so long as he believed it could be used to defend Soviet Communism and other Red enterprises. His writings, speeches, and activities show he was one of Stalin's most slavish followers—albeit one of his most talented propagandists. And this is the man the Hollywood Left will always consider an authentic American hero.

CHAPTER THIRTY-TWO

LILLIAN HELLMAN: SCARLET WOMAN, SCARLET LIES

illian Hellman died on June 30, 1984, of heart failure. She was seventy-nine. Born in New Orleans of struggling Jewish parents, she became a hugely successful playwright, screenwriter, author, and left-wing polemicist. She had penned such Broadway hits as *The Children's Hour*, *The Little Foxes*, and *Watch on the Rhine*. *Little Foxes* and *Watch* were turned into successful movies, and, as we have seen, Hellman's wartime picture *The North Star*, hailing the Soviet collective farm, became a favorite of Moscow's Party members.

Hellman also wrote three provocative memoirs: *An Unfinished Woman* (1969), *Pentimento* (1973), and *Scoundrel Time* (1976), which give a strong sense of her radical views. Dazzled by her literary achievements and radical politics, her Hollywood peers furnished her a thunderous standing ovation at the 1978 Academy Awards ceremony. For many years she was an iconic figure on the Left.

HIDING BEHIND THE FIFTH

What is often overlooked by her admirers is that she had been a Communist Party member for an important part of her adult life, even though she would repeatedly deceive her fans, friends, and associates about that association, outrageously so in *Scoundrel Time*. The mountain of falsehoods in that 1976 memoir begin with a laborious and specious introduction by her enabler Garry Wills, who covers for her by deceiving readers about her CP membership and allowing her to get away with implying that Whittaker Chambers slandered Alger Hiss. She tells so many untruths that Mary McCarthy's famous line that "every word she writes is a lie, including 'and' and 'the'" appears almost understated.

Hellman's reputation for telling fabrications about herself was legendary. And nowhere did she seem to prevaricate more than when discussing her ties to the Party. We know she was a longtime Party member from her FBI files, the testimony of ex-Communist screenwriter Martin Berkeley, her appearance before HUAC in 1952, and an illuminating peek into the collected papers of her attorney, Joseph Rauh.

Despite her efforts to fog over her Party membership, her 1952 HUAC testimony should have laid all doubts to rest. The testimony in which she issued her famous challenge to Chairman John S. Wood, who was questioning her about her radical activities, has long been seen by her fans as a highlight of her life.

"I am most willing to answer all questions about myself," she had written Wood just prior to her public hearing. "I have nothing to hide from your committee and there is nothing in my life of which I am ashamed." She assured Wood that she "did not like subversion and disloyalty in any form, and if I had ever seen any I would have considered it my duty to have reported it to the proper authorities."

But there were limits to making her life an open book, she explained. She would not carry out her promise to testify about herself if, as the existing

Committee rules demanded, she would then have to testify against others. She would reluctantly have to take the Fifth under such circumstances, but only to protect the innocent from possible harm. To hurt "innocent people whom I knew many years ago in order to save myself," she went on, "is, to me, inhuman and indecent and dishonorable. I cannot and will not cut my conscience to fit this year's fashions...."[1]

That last sentence was memorable, and the impression burned into the public's mind over the years by Hellman's apologists is that she courageously defied the Committee when she was asked about her radical politics and activities. But that is not precisely what happened. What Hellman did was to truthfully answer questions about herself, but only when her responses wouldn't implicate her as a Party member. She took the Fifth, however, when a truthful answer would have revealed that she had been a longtime member and would have incriminated not "innocent people" but a very guilty Lillian Hellman.

She didn't take the course that would have revealed true courage, at least by her own lights. She could have discussed only her own activities, never named names, and never taken the Fifth. But that might have drawn a contempt charge and time in jail, the prospect of which, she has acknowledged, filled her with enormous fear.

Hellman had been called before the Committee for a valid reason. Screenwriter Martin Berkeley, an ex-Red himself, testified in September 1951 before HUAC that the first meeting of the Hollywood section of the Communist Party was held in his Los Angeles home "out on Beverly Glen" in June of 1937, with many high-powered Party functionaries present, including John Howard Lawson and V. J. Jerome. Also attending, he said, were such left-wing Hollywood luminaries as Dorothy Parker, Donald Ogden Stewart, "my old friend Dashiell Hammett, who is now in jail in New York for his activities, and that very excellent playwright, Lillian Hellman."[2]

When Hellman appeared before HUAC on May 21, 1952, Committee counsel Frank Tavenner asked her of Berkeley's testimony, "[W]hether or not you agree that that is a correct statement, and if it is not, wherein it is in error." Hellman balked, saying she "would very much like to discuss this with you," but then refused, referring Tavenner to her letter to HUAC in which she indicated she would take the Fifth Amendment rather than become an informer. Chairman Wood acknowledged that if she admitted Party membership she would be asked about her associates.

After this exchange, Tavenner pressed her, "Now the question was asked you of whether or not you attended this organizational meeting of the Communist Party that was described by Mr. Berkeley." Hellman then took the Fifth, saying, "I refuse to answer on the ground that it might incriminate me." Berkeley had also said she was made "a member at large" of the Communist Party, meaning she had a special relationship with the Party not bestowed on most CP members, such as not having to attend regular CP meetings with less talented and less important Party members. (Stewart, Parker, and Hammett, said Berkeley, had also been made Party members "at large.")

So, asked Tavenner, "Were you at any time a member at large of the Communist Party?"

Hellman repeated, "I refuse to answer."

Prodded Tavenner, "Are you now a member of the Communist Party?"

Hellman: "No, sir."

Well, Wood interjected, what I would like to know is "can you fix a date, a period of time in the immediate past, during which you are willing to testify that you have not been a member of the Communist Party?"

Again, Hellman said, "I refuse to answer...."

But Wood then unlocked the puzzle with this series of questions:

> **Mr. Wood**: Were you yesterday?
> **Miss Hellman**: No, sir.
> **Mr. Wood**: Were you last year at this time?
> **Miss Hellman**: No, sir.
> **Mr. Wood**: Were you five years ago at this time?
> **Miss Hellman**: I must refuse to answer.
> **Mr. Wood**: Were you two years ago at this time?
> **Miss Hellman**: No, sir.
> **Mr. Wood**: Three years ago from this time?

Miss Hellman: I must refuse to answer....[3]

Surely Committee members and the public were right to draw this inference: Hellman had been a Communist Party member from at least the approximate time that Berkeley had said she was a founding member of the Party's Hollywood section in 1937 until sometime in 1949 or early 1950, some two years prior to her HUAC testimony. To take the Fifth if she had never been in the Party, as she frequently implied and subsequently would insist was gospel, would not only have been a lie and an abuse of the Fifth Amendment—it would also have been terribly foolish from her own point of view.

A firm and truthful denial of Party activities by Hellman would have been a ten-strike for the Left. It would not only have removed any blood-Red clouds hanging over Hellman's head, but it would also have shattered the credibility of the Committee and the testimony of "informers" such as Berkeley. If Hellman could have given an honest "no" answer to the $64,000 question, she would *not* have had to hurt "innocent" people, because she was an innocent herself and was in no position to finger anyone as subversive.

Her HUAC testimony, in short, proved beyond any reasonable doubt that Lillian had been lying for years—but it wouldn't prevent her from blatantly lying again in *Scoundrel Time*. Nevertheless, Hellman became convinced she had been a hit, that she had somehow bested the Committee. After all, she never did name names, nor did she flatly concede she had been a Party member. And plenty of folks on the Left were telling her that her performance was brilliant.

Her able attorney, the liberal Joseph Rauh, told her she did "nobly" on the stand; he would later insist that her testimony "is one of my proudest moments." Brooks Atkinson, the chief theater critic for the *New York Times*, wrote Hellman that she was to be "earnestly commended for your unwillingness to testify about other people before the House Committee on Un-American Activities." His wife, too, thought Hellman's letter showed "courage and probity." And Hellman was able to write Rauh ecstatically eight days after her appearance,

The reaction here has just been too good to believe and I thought you would want to know about it....

There has been the largest amount of mail I have ever received about anything, and an equally large number of phone calls [all favorable]. The small and excitable world of the theater is getting itself very excited, chiefly because they are all up in arms about Kazan and Odets.[4] [Kazan and Odets had both named names.]

A MOUNTAIN OF LIES

Hellman's pledge to the Committee—that she was prepared to tell all about herself if she didn't have to name innocent parties—was almost certainly another one of her famous falsehoods. She never, ever wrote or talked in a truthful and substantive way about her activities with the Party—before, during, or after her HUAC appearance. And she flatly lied about her Communist past in *Scoundrel Time*.

In that astoundingly false 1976 memoir, she says, "I am fairly sure that Hammett [Dashiell Hammett, her longtime lover and the writer of such mystery classics as *The Thin Man*] joined the Communist party in 1937 or 1938. I do not know because I never asked...."[5] She never asked the love of her life if he was a Party member? She was not even curious? Who can believe such nonsense?

It's also impossible to accept her assertion in *Scoundrel Time* that she had "never" met her accuser, Martin Berkeley, at his house, since she took the Fifth when HUAC confronted Hellman with his testimony. She had had an opportunity to destroy Berkeley's testimony but wouldn't take the chance when under oath.

Scoundrel Time then serves up another enormous and proven lie: "I did not join the party, although mild overtures were made by Earl Browder and the party theorist, V. J. Jerome."[6] We know this is another one of Hellman's stunning fabrications, not only because of her back-and-forth with Chairman Wood before HUAC but also because of a most revealing exchange of letters with Rauh, included in his papers registered in the Manuscript Division of the Library of Congress.

Hellman had initially intended to go before HUAC, decline to answer any questions about people whom she had known to be Communists, and then read a statement justifying her stance to the press. This would have been a daring act; she would have been risking a contempt citation and jail for her convictions.

Based on his initial prep talks with Hellman, Rauh then sent her a detailed statement on what he thought she might tell the media after she testified before HUAC. In his April 14, 1952, draft, he has Hellman waxing at length about her determination not to name anyone she knew who may have been a Party member, but he also has her admitting, "I joined the Communist Party in 1938, with little thought as to the serious step I was taking."

In her revised version of Rauh's draft, Hellman says she had "nothing to hide and nothing to be ashamed of," but that she will not answer questions "about myself," because she would then "be forced to answer questions about other people." She then proclaims, "I am not willing now or in the future to serve as an informer and thus to save myself at the expense of people who committed no wrong except that they once held unpopular political opinions."

She goes on to assert, in accordance with Rauh's draft statement, "My own story is simple. *I joined the Communist Party in 1938* [emphasis added]...." There you have it. No inferences have to be drawn. We get a clear confession to her attorney in her own words, which, of course, means she baldly lied in *Scoundrel Time*—no doubt thinking her letter to Rauh would never be unearthed for public scrutiny.

But she concealed critical portions of the truth even from Rauh. Hellman informed him that she had left the Party sometime late in 1940—another obvious falsehood, given her refusal to answer under oath before HUAC whether she had been a Party member three years before 1952.

"I was a most casual member," she remarks breezily in the draft to Rauh. "I attended very few meetings and saw and heard nothing more than people sitting around a room talking of current events or discussing the books they had read. I drifted away from the Communist Party because I seemed to be in the wrong place." Even Rauh viewed her claims as unconvincing, urging revisions on the grounds that her explanations were not sufficiently credible or regretful. On April 30, he critiqued her effort this way:

The more I read your draft statement, the more it seems to me that it is so little critical of the Communist movement in America that it will be generally considered an acceptance of it.... The statement almost seems to equate membership in the Communist Party with membership in a ladies' literary society or "good works" club. This may have been your experience, but few will accept it.

Let me ask you a couple of specific questions about your statement that will help make this point clear: Isn't it a little naive to say that the Communists at their meetings just talked about the latest books they had read or at least naive to suppose this would be believed? When you say that you drifted away from the Communist Party because you seemed to be in the wrong place, doesn't it have a certain air of getting into Schubert's when you wanted to be at the Majestic? When you refer to the Communists as people who were going your way, don't you just confirm what the House Committee is setting out to prove about you?[7]

Hellman eventually decided to abandon any sharp challenge to the Committee, politely testify before it on May 21, and then take the Fifth when asked about her years under Party discipline. She also accepted Rauh's tactical wisdom as to what to say. The final statement she submitted to HUAC, far better written than her earlier drafts, admitted nothing at all about her past Communist activities but focused largely on her desire to shield others. The words "Communism" and "Party" were nowhere mentioned. She would "decline to answer questions" about her "political opinions and activities"—not Communist opinions and activities, mind you—if that meant she would have to unfairly tarnish others.

Despite her Big Lie in *Scoundrel Time*, Hellman was an important CP member, and it would have been nice, even patriotic, if she had been willing to discuss her Party experience and what it meant to be a "Communist at large," as Berkeley had called her. What were her connections with Earl Browder and V. J. Jerome, who she admits asked her to become a Party member? What, if anything, did they instruct her to do? Alas, she never lets us in on what would have been a fascinating piece of history.

We do know today from the public record and her FBI files that for a critical part of her adult life, Lillian Hellman was not only a Party member, but a thoroughgoing Stalinist who joined the Party in the late 1930s (as she admitted to Rauh), attended the Tenth Party Convention in 1938 (according to her FBI file), remained in the Party until at least 1949 or possibly early 1950 (as can clearly be deduced from her HUAC testimony), and flocked to a multitude of Red fronts for over a dozen years (according to the public record), lending her vast prestige to dozens upon dozens of Stalinist causes, big and small.

In the 1930s Hellman frenetically backed the Soviet effort to take over Spain. She visited the Loyalist side near the front, then returned to America to glorify the Communist cause. No pro-Loyalist group seemed too Red for her to ignore, including the Abraham Lincoln Brigade, a military group birthed and controlled by American Communists, whose members fought on the Communist side in Spain.

She worked closely with the Communist Party in the Red-controlled League of American Writers and the Theater Arts Committee, both inspired and under the thumb of the Party. She signed a *New Masses* ad defending the notorious Soviet purge trials and attacked those who opposed her view. She hailed Communist union leaders like Harry Bridges, rushed to the defense of Party bigwigs like Earl Browder, and urged actions to stop the Nazis—until, of course, Stalin embraced them himself in that infamous Pact in August of 1939.

BLAMING THE VICTIM

When the Soviets attacked Finland on November 30, 1939, where did Lillian Hellman, the great foe of aggression and champion of oppressed people, stand? Not with Finland, you can be sure. Much of the world was appalled by the invasion, including American liberals. Even the League of Nations kicked the Soviets out of the club for their aggressive war. Tallulah Bankhead, who was starring at the time in Hellman's *The Little Foxes*, a smash Broadway hit, was so concerned that she and several of the cast announced they would do a benefit performance for this beleaguered country. Bankhead was hardly alone in her sentiments. Helen

Hayes chaired the entertainment committee for Finnish relief, while other Broadway casts were pitching in to help. Such movie and Broadway stars as John Barrymore, Edward G. Robinson, Ethel Merman, Joan Fontaine, Bert Lahr, Jimmy Durante, and Abbott and Costello were eager to help the Finns as well.

Thus Bankhead was dumbfounded when Hellman and director Herman Shumlin yanked the rug out from under the cast, insisting there would be no benefit performance and that America had no dog in the Soviet-Finnish fight. Hinting that their Soviet sympathies were at the heart of the problem, Bankhead reacted with some heat. "I've adopted Spanish Loyalist orphans and sent money to China, causes for which both Mr. Shumlin and Miss Hellman were strenuous proponents," she told the press. "They were questions of human suffering and we were glad to play benefits for them.... If Spanish refugees, the Chinese dispossessed and German refugees are deserving of aid, why not the Finnish women and children who are suffering privations caused by wanton invasion?" Why, she wondered, had Hellman and Shumlin "suddenly become so insular?"[8]

Hellman countered in a *New Yorker* interview by claiming that Bankhead had refused her request for a benefit for the Spanish Loyalists and thus no Finnish benefit was required. (Bankhead called this story a "brazen invention," and Hellman had to back off her claim because it was so obviously a lie.)

Hellman then decided to take a whack at the victims. "I don't believe in that fine, lovable little Republic that everyone gets so weepy about," she said.[9] She would later justify her position on the grounds that when she had been in Finland in 1937, it resembled a pro-Nazi Republic, another likely falsehood.[10] Hellman also complained that playing a benefit would stir the war embers smoldering in America.

The real reason, of course, was that Hellman was a stout backer of the Soviet-Nazi Pact, in which two totalitarian nations conspired to annihilate Poland, and one of them, Nazi Germany, was given the green light by Hellman's beloved Moscow to then conquer Western Europe. The deal also blessed the Soviet conquest of Finland. Few supported the deal that unleashed World War II with more gusto.

Hellman's defenders argue that her anti-Nazi play, *Watch on the Rhine*, first shown on April 1, 1940, did not follow Soviet policy during the Pact period, but Hellman had hardly abandoned the main Party line, which was to ensure that this country would not assist any group or nation challenging Adolf Hitler while Stalin considered the Nazi warlord his ally. "With her friends," notes Carl Rollyson in his well-researched and frequently sympathetic biography, "Hellman was candid about her support of the Hitler-Stalin alliance."[11]

When the *Daily Worker* printed the "call" to the "Fourth Congress of the League of American Writers to be held in New York City, June 6-8, 1941," it was a complete reversal of the "calls" to the last two pre-Pact Congresses and wholly in line with the current Soviet position. As we have seen, the 1941 meeting would be a pro-Hitler Congress. The "call" said, "*Today, we must ask whether the present policy of the administration*" to aid England and rebuild our military is "*not leading us to war and fascism*" at home [emphasis in original]. Among the prominent signers: the author of *Watch on the Rhine*.[12]

The Congress itself condemned the "criminal war" in Western Europe, insisting that Hitler's Germany and Churchill's England were in a "shameless struggle for the redivision of empire." Hellman conspicuously supported this Congress, and her lover, Communist Dashiell Hammett, was "elected" by it to head the Communist-controlled League of American Writers, which poured forth the same anti-British, anti-interventionist, pro-Soviet line. The Congress backed yet another Communist front, the American Peace Mobilization, which was relentlessly picketing the White House in fierce opposition to America's furnishing aid to England and even to rebuilding our own defenses. Hellman's profound anti-fascist beliefs were clearly in deep remission.

In a twinkling, however, they were revived! Within weeks after the Fourth Congress ended, Hellman and Hammett dramatically revised their views and now called for massive aid for Russia and even "imperialist" England.[13] The sole event that had magically transformed their fervent anti-interventionist beliefs: *Hitler's invasion of Hellman and Hammett's cherished Soviet Union*.

GLOWING SOVIET REVIEWS

Like all good Communists, Hellman was now bubbling with enthusiasm for plans to aid the Soviets after the Nazi invasion, and the Kremlin reciprocated her generosity. Her plays received official Soviet approval, and her wartime film, *The North Star*, was lavishly praised by several Russian screenwriters. Hellman championed war relief for Russia and demanded a quick opening of a "second front" to relieve the Soviets from the Nazi onslaught. So well did the Soviets think of their most ardent advocate, they invited her to Moscow in 1944 on a three-month cultural mission (where she instantly and notoriously bedded John Melby, a high-ranking American foreign service officer).

Treated as a privileged diplomat, Hellman returned home tremendously excited about her favorite country. She praised the Red Army for its extraordinary "discipline," hailed the Yalta agreement that many believe surrendered Poland and Eastern Europe to Soviet occupation, and found it pleasant that her plays and pictures were now or were about to be hot items in Moscow. She proclaimed that "artists are treated like kings in Russia in the respect and remuneration accorded them."[14]

The *Daily Worker* was delighted with her remarks, printing its story with a bold, black headline: "Lillian Hellman, after USSR Trip, Hits Soviet-Baiters." Hellman, the *Worker* reported, "branded as 'red-baiters' those who claim the Soviet Union is laying the foundation for a third world conflict and said these people were 'willing to risk involving the West in another war just to air their foolish, irresponsible notions.'"[15]

Hellman remained fully devoted to Stalin's policies in the postwar period, hosting Soviet-inspired May Day parties in 1947 and 1948, praising the Kremlin on various occasions, denouncing the Truman policy of checking Soviet aggression in Europe, attending Soviet-dominated "peace" conferences, backing the Red-saturated, pro-Soviet Henry Wallace campaign in 1948, and, according to her FBI file, even giving "a dinner party" in 1949 in honor of Gerhart Eisler, the Soviet Comintern agent.

She also became a major organizer in 1949 of the Communist-controlled "Cultural and Scientific Conference for World Peace." The major aim of that conference: to weaken and demilitarize America, to mobilize public opinion against U.S. assistance to nations threatened by Moscow, and to promote Soviet foreign policy. The *New York Times* reported that the conference's theme was set by Alexander A. Fadeyev, "poet and novelist and spokesman" for the Russian delegation, who assailed American foreign policy and insisted the Soviets were only seeking peace.

Fadeyev received the loudest applause at the conference's final session, a mass rally of eighteen thousand at Madison Square Garden. That session also heard both American and Soviet representatives denounce the formation of a military alliance against the Soviets in Europe as well as the Marshall Plan, which had offered foreign aid to the Soviet Union, its European satellites, and the Western democracies. Famed composer Dmitri Shostakovich called for artists all over the world to lead the war on the new "Fascists," that is, anyone opposing Stalin.[16]

Hellman never publicly criticized the Soviet Union for any of its actions while Stalin was alive: the purges, the manmade famine, the show trials, the mass murders, the Pact with Hitler, the seizure of Eastern Europe, the Berlin blockade, the Korean War, the prison camps, the imprisonment and murder of writers and artists. All these things she excused, dismissed, or fervently supported.

Her Stalinist convictions appeared to linger long after other vociferous Stalinists had finally acknowledged the Soviet dictator's evil deeds. When Nikita Khrushchev gave his famous speech in 1956 thoroughly condemning Stalin's crimes, how did Hellman react? As one might expect from a Stalinist. Rollyson informs us, "Hellman condemned Khrushchev for turning on the very leader who had been responsible for Khrushchev's successful career."

He adds, "She even predicted that Stalin would be vindicated someday."[17]

CHAPTER THIRTY-THREE

DONALD OGDEN STEWART: HOLLYWOOD REVOLUTIONARY

Donald Ogden Stewart was one of the best screenwriters in Hollywood. He won an Oscar for *The Philadelphia Story*, starring James Stewart and Katharine Hepburn, and received plaudits for *A Woman's Face* with Joan Crawford and Melvyn Douglas. He adapted for the screen that warm and humorous play about an imperious, upper-class family autocrat, *Life with Father*, starring William Powell, Irene Dunne, and Elizabeth Taylor. Stewart had a wonderful career, was surrounded by such good Hollywood friends as Hepburn and Bob Benchley, and celebrated a rich life in his autobiography, *By a Stroke of Luck!*

Stewart was also "blacklisted" and in the late '40s moved to Europe, where he mingled with anti-Americans including Paul Robeson and the Chaplins and hobnobbed with African "socialist" soon-to-be-tyrant Kwame Nkrumah of Ghana. The conventional wisdom of Hollywood is that Stewart's taking refuge abroad to avoid being subpoenaed by HUAC was a terrible tragedy, but the truth is that he was blacklisted with cause. Apologists customarily portray Hollywood's Red community as composed largely of romantic visionaries—"tender comrades," in the popular phrase—not dedicated revolutionaries.

But this hardly does justice to the acknowledged views of so many of these committed American Communists. Certainly not to Stewart's. For despite his warm and witty prose style and his general affability, Stewart was clearly one of those who encouraged the violent men, those who prodded others to bring our economic and social system down with a bang. We know a lot of what Stewart believed because he informed the world in his autobiography.

Stewart was a product of Phillips Exeter Academy in New Hampshire and a graduate of Yale University, where he became an editor of the *Yale Daily News* and was tapped for the prestigious Skull and Bones society. After a stint as a navy instructor in World War I, he dabbled in business, found it boring, and, lo and behold, discovered that Edmund Wilson—the editor of *Vanity Fair* who would become a famous literary critic—thought his writings frightfully funny. From then on, Stewart earned his living as a writer. He was well paid, palled around with wealthy people, wrote scripts for MGM's Irving Thalberg, and was considered a major asset at social events. Yet he had a nagging sense that his life lacked meaning.

HOW STEWART BECAME A COMMUNIST

In his very early forties, Stewart had become dissatisfied with his Hollywood career. He loved the glamour and the money, yet he felt his "quest for security through social and financial success had led me up the garden path—a very pleasant path but one which seemed to have come to a dead end. The jackpot had brought security but no inner satisfaction."[1]

So, circa 1934, he temporarily left Hollywood and went to London, where he thought he would write a play about this theme of successful but unfulfilled men. One of the minor characters, he says in his memoir, "was to be a Communist," but since he didn't know much about the subject, he asked in a London bookshop for "the latest book on communism." They gave him two books by John Strachey, *The Coming Struggle for Power* and *The Nature of the Capitalist Crisis.*

Those books had a powerful impact on Stewart's thinking. When he returned to America, he started to read rather religiously such left-wing fare as the *New Republic,* the *Nation,* and the *New Masses.* Soon he was inspired to join the "coming struggle against the Nazis and the Fascists. If this meant being called a Socialist or a Communist (I didn't know there was a difference), I was ready for that too. I even began romantically to think of myself as a Communist."[2]

Stewart insists he "had no idea" of what was involved, but the Soviet Union, he had come to believe, "was the country where the underdog had taken power into his own hands, and I wanted to be on the side of the underdog." He had "won all the money and status that America had to offer—and it just hadn't been good enough. The next step was Socialism."[3] Stewart says he was deeply indebted to Herb Kline, "a young left-winger who had started a Broadway magazine called *New Theater*" and "my first real honest-to-Marx Red." Kline showed him "the glory of the Marxist ideal of bringing to the underprivileged of the world an insight into their true position in that world, an historical understanding of the reasons for that position, and an assurance of its betterment through a realization of their united power."[4]

Stewart never really looked back. He joined the Party, was active in Communist fronts, struggled to write Marxist plays and pictures, and supported whatever Stalin's malignant heart desired. Everything. The famine, the purges, the slaughters, the Pact—everything. His radical politics helped put an end to his ten-year marriage, and in 1939 he married Ella Winter, the widow of muckraker Lincoln Steffens and a busy Communist activist in her own right.

Ceplair and Englund, though camouflaging many of Stewart's pro-Stalinist and pro-revolutionary statements, inform us in *The Inquisition in Hollywood* of many of his activities, including his seeking out friends among American Communists. According to these authors, Stewart "decided that the Communist Party was the best link with the proletariat and the backbone of meaningful political activism. He therefore attached himself to any 'real Communists' who crossed his path, and, by 1936, there was a good-sized nucleus of them in the Screen Writers Guild...."[5]

Associating himself with the Party—first as a sympathizer, then as a member—Stewart became the archetype of the Hollywood Communist activist. In the Popular Front period he was the Energizer Bunny. He was active in the Screen Writers Guild, became head of the Hollywood Anti-Nazi League, and was president of the League of American Writers (LAW). The SWG was saturated with Communists, while the other two organizations, extremely influential Popular Front groups, were under Party control.

STEWART: REDS DID THE REAL WORK

Stewart's most important role for the Left, as Ceplair and Englund note, was as "joiner, lender (of money, fame, leisure), and speaker *par excellence*. The mind boggles at how much activity he squeezed into a twenty-four hour day. Ella Winter, Stewart's second wife...recalled that: 'His sponsorship of so many committees and delegations gave rise to a satiric story: when President Roosevelt awoke in the morning, he would ring for his orange juice, his coffee, and the first eleven telegrams from Donald Ogden Stewart.'"[6]

All these frenetic activities, of course, were directed by Moscow's pawn, the American Communist Party, which greatly eased the burdens of Stewart's leadership roles. As Stewart himself admits in discussing his presidency of the League of American Writers and the Anti-Nazi League: "it was largely the Communists who did the work."[7]

Stewart found Communism's revolutionary ideology enormously appealing. When the Second Congress of American Writers in 1937 was under way, he delivered a bitter speech about America and capitalism, advising his colleagues to do their utmost to destroy fascism, which, he had clearly been convinced by Marxists, was the result of the kind of capitalism that prevailed in the United States.

Stewart mockingly informed his audience, "I hope that nothing that I say can give anyone the slightest possible cause to report back in Hollywood that I am in the least bit radical." He explained what he meant when he complained about "slavery" in America—just the "Communists' way of expressing the conditions of ninety-five per cent of the people in America."[8] He observed that "[W]e have the word of many intelligent fellow writers that it [capitalism] is a monster—a dying monster which is giving birth to fascism in its death agonies." If this is so—and he left no doubt that it was—then it must be "the purpose of every writer and every human being to fight fascism with every weapon at his command." For Stewart, that included using revolutionary violence in America.[9] Because of his hard-line opinions, the Party apparatchiks eagerly installed him as the second president of the League of American Writers in 1937 and "re-elected" him in the spring of 1939.

As we have seen, Stewart candidly elaborated on his views on violence in his memoir: "I wanted to fight for Socialism in America as the next step toward Abraham Lincoln's speech about the 'revolutionary right of any people to overthrow their government' in their march toward liberty and justice...I accepted with it the Marxist doctrine of the need for a 'final conflict' in view of the fact that those in possession of the means of production were not going to surrender them without a hell of a fight."[10] In case the reader isn't clear on his political inclinations, Stewart refers to himself as a "revolutionary Socialist."[11]

When the Hitler-Stalin Pact was signed in August of 1939, triggering Hitler's violent war against Poland and then the Nazi invasion of Western Europe, Stewart dutifully went along. "[B]ecause I trusted the Soviet Union to have the correct Marxist understanding of the situation," he admits, "I refrained from publicly criticizing the pact and the party's theory about the war."[12]

Stewart addressed the Fourth American Writers' Congress, a project of the LAW, of which he was the outgoing president, when it gathered in June of 1941 to hail the Hitler-Stalin embrace. It turned "out to be a rather sad affair," Stewart recalls. "Four years ago I had proudly stood up in Carnegie Hall and nailed my flag to the left-wing mast." But now the "anti-Hitler struggle" had turned into the "mobilization for peace,"[13] led, of course, by his Communist friends and mentors.

Despite some qualms about the Pact, Stewart permitted his name to be used on materials shilling for the alliance and, though he stepped down as LAW president, he was "elected" by the Congress as one of its seven vice presidents when the LAW was still in Hitler's corner. Whatever his misgivings on the Pact, he had "no intention of resigning from the Movement."[14]

Stewart's somewhat melancholy spirit, however, was instantly lifted several weeks later when Germany invaded Russia. He was imbued with enthusiasm for a new cause: frantically pushing America into harm's way to save Stalin from total destruction. A violent revolution was still essential for America's future, but for the moment the increasingly "fascist" United States—not yet at war, though Pearl Harbor loomed—was needed to rescue the world's only socialist country. America's destruction, so far as Stewart and his fellow comrades were concerned, could wait for a more opportune time.

When America was attacked on December 7, Stewart, like so many of his Communist colleagues, was in near ecstasy. Now the United States would eagerly contribute to the Soviet war effort. Stewart himself pitched in by working on patriotic radio programs and speeches and crusading for the immediate opening of a "second front" to relieve Soviet forces from the Nazi invaders.

During the war, Stewart began to think a bit better of Hollywood. He was encouraged by its embrace of the Soviet Union as a stout ally and praised the industry for releasing such wartime films as *Mission to Moscow*, *The North Star*, and *Action in the North Atlantic*. Each, of course, had a pro-Soviet tilt, and each had been written by Communist or super-fellow-traveling writers. He was surprised by Warner Brothers' release of *Song of Russia*, a picture full of praise for Moscow and penned by two Red writers, Dick Collins and Paul Jarrico. But what Stewart recalled with a special thrill was that the technical advisor to that picture was Anna Louise Strong, "throughout her long life one of the most ardent friends of communism and the Soviet Union." Was Hollywood, he wondered, now moving in his direction?[15]

KEEPER OF THE [RED] FLAME

Stewart was pleased that Hollywood allowed him to strike a blow for the Left in scripting the 1943 MGM film *Keeper of the Flame*, starring Spencer Tracy and Katharine Hepburn. Stewart hoped "to contribute to an understanding of democracy's war by exposing the danger of un-Americanism within our own gates." By "un-Americanism," Stewart meant the views of anyone to the right of Stewart.

He describes his film, of which he was "most proud," as an attack against a "General MacArthur"–type figure who was backed by the country's major industrialists and newspaper publishers (including William Randolph Hearst) and who was intent on imposing fascism through a military coup. The purpose of the coup plotters, in Stewart's words: "to overthrow the Roosevelt-like government and substitute a Mussolini-type of dictatorship."[16]

Apparently American "militarists," the Hearst press, Taft-Hoover Republicans, Big Business, Congressman Martin Dies—in short, virtually any and all groups and individuals who were anti-Communist or had opposed FDR's domestic policies in the prewar period—were yearning to mount an anti-Roosevelt *putsch*. Meanwhile they were deliberately dividing the country, as the movie's heroine (Hepburn) proclaims, through writings that were "anti-Semitic... anti-Negro, anti-labor, anti-trade union."

As Hepburn's character says, they didn't call what they wanted by its proper name, "fascism." Instead, they dressed up their ideology in "red, white and blue and called it Americanism." Inspired by well-developed Marxist fantasies, Stewart had smeared a considerable segment of the American public, large numbers of whom were fighting and dying in a war against Hitler's armies.

By calling his villains all sorts of names, Stewart was able to settle scores against American anti-Communists and against military men like MacArthur (who would win the war in the Far East). No wonder he was becoming increasingly fond of Hollywood. When the war was won in 1945, Stewart observed that he "had been in the movement for ten years" and had "not lost my belief in Socialism." He would also acknowledge (apparently not counting his flickering doubts about the Pact), "My belief in Stalin had not wavered."[17]

Then on April 25, 1945, "came the beginning of the formation of the United Nations in San Francisco and in May the unconditional surrender of Italy and Germany. There were newspaper photographs of the fraternizing of Russian and American troops. No one knew what deals had been made at Yalta, but there was alarm at the Red Army occupation of Poland, Hungary, Bulgaria and Romania. I saw it as the spread of Socialism and was delighted."[18]

Surely it was not illogical for the House Un-American Activities Committee to be concerned that men such as these were flourishing in an industry that had such a strong influence on the American people.

CHAPTER THIRTY-FOUR

JOHN HOWARD LAWSON: THE CP'S "GRAND POOH-BAH"

"**I**n the formidable history of progressive and radical consciousness in the Hollywood film community, there are notable names—Donald Ogden Stewart, Dudley Nichols, Eddie Cantor, Edward G. Robinson, Oscar Hammerstein II…but by general agreement among them, as well as their enemies, there was always one 'strongest of the strong': John Howard Lawson…. He acted the part of fearless, eloquent, unyielding, tireless, Communist."[1]

This description of Lawson's Communist ideology does not come from some ardent "red-baiter" but from a 1977 *Los Angeles Times* obituary on Lawson by those two very friendly chroniclers of Hollywood's "progressive community," Larry Ceplair and Steven Englund.

Though Ceplair and Englund called him a Communist, their book and articles romanticize Lawson's work by dressing up his activities with such euphemisms as "indefatigable organizer of labor" and "unrelenting organizer of sociopolitical causes" and lumping him with such soft left-wingers as entertainer Eddie Cantor and famed lyricist Oscar Hammerstein II (*Oklahoma, South Pacific, The Sound of Music*).

Lawson was in fact a bitter-end agent of Stalinism who had been dispatched by the Communist Party's Central Committee to Hollywood to recruit Party members and cajole and intimidate writers into hewing to the Soviet line. A successful playwright and screenwriter himself, he had early on loudly championed those urging a bloody revolution in America. He was a founder of the Screen Writers Guild and a leading player in its hard-left faction.

He was also an enthusiastic founder of the Soviet-controlled League of American Writers, embracing it when the League was calling for a Red revolution in America and encouraging Hitler's deadly assault on the West. In fact, he decorated virtually every important Soviet front from 1934 until his appearance before the House Un-American Activities Committee in 1947, when he was siding with the Soviet Union at the beginning of the Stalin-instigated Cold War.

HOW TO REDDEN A PICTURE

Despite the liberal myth that no Red propaganda was inserted into Hollywood's movies, Lawson consciously put Communist propaganda into his own works and was determined to infuse other writers' projects with the Soviet line as well. He wrote numerous plays that promoted violent revolution, and he scripted movies—*Blockade, Action in the North Atlantic, Counter-Attack*—intended to make American audiences cheer for Moscow.

He is also recalled as the lead unfriendly witness before HUAC in 1947—an appearance so disruptive and poisonous that it prompted the movie industry to formally blacklist Communist writers.

The third child of Belle Hart and S. Levy Lawson, Lawson was determined to become a playwright from the age of thirteen. He went to Williams College and wrote for the student newspaper and literary magazine there (although biographers say he couldn't join the news staff or edit the magazine, because he was Jewish).

After graduating from Williams, Lawson worked for Reuters and became the news agency's general manager for North America. But he soon abandoned journalism for his first love, playwriting. When World War I broke out, Lawson, though opposed to the war, joined the volunteer ambulance service, where he would meet and befriend then radical and future literary luminary John Dos Passos. (Dos Passos would move rightward in later years and even write for William F. Buckley's *National Review*.)

From the outset, Lawson was a man of the Left. After the war he wrote several plays, most of which had a reddish tinge. In *Processional* (1925), the protagonist is oppressed by a cartoon figure of a capitalist; in *The International* (1928), Alise turns her boyfriend David's "anarchic feelings into an acceptance of Marxian revolution," as Lawson biographer Gary Carr puts it.[2]

MIKE GOLD'S SCATHING REVIEW

Lawson, however, was still struggling to get in touch with his inner Stalinist until 1934, which would become a pivotal year for him. That March, Lawson saw two of his plays, *The Pure in Heart* and *Gentlewoman*, open in New York and then fold within less than a dozen performances. The critics in general were harsh, but what particularly traumatized the playwright was a scathing review by Mike Gold in the Communist *New Masses*.

Gold, who would be a featured *Daily Worker* columnist for thirty-two years, characterized Lawson as "A Bourgeois Hamlet of Our Time." Gold assailed not only the two failed plays but Lawson's entire career, insisting that he had been a man of "great potential talent" but had achieved no better set of principles than "futilitarianism."[3] Stung to the quick, Lawson responded immediately.

He acknowledged the "truth of 70 percent of Mike's attack" in his *New Masses* reply. "I readily admit, that my plays have achieved no real clarity," but he was convinced his work had shown steady progress toward full-throated Marxism; he was only sorry that he hadn't yet been able to achieve it. "*The Internationale* was a serious attempt to portray a world revolution," he argued, but conceded that "my lack of theoretical background betrayed me into many inexcusable errors and a general air of anarchistic sentimentality."

But the more he continued to delve into Marxism, Lawson suggested, the better his plays were sure to become. He knew that his work to date was "utterly unsatisfactory in its political orientation" and that "the only justification for any existence as a dramatist will be in my ability to achieve revolutionary clarity."[4]

Shortly after this extraordinary exchange, Lawson fully embraced the Soviet Union, the Soviet-controlled American Communist Party, and the need for violence and class struggle to bring on a Marxian utopia. Indeed, even before Gold's sharp criticism, Lawson said it had been his conviction that in America "violent social struggles involving masses of people seemed inevitable." Post the Gold critique, he was no longer in doubt.

Lawson gives some hints of his revolutionary fervor in the 1930s in a woefully inadequate autobiographical account written in the late 1960s that sits among his papers in the Morris Library at Southern Illinois University. In that account he remarks that his deep commitment to an "activist role led [him] into time-consuming responsibilities" and that the "Communist party was the guiding force" in his participation in the social struggles of the day.

LAWSON SECRETLY JOINS THE PARTY

"My public role," he allowed, "was that of a sympathetic intellectual who expressed his independent conviction. This was exactly what I did, but I wanted to do more...." And doing more—that is, joining the Party and chucking any conviction independent of it—was just around the corner. At a meeting in New York (circa 1934) at which he spoke, Lawson recalls that "a young man walked down the aisle toward the platform, waving a paper. It was an application for membership in the Communist Party, and he asked me to sign it. The crowd roared approval, and I explained that I supported the Communist position, but could be more useful outside the Party."

The audience was cool to his rationale, and Lawson felt more than a twinge of guilt for not joining. But the argument "that I could be more useful outside the organization was irrefutable common sense.... It was ridiculous, but true that I would lessen my usefulness if I joined the party publicly. Indeed, a public action was out of the question."

But when "a writer invited me to join a private group"—he refuses to say who the writer was or the year he joined (it was almost certainly 1934)—Lawson leapt at the chance. "So did a lot of other intellectuals" join "private" or "secret" Communist cells, he writes, including writer Granville Hicks, play-wright Clifford Odets (*Waiting for Lefty*), and actor Elia Kazan, who would go on to become a famous stage and motion picture director (*A Streetcar Named Desire, Death of a Salesman, On the Waterfront*).[5] Lawson's formal Party membership was kept under wraps for many years, though few were fooled, because his support of Party causes was so pronounced. Martin Berkeley testified before HUAC that he met Lawson in Hollywood at a left-wing meeting (circa 1937), but that he—Berkeley, then a Communist himself—was informed that Lawson "was not a party member," even though he was constantly referred to as "Comrade Lawson." Subsequently, said Berkeley, "I learned that that was untrue."[6] Although he wished to proudly proclaim his CP credentials, Lawson writes, he "functioned 'secretly,'" but just joining the Party "was a 'revolutionary' act—and it made me part of a great movement which I assumed was cohesive, democratic—and objectively it had results which changed many lives."[7]

CHEERING FOR A "SOVIET AMERICA"

Shortly after Gold's sharp critique of his commitment, Lawson visited Earl Browder, the general secretary of the Communist Party, in his ninth floor office in New York. Though Lawson was already on assignment from *New Masses* to gather material on the Tennessee Coal and Iron strike in Alabama, Browder suggested that he do some pieces for the *Daily Worker* as well.

Lawson agreed and, according to Carr, received from Browder "a letter of introduction to Communists in the south."[8] This was in early 1934. Ceplair and Englund say Lawson formally joined the New York CP in the same year (although they don't give a precise date). Indicative of his newly focused militancy was a report he filed from Birmingham as a "special correspondent" for the *Worker* on May 17, 1934, on a union organizer named Harold Ralston. Ralston, along with five others, had been arrested for reasons that Lawson inexplicably failed to describe in his front-page dispatch. His reporting was light on facts but heavy on Marxist rhetoric.

"For the first time in an Alabama jim crow court, the program of the Communist Party rang out in Judge Abernathy's kangaroo court today," Lawson's

Daily Worker piece began, "as Ralston and five other workers militantly defended themselves against the frame-up attempt of the steel bosses."[9]

Just why this was a "kangaroo court" Lawson never mentioned. How the "steel bosses" had railroaded Ralston was never described. Even what crimes Ralston and the others had allegedly committed were never discussed. These minor details were apparently irrelevant to the more important point: Lawson, no longer a bourgeois Hamlet, was revealing how eager he was to hoist the Red flag.

Lawson then approvingly quoted Ralston's incendiary cry from the witness stand: "The Communist Party is actively participating in strike struggles and building a powerful trade union movement as part of the struggle of the working class for the overthrow of capitalism, confiscation of the factories, mines, railroads and wealth of the Southern bourbons and the Wall Street oligarchy *in order to establish a Soviet America as part of the world struggle of the toiling masses for Communism* [emphasis added]."[10]

Ralston's speech was a revolutionary mouthful—and Lawson was ecstatic. There were other union organizers Lawson could have decided to identify with, but he chose to champion Ralston, the man who had, in "ringing tones" (Lawson's description), called for a Red revolution and "a Soviet America." One day Hollywood studio heads would be appalled that the founder of the Screen Writers Guild had held such views, but back at the *Daily Worker*, Mike Gold must have been riding on cloud nine.

Just eleven days after Lawson filed his *Worker* article, he and Ralston were featured speakers at an "Alabama Strike Protest Meeting" in New York City sponsored by the John Reed Club and the *New Masses*. The sponsors were outright Communist enterprises, each of which Lawson openly supported. (Ralston was described in an ad for the meeting in the May 29 *New Masses* thus: "an Alabama organizer for the Communist Party, recently arrested and *released* [emphasis added]." Apparently Judge Abernathy's court was not quite the "kangaroo court" that Lawson had maintained.

LAWSON GROWS THE PARTY

Lawson never appeared to waver after his post–Mike Gold commitment. He not only was the first president of the first Screen Writers Guild (elected in his pre-CP membership days) but became a member of the Communist Party "fraction" of the Guild. He emerged as a dominant figure in scores of Communist Party enterprises, attended Party fraction meetings in New York and Hollywood, and wound up as head of the Hollywood chapter of the Communist Party, dispatched by the CP bosses in New York in 1937.[11]

Nor did he shy away from openly embracing a Red revolution in America. His support of Ralston's militant views was not an aberration. In the *New Theatre* magazine of June 1934, Lawson asserted that "the vital forces at work [in America] are the growing strength of the revolution, the upsurge of a new class...." There is "only one direction in which the drama can move forward: it must join the march of the advancing working class; it must keep pace with the quickening momentum of the revolution."[12]

When the First American Writers' Congress was held in 1935, Lawson found it so "memorable that it stands amidst all the clamor and controversy of the thirties as the decade's central cultural event...." He embraced the revolutionary rhetoric and the writers' commitment to Communism, singling out for approval Waldo Frank's statement that it was "my premise and the premise of the majority of writers here assembled that Communism must come, and must be fought for." Such words, Lawson declares with admiration, "had never been spoken before in a large gathering of writers."[13]

Nineteen thirty-seven was a banner year for Lawson as a CP member. He writes that he was "preoccupied throughout... with the organization of the Communist party in Hollywood," which quickly grew to several hundred members under his leadership. (He gives no names.) In the same year, the left-wing Theatre Union in New York produced his play *Marching Song*, which garnered glorious reviews from the Communist Party, whose approval he always seemed to cherish the most.

The headline in the *Daily Worker* could not have been more fulsome: "Marching Song Finest Labor Play—Lawson's Drama the Most Eloquent and Poetic Dramatization of the Class Struggle in Our Time." Lawson had also begun to write the film *Blockade* in an attempt to advance the Stalinist cause in Spain.

HOLLYWOOD'S ENFORCER OF THE PARTY LINE

Lawson had been a successful leftist in New York, but he became a Red powerhouse on the West Coast. He was sent from New York to Hollywood by the Central Committee of the Communist Party, accompanied by V. J. Jerome, a member of the Communist Party's National Committee.[14] Jerome introduced him to the Party comrades in Hollywood, and Lawson became the "cultural czar" and the chief enforcer of the CP line. He raised potfuls of money for the Party and shilled for Stalin whenever he got a chance. No project was so Red or so Soviet-controlled that Lawson wouldn't fully embrace it.

When the California Senate Committee on Un-American Activities released its report in 1945, replete with documentary evidence and eyewitness accounts, it labeled Lawson "one of the most important Marxist strategists in Southern California." Ex-Communist Martin Berkeley described him in the 1951 HUAC hearings as "the grand Pooh-Bah of the [Hollywood] Communist movement.... He speaks with the voice of Stalin and the bells of the Kremlin."[15]

Rena Vale, a playwright and onetime Party member, testified that Lawson helped her and others write the Federal Theatre project *The Sun Rises in the West*, a play on migratory workers that apparently became the model for John Steinbeck's *Grapes of Wrath*.

"Did you have some help from people in Hollywood in working the play up?" she was asked.

Vale replied, "Yes, sir.... There was one person in Hollywood assisted in the writing of it, and that was John Howard Lawson, a screen writer, who met in a Communist fraction meeting with us, and he was identified as a Communist party member." Lawson, she said, discussed with the writers various ways of "translating the Communist party line into drama."[16] (Lawson told a California committee in 1945 he didn't recall the encounter, but he didn't deny it either.)

So moved was Lawson by Soviet ideology that he tried to persuade writers they could improve their craft by steeping themselves in Marxist doctrine. In his 1936 book, *Theory and Technique of Playwriting*, Lawson hails the "rapid economic and cultural growth of the Soviet Union"—due, he maintains, to the Russians' embrace of "dialectical materialism." The recent achievements of the Russian theater and films, Lawson insists, have involved the application of this important principle "to the specific problems of esthetics and technique."[17]

HOLLYWOOD'S TRIBUTE TO A TOTAL STALINIST

Lawson remained enthralled with all things Soviet and Stalinist even while many of his friends on the Left were becoming disillusioned. Oswald Garrison Villard, publisher of the left-wing *Nation* magazine, ventured, in writing Lawson about the Soviet purges, "I do consider the executions in Russia as being exactly as villainous as those of Hitler; they have done more to alienate liberal American sympathy than anything which has happened in Russia."[18]

Lawson's faith, however, was not dented. When American Communists began to drift from the Party after Nikita Khrushchev exposed Stalin's crimes in 1956, Lawson appeared as charmed as ever by Soviet Communism.

"John Howard Lawson is back," announced the anti-Communist *Tocsin* publication in June of 1963. "After two years spent conferring with his bosses in the Soviet Union," *Tocsin* reported,

> the one-time Hollywood screenwriter and still active Communist has returned to California. A welcome-home program was announced for Lawson, June 16, to be held at that reliable old party gathering place, the Los Angeles Park Manor Ballroom, 607 South Western Ave. Appropriately, the sponsor was the Southern California Committee for the *People's World*....
>
> Lawson's creative activity has largely been limited in the past 15 years to propagating the Communist line through speeches, articles and books. The author of such World War II hits as *Sahara* and *Action in the North Atlantic* (both with Humphrey Bogart), Lawson wrote his first script since the "Hollywood 10" case two years ago on a ship bound for the Soviet Union. Dealing unfavorably with an American "bourgeois" family, the play has already been applauded in Communist East Germany and is in rehearsal in the Leningrad Pushkin theater, according to the *Worker* of May 28.[19]

Lawson died in 1977, still "the strongest of the strong," as Ceplair and Englund put it. That is, the strongest of the strong *Stalinists*. Still, he remains a hero to much of Hollywood. A few years ago, Jim Carrey starred in the film *The Majestic*, in which an up-and-coming screenwriter is blacklisted because it is discovered that in his college days he attended a single meeting that was possibly run by Communists. (The premise itself is absurd; no credible case of this kind has ever been unearthed.)

The Carrey character suffers amnesia in an accident and winds up in one of the nicest ever of America's small towns, virtuous and patriotic, complete with a cemetery filled with World War II soldiers who died to preserve our freedoms fighting Nazism. The creators of the film, Frank Darabont and Michael Sloane, name this wonderful town *Lawson*, after the one and only John Howard Lawson, Sovieteer Extraordinaire (Lawson's loyalty to Moscow is, of course, not mentioned). An authentic film clip of the 1947 HUAC hearings shows this Hollywood Communist defying the Committee and its allegedly "Gestapo" tactics. The film's aim, of course, is to transform this loyal Stalinist and Nazi ally into an American hero.

Lawson remained a stout Stalinist to the very end (though his memoir very occasionally and very halfheartedly acknowledges that some unpleasant things did occur when Stalin ruled the USSR). He died still yearning for what Howard Ralston had called for in that Birmingham courtroom in 1934. Not a liberal America or a progressive America but the kind of regime Stalin had sought to impose: a Soviet America. Why Hollywood is still hailing this ferocious enemy of American freedoms as a champion of human liberty remains an inexplicable mystery.

CHAPTER THIRTY-FIVE

ELIA KAZAN DESERVED HIS OSCAR

The Academy of Motion Picture Arts and Sciences (AMPAS) gave its lifetime achievement award to Elia Kazan more than half a century after those incendiary 1947 hearings. However belated, that was still something remarkable for the celluloid crowd.

Through the tenacious lobbying of Karl Malden (*The Streets of San Francisco*), AMPAS finally relented and honored the man responsible for directing such celebrated films as *East of Eden, A Streetcar Named Desire, Gentleman's Agreement, Panic in the Streets, Viva Zapata, Splendor in the Grass*, and, perhaps his greatest triumph, *On the Waterfront*.

Kazan had already won two Academy Awards for Best Director. He had also guided ten different performers to Oscars for acting, and his pictures had accounted for fourteen other nominated performances. Kazan had directed several smash Broadway hits as well, including Arthur Miller's *All My Sons* and

Death of a Salesman. His novels had also been extraordinarily successful, and his lusty autobiography, *Elia Kazan: A Life*, provides fascinating details of the drama and movie world.

THE UNFORGIVABLE SIN

Nobody deserved the AMPAS lifetime achievement award, a quintessentially American honor, more than the Greek immigrant and eighty-nine-year-old icon Kazan. Yet until 1999 he had been passed over and excluded by his colleagues for much of his adult life because on April 10, 1952, he committed an unpardonable sin in the eyes of the Hollywood Left.

Kazan not only testified before the hated House Un-American Activities Committee, the panel that had exposed the Hollywood Ten as card-carrying Communists, but he also named eight people who had been in the Party with him for eighteen months in the 1930s. Other former Party members in the entertainment world—Larry Parks, Lee Cobb, Leopold Atlas, Sterling Hayden, and Budd Schulberg—had also appeared before the Committee and named names. But none was as reviled as Kazan.

There were reasons for the focused anger. The Kazan award rekindled the Left's enormous enmity toward a man who had generously cooperated with Congress in exposing Communism in Hollywood *and seemed to relish his role in exposing the CP.*

Kazan was not only the most illustrious former Communist from the entertainment industry to have cooperated with HUAC. What really galled the Hollywood Left was that Kazan appeared to have become a *believing* anti-Communist who thought cooperating with the Committee, even if one had to name names, was absolutely justified. That is what the Left has never been able to forgive.

And it wasn't just his testimony alone that got under their skin. Two days after his HUAC appearance, Kazan rubbed vinegar into the wounds of his former comrades. Prompted by his wife, Molly, he took out an ad in the *New York Times* urging others who knew about Communism to follow his lead. The Kazan ad—titled simply "A Statement"—said that he had placed the facts he knew about this "dangerous and alien conspiracy" before the "House Committee on Un-American Activities without reserve"—*without reserve*—and "that any American who is in possession of such facts has the obligation to make them known, either to the public or to the appropriate government agency."

The American Communist Party, his ad continued, "was abjectly taking its orders from the Kremlin," attempting "to dictate personal conduct," and "habitually distort[ing] and violat[ing] the truth." To be a Party member, he stressed, "is to have a taste of the police state." Firsthand experience with the Communist Party not only "left me with an abiding hatred of Communist philosophy and methods," but with the conviction that we must fight to preserve "the very things which [Communists] kill" in the countries they already rule. What things? Well, said Kazan, they suppress "free speech, a free press, the rights of property, the rights of labor, racial equality and, above all, individual rights."[1]

The Left was aghast. Kazan, after all, had been one of them. Even at the time of this testimony, he was still thinking like a left-winger. He had initially been reluctant to name names. He had never been—and never became—a "man of the Right." His enemies accused him of betraying his former comrades so he could make pictures in Hollywood. But while that may well have been a motive, it was clearly not the whole story.

In his autobiography, Kazan elaborates on this pivotal moment of his life. On the morning of January 14, 1952, he furnished testimony to HUAC in a closed executive session. Kazan was torn between wanting to testify about the Party he now had such contempt for and his reluctance to face the scorn of prominent liberals and leftists for being an "informer." His wife had urged him to "tell them the truth" about the Party, but he couldn't yet bring himself to "name names."

The friendly and relaxed Representative Richard Nixon appeared to be his chief questioner: Had Kazan been a CP member? Who recruited him? Were Clifford Odets and John Garfield in the Party? Kazan admitted his own CP membership, but at first he was mute about the activity of most of the others. (He did say he didn't think Garfield had been in the Party.) Did Kazan know about the risks of contempt? Nixon asked. Yes, he did, Kazan replied. When the questioning was finished, Nixon indicated the Committee wasn't satisfied with his responses. Kazan feared quite rightly that he would be called back into open session and would have to…name names.

The *Hollywood Reporter* printed an item about Kazan's "secret" testimony: "Elia Kazan, subpoenaed for the Un-American Activities Committee session, confessed Commie membership but refused to supply any new evidence on his old pals from the Group Theatre days, among them John Garfield." The *Reporter's* publisher, William Wilkerson, also informed an inquiring Darryl Zanuck of Twentieth Century-Fox that Kazan would soon be recalled, which could only mean he would be asked to "out" his former comrades.[2]

Kazan felt himself in a terrible quandary. He was not eager to testify in public, answering questions about his friends and one-time co-conspirators. Yet he had come to see Communism as an evil that should be exposed. And then there were other arguments for speaking out. Twentieth Century-Fox's Zanuck encouraged him to "name the names, for chrissake. Who the hell are you going to jail for? You'll be sitting there and someone else will sure as hell name those people. Who are you saving?"

The men Kazan would name had been his close friends, and he didn't want to do them any injury, but he also knew that the Party *was* repressive and a tool of Moscow. Surely the good liberals who had joined the Party must have left this Stalinist outfit by now. Kazan himself had jumped ship in 1936, having lived in the confining Soviet straitjacket for only a year and a half.

The famous director would talk to a lot of people before deciding to go before HUAC and spill the names of old friends. Zanuck had given his okay, and his lawyer, Bill Fitelson, had relentlessly argued that he could be a good "progressive"—like Sidney Hook, for example—and still be an outspoken anti-Communist.

After considerable soul-searching, Kazan decided that the Stalin-controlled CP and those who still clung to this thoroughly corrupt and un-American enterprise were no longer worth protecting—certainly not at the price of being excluded from a career in the Dream Factory.

NAMING NAMES

Kazan also knew that anyone who had been a Party member but insisted it was a mistake could still make it in Hollywood. In other words, naming some of his fellow conspirators from the '30s would hardly bring them to ruin—*unless they still remained hell-bent on participating in the Stalinist conspiracy against America*. So Kazan decided to "inform."

His April testimony, coupled with his ad in the New York Times explaining his rationale for "naming names," completely unhinged the Left. The *Daily Worker* was apoplectic about Kazan's alleged betrayal, branding his testimony a "belly-crawling," "goose-stepping" statement and the "lowest moment of Kazan's life." He was a "stoolpigeon" who had toadied to the "white-supremacist, union-busting Un-American Activities Committee." Just in case you missed the point, the *Worker* insisted Kazan had "earned the undying contempt of all decent people."[3] Very soon, Kazan recalls in his autobiography, "I heard of meetings organized by the Communist party...to isolate me for attack. I'd become the primary target."[4]

Other leftist publications including the *Nation* and the *New York Post* (at that time on the far Left), went after Kazan with particular zeal, while playwright Arthur Miller, Kazan's longtime friend and collaborator, and Stalinist writer Lillian Hellman were to join in the assault. Even Kazan's secretary left him.

Kazan refused to be cowed, however, informing one harsh critic who suggested he didn't envy Kazan's sleepless nights, "I'm sleeping fine. How are you?" Indeed, Kazan not only refused to fold but in 1954 directed *On the Waterfront*, which he considered a metaphor about his life.

That film was actually the product of *two* "informers," as the Left has always contemptuously referred to those who named *Communist* names. (Those who inform against fascists, capitalists, or anti-Semites are to be admired.) Kazan directed the film, and Budd Schulberg (*What Makes Sammy Run?*), an ex-Communist who had pulled a Kazan in 1951, wrote the script. It dazzled the public and even a Hollywood community furious with Kazan. Marlon Brando won the Oscar for Best Actor, Kazan for Best Director, and Schulberg for Best Script. The film established that ex-Communists who named names could still work in Hollywood, and even receive honors.

Kazan viewed *Waterfront* as a justification of his own testimony. In the movie, longshoreman Terry Malloy (the part made famous by Brando) testifies against his friends in the mob-controlled union, having been persuaded to do so by Father Barry, played by Karl Malden. Barry pleads with Malloy to come out publicly "for what you know is right against what you know is wrong." What's "ratting" to them, he says, "is telling the truth for you."

"When Brando, at the end, yells at Lee Cobb, the mob boss, 'I'm glad what I done—you hear me—glad what I done!'" writes Kazan, "that was me saying, with identical heat, that I was glad I'd testified as I had.... So when critics say that I put my story and my feelings on the screen to justify my informing, they are right."[5] Hollywood's Reds were well aware of the message Kazan was trying to convey. John Howard Lawson accused both Kazan and Schulberg of pouring out "McCarthyite poison" and wearing the "livery of the informer." Lester Cole, another Hollywood Ten figure, insisted the film was "designed to justify stool pigeons and slander trade unionism." His long-time friend, Arthur Miller, who split with Kazan over his HUAC testimony, the next year wrote *A View from the Bridge* to demonstrate that "informers" were the scum of the earth.

In his outsized autobiography, Kazan exposes the Communist Party as largely comprising a vicious, narrow-minded, and oppressive crew who were controlled by Moscow and who bullied members unmercifully if they failed to toe the Party line.

Kazan implies that Hollywood artists who remained Communists after it was all too clear what the Soviets were up to even deserved to lose their jobs. They weren't fighting for civil liberties when they took the First or Fifth Amendment before HUAC, he contends, but were "protecting the party" and "their own pasts." When discussing an ex-CP friend dismissed from CBS, he voices no sympathy, insisting that "Communists should not be in positions of control in communications."[6]

Did he believe that "everyone who defended himself by calling on the 5th Amendment—constitutional right though it was—was a Communist? I must confess I did believe that. Why else would they resort to the 5th? I'd known them all too long and too well, been scornful of their disguises, and often thought their public postures hypocritical."[7]

THE RED CRUSADE AGAINST KAZAN

For such unapologetic anti-Communist behavior over several decades, the Hollywood Left waged a vendetta against Kazan, determined to block him from acquiring tributes for his body of splendid work. Prior to securing his lifetime achievement award from AMPAS, for instance, he was on the brink of receiving the same award from the American Film Institute on three different occasions, but each time the tribute was scotched.

Charlton Heston, who attended the AFI's 1989 gathering, said the Kazan award had "looked like a done deal," until producer Gale Anne Hurd said, "'We can't give this award to him. He's a great director, but he named names.'" There was a "stunned silence," Heston recalled, and "that effectively killed it." Kazan's foes had also blocked an effort by the Los Angeles Film Critics Association to honor him.

Hollywood's hard-core radicals tried mightily to stop the AMPAS award as well, but they were unable to do so—which suggests that at least a little bit of the steam may have gone out of the relentless determination to portray HUAC's hearings against Communism in the movie industry as some kind of Nuremberg war crime.

When Malden, a former president of AMPAS, urged the board to give Kazan its lifetime achievement award, not only was his speech greeted with applause, but the proposal was approved unanimously. Even board member Haskell Wexler, who considered himself a victim of anti-Communist hysteria, voted for Kazan, though he still thought Kazan's testimony was wrong. This was not the first time Malden had been in Kazan's corner, for he stoutly defended Kazan in 1952 when the famed director was taking unmerciful flak for his HUAC appearance.[8]

Still, the Kazan detractors were hoping to stir up trouble for the famous man on Oscar night, with an invincibly ignorant media giving them a helping hand. The *New York Times'* Maureen Dowd helped fuel the anti-Kazan fire with a column headlined "Streetcar Named Betrayal," letting her readers know where she stood on the issue of Kazan versus the Communists.[9]

The *Los Angeles Times'* Robert Koehler, apparently convinced that tying Kazan to the late Senator Joe McCarthy was a surefire way to enrage liberals and leftists alike, wrote that Kazan was "an informer for Sen. Joseph McCarthy's House Un-American Activities Committee."[10] (Koehler was apparently oblivious to the fact that under our form of government, senators don't chair House committees.)

The *Washington Post*'s Sharon Waxman, who does know that McCarthy never headed HUAC, complained that Kazan "denounced eight colleagues as onetime Communists" before the House panel and that "those stung by his betrayal" can never "forgive or forget."[11]

WHAT KAZAN REALLY SAID

Had Waxman read Kazan's testimony? Not likely. The transcript for the HUAC hearings on April 10, 1952, contains Kazan's statement amending his earlier closed-door testimony in which he had declined to name anyone who had served with him in the Communist Party. His amended testimony, a written statement beginning on page 2407 and ending on 2414, named eight members of his Communist unit "who were, like myself, members of the Group Theatre acting company."

Kazan's statement is descriptive, not condemnatory, and suggests the eight may have joined the Party because, like him, they thought the Party was anti-Nazi and "had at heart the cause of the poor and unemployed people whom I saw on the streets about me."

Here, precisely, is what he said about the eight:

> Lewis Leverett, co-leader of the unit.
> J. Edward Bromberg, co-leader of the unit, deceased.
> Phoebe Brand (later Mrs. Morris Carnovsky): I was instrumental in bringing her into the party.
> Morris Carnovsky.
> Tony Kraber, along with [Ted] Wellman, he recruited me into the party.
> Paula Miller (later Mrs. Lee Strasberg): We are friends today. I believe that, as she has told me, she quit the Communists long ago. She is too sensible and balanced a woman, and she is married to too fine and intelligent a man, to have remained among them.
> Clifford Odets: He has assured me that he got out about the same time I did.
> Art Smith.[12]

That's it. That's what all the brouhaha is about.

There is nothing else Kazan said—good or bad—about *any* of these eight in seven pages of carefully crafted testimony. In short, he clearly had not, as the *Post*'s Waxman suggested, "denounced" his colleagues.[13]

Waxman also wrote of "his repudiation before HUAC in 1952 of former friends," including "playwright Clifford Odets, actor Paula Strasberg...." Not only is it clear that Kazan didn't repudiate any of the eight before HUAC, but in his autobiography he lays out in considerable detail how, in advance of his written testimony, he asked both Odets and Strasberg whether it would be okay if he named them before the Committee. Both, says Kazan, gave him permission.

Was Kazan lying? To my knowledge, his account has never been substantively refuted. Moreover, the Committee knew the names of all eight persons he identified before Kazan testified. Two had given him permission, and two more, Bromberg and Carnovsky, had already taken the Fifth before HUAC in 1951, so Kazan's testimony could hardly have harmed them. No wonder so much of Hollywood, and indeed America, is still confused about what Kazan did or did not do.

What Kazan's testimony did accomplish was to enlighten the public on how the Communists deceptively manipulated groups and people. He revealed how key Communist Party officials such as "cultural commissar" V. J. Jerome were assigned to his unit to "hand the party line to us new recruits."

The members were told to "educate ourselves in Marxist and party doctrine," help the Party "get a foothold in the Actor Equity Association," support "various 'front' organizations of the party," and "try to capture the Group Theatre and make it a Communist mouthpiece."[14] Kazan went on in this vein, making an important contribution to our knowledge of how the Communists operated in the entertainment field. Nor have those who continue to attack Kazan ever been able to refute his testimony.

LONGTIME STALINISTS PROTEST KAZAN'S AWARD

The die-hard Left could not allow Hollywood to honor a man making such vigorous anti-Communist statements without a fight. Yet not a single soul who led the charge to protest Kazan's AMPAS award had ever been "harmed" by his testimony. Those ganging up against him were onetime—and longtime—Stalinists who, at least at the time of the Oscar ceremony, still appeared to have dreamy ideas about Communism, if no longer about the Soviet Union.

The Committee against Silence, larded with hard leftists, issued a statement about the Kazan award saying, "There will be a protest demonstration among all the lovely gowns and black ties at the Academy Awards ceremony." The group asked the audience to remain silent and "sit on their hands" when Kazan received his award.

Who were these folks so outraged by Kazan's nearly half-century-old testimony? Bernie Gordon, for one, whom Maureen Dowd celebrated in her column attacking Kazan. The key organizer of the Committee against Silence, Gordon—who coscripted the 1957 movie *Hellcats of the Navy*, starring Ronald Reagan and his wife, Nancy Davis, under a pseudonym—was once one of those true-believing Stalinists.

Gordon admitted as much to me, albeit reluctantly, when I spoke with him by telephone at his home in Los Angeles just days before the Oscar ceremony. He had been named as a Communist in the 1947 hearings, Gordon said, but he wasn't "blacklisted"—that is, deprived of working in Hollywood under his own name—until 1952 when he refused to become an "informer" for the House Un-American Activities Committee.

Well, had he been a Communist? Gordon danced all around the question, insisting it wasn't "relevant" and that I was putting him in the same position that the House Committee had when it asked: "Have you now or have you ever been...?" But when it was pointed out that he was no longer in any legal or professional jeopardy, Gordon finally acknowledged, "I was a member of the Communist Party, from the mid-'40s to the mid-'50s" and said that he decided to break with the Party "when I learned what was happening in the Soviet Union under Stalin," probably "sometime in the 1950s, maybe it was when Khrushchev spoke."

Khrushchev did not deliver his anti-Stalin speech until February 25, 1956, so Gordon admits he was in Stalin's corner for quite a long time, especially considering that so many of his comrades had already turned against one of history's mass murderers in the previous decade. By his own reckoning, Gordon probably didn't spurn Russia's Supreme Butcher, the sworn enemy of the United States, until someone he really trusted—Nikita Khrushchev, also a long-time Stalinist—told him it was all right to do so.

When he discovered Stalin's sins, did he speak out? "Oh, yes, we all felt that this was a terrible betrayal of our idealistic reasons for having joined the Party, which we joined, not to help the Soviet Union, but to fight all of the evils in this country." What had he said, on the record, after this traumatic revelation? "Nobody was listening to me. I couldn't even work as a screenwriter," he lamented. But this was not precisely true, for he did work as a screenwriter post-1952, though under a pseudonym. In fact, he could have written scripts under his own name if he had—like many, many other writers and actors—just publicly renounced the Soviet-controlled CP.

Gordon became testy over this line of questioning, exclaiming, "Where did you want me to do this? You wanted me to take out an ad in the *New York Times*, the way Kazan did? You're being very provocative." Gordon clearly didn't like being cornered into admitting that he had *never* publicly spoken out against Stalin (somewhat ironic for a founder of the Committee against Silence), but he didn't seem to mind apologizing for the CPUSA, the Communist Party of the United States of America.

"A lot of people," Gordon said, "disagree strongly with me for having been a member of the Communist party. I disagree with a lot of people strongly who are members of the Republican party." Apparently Gordon still couldn't see much real difference between the GOP and the Communist Party, whose members had moved heaven and earth to aid the Soviet Union and destroy America. In fact, he still seemed to prefer the CP.[15]

Norma Barzman, who lent her name to the Gordon group, is another Kazan-hater: "He's being honored as if he were a hero, when in fact he was a heel," she allowed. The *Post*'s Waxman described screenwriter Barzman as a "former" leftist and a "blacklisted writer who lived in France for several years." Barzman was not in fact a "former leftist" but a longtime *Communist* who was still spouting the Communist line in the year 2002 in the magazine *Written By*, put out by the Writers Guild of America, West. ("Former leftist" is the media's usual euphemism for Stalinist. No wonder it is so difficult for the average newspaper reader or TV listener to comprehend why the Kazans of the world became so infuriated with the Barzmans of the world.)

Barzman tells a lot about herself in her interview for the 1997 book *Tender Comrades*. In 1942 she met Ben Barzman, who "had already been in the party for three years"—that is, during the Hitler-Stalin Pact—and married him three years later. He persuaded her to join the Party, although she had confided to him that she didn't think she was "worthy...I'm still so bourgeois," meaning, one supposes, that she still didn't think the United States should be crushed by Marxist revolutionaries. But in fact she proved exceptionally worthy, dedicating much of her life to the CP.

Both Barzmans, fearing the rise of anti-Communist sentiment in Hollywood, left the country in 1949 and settled for many years in France, where "we inhabited a Communist milieu" and "continued to feel like Communists."[16]

And so it goes with the most prominent names associated with Gordon's Committee against Silence. Abe Polonsky? Polonsky, who wrote such successful films as *Body and Soul*, starring John Garfield, and *I Can Get It for You Wholesale*, had taken the Fifth in 1951 rather than tell HUAC whether he or his wife was at that time a Communist or whether he would even fight for the United States if we were invaded.

Asked by Representative Charles Potter, a Republican from Michigan, "if the United States should be invaded by the Soviet Union, would you bear arms to defend the United States?" Polonsky couldn't bring himself to answer "yes," saying only that he didn't think a positive response was "the way to get peace."[17]

Nearly half a century later, he was still spouting great things about the Party. When the Academy honored Kazan, Polonsky, who had been so peace-loving that he couldn't commit to defending the United States in a war with Soviet Russia, told *Entertainment Weekly* about the Oscar presentation to Kazan that "I'll be watching, hoping someone shoots him."[18]

Then there's Robert Lees, who had scripted some successful Abbott and Costello comedies. Regarding the famed director, he said, "Kazan crawled through the mud for a contract at 20th Century Fox. He should apologize." Lees, however, was hardly unbiased. He took the Fifth in 1951, but later acknowledged, nay boasted about, his CP membership.

When Hollywood celebrated blacklisted Communists in a spiffy ceremony in Beverly Hills in 1997, a half century after the first big HUAC hearings into the movie industry, Lees popped up in a film clip. He merrily told how he had once been a "San Francisco Republican," but that when he got to Hollywood, the Communists in the entertainment industry "were making such sense, that I figured, what the devil, maybe that's where I should be. And that's how I became a member...."[19]

Frank Tarloff? He teamed up with Gordon's anti-Kazan committee as well. Here's what he said in *Tender Comrades*: "I must say, I have never regretted to this day, having joined the Party."[20]

Earlier in the day, before the pageant began, about five hundred protesters, including members of Gordon's committee, had been picketing the Dorothy Chandler Pavilion, hoisting placards reading: "Elia Kazan: Nominated for the Benedict Arnold Award" and "Don't Whitewash the Blacklist."

When Kazan was actually given the award, the majority in the audience stood up to give the great man an ovation. Kazan gave a big hug to Martin Scorsese and Robert De Niro, who introduced him. But others remained sullen. Producer extraordinaire Steven Spielberg did applaud but remained in his seat. Actors Nick Nolte, Ed Harris, and Amy Madigan stayed glued to their chairs and conspicuously refused to clap.

The movie colony still hates Kazan's 1952 testimony, but he snagged the lifetime achievement Oscar anyway. His exceptional talent, the wealth of material he produced, his advanced age, and the unbending support of Karl Malden managed to trump what Hollywood still considers his most terrible deed. In truth, however, Kazan had committed a supreme act of patriotism. And he very much deserved his award.

CHAPTER THIRTY-SIX

ARTHUR MILLER— WAS HE OR WASN'T HE?

"Arthur Miller, Moral Voice of American Stage, Dies at 89." The *New York Times'* adulatory front-page obituary was typical. Within hours of Miller's passing, the famed playwright was being lavished with praise for his prodigious literary output. With his prolific writings, he had managed to capture a Pulitzer, four Tony awards, and a host of other honors.

The man who had once married Marilyn Monroe was celebrated for several important dramas, including *All My Sons* (1947), *Death of a Salesman* (1949), *The Crucible* (1953), and *A View from the Bridge* (1955). He had obtained icon status among liberals just for having written *The Crucible*, his allegorical tale ripping Joe McCarthy, and he was also lauded for his refusal to "name names" of those he had met in various Red groups before the House Un-American Activities Committee (HUAC). Few folks have had a more effusive media send-off from their earthly moorings.

WILLING PAWN

What has been obscured by all this adoration is Miller's role as willing Soviet pawn. Miller's plays savaging America's free-enterprise system were lovingly staged in Communist countries. In a broadcast over Radio Hanoi (August 22, 1972), Jane Fonda told of her euphoria when she "saw Vietnamese actors and actresses perform the second act of Arthur Miller's play, 'All My Sons.'" Hanoi Jane found it "very moving" that Vietnamese artists were so forgiving that they were "translating and performing American plays while U.S. imperialists are bombing their country."[1]

Fonda didn't have a clue. Ho Chi Minh's ideological warriors were staging Miller's drama because they saw it—accurately—as agitprop against America. The protagonist of Miller's play is a corrupt American manufacturer who causes American pilots to die by deliberately selling faulty equipment to the U.S. armed forces. When *All My Sons* was first produced in 1947, the Communist *Daily Worker* gave it a vigorous thumbs-up, hailing Miller as a "leading figure" in a new generation of playwrights. It has been admired in Red circles ever since. *Death of a Salesman*, another terrific punch tossed at the American way of life, became a favorite of the Left as well.

Miller also used his writing talents to zing disillusioned ex-Communists, such as his longtime friend and collaborator, Elia Kazan. Miller got even with such "turncoats" and "informers" in *The Crucible* and *A View from the Bridge.*

What the obituaries failed to report was that Miller had provided substantial support for Joe Stalin's fifth column operations here in America. And when finally faced with his own crimson past before the public, Miller chose to mislead. In his famous June 1956 appearance before HUAC, he vowed—to the eternal cheers of the Left—that he would never inform on fellow Red and pro-Red conspirators. But he also proclaimed he would be "perfectly frank with [the Committee members] in anything relating to my activities."[2]

Miller kept the first promise but conspicuously crawfished on the second. Even the crumbs of "admissions" he coughed up had to be pried out of him by HUAC's pit bull staff director, Richard Arens.

SUPPORT FOR RED CAUSES—AND A RUSSIAN AGENT

Had Miller, Arens asked, signed a 1947 statement, released by the notoriously Red-controlled Civil Rights Congress, giving a *carte blanche* defense of the Communist Party? At the time that ad was published, several lawmakers were arguing that the Communist Party, as a wholly owned and operated subsidiary of Stalin's USSR, should be outlawed. But Miller, along with numerous CP cosigners, decided to coat the Party with whitewash, insisting there was "nothing in their program, record or activities, in war or in peace" to justify any "repressive legislation." Apparently committing espionage and subversion and taking orders from Stalin amounted to nothing.

When Miller fumbled over whether he'd been a signatory, Arens pushed the *Daily Worker* of April 16, 1947, under his nose. This issue of the CP's flagship publication, Arens pointed out, says "that 100 prominent Americans had issued this statement, including a person described here as Arthur Miller. I lay that before you and ask you if that refreshes your recollection?"

Cornered, Miller conceded—sort of: "I see my name here," so "I will not deny I signed it."[3]

Arens then directed Miller's attention to a similar ad defending the Party that had appeared in a May 20, 1947, advertisement in the *Washington Post*. The ad's sponsor: the same Communist front that had vouched for the innocence of the CP—the Civil Rights Congress. Miller suffered another spasm of amnesia but did allow, "I see my name here. I would not deny I might have signed it."[4]

Arens pushed Miller on another front: "Did you sign a statement in protest of the prosecution of Gerhart Eisler?"

Miller responded, "I don't recall that, sir."

So Arens produced a 1947 press release, again from the Communist Civil Rights Congress, protesting the persecution of the German anti-fascist refugee, Gerhart Eisler.

"I recall this," Miller piped up, his memory refreshed.

But Arens then posed a more interesting question: "Did you know at the time you signed that statement protesting the persecution of Gerhart Eisler that he was a top-ranking agent of the Kremlin in this country, and that, among other things for which he was being pursued by our government, was passport fraud?"

Miller obfuscated. "I would have no knowledge of that," he said, pointing out that he was neither an "investigator or a lawyer."[5]

But did Miller regret having given aid and comfort to a dedicated Soviet agent interested in destroying the United States? Miller never expressed the least bit of remorse for his support of this agent of Stalin's Comintern in his testimony or in later writings.

Despite Miller's effort to muddy his past, Arens produced enough material to show that in the '30s, '40s, and '50s, the esteemed playwright hung around with Communists, cowrote scripts with them, received high praise from the Red press, rose to the defense of active subversives, and supported or joined a host of prominent CP fronts and causes, which were all dutifully attempting to serve the Soviet Union and undermine the United States.

As late as 1952—in the midst of the Korean War—Miller joined yet *another* Communist front, signing a statement in defense of the twelve top Party leaders convicted under the Smith Act of knowingly conspiring to teach and advocate the violent overthrow of the U.S. government. He was still opposed, he told the Committee, "to the prosecution of anyone for advocating anything." He was not "defending Communists" as such, he wanted HUAC to know, but "the right of an author to advocate, to write," and to engage in "creative literature."[6]

Committee members thought the notion that the Smith Act was somehow inhibiting creative artists from anything but an organized conspiracy against our government was a fantastic stretch. But Miller maintained that the act—which he admitted he had never read, and seemed to misconstrue—should be repealed. As Miller would have it, the untrammeled freedom of the literary class trumped the need of the U.S. government to protect itself against agents of a deadly foreign power.

MILLER DOESN'T "RECALL" APPLYING FOR MEMBERSHIP

Had Miller ever joined the Party? HUAC never came up with a card, as they had with each of the Hollywood Ten. But Miller seemed, at the very least, to have come right up to the precipice. The U.S. State Department was concerned enough about Miller to deny him a passport for a while. And seven months before Miller's HUAC appearance, the Communist writer Howard Fast wrote a lengthy piece for the *Daily Worker* hailing Miller "as the American dramatist of our time," better than Clifford Odets, Elia Kazan, and Lillian Hellman[7]—each of whom had been in the Party. Fast's flowery salute raised obvious suspicions that Miller's links with the Party had been extremely close, if never formalized. In his autobiography, *Timebends*, Miller himself confesses that he had "at times believed with passionate moral certainty that in Marxism was the hope of mankind."[8]

Kazan said he didn't believe Miller was ever a Party member, but he sprinkled his autobiography with enough tales about Miller to make the reader wonder. He recalls Miller's curious behavior in suddenly abandoning his movie script, *The Hook*, which had also been extensively revised by Kazan, in 1951. Harry Cohn, president of Columbia Pictures, had agreed to back the movie, but he was under pressure to give the picture an anti-Red tilt, largely because both Kazan and Miller had left-wing backgrounds: if the movie was perceived as pro-Left, the nation's anti-Communist organizations could seriously damage the film's box office appeal with bad publicity.

To head off such a possibility, Cohn brought in labor leader Roy Brewer, who had crushed the pro-Red Conference of Studio Unions, to sit in on a script conference with Kazan and Miller. Brewer suggested that Cohn ensure that the key character, a longshoreman, be viewed as an anti-Communist.

Cohn was willing to plow ahead with the project with script revisions reflecting some of Brewer's thinking—if not his proposed heavy-handed dialogue. Kazan worked hard on the script, and Miller had pledged to go along, though he was far more hesitant. When Miller suddenly—and unilaterally—pulled out of the project, Kazan was "sick at heart" and "too shocked to ask questions."

When Kazan informed Cohn, Cohn was apoplectic. "Miller is a Communist," he barked. When Kazan said he didn't believe it, Cohn exclaimed, "Then tell me what other explanation could there be for what he did? ... I could tell just by looking at him. He's still one of them."[9]

HUAC staff director Richard Arens also thought Miller had been a Red, but he never proved it. He did, though, uncover some tantalizing pieces of information. When Arens asked the playwright if he had ever applied for Party membership, Miller—no doubt wondering what revealing document Arens would next pull out of his magic hat—gave a curious reply. "In 1939, I believe it was, or in 1940," he said, "I went to attend a Marxist study course in the vacant store open to the street in my neighborhood in Brooklyn. I there signed some form or another."[10]

Signing "some form or another," Arens must have thought, was a rather understated way of describing what Miller had done. Wasn't what you signed, asked Arens, "an application for membership in the Communist Party?"

Miller wasn't quite sure, responding, "I would not say that. I am here to tell you what I know."

Then, said Arens, "tell us what you know."

But Miller had nothing to tell: "This is now 16 years ago. That is half a lifetime away. I don't recall and I haven't been able to recall and, if I could, I would tell you the exact nature of that application."

That reply defies credulity. How could Miller not recall if he had ever applied for membership in the Communist Party? This was not something one did every day—not even reliable joiners of Red-controlled fronts like Miller. And what was it that convinced Miller to say that he just might have applied for membership at this particular meeting? Miller, alas, never lets us in on the secret.

There was a particular reason Miller should have recalled applying for Party membership if he applied in late 1939 or 1940. That was shortly after Stalin had cut a deal with Adolf Hitler—a convulsive event in both world history and on the Left. Could a smart Jewish boy from Brooklyn really fail to remember applying for membership in the Communist Party at just the moment when it was embracing the brutally anti-Semitic Fuehrer? Not likely.

Arens also asked Miller if he had ever attended any Communist Party sessions with playwright Arnaud d'Usseau.

Miller replied, "I was present at meetings of Communist Party writers in 1947, about 5 or 6 meetings...." But as an inquirer and even a critic, not a slavish devotee, he maintained. He added, "I went there to discover where I stood finally and completely" in relation to Marxism. Miller even claimed to have composed an essay for the group setting out his differences with the Party members, but when asked by Chairman Francis Walter to produce it, Miller lamented that he had somehow lost what he believed was "the best essay I ever wrote."[11] Still, long after his supposed critique of Marxism, Miller remained a faithful Stalin camp follower, promiscuously joining or backing one Red enterprise after another, almost until the day he appeared before HUAC.

ESTRANGEMENT FROM KAZAN

Miller's friendship with Kazan and their eventual estrangement also illuminate Miller's history with the Party. The two men had become great friends over the years, with Kazan having directed two of Miller's plays. Kazan had even introduced Miller to Marilyn Monroe. But the two parted company in 1952, and the only reason ever given was this: the famed director had willingly named before the House Un-American Activities Committee in 1952 those who had belonged to a Communist cell with him in the 1930s. Miller was reportedly outraged at Kazan for "informing" on his fellow conspirators.

Kazan's autobiography gives his side of the story. After Kazan testified before HUAC in April 1952, Miller didn't talk to him but let it be known that he was angry about his testimony. Kazan said he had heard that Miller had accused him of testifying for money, but then "I received his public dismissal through the newspaper. The *New York Post*'s headline: 'KAZAN SLAP AT REDS COST HIM MILLER PLAY'. ... 'since then, Mr. Miller has expressed strong disapproval of that stand to Broadway intimates and cut off all communications with his theatrical teammate.'"

Kazan said that the only explanation he got from Miller "came indirectly through Arthur Kennedy, who played the lead in *The Crucible*. Kennedy told me that at the opening night party for that play, Art raised a glass of spirits and, in a tone of vindication, said, 'This one's for Gadg [Kazan's nickname]!' And so we separated."[12] *The Crucible* showed "informers" like Kazan as villains and those they informed on as heroes.

Knowledgeable people in the theater and the film world, and on the Left in general, knew for a fact that the split had occurred because of Kazan's testimony and his strong defense of what he had done. But surprisingly, Miller, despite repeated hammering by Arens, insisted that he had never attacked Kazan for his testimony or for being an informer. He reluctantly acknowledged there had been a "break"—though he didn't like to use that term—but he claimed it had nothing to do with Kazan's testimony. Then why *did* they have a parting of the ways? Arens never asked that critical question directly, and Miller never provided an answer.

The truth is that Miller never completely forgave Kazan for "informing," although there was a reconciliation of sorts over a decade later. Victor Navasky, a man of the Left, in his comprehensive and highly informative *Naming Names*, makes the case that Miller thought Kazan a "stool pigeon." The liberal critic Richard Rovere insisted that Miller took the view in his own writings that "informing" was "the ultimate in human wickedness."[13]

When Kazan and Budd Schulberg's 1954 Oscar winner *On the Waterfront* celebrated the hero who "informs" on union racketeers, Miller tried to trump it the next year with *A View from the Bridge*, in which the informer is depicted as a despicable human being. In *Timebends* Miller repeatedly expresses his disgust for "informers," with such contemptuous asides as, "Certainly, I felt distaste for those who groveled before the tawdry tribune of moralistic vote-snatchers"—that is, those who testified against fellow Red conspirators before HUAC. And when Miller wasn't expressing his anger, he was feeling "pity" for these weak men and women.[14]

The Committee did not go after Miller for his dodgy responses about whether he was a Party member, but it did cite him for contempt because he refused to "name names" of those he had known as actual Communists. The contempt case was tossed out by the U.S. Court of Appeals on a technicality. Meanwhile, Miller's HUAC performance—because he had refused to "inform"—had only enhanced his hero status on the Left.

HUAC MADE HIM APPRECIATE SOVIET DISSIDENTS

Arthur Miller remained a man of the Left until the day he died, though he did, after his HUAC experience, become a critic of Communist countries' suppression of dissident writers. Even during his HUAC hearing, he said that he had stopped joining fronts that were Red-controlled, though he never seemed to regret the causes of the fronts that he had championed.

Why had Miller finally become critical of Communism, or at least some of its practices? It's unclear. But when he testified in June of 1956, he must have felt the impact of Khrushchev's brutal denunciation, four months earlier, of Stalin's crimes—a traumatic event in the lives of many on the Left that caused some of them to leave the Party and others to reject Communism altogether.

But Miller gives a different explanation. He credits Chairman Francis Walter and HUAC for his sympathy with dissidents. The great ease "with which I could, in the sixties, understand the fear and frustration of the dissident in the Sovietized world was the result, in some great part, of my experience before the Un-American Activities Committee in the fifties." Miller averred that the same totalitarianism that foreign journalists believed "had almost murdered European culture" during Nazism "was sitting in this [HUAC hearing] room under the almost palpable power of the American flag, and I wanted to reassure them that it was not going to happen here, at least not today."[15]

Apparently Miller wanted the world to believe that only when he faced the terrors of a committee investigating his close adherence to Communism, Stalinism, and Soviet Russia—sworn enemies of America and all its freedoms—could he finally comprehend the Gulag! But not a moment before.

In 1965, Miller was elected president of the international literary organization PEN and in his new role went to bat for dissident writers in Communist countries. The Soviets were sufficiently annoyed with Miller that his works were banned in the USSR in 1970. (But not in Communist Hanoi, as Jane Fonda's broadcasts remind us.)

But Miller always remained soft on Communists and Communism and harsh on anti-Communists. In *Timebends* he proudly recalls that at one performance of *The Crucible*, the audience, upon the execution of the innocent leading character, John Proctor, "stood up and remained silent for a couple of minutes, with heads bowed." The reason? Julius and Ethel Rosenberg, the Soviet spies who gave Stalin the secrets of the atomic bomb, were at that moment being executed in Sing Sing.[16]

Arthur Miller was a great playwright whose works frequently transcended their political slant. But in the great battle that was waged against Soviet Communism in the twentieth century, Miller was on the side of Joe Stalin when it really counted. You wouldn't have learned much about that aspect of his life from those glorious media tributes.

CHAPTER THIRTY-SEVEN

THE CURIOUS CASE OF MICHAEL BLANKFORT

Michael Blankfort was an accomplished novelist, biographer, TV scriptwriter, and screenwriter. He wrote *Halls of Montezuma*, a World War II film honoring the U.S. Marines—he joined up soon after Pearl Harbor—*Lydia Bailey*, and *The Juggler*. He contributed to the 1954 classic *The Caine Mutiny*, starring Humphrey Bogart, and later did scripts for TV. Honored by his fellow writers, he was president of the Writers Guild of America, West, from 1967 to 1969.

Blankfort would not go totally unscathed by the congressional probes into Hollywood, though apparently he never wound up on the blacklist, for reasons that remain curious and tend to disprove the myth that HUAC pursued radical writers with the same zealotry with which Captain Ahab pursued Moby Dick.

In testimony before HUAC on January 15, 1952, former *Daily Worker* managing editor Louis Budenz made damaging charges against the Hollywood writer. He said he met Blankfort at the *Worker's* editorial offices in 1935, knew him as a "concealed member" of the Party—though Budenz also said Blankfort had been fairly open with him—and was aware that he had written theater reviews for both the *Daily Worker* and the *New Masses*.

Budenz further recalled that he had had a three-hour meeting with Blankfort, at Blankfort's request, before Blankfort left for Hollywood in 1937. Budenz insisted that Blankfort had personally informed him during that meeting that he had received instructions straight from the American CP's Politburo "to penetrate," in Budenz's words, "the ranks of the Catholics on the West coast."[1]

BLANKFORT DENIES RED CHARGES

When Blankfort took the witness stand two weeks later, he insisted that he had been unfairly accused. He swore that he had never been a member of the Party, concealed or unconcealed, and that nobody but Budenz had ever made such an accusation. In fact, he testified, he had been part of the V. F. Calverton literary circle in the early 1930s, whose "distinguishing characteristic...was that it was anti-Communist." The group included Sidney Hook, Max Eastman, and John F. Dewey, each of whom had flirted with Communism but had turned against it. The people in this gathering, Blankfort claimed, "compared me with Eugene Lyons," the famous anti-Soviet journalist.

Blankfort also categorically denied that he had ever talked to Budenz, at the paper or anywhere else, about infiltrating Catholic groups. True, he had a passing acquaintance with Budenz, but that was as a member of the Calverton group before Budenz had become a Communist. And, yes, he had written a few pieces for the *New Masses* in 1934 and the *Daily Worker* in 1935 as a young freelance writer with liberal and left-wing views, but the editors of both publications had eventually started to reject his work because his positions were not compatible with theirs.[2]

But as the hearings chugged along, Blankfort's portrait of himself as a stout "anti-Communist" whose work had been rejected by two Communist publications began to erode. Blankfort, for instance, claimed he had never been on the staff of the *Daily Worker*. Well, then, asked Frank Tavenner, HUAC's very thorough counsel, how come the *Worker* carried an article, "Introducing the

Staff," on December 21, 1935, naming Blankfort as the "theater editor"? Blank-fort couldn't account for the designation, though he conceded he was so listed in several issues.[3]

BUT HIS STORY QUICKLY UNRAVELS

Covering the Red-dominated New Theater League's conference in April 1936, the *Daily Worker* reported that "Greetings from John Howard Lawson, Michael Blankfort and from a number of German playwrights now in the Soviet Union received prolonged applause from the delegates." Blankfort said that he was "pretty certain I wasn't there." But the point wasn't that he had attended but that he had sent greetings that were enthusiastically received—possibly in conjunction with Party member Lawson and several pro-Soviet German play-wrights. Blankfort told HUAC that he guessed that he might have agreed to send greetings in some offhand remark, but his memory was rather dim on that score.[4]

Wasn't it true, asked Tavenner, that he was a member of the Red-controlled League of American Writers and that he had contributed an essay on drama at the Congress of American Revolutionary Writers when it was founded in 1935? Well, yes, on both counts, Blankfort allowed.[5] (Recall that the final session of that Congress closed with the singing of the Comintern's theme song, *The Internationale*.)

Tavenner disclosed that Blankfort's name had appeared in the *Daily Worker* as the coauthor, with Michael Gold, of an article about a play they had written together. The piece had appeared on June 6, 1936, even though Blankfort had insisted before the Committee that he had not written for the *Worker* since 1935 and that his opinions were not in sync with Party members' views.

The joint byline made it appear as if they had written the article together, Blankfort agreed, but he was certain—for reasons he could not adequately explain—that Gold had put Blankfort's name on the essay without his permis-sion.[6] From the article it appeared that Gold and Blankfort had apparently teamed up a short while before to write the 1936 play *Battle Hymn*, discussed in the *Worker* piece. The play celebrated the violent anti-slavery hero, John Brown, a favorite figure of the Communists.

But Blankfort chose to distance himself from Gold, claiming the two were barely in touch when *Battle Hymn* was produced, even though both were listed as coauthors. "I knew him," he informed HUAC, "but I didn't have contact with him. I didn't talk with him." Nor, apparently, did he really "collaborate" with him on the script. Blankfort claimed that he had just rewritten an unusable product that Gold had given him without securing Gold's input on the rewrite. And though he knew Gold was a Communist, his association with him didn't mean much, he later implied, since Gold, for reasons unexplained, had advised him never to join the Party.[7]

So it went, through Blankfort's lengthy testimony. No matter how clearly the public record might seem to establish that he was close to Party members, Party events, and the Party line, he chose to downplay his friendship with various comrades, claimed his name had been mysteriously appropriated for a myriad of Red causes without his permission, and insisted that Party members knew he was critical of their activities.

As Blankfort would have it, the more he informed people of his disillusionment with the Party, the more it seemed that America's Communists kept asking him for support. Blankfort repeatedly said that he had been "dropped" by the Communist *New Masses* in 1934 because his opinions were not in harmony with those of the editors, but for its twenty-fifth anniversary in 1936—two years later, as Tavenner's questioning brought out—the *New Masses*' editors sought Blankfort out to write a history of the publication. Called "The Anniversary Cavalcade," Blankfort's history was even dramatized at the celebratory event for the magazine's anniversary.[8]

The "anti-Red" Blankfort also became a board member of the American Society for Technical Aid of the Spanish Loyalists, some of which aid, Tavenner pointed out, "was the recruiting of Americans to fight in the Loyalist Army during the Spanish Civil War." The Loyalist Army was controlled by Moscow, and the Society was an obvious Red front. Blankfort admitted he had favored the Loyalists, like many Americans, but he wanted to make it clear that "I never attended as a member of the board, I never attended as a member of the committee." In fact, "I have no recollection of anyone asking for my name or giving it."[9]

Tavenner kept rolling out a long list of Red fronts that prominently displayed Blankfort's name. It ought to have been embarrassing to a man who kept insisting he was not close to the Party or Party people and was even known for his anti-Communist views.

"Mr. Blankfort," Tavenner said, "I show you a photostatic copy of the program of the banquet given Mother Bloor on the 45th anniversary of—and I quote—'your never-ceasing fight in the ranks in the revolutionary movement for the liberation of the American toilers.'" Blankfort's name was not only shown as a sponsor, Tavenner added, "but personal greetings by Michael Blankfort appear in the form of 'All Power to Mother Bloor.'"[10]

A famous American Communist, Mother Bloor had helped found the Communist Party USA, traveled to Moscow to attend Comintern meetings, and from 1932 to 1948 was a member of the American Party's Central Committee.[11] She was also the mother of Harold Ware, named by Whittaker Chambers as a Soviet spy.

Blankfort, the self-proclaimed anti-Communist, appeared to have personally honored this Communist icon, or so the banquet program suggested, but his memory failed him once more. He could not recall lavishing his blessings on this dedicated Communist lady. Tavenner reminded Blankfort that he had initially told investigators in 1951 that he never sponsored the banquet. "Does this photostatic copy of the program refresh your recollection?"

"No, it doesn't," Blankfort replied, adding: "I don't remember ever being asked to be a sponsor. I don't remember ever sending a message of greetings. I don't remember whether I ever met Mrs. Bloor or not."

Could he think of any reason his name might have decorated the program, any reason at all? It is "not unlikely," Blankfort speculated, "that someone may have said to me, 'They are having a conference or an anniversary or a birthday party for Mother Bloor,' and I might have said, 'That is fine, all power to her.' I don't go beyond that."[12]

Nothing separated Communists from non-Communists during the 1930s more than the Hitler-Stalin Pact. When Stalin allied himself with Hitler, and liberals and even many on the far Left began to split with the Party line, Blank-fort apparently felt no such urge.

Tavenner unveiled the copy of a circular showing that Blankfort was a sponsor of an April 5, 1941, peace rally sponsored by the American Peace Mobilization, the blatant Red operation formed during the Soviet-Nazi Pact and run by Communist Frederick Vanderbilt Field. As we have seen, the APM, following orders from Moscow, launched a relentless campaign to block aid to Hitler's enemy, England; roll back this nation's defense buildup; and prevent America from embracing any policy that might conceivably hamper the fero-cious warlord in Berlin in any way.

Blankfort found his gray matter failing him again. "I do not recall ever sending permission or greetings or anything of that kind to the American Peace Mobilization." He said he was opposed to its agenda and couldn't imagine lend-ing his name to the group and would be "ashamed" if he actually had, which he doubted was the case.[13] Yet the circular wasn't the only piece of evidence that made it seem as if Blankfort had lent his name to fronts supporting the Hitler-Stalin alliance.

In *The Inquisition in Hollywood*, Ceplair and Englund have this to say about Blankfort's position during the Pact: "Keep America Out of War committees were formed in all branches of the League of American Writers," of which Blankfort was still a member when the Pact was in full bloom. So-called "peace" rallies, run by Reds and in tune with the Party line, were widespread, and one of them, "America Declares Peace," was said to have drawn "eight thousand people to the Olympic Auditorium in Los Angeles (on April 6, 1940) to see a 'Living Newspaper on Peace,' written by Michael Blankfort, Gordon Kahn, and other leftist screenwriters...."[14] Kahn, of course, was not just a leftist, but a Communist Party member.

On and on Tavenner went, uncovering details from before, during, and after World War II, all demonstrating that Blankfort or his name was continu-ally adorning notorious Red-controlled outfits and events. He taught at a school established by the Red-controlled League of American Writers, joined the notorious Communist-run National Council of Arts, Sciences and Professions after the war, embraced various Red groups demanding that the House Un-American Activities Committee be shut down, and wrote a pro-Soviet, pro-Mao book distributed through Communist book stores.

In the May 2, 1947, edition of the Communist *People's World*, the Civil Rights Congress, a notorious Red front, took out an ad that proudly proclaimed it was "defending Gerhart Eisler—world renowned anti-fascist fighter framed by the Thomas-Rankin Un-American Activities Committee." Blankfort's name, along with those of Lawson, Cole, Trumbo, and Maltz—each of whom would emerge as Hollywood Ten members—was prominently displayed in this advertisement in support of Eisler, previously revealed in the *New York Times* to be a Soviet agent.[15]

How, if Blankfort had been an anti-Communist or even just a non-Communist, did his name keep cropping up in connection with numerous and major Communist groups? HUAC panel members were eager to know. Blankfort had a response. His name had wound up on publications for fronts for various reasons, he allowed. He had unwisely given permission to some groups to use his name, but others, it became clear to him, had used his name without his okay. He was also "intellectually lazy," meaning he just didn't pay much attention to the causes he supported.

Other than a few unsubstantiated remarks, however, Blankfort offered little evidence to buttress his claim that despite the multiple times his name had been used to push Communist causes, he was, underneath it all, a stout opponent of Communism.

CELEBRATING THE COMMUNIST EVANS CARLSON

Blankfort's claim to be an anti-Communist looked even shakier when Tavenner presented evidence from Blankfort's biography of Evans Carlson, a World War II Marine hero. Blankfort's 1947 book, *The Big Yankee*, took note of Carlson's WWII exploits but largely dwelt on Carlson's time in China in the late 1930s, when then-colonel Carlson attached himself to the Chinese Communist army.

Carlson was a tough Marine who would be saluted in the World War II film *Gung Ho!* for his derring-do against the Japanese. But Carlson had also become a champion of the Chinese Communists in the late 1930s and a strong apologist for the Soviet Union. Carlson's own book, *Twin Stars of China*, published in 1940, was a glorious tribute to the Chinese Reds.

In his closing chapter, Carlson says, "From the Communist party and its brilliant, self-effacing leaders, Mao Tse-tung, Chu Teh, Chou En-Lai, and others, has come the rich, leavening of liberal thought and action" in China and "the insistence on recognition of the nobility and rights of the individual...."[16] This appears a particularly ludicrous claim in hindsight, but even at the time a huge number of journalists, missionaries, educators, and historians had the foresight to predict that once in power, Mao was likely to become one of history's most ruthless and murderous despots.

Using quotations from Carlson to press his own political agenda, Blankfort in his biography pushes the view that Mao and his brave band of Reds are the likely saviors of China and that the United States must rally behind them to overthrow the pro-American Nationalists led by Chiang Kai-shek. (Carlson was kinder to Chiang in his own book, but Blankfort suggests that this heavily decorated Marine likely changed his mind before his death in 1947.)

More curious still for a supposed "anti-Communist" is Blankfort's obvious desire to defend the Soviet-Nazi Pact using Carlson as his mouthpiece. Carlson wrote very favorably of the deal the day after it was signed—and Blankfort treats his rapid approval of the agreement between the two bloody dictators with sympathy and respect. Quoting Carlson on the Pact, Blankfort reports: "'Well,' Carlson remarks in a letter to friends, 'Russia evidently has the boys guessing now. The Russo-German Pact was one of the shrewdest moves made in many a day. I am inclined to believe that it may mean the end of the old type French and British imperialism as I have known it in China.... America will be well advised to keep out of Europe and turn her face to the south and to the west.'"[17]

Carlson was echoing the precise Soviet line at the time: America should not help those in Europe resisting Stalin's new ally, Adolf Hitler, but instead should challenge Stalin's potential enemy to America's west, Japan. Of course, this "shrewd" Stalin maneuver triggered World War II, enabled Hitler to conquer Western Europe, and unleashed the Holocaust. And while it may have weakened British and French "imperialism" in the postwar period, it enabled the Soviet Union to engage in a far more brutal form of imperialism by vanquishing one hundred million people in Eastern Europe.

In his acknowledgments to the Carlson biography, Blankfort lavishes praise on several Maoists and Stalinists who assisted him. He writes that "Edgar and Peg Snow helped me formulate the idea for this book from the beginning, and I am indebted to them." Both Snows were notoriously pro-Mao. Blankfort then proceeds to thank a number of outright Communists for helping him with his book, including Samuel Ornitz, one of the Hollywood Ten.[18] "To Albert Maltz and George Sklar," he also writes, "I herewith offer my gratitude, not only for their friendship, but for their encouragement during the days when the going was toughest."[19] Maltz, too, became a prominent member of the Ten.

Could someone who had been an anti-Communist from the mid-1930s, as Blankfort had testified he had been, have been so chummy with so many fervent Communists, taken up their causes before, during, and after World War II, supported the Soviet-Nazi Pact, allowed at least a dozen blatant Red fronts to use his name so promiscuously, and heartily championed Mao? Were his actions, as Blankfort would have had the Committee believe, reminiscent of those anti-Communists such as Sidney Hook, Max Eastman, and Gene Lyons? The idea is beyond absurd.

Nevertheless, Blankfort was neither pilloried by the Committee nor, apparently, was he blacklisted by the studios. In *Naming Names*, Victor Navasky, the famous left-wing writer, recounts interviewing Blankfort on how he managed to escape any dire consequences for his left-wing activities. It appears that Blankfort's able left-wing lawyer, Martin Gang, arranged a deal with the Committee, though it is not entirely clear why the Committee went along.

At the end of the hearing, Democrat Francis Walter of Pennsylvania, who chaired the Blankfort session, was scheduled to make a statement that would thank Blankfort for his testimony and thus get him off any blacklist. Representative Walter, Blankfort informed Navasky, "forgot to thank me for appearing. So Martin Gang got hold of him after the session and said, 'You forgot to thank Blankfort.' Walter called the court reporter of the Committee over and told him to put in a thank you so that I could be clear of the blacklist...."[20]

Walter's insertion was a handsome encomium to a duplicitous witness. "We appreciate your cooperation," Walter's post-hearing insertion appears at the hearing's conclusion, "and it is only because of the willingness of people like you to come here and give us a full statement of the facts as you know them that we are able to point up to the American people the danger of this conspiracy. We are deeply appreciative of your efforts to assist us."[21]

Blankfort had been clearly feigning ignorance during the hearing, and he had shed no light whatsoever on the Communist conspiracy in Hollywood or anywhere else. He had deliberately withheld information and had doctored his past. After the hearing he told his Red friends that, while he may not have been an unfriendly witness, he never named names.

Yet even this remarkably uncooperative performance caused Blankfort to be shunned by a number of comrades, particularly his good friend Albert Maltz. Navasky writes that Blankfort and Maltz had been close for years, with Maltz even "dedicating his first novel, in part, to Blankfort." Navasky adds, "They were contemporaries, politically sympathetic, inseparable."[22] Blankfort had also put his name on the 1950 movie *Broken Arrow*, reportedly written by Maltz, after Maltz had been blacklisted.[23]

When Blankfort talked to Navasky about Maltz's refusal to renew their friendship, Navasky reports, "one can see that the wound still festers. 'As I say, [said Blankfort], there were a few people who were very angry with me for cooperating with the Committee, to whom I would say, 'But I didn't name names,' who would say, 'Yes, but you betrayed us because you were willing to answer their questions,' and the one man who has never forgiven me is Albert Maltz.'"[24]

The Blankfort case is curious. Important anti-Communists on the Committee and in Hollywood, despite Blankfort's blatant Red record, easily forgave him, but many of his Red friends put him in Coventry, though he had helped them out over the years and had never said anything that jeopardized their careers. The anti-Communists, it seems, were far more generous in spirit than Blankfort's Communist friends.

Still the episode remains a puzzle, and it would be interesting if some Hollywood historian would someday enlighten the world as to just how close Blankfort was to the Party and precisely why the anti-Communists really let him off the hook. In the meantime, Louis Budenz's view that Blankfort was a "concealed" Party member seems to have the ring of truth.

CHAPTER THIRTY-EIGHT

REDS ON THE BLACKLIST

In the eyes of HUAC's critics, the most tragic result of the Hollywood hearings is that they ended the careers of hundreds of talented folks who had worked long and hard at a craft they deeply cherished. Millions of words and numerous films have been written about these unfortunates who lost their jobs in the movie industry, faced financial ruin, and even had to flee to other countries to eke out a living.

The tales are frequently moving, but they customarily omit a crucial fact: the men and women who are defended with such zeal were not innocents being persecuted for innocuous "political views" but dyed-in-the-wool Communist activists who had embraced all that that belief system entails.

When the literary elites and the Left howl about the terrible injustices allegedly inflicted on the screenwriters, actors, directors, and others in the industry, they almost never bring up the name of someone unfairly charged with Party membership. Usually they are wringing their hands about those who were dedicated Party members for much of their adult lives. To put it less delicately, the defenders of those on the Hollywood blacklist believe HUAC had no right to pry into the activities of agents of a foreign power bent on America's destruction.

THEY WERE REAL COMMUNISTS

Hollywood has loudly—and ceaselessly—condemned the major studios for having denied employment to the Hollywood Ten, the first to be formally barred from working. But none had been *falsely* identified as a Communist. At least nine of the ten were devoted, enthusiastic Communists at the time of the 1947 hearings, and the tenth, Edward Dmytryk, didn't make a clean break with the Party until he was about to leave prison in 1950.

The relaunching of the HUAC hearings into Hollywood in March 1951 turned out to be far more devastating to the radicals, with names on the blacklist soaring exponentially. Left-liberal activists were in shock. As authors Ceplair and Englund put it, the Committee "resumed its project of political inquisitions and repression with renewed vigor." The Committee heard not only from recalcitrants as in 1947 but also from those willing to talk about their time as Party members in Hollywood. Witnesses with scarlet pasts were now freely confessing their sins and, in many cases, naming scores of those who had participated in the conspiracy with them.

Still, the new hearings simply did not create cases of the kind that would justify liberals and Hollywood leftists in describing the blacklist as a genuine tragedy involving innocent people: writers and artists who were *bona fide* victims—that is, who were named as Party members and lost their jobs as a result but turned out to have been unfairly accused of Party activity.

Even Ceplair and Englund seem to acknowledge in *The Inquisition in Hollywood* that the list of unemployables was not being swollen with authentic innocents—a major concession to HUAC's supporters. "HUAC's project was...more of a mop-up than a vengeful assault," they note. "Only the unwilling, the unrepentant or the dissembling would feel the Committee's steel; the cooperative had nothing to fear from HUAC or the studios."[1] They also admit, "The blacklist, however, was rather exclusive. One's name could not be inscribed on the rolls, unless one had refused to cooperate with HUAC, either by taking the Fifth or by refusing to appear after being named by an informer."[2]

Over one hundred people in the industry were called before HUAC in the early '50s, with more than half deciding to cooperate. Altogether, cooperative witnesses named some three hundred people who were Communists at the time of their testimony or whom they knew had been Party members in the past. Virtually all of those named were blacklisted. Martin Berkeley alone, according to Ceplair and Englund's account, named over 150 individuals; Pauline Townsend, 83; and David Lang, over 70. Of the 58 cooperating witnesses, 31 had made substantive contributions to Hollywood, and over 60 percent of these were writers.[3]

The 1956 Fund for the Republic–financed study, *Report on Blacklisting I: Movies*, directed by John Cogley of the liberal *Commonweal* magazine, remains the most thorough investigation of the movie blacklist. Much of this report, cited frequently throughout this book, is informative, well documented, and even balanced. But the discussion of specific blacklisted individuals is heavily tilted in their favor. The authors depict virtually all who were blacklisted as victims no matter how committed they were to the Communist cause or how many times they took the Fifth.

The Fund study strongly suggests that taking the Fifth was more honorable than "naming names"—and no grounds at all for depriving anyone of a job. The report also does its best to gloss over the histories of stonewalling witnesses, playing down or obscuring their past and present Party connections.

HOWARD DA SILVA

The Fund report treats Howard Da Silva, the first witness from the film industry to invoke the Fifth Amendment when the hearings were renewed in 1951, rather sympathetically. Da Silva, whom Cogley notes was as well known on Broadway as in Hollywood, had appeared in the original casts of *Oklahoma!* and *Waiting for Lefty*. He had had roles in *The Lost Weekend*, *The Great Gatsby*, and *Keeper of the Flame*.

When a Committee member asked actor Robert Taylor in 1947 if he recalled the names of those in the Screen Actors Guild who were "disruptive" and "follow the Communist party line," Taylor referred to Da Silva as one who "always seems to have something to say at the wrong time." Da Silva's star began to descend shortly afterward, according to the Fund for the Republic study— but the evidence is not strong that this was caused by HUAC.

Da Silva was called before HUAC in March of 1951. Cogley's version of his testimony is that Da Silva protested that the First and Fifth Amendments— indeed, the entire Bill of Rights—shielded him from "any inquisitorial proce- dure" designed to produce evidence that would incriminate him and "drive him from" his profession as an actor. After his appearance, the report states, "Da Silva found no more work in Hollywood."

The reader feels more than a few twinges of sympathy for Da Silva as his story unfolds. Every paragraph of the Fund report seems designed to blur over his Party membership, emphasizing instead his unhappy circumstances and the seemingly harsh decision by the studios to no longer hire him. The word "Communist" appears only once in the pages devoted to his tale of woe, and then only to suggest that the accusation was in the nature of rumor, at best.[4]

When one reads the transcript of the HUAC hearings themselves, however, the sympathy for Da Silva aroused by the Fund study begins to wane. Da Silva appears to have modeled his demeanor as a witness on the behavior of the worst howlers and epithet-tossers among the Hollywood Ten. He was vituperative and self-righteous, pouring vitriol on HUAC and accusing its members of attempting to "control every concept of free thought throughout the country."

Had he been a Communist? Had he been married to a Communist? Was he a Communist today? Had he recruited folks into the Party? On all such questions, Da Silva embraced the Fifth. Republican representative Charles Potter of Michigan, who had lost his legs in World War II, then asked Da Silva the question he would often ask of hostile witnesses in these HUAC hearings: "If the Soviet Union should attack the United States, will you support and would you bear arms for the United States?"

Da Silva found the question difficult. "Any word 'peace' today is considered subversive by this committee and by those who prefer war to peace." He con- cluded, "I decline to answer this question on the grounds previously stated." The grounds previously stated included the Fifth Amendment. Perhaps Da

Silva thought a truthful answer to the question would be shocking as well as incriminating.[5]

PAUL JARRICO

Paul Jarrico is treated as another sympathetic figure in the Fund study. He had cowritten *Song of Russia* and *Thousands Cheer* with fellow Communist Dick Collins. The Fund allows him to explain his side of the story. Jarrico, whose leadership in the Party is camouflaged by the Fund's report, says he was treated unjustly by the studios, especially by RKO. Jarrico notes he was let go by the studio in March of 1951, shortly after he had been subpoenaed by HUAC and told the press that if he had to "choose between crawling in the mud with Larry Parks [an actor who named names] or going to jail like my courageous friends of the Hollywood Ten, I shall certainly choose the latter." He says he was "fired that very day" for his remarks and "was forbidden to come onto the studio lot even to pick up my personal belongings."

Jarrico then congratulates himself on what he thought was a bravura performance before HUAC in April of 1951, preening that he was a "most unfriendly witness. I not only exercised my privilege under the Fifth Amendment. I assailed the Committee for trying to subvert the Constitution." Jarrico then relates that his name was removed from an RKO film in 1952 by a vindictive Howard Hughes. Jarrico had worked as a screenwriter "more or less steadily for almost 14 years prior to that date on which I was subpoenaed," he informed the Fund, but he had "not been employed by any Hollywood studio since."[6]

In the Fund study, Jarrico comes off almost as a rebel hero: standing up for his constitutional rights, telling off the witch hunters at HUAC, refusing to name names, and revealing the supposed small-mindedness of Howard Hughes and RKO. It seems unjust that, despite his obvious talent, he could no longer find work.

The fact that he was identified as a Communist, interestingly enough, is nowhere to be discovered in this lengthy treatment of Jarrico's plight. Jarrico later admitted that not only had he been a Communist but he had become head of the Party's Hollywood chapter in the 1950s. The screenwriter's robust Communist beliefs, moreover, were wholly available to Cogley, in charge of the study for the Fund, in the proceedings of the '51 hearings, since Jarrico's collaborator, Dick Collins, had given voluminous and important testimony on Jarrico and also on how the Communists operated in Hollywood.

Collins testified that Jarrico was an enthusiastic Communist Party member, that he tried to persuade Collins to return to the Party after Collins had drifted away, and that he frantically tried to dissuade Collins from giving any names to the Committee. According to Collins, Jarrico was still convinced in 1951 that the Soviet Union "is devoted to the interests of all people and is peaceful." In a somewhat unclear manner, Collins also indicated that Jarrico would not defend this country if the Soviet Union and the United States ever got into a war.[7] None of this is reflected in the Cogley study.

Was Collins lying? Jarrico couldn't wait to accuse Collins of "perjury" when he appeared before HUAC the next day. But then he engaged in an illuminating exchange with HUAC counsel Frank Tavenner:

> **Mr. Tavenner**: Did he [Richard Collins] perjure himself in regard to the statement that you were a member of the Communist Party?
>
> **Mr. Jarrico**: I refuse to answer that question on the grounds that it may tend to incriminate me.
>
> **Mr. Tavenner**: Then what did you mean by stating that he perjured himself in his testimony here?
>
> **Mr. Jarrico**: I refuse to answer that question, also, on the same grounds.
>
> **Mr. Tavenner**: And what is that ground?
>
> **Mr. Jarrico**: That it may tend to incriminate me.

Chairman John Wood, the Georgia Democrat, then pressed Jarrico as to his charge that Collins had committed perjury:

> **Mr. Wood**: You are under oath now. Under oath you have sworn that he [Collins] committed perjury. One or the other of you is swearing falsely. He has pinpointed his testimony. Don't you think you ought to pinpoint yours?

Mr. Jarrico: This is not my forum, Mr. Chairman, and this is not the place for me to discuss my differences with Mr. Collins. I don't choose to do it here.[8]

Jarrico was also asked: "Do you believe the Communist Party is dedicated to the overthrow of the United States Government by force and violence?" Jarrico's response: "I refuse to answer that question on the grounds previously stated."[9]

Jarrico, in short, was unwilling to respond to any of Collins's sworn testimony or to questions put to him by the Committee. He took the Fifth rather than say whether he was a CP official or believed the Party favored overthrowing this government by force and violence. Nor would he say whether Collins was right when he accused Jarrico of saying he would not defend America in a war with the Soviet Empire. His HUAC appearance should at least have diminished his status as a full-blown martyr for the First Amendment.

WALDO SALT, MICHAEL WILSON, AND ABRAHAM POLONSKY

Da Silva and Jarrico weren't the only "martyrs" unwilling to say they would defend the United States if attacked. Republican representative Morgan Moulder of Michigan had asked writer Waldo Salt a Potter-like question: "In the event of an unprovoked military attack upon this country by the Soviet Union, would you feel your allegiance to this country and join the defense of our country against such an attack?"

Told that this seemed like a simple question, Salt retorted, "I don't believe this is a simple question at all"—and then took several minutes to avoid responding, still saying—along the lines of the Hollywood Ten in the 1947 hearings—"I am responding to the question."[10]

Screenwriter Michael Wilson launched a preemptive strike against "The Question," bringing the subject up first to condemn the query as recklessly inappropriate. "It seems strange to me," he said, "that you are always asking people whether or not they are willing to bear arms to kill people. Why don't you ever ask them if they are willing to fight for peace?" With this diversionary tactic, Wilson managed to avoid the question altogether—and never had to answer.[11]

"Assuming a hypothetical," remarked Representative Potter to writer Abraham Polonsky, "if the United States would be invaded by the Soviet Union, would you bear arms to defend the United States?" Polonsky began, "I have thought very long and deep on that question, because it has been asked many times before by this committee." But Polonsky's long and deep thoughts never yielded an unambiguous response. "I do not think by committing ourselves to a war we can get peace," he replied.[12]

But that answer deliberately evaded the point: If the Soviets launched an aggressive war against the United States, would he defend his country? The Stalinist Polonsky could not summon up enough latent patriotism to just say "yes."

Nowhere do HUAC's critics get to the heart of the matter with these Fifth Amendment witnesses. The studios were letting go the Da Silvas, the Jarricos, and the Salts because they were in violation of the 1947 Waldorf Statement. In that statement, the studios had made it clear that Hollywood was no longer in the business of hiring Communists or those who took the Fifth Amendment before HUAC, because of their loyalty to a dangerous foreign enemy of America. These witnesses knew the rules of the game and chose to defy them brazenly—a fact that Cogley's report for the Fund for the Republic muddies over.

ANONYMOUS CASES

The Cogley study is also largely unconvincing in its effort to discredit studio blacklisting practices even when addressing the situations of those whose past or present Party membership was a little more ambiguous.

Take the study's discussion of *R*, who had worked as an actor in theater and motion pictures since 1925. Even *R*'s side of the story does not prove the studio was in the wrong.

During the Korean War, *R* was called for a part in the MGM production of *Julius Caesar*. An executive then asked *R* about his various left-wing activities, including a subscription to the *People's World*, a Communist publication. *R*'s responses seemed inadequate, and he refused to write a letter to a higher MGM official explaining his associations.

The executive then said, "Then, I will ask you, are you a member of the Communist Party?" According to Cogley, "R answered, 'You have no right to ask that question or any other like it, and I will not answer it.' The executive concluded the interview. 'Then you are no longer employed by M-G-M.' After that R was called but not hired for one brief part at another studio, but he has not appeared in films since."[13]

The story of L is also unconvincing about the supposed unfairness of studio practices. In 1953, L, according to Cogley, began working in a part in a major Hollywood production. When there was information that he had belonged to several Red fronts and had backed the defense of Dalton Trumbo and John Howard Lawson, he was asked to take out an affidavit denying he was a member of the Communist Party.

He refused to do so, supposedly on principle, and claimed he had never been named as a Communist by any committee. He was permitted to finish the film anyway, but his agent said that unless he signed a statement denying Party membership, he would get no more jobs. He refused again. "Since then," according to the Cogley report, "L has had no work except one tv commercial, some tv films directed by a close friend who was brought into Hollywood from New York and one part in a movie made by an independent group. His agent has given up. L now makes his living as a manual laborer."[14]

The travails of the Fifth Amendment witnesses—supposedly symptomatic of the terrible oppression in Hollywood at one time—are considered a form of martyrdom by liberals and left-wingers. But this is hardly a martyrdom to be admired, unless one thinks that sacrificing oneself out of loyalty to the Communist Party and Joseph Stalin is an activity to be commended. Assuming there were individuals who refused on principle to sign anti-Communist affidavits, they were foolishly chucking their careers for an awful principle and a subversive cause.

Yet for decades torrents of tears have been shed over the actions of the studios for firing (or not hiring) those who took the Fifth or refused to sign anti-Communist affidavits, many of whom, as we know, were even refusing to pay lip service to the defense of their country.

Hollywood's anti-Communists, however, were encouraged by what the studios were doing. At a meeting of the Motion Picture Alliance on May 15,

1952, Roy Brewer declared that not one of the witnesses who had hidden behind the Fifth Amendment since the hearings had been renewed in 1951 was working in the movie industry.

"Later," notes the Fund study, "it became apparent in Hollywood that workers who were named as Communists but had neither been called to testify nor come forth to answer the charges made against them, were also blacklisted."

All this was accurate enough, but this was not a source of sorrow for the anti-Communist contingent in the movie industry. Blacklisting meant that Hollywood was no longer the haven for Soviet acolytes it had been in the 1940s. It also meant that the studios were no longer shoveling out huge sums of money to Communist writers and others who would in turn dump their money into Communist causes.

Hollywood's anti-Communists found it difficult to empathize with these liberal and left-wing heroes—especially when they could come in from the cold through a relatively mild form of contrition: cooperate with HUAC in exposing the Red conspiracy they had been involved in. The Fifth Amendment supporters, however, as the next chapter discloses, would go after the men and women who did just that—with a vengeance.

CHAPTER THIRTY-NINE

REHABILITATING
EX-REDS

HUAC's critics showed no concern for the plight of the *ex*-Communists who testified before the Committee and furnished a cornucopia of data on the Party's activities and subversive ends. They were mostly viewed as turncoats, their testimony supposedly self-serving and drenched in hypocrisy. Many of their liberal and left-wing colleagues snubbed them and refused to help them when they were in distress.

The Fund for the Republic study concedes that "social life became extremely difficult" for the "informers." After his appearance before HUAC, Collins says he was cut dead by most of those he met at Screen Writers Guild meetings. Other cooperative witnesses experienced a similar social ostracism from both liberals and leftists.

This Fund finding is ironic:

Many of the "friendly" witnesses tell stories of how they were insulted and avoided. The wife of one witness says that the only people who offered any sympathy or financial help during this period were members of the Motion Picture Alliance for the Preservation of American Ideals. The MPA was the anti-Communist group despised by the Left.

"When we needed friends as we never needed them before, Ward Bond [a major MPA figure] telephoned and asked how we were doing," she recalls gratefully. Rebuffed as they were by liberal Hollywood, a number of the cooperative witnesses completed the full circuit from the Communist Party to the right-wing Motion Picture Alliance....[1]

DMYTRYK SEEKS OUT BREWER

The case of the famous director Edward Dmytryk is instructive on this score. After the 1947 hearings, Dmytryk married actress Jean Porter, with Hollywood Ten writer Albert Maltz serving as best man. On his wedding night, Dmytryk traveled to Philadelphia where he, Maltz, and Paul Robeson, the famous singer and outspoken Stalinist, addressed a gathering of the Ten's supporters. He and his wife then left in 1948 for London, where he worked with the Communist writer Ben Barzman on a film called *Christ in Concrete*, a bizarre tale that appeared to express a sardonic view of things in a capitalist society.

Dmytryk returned to the States, found no work, and was then sentenced for six months at a prison in Mills Point, West Virginia, for conviction for contempt at the '47 hearings. Despite having Red friends, sticking with the Ten after the HUAC hearings, and supporting several Communist causes after the time he said he left the Party, Dmytryk received help from the anti-Communist community.

Dmytryk told me that he had not really changed his socialist views over the years, but he had been bugged by Communism's rigid ideology and its unbending defense of the Soviet Union. He has always maintained, as he did with me, that he actually left the Party—though not his left-wing views—in

1945 when John Howard Lawson tried to force a heavy dose of Red propaganda into the film *Cornered.*

While in jail, Dmytryk said, he didn't wish to remain a martyr for a cause he no longer supported. He wanted to get back to work and decided to divorce himself publicly from the Party. First off, he signed a statement on September 9, 1950, witnessed by the prison warden, saying he was not a Communist or a Communist sympathizer and that he had not been a Communist at the time of the '47 congressional hearings. His affidavit also said, "I recognize the United States of America as the only country to which I owe allegiance and loyalty."[2]

When Dmytryk got out, he asked a friend, an independent producer, to arrange a meeting with "the toughest anti-Communists in town." Roy Brewer, the extremely influential labor leader, attended the meeting and heard Dmytryk explain why he joined the Party and why he left. Dmytryk also answered pointed questions put to him by the anti-Communist labor leader.

BREWER: EX-REDS "HAD TO BE HELPED"

Brewer was impressed. As a result, he came to the conclusion that "the people who had broken with the party had to be helped, both because it was the right thing to do and because it hurt the Communist Party." With Brewer's assistance, Dmytryk became the first of the ex-Communists to go back to work, but he would not be the last.

Brewer had become a major figure in Hollywood after having successfully beaten Herb Sorrell and his radical Conference of Studio Unions. He was viewed by business leaders as reasonable, he was liked by his fellow labor leaders in the AFL, and he was active in Democratic politics. As chairman of the AFL Film Council, he coordinated collective bargaining in Hollywood. He had helped set up the Motion Picture Industry Council (MPIC), which recommended anti-Communist policies to the producers. Brewer was also a powerful figure within the highly influential anti-Communist Motion Picture Alliance.

Using these and other fora, Brewer became the most important anti-Communist force in Hollywood. The connection between Brewer and Dmytryk turned out to be enormously helpful as anti-Communist Hollywood decided how to deal with ex-Communists and those willing to become ex-Communists.

Through Dmytryk, Brewer met Dick Collins, a member of the original Hollywood Nineteen. Collins, as the Fund study discloses, "put Brewer in touch with other ex-Communists who were finding it impossible to go back to work." In his effort to assist these former Party members, Brewer customarily turned them over to a key member of his staff, an ex-Communist named Howard Costigan.

Costigan had a "to do" list for the "Exes." They would have to go to the FBI, then get in touch with HUAC, and, finally, testify against the Party and name fellow conspirators. If any of the "Exes" was prominent enough, he might have to make a public statement or write an article condemning the Party. (Dmytryk had written a seminal article on his experience in the Party for the *Saturday Evening Post* in April 1951.)

Brewer's compassionate anti-Communism proved a spectacular plus for the entire industry. He had even persuaded the hard-boiled Motion Picture Alliance to get behind his "rehabilitation" program. The American Legion and other anti-Communist organizations sided with Brewer's position as well.

As the Fund study grudgingly (and not-so-approvingly) relates, "Costigan's and Brewer's contact with so many ex-Communists not only gave them access to names not yet publicly revealed but an intimate knowledge of the party's operations in Hollywood. And when graduates of the 'rehabilitation' course appeared before the House Committee, they testified with a degree of 'cooperation' unknown during the first Hollywood probe. After they testified, *most of them went back to work* [emphasis added]."[3]

Brewer, in short, helped the industry remove its Red taint, created a path back to work for Hollywood's disillusioned and blacklisted Communists, and persuaded pragmatic liberals to climb aboard the anti-Communist bandwagon.

The Left had a grudging respect for Brewer, but they never reconciled themselves to his brand of anti-Communism or his program allowing former Communists to remain in the movie industry.

PRAGMATIC LIBERALS

Brewer and his allies weren't the only folks helping the ex-Communists—or the only ones taking the heat for doing so. So were many pragmatic liberals, but only after HUAC and Brewer had won the fight over whether ex-Reds needed to show their bona fides by naming fellow conspirators. Martin Gang, for instance, of the firm of Gang, Kopp & Tyre, was a prosperous lawyer in Hollywood. In 1950 prominent actor Sterling Hayden called on Gang to help him with his "Communist" problem. Gang tried to resolve it by sending a letter about his client to FBI director J. Edgar Hoover.

The letter claimed that Hayden, "in a moment of emotional disturbance," joined the Communist Party in the state of California in June of 1946 but ended his membership six months later. He discussed Hayden's war record, including his enlistment in the Marines as a private and leaving as a captain. Hayden had also won the Silver Star for gallantry in action.[4]

Gang didn't mention it, but Hayden had joined the Office of Strategic Services (OSS), fought behind enemy lines, and worked closely with the Partisans in Yugoslavia, controlled by the Communist Marshal Tito. Tito, with Stalin's help, eventually seized power and turned Yugoslavia into a Communist state. So important was Hayden's assistance in World War II that the Tito government awarded him the Order of Merit, the "second highest decoration" that could be awarded to a foreigner.

Hoover told Hayden to tell his story to the FBI offices in Los Angeles, which Hayden dutifully did. In April 1951, with Gang's assistance, he appeared before HUAC and told a fascinating story of his life in the OSS, his support of the Partisans, and his joining a secret Red cell in Hollywood in June 1946 at the behest of Bea Winters. This cell, which included Communist writers Robert Lees and Abraham Polonsky, met weekly and backed Red causes. At Party direction, Hayden was told to line up actors and actresses behind the 1946 strike conducted by the Red-saturated Conference of Studio Unions. Hayden told Committee members that he quit the Party in December of 1946 partly because he had come to the conclusion that there was no freedom in the Party, that everything "was predetermined,"[5] and that its "ultimate objective" was the overthrow of the American government.[6]

Hayden remained a left-winger his entire life and, in his memoir, *Wanderer*, appears to regret his confessions, calling himself "a real daddylonglegs of a worm when it came to crawling."[7] Still, the major anti-Communist forces put up no obstacles to Hayden's employment despite his radical politics, and he began starring in a score of pictures after his testimony. Walking the "Gang plank" had worked wonders. Thus Gang became the "go-to" guy for ex-Communists and troubled radicals.

Gang was a liberal and a Democrat and had been a member of the far-Left National Lawyers Guild, which wound up on the attorney general's list as Communist controlled. Among his clients in the 1940s were members of the original Hollywood Nineteen, including CP members Larry Parks and Dalton Trumbo. He also signed, as Victor Navasky tells us in *Naming Names*, an *amicus curiae* brief on behalf of the Hollywood Ten. But he became a beacon of hope for those who wanted to divorce themselves from the Party.

Prior to the 1951 hearings, Gang frequented Washington to feel out how HUAC would react to Hayden and his other left-wing clients who had been subpoenaed, including Collins, former screen editor Meta Reis Rosenberg, and musical comedy writer Abe Burrows. Gang said he didn't like HUAC's demand for "public exposure," but he was satisfied that its staff was comprised of "decent people," and he advised his clients to tell the truth about their time in the Party.

According to the Fund, Gang represented fifty people called by the House Committee, twenty of them in the motion picture industry. He successfully advocated the cause of both ex-Reds and those who had joined numerous Red fronts with considerable abandon. Committee members were grateful to him because he had persuaded clients, particularly Collins and Meta Reis Rosenberg, to furnish extensive information on the Party's activities.[8]

In assisting the ex-Communists, including those still on the Left politically, Gang, many might think, should have won kudos even from the toughest critics of HUAC and the blacklist. But Gang found himself condemned by many on the Left. Navasky charges Gang with viewing the issue of "informing" as one of "tactics rather than ethics, style rather than substance, of immediate benefit or loss rather than long-range principle."[9] He calls Gang HUAC's "collaborator," "Torquemada's adjutant," and a tolerator of the Nazi tactic of compelling German citizens to inform on their neighbors.

In fact, Gang had just told his clients the truth: as a result of the Waldorf Declaration establishing the blacklist, they couldn't get movie industry jobs unless they repudiated Communism and named some CP conspirators they had worked closely with over the years. And Gang was going to do his darnedest to help his clients get back to work.

That was the nub of the problem for the Left. They believed the only truly respectable form of conduct, even for those who wanted to break with the Party, was to stonewall HUAC completely. The next best option was to admit your Party membership but never "inform" on fellow cell members. Any other position was said to be cowardly and dishonorable.

As Gang and others developed strategies to avoid the blacklist or the gray list (for non-Party members with scarlet associations), the Left became increasingly incensed. They objected even in cases where Communist sympathizers weren't asked to inform on former comrades but only to prove their own loyalty. Take the case of Paulette Goddard, the ex-wife of the very pro-Communist actor Charlie Chaplin (then in exile), and a client of Gang's.

Paramount was upset with Goddard because her detailed letter about her left-wing activities "does not give us the kind of declaration that we would want from her, namely, that she is not and has never been a Communist and that her allegiance is to the USA." The studio, according to Navasky, finally gave her a pass because she was big box office and they didn't want to fire her and stir up a fuss that might backfire. But even so, the Hollywood Left was indignant. In *Naming Names*, Navasky clearly implies that the studio had no right to ask such a pledge of allegiance in the first place.[10]

Screenwriter Philip Dunne, a good guy, but always a patsy for the Hollywood Reds, also came under fire from left-wingers for cooperating with Brewer to help some of his radical friends get back to work. He suggests he was viewed as a "harlot" for his good deeds—and even he himself seems conflicted about his conduct.

No one was more supportive of the Hollywood Ten and more opposed to the blacklist than Dunne. Dunne reminds readers of his book that he went to the mat for the Ten. When his ad hoc Committee for the First Amendment folded, he helped found the successor Committee of One Thousand, signed an *amicus* brief on behalf of the Ten after they were indicted, flew to Washington to testify for his Stalinist friend Dalton Trumbo, and "contributed to the support of the families of the blacklisted."[11]

Nevertheless, Dunne, like Gang, was willing to work with Brewer to help his friends get back into the movie industry. Dunne had come to know labor leader Brewer a bit because Brewer had become a member of the Hollywood for Stevenson group—but only after Dunne had stopped an effort to prevent Brewer from joining.

Dunne met with Brewer and his chief aide, Howard Costigan, also a relentless anti-Communist, at a bar. Dunne told them that he opposed the blacklist "with all my heart and soul," but Brewer promptly offered to clear anyone whose innocence Dunne could prove. Dunne said he decided to cooperate to "put many good and deserving people back to work."

These people would write letters to Dunne explaining their past radical political activities, and the letters would be forwarded to Brewer. "As it happened," writes Dunne, "every single one of those I approached eagerly accepted my proposal, and I obtained clearance for fifteen people in all, including two prominent actors. If this was an act of political prostitution, I can claim that, like many a movie harlot, this one was motivated by a heart of gold."[12]

Still, for the far Left, Dunne, like Gang, had committed the cardinal sin of working with Brewer and accepting the idea that there should be a clearance system in the first place. For the Navaskys, active Communists should have been welcomed with open arms by the movie industry; ex-Communists, however, were to be scorned, mocked, or reviled, especially if the price of getting a job was to "inform" on fellow conspirators. And those who helped them get jobs were considered narrow and zealous anti-Communists (like Brewer) or liberal "collaborators" (like Gang), whose work could be compared to that of informers in Hitler's Germany.

The blacklist's harshest critics over the years have shown an enormous concern for the welfare of the Communist stalwarts who "stood up" to HUAC and refused to bow down to the studio demands to renounce the Party. This is why the Hollywood liberals today are so enamored of Dalton Trumbo, the highly celebrated screenwriter who was the first to break the blacklist without having to apologize for a single unpatriotic action taken during his years of subservience to the Party.

The plight of those who changed their mind about belonging to a conspiracy to overthrow the constitutional government of their country in a bloody revolution and were willing to try to make amends, on the other hand, doesn't seem to concern them at all.

CHAPTER FORTY

RED REMINISCENCES

ommunists who remained Communists for most of their lives frequently tell at least a portion of the truth in their more reflective moods. Virtually all of the major Hollywood Reds—not the "informers" but the bitter-enders—have, in the end, said quite a lot that is less than helpful to their side of the argument. Not one of these aging leftists, many of them now deceased, ever made a clean breast of his or her ties to the Party, but together they have granted a good deal of the case that the anti-Communists made against them.

They concede that they joined the Party, conspired to take over the movie industry, salted films with Red propaganda, recruited comrades into Hollywood, and were completely in the tank for the murderous Stalin. Some have said that post-Stalin they still hungered for revolutionary Communism (Norma

Barzman, for one, was disappointed that the Communists in France had lost their insurrectionary zeal).

Many of their reflections can be found in *Tender Comrades*, a 1997 collection of interviews with blacklisted movie writers and directors that contains a wealth of reminiscences—and damning admissions.

PAUL JARRICO

Paul Jarrico, Richard Collins's partner in writing *Song of Russia* and *Thousands Cheer*, was a thoroughgoing Red till his dying day. He admits that the Party betrayed him over and over again. But he remained a faithful spouse no matter how many times he was cuckolded. In an insightful interview in *Tender Comrades*, he says he joined the Young Communist League as a sophomore at UCLA in 1933, transferred to Berkeley in his junior year, and became a Party member. (He heard the French author André Malraux speak on behalf of the Spanish Loyalists at the LA Philharmonic and met a friend there who talked him into joining the Party.)

Jarrico became a prominent Hollywood screenwriter, was "outed" as a Red by his writing partner Richard Collins, took the Fifth before the House Un-American Activities Committee, refused to say whether he would defend the United States in a war with Russia, and was blacklisted. No one on the Left can accuse him of being a "collaborator" with the anti-Communists or an "informer," but he concedes quite a lot of the case of those who vigorously battled the Hollywood Communists. Discussing the "worst mistakes" of the Party in Hollywood, Jarrico said they were probably the same "as the mistakes of the Party everywhere in the United States. It was looking to the Soviet Union for leadership."

He stresses that the Soviet-Nazi Pact "was a disaster for the Party. Or, rather, the Party decision to accept 'What is good for the Soviet Union is good for us'...was a disaster. Clearly, we lost whatever prestige we had built up in the course of the anti-Fascist fight...." Jarrico confides that the Communists "had been the chief organizers" in the Hollywood Anti-Nazi League, but then concedes that after the Pact they were no longer opposing Hitler's predatory policies and instead calling for a change in the organization's name. They also began to excuse Hitler's brutality by claiming that the "war is imperialist on both sides." After the Soviets made that Pact with the devil, the Party, Jarrico remarks, never fully recovered, even when it switched back to the "anti-fascist" line.

Serious anti-Nazis, he laments, could no longer follow the Communist Party leadership. And though many quit in the wake of the Pact, Jarrico acknowledges that he personally remained a Party member in good standing through all its acrobatic antics. The Party enthusiastically backed the war effort, but only after Hitler had betrayed the Soviet Union. So, Jarrico admits, the belief held by many that Hollywood's Reds became "patriotic on June 22, 1941, when the Soviet Union was invaded was well-founded." After Pearl Harbor, America's domestic Communists focused on opening a second front to relieve the Nazi pressure against Stalin, which made people think Hollywood's Reds were "looking out for the interests of the Soviet Union, not the United States."

The Albert Maltz episode—in which, as we have seen, Maltz was browbeaten into publicly recanting his mild questioning of the Communists' determination to reduce all art to agitprop—was itself unsettling, Jarrico acknowledges, and underscored the ham-fisted Party control over writers and artists. And yet he defends the Communist principle that was at stake. The issue was whether writers and artists should focus "more sharply" on political events or create works that dwell more on positive human values, he explains. If the war against fascism should be of high priority, then, the Party believed, "your cultural work ought to be about the war against fascism" and not about less important issues.

The Soviet Union had embraced the view of cultural "theorist" Andrei Zhdanov, whose intent was to compel artists to serve the political needs of the moment rather than dwell on side issues such as poverty and the creation of great works of art. The Zhdanov line "became the dominant line in the Soviet Union," Jarrico notes, "and, by extension, in the American Party as well."

Maltz was rebelling just a bit against the "Zhdanov line," Jarrico points out, but got walloped for it and finally surrendered. The Zhdanov line was being pushed everywhere, even in China. Mao Tse-tung was enforcing the Zhdanov line, Jarrico recalls, insisting, for example, that the writer Ding Ling had to use her talents to directly pursue the Party's message of the moment. She rebelled, got tossed into various prisons, and was finally exiled.

Despite these disturbing cases, Jarrico was never really disillusioned with Communism. He headed the Party in Hollywood in the 1950s, though he concedes that by then he was presiding over a lost cause. "When the Khrushchev report came along in 1956, even the slowest of us realized that the accusations against Stalin and Stalinism had been true—though we had denied they were true—and that we had been defending indefensible things. That, I would say, was the end of the Party."

Jarrico says that he and some of his comrades made a last-ditch effort to get the American Communist Party to declare itself independent of Soviet leadership, but after a temporary win in 1958, the hard-line Soviet supporters prevailed. So, he says, he finally quit—but he never apologized for his longtime CP membership.[1]

JULES DASSIN

Jules Dassin had directed several well-received films—*Brute Force, The Naked City,* and *Night and the City*—before he was blacklisted in 1950 and decided to live in Europe. Beginning in 1957, while living in Greece, Dassin wrote and directed movies for the famous actress Melina Mercouri, a political soul mate whom he eventually married. The best-known films he penned for her to star in were *Never on Sunday* (1960) and *Topkapi* (1964). *Never on Sunday* earned Dassin an Oscar nomination for Best Original Screenplay.

In recalling his experience with the Party, Dassin makes many of the same points as Jarrico, especially about the Party's slavish attachment to the Soviet Union. The Party worked hard, Dassin informs Patrick McGilligan in *Tender Comrades,* to present Communism as something that was rooted in American traditions. But Americans couldn't be persuaded to the Party's point of view, because the Party's "association with the Soviet Union was too powerful."

Dassin suggests that it would have been far better if the Party had shed the slogan "Defend the Soviet Union" for something along these lines: "Defend a Fairer System." He admits the pro-Soviet slogan became "very dangerous" and was used by opponents who wondered why it was important for Americans to be defending Bolsheviks.

Did he speak out against the Party when he thought it was mistaken? Dassin says the Party did many "stupid things" and that he was "on the verge of expulsion many times," but he apparently never spoke out publicly. Dassin says he complained that the Party line was too soft on Hitler after the British were kicked off the Continent and that he disagreed with its harsh treatment of Albert Maltz. Nevertheless, he dutifully stayed the course.

The Party's contemptuous attitude toward John Wayne was also a major mistake, he claimed. "Even if he was naïve and a red baiter," he argues, "it was a mistake to label John Wayne a Fascist, when he was really, on his own terms, an American patriot and nationalist."[2]

JOHN BRIGHT

"In Hollywood since 1929, John Bright was a founding father of the Screen Writers Guild as well as one of the original 'secret four' members of the Hollywood section of the Communist Party. At the same time that he was building his early reputation as an uncompromising, hard-boiled writer, he participated in every left-wing cause that came along." So say left-wing sympathizers Patrick McGilligan and Ken Mate in *Tender Comrades*. Among the movies Bright wrote or helped write were *She Done Him Wrong* (1933) with Mae West, *San Quentin* (1937), *Sherlock Holmes and the Voice of Terror* (1942), *The Brave Bulls* (1951), and Dalton Trumbo's *Johnny Got His Gun* (1971).

Asked by McGilligan and Mate how the Party was organized in Hollywood, Bright was forthcoming enough to give the world an interesting but very restrictive glimpse. He wouldn't give names and never elaborated on the Party's various crusades. "By 1934," he says, "I was pretty well established as a writer in Hollywood, and I was also looking for a political home." He had worked for the radical novelist Upton Sinclair in his failed campaign for California governor, but then he met Stanley Lawrence, "with credentials from the general headquarters of the Communist Party in New York."

Lawrence, who taught Marxism to Hollywood scriptwriters and others, informed Bright and his partner, Bob Tasker, that the

> Party nationally had decided on the organization of a Hollywood studio section which would not be answerable to the state or the county but only to headquarters in New York.

I, Tasker and two other people became the first four members of the Hollywood studio section. Very soon after that, the section grew to three hundred within two or three years. We established a direct linkage with New York, and "Commissar" V. J. Jerome, the cultural head of the party, came out to advise us. John Howard Lawson assumed the position of the indigenous Hollywood person who was the head of the section.

What did he think of "Browderism" and the patriotic tone of Hollywood Communism during the Second World War? Bright said he viewed it as "backsliding, as a betrayal, really, of revolutionary purposes." Earl Browder, the head of the CPUSA during the war years, was an amiable fellow, but he became "a reformist liberal who talked in Marxist phraseology." According to Bright, Browder's message amounted to "collaboration" with the U.S. administration. But after French Communist Party leader Jacques Duclos's sharp criticism of the Kansas-born Browder in 1945, the Party, as Bright would have it, "woke up" to the disaster Browder was creating and went in the other direction.

Bright was often frustrated by various Party positions, usually because they weren't revolutionary enough for him. He was also upset by the concept of "democratic centralism," according to which individual members were to submit to the policy decisions of the Party. Bright relates that he went to a Party school presided over by V. J. Jerome, a defrocked rabbi, "who lectured at interminable length" and repeated the same thing over and over again. He once challenged Jerome on democratic centralism, "Comrade Jerome, what if a Party decision is made that you cannot go along with?" Jerome responded that when the Party makes a decision, "it becomes your decision." Bright said he didn't like the answer but that he "swept it under the rug."[3]

MAURICE RAPF

Maurice Rapf was hardly a prodigious scriptwriter, though he wrote, cowrote, or was involved with several well-known pictures, including *Jennie* (1940), Disney's *Song of the South* (1946), and *Cinderella* (1950). He had joined the Communist Party in the 1930s and says he left it in 1946 because he felt he had to choose between being a successful moviemaker or being a dedicated Communist. He chose being a moviemaker, but he remained a Party defender and a cheerleader for Stalin during much of his adult life.

Rapf tells Patrick McGilligan in *Tender Comrades* that his main job in the Party was to steer the Screen Writers Guild toward Communist objectives. The Party "put me on the board and made me secretary of the Guild," he relates. "The party could control an election, you know. Otherwise, people like me and Harold Buchman and even Ring [Lardner Jr.] would never have been elected to the board of the Screen Writers Guild. We didn't deserve to be on the board."

Rapf says the Party took control by "passing out a slate and urging people to vote for it." Since not everyone would vote and others could be manipulated, a concerted group of activists could determine the outcome. Rapf had gone east in 1947 and insists that he had stopped going to Party meetings six months before he left Hollywood. He had no political differences with the CP, he stresses, but he just didn't want to spend the "time and energy" that it took to be a Party member.

There were some people who used the Party "very strongly for their professional ends. There's no doubt about that—people hired Party people; they read each other's scripts and were helpful." But even when he stopped going to meetings, he didn't stop his Guild activities, and he still considered himself a Communist. During an interview in New Hampshire in the 1980s, Rapf said he had just got back from some academic conference in Toledo where he had shocked everyone by saying that he remained "an unrepentant Communist."

Rapf was one of those unrepentant Reds who didn't much believe in the crimes of Stalin. He concludes his interview with McGilligan this way: "As for all the revelations about the atrocities that took place in the Soviet Union—the so-called exposé of Stalin—by the time it began, I was no longer a member of the Party anyway—and I don't believe half of it, either. I tend to be pro-Soviet...."[4]

NORMA BARZMAN

In her memoir, *The Red and the Blacklist*, Norma Barzman begins by reminiscing about a Halloween party in October 1942. The purpose was to raise money for Russian war relief. The gathering was held at the home of Communist writer Robert Rossen, where Barzman was surrounded by CP members and tingling with excitement at the big names she encountered.

Among the Party writers she was hobnobbing with was Gordon Kahn ("my screenwriting teacher from the School for Writers"), sandwiched on a sofa between Paul Jarrico and Ring Lardner Jr. Jarrico's screenplay, *Tom, Dick and Harry*, had been nominated for an Oscar in 1941, while Lardner had won the Oscar that year for *Woman of the Year*. The "pompous" Herbert Biberman, as Barzman describes him, was in attendance, as well as *Scarface* star Karen Morley. All were CP members.

"Within a few years," writes Barzman, "most of the people would be summoned before the House Un-American Activities Committee" to be asked about their Party membership. But on that evening, she was dazzled "by the star-studded room." She was also dazzled by Ben Barzman, whom she had just met, and who had been a Party member since 1939, when Hitler and Stalin had agreed to that infamous Pact.[5]

Norma Barzman studied Marxist ideology, including Friedrich Engels's *The Origin of the Family, Private Property and the State*. And she strongly believed that "art needed to serve the revolution." She was "busy all the time: a branch meeting every week and selling a number of copies of the [Communist paper] *People's World*." She tried hard to recruit Party members.

Her husband Ben and future Hollywood Ten member Edward Dmytryk were very close, with Dmytryk having directed Ben's screenplay *Back to Bataan* (1945), starring John Wayne. Norma relates that Ben so detested Wayne's "outrageous reactionary comments"—though never reprising them for the reader—that he "got even" with the famous movie idol. A furious Ben, she says, "devised and wrote into the script agonizing stunts that Wayne, who worked without a double" would have to perform. Wayne managed to survive the ordeal.

After the '47 hearings and the blacklist, the Barzmans went abroad in 1949 rather than risk a subpoena from HUAC. They settled in France with a colony of Red writers including Jules Dassin and Jack Berry. "Socially," she says, "we inhabited a Communist milieu." She and Ben felt good about themselves, "since we were in a country where the Communist Party was a mass party" and we were "part of the mainstream, not off in a corner." Friends believed that "by standing up to HUAC, we had done something wonderful."

When Nikita Khrushchev delivered his 1956 speech disclosing Stalin's awful crimes, Barzman concedes that Ben and she were "shocked" but thought it was "wonderful" that the Soviet Union would admit such error. Even when their doctor friends and other left-wing intellectuals broke with the French Communist Party, the Barzmans didn't budge in their support of Red Russia. "It took us until 1968 to admit the many things wrong with world communism."[6]

Curiously, what bothered these American Communists the most about "world communism" was its supposed lack of revolutionary ardor. Yes, Stalin may have done some terrible deeds, but the Barzmans still hoped that revolutionary Communism would triumph somewhere.

In her memoir, *The Red and the Blacklist*, Norma waxes eloquent about the May 1968 near-revolution in France. What began as a student protest morphed into massive protests and a general strike. Students mounted barricades, tossed firebombs at police, and joined left-wing workers in flying red flags over seized factories and public facilities. *Facts on File* described the civil unrest as raising "the threat of social revolution."

Barzman discusses how excited she was by the unstable conditions in the country, applauding the students engaged in mass protests and the rapidly spreading labor strike that was beginning to paralyze the nation. After student protesters were arrested in Paris, she happily states, some twenty thousand marched down the streets, crying, "Free our comrades" and "singing the *Internationale*."[7] The Barzmans loved it all.

Toward the end of May, when they arrived in Paris, their son Aaron, who was "busy with the battle," handed them a leaflet of the March 22 Movement, a central organizer of the student protests. The leaflet explained to the striking workers, whom many of the students had joined, the importance of their fight:

> When a worker's son becomes a student, he leaves his class. When the son of a bourgeoisie goes to the university, he may learn the true nature of his class.... We want to build a classless society.... Your struggle is more radical than our legitimate demands

because it not only seeks an improvement of the worker's lot within the capitalist system, but it implies the destruction of that system.

Your struggle is political...you are *not* fighting to replace one prime minister by another, but to deprive the owner, the boss, of his power in the factory and in society; the appropriation of the means of production and of the power of decision by the working people.

Her husband Ben, says Barzman, "was revitalized" by the turmoil and their son's fight for "socialism." Bordering on a state of ecstasy, she writes that in Paris, "in the midst of May '68, when I was forty-seven and Ben fifty-seven, I fell in love with him all over again."[8]

The Barzmans' bliss was, alas, short-lived. She notes that the revolution never materialized, because the French Communist Party and the Communist-controlled CGT (the Confederation of Labor) had become concerned about the anarchy that threatened to devour the nation. The Communists had turned against a potential revolution. The outcome "was a vast conservative Gaullist majority in the elections."

The Barzmans were devastated. "Why didn't the Communists support the strike?" she asks. "Because, according to them, the students would lead the revolution into an 'irresponsible leftist direction.' For Ben and for me, the Party's position was untenable. We felt betrayed, as if they were aiding and supporting de Gaulle."[9] After these great events only strengthened de Gaulle's position, Norma Barzman came down with hepatitis. "Though I did not yet know it, I was recuperating from massive betrayal and self-delusion." Still, Barzman managed to remain hopeful when she thought about the student movement's primary leader, Daniel (Danny-the-Red) Cohn-Bendit, who was "tossed over the border into Germany by the French government," with thousands of Parisians, young and old, rallying to his cause.

She concludes her chapter, "I could visualize the terrible June when de Gaulle was back in power. Yet students and workers, by now maybe only 30,000, their red flags flying, bravely marched down Montparnasse, chanting the slogan that will stay with me forever: 'It's only a beginning.... Let us continue the struggle.'"[10]

CHAPTER FORTY-ONE

HOLLYWOOD TODAY

ollywood may no longer be enamored of Stalin, but troops of the town's stars remain enamored of Stalin's defenders. The Hollywood Ten, Stalinists all when they were cited for contempt by Congress in 1947, continue to be honored—with the notable exception of Eddie Dmytryk, the only one to decisively turn his back on the Party. The Soviet Union is gone, Eastern Europe is no longer under Moscow's heel, and Communist China has scrapped Maoist economics. Much of Hollywood, however, is still lured by the romance of Marxism, and its films are still filled with heavy doses of anti-American propaganda.

ANTI-AMERICAN HOLLYWOOD

How many movies, for instance, show Americans bravely routing Islamic terrorists? How many films offer any justification for the harsh interrogation techniques or important internal security measures we have used to keep our country safe since 9/11? Almost none, of course. It's easy to rattle off the anti-American films—*Lions for Lambs, The Valley of Elah, Rendition, Redacted*, and so forth—where the United States is invariably portrayed as the villain.

Observing Hollywood's anti-American slant, Mark Steyn has wryly noted, "Every Friday night at the multiplex, Mr. and Mrs. America are saying, 'Hmm, shall we see the movie where our boys are the torturers? Or the one where our boys are the rapists? How about the film where the heroic soldier refuses to fight? Or the one where he does fight and the army covers up the truth about his death?'"

Take the film *Syriana*, for instance, for which George Clooney won an Oscar for Best Supporting Actor. A heroic Arab prince wants to end corruption and oppression, especially of women, and modernize his country. And wouldn't you know it, the CIA obliterates him and his family with a remote-controlled missile.

The film also features a wonderfully humane Pakistani who feels impelled by America's heinous policies to become a suicide bomber and carries out a mission similar to the terrorist assault on the USS *Cole*. (Just for the record, the suicide bombers that severely damaged the *Cole* and murdered seventeen American sailors were directed by Osama bin Laden's "idealistic" group, al Qaeda.)

TINSELTOWN STILL LOVES MARXIST THUGS

Then there is the curious way that Hollywood's elite have been drawn to the saintly spirit that is Fidel Castro. In 2002, filmmaker Steven Spielberg visited Castro's totalitarian regime (described so even by our own State Department), dined with its bloodstained dictator until the wee hours of the morning, and pronounced that dinner with Fidel "was the eight most important hours of my life."

Actor Jack Nicholson, equally mesmerized, informed *Daily Variety* that Fidel "is a genius. We spoke about everything." Model Naomi Campbell has declared the Cuban dictator "a source of inspiration to the world." Chronicling the numerous stars swooning at Castro's feet, Marc Morano noted that comedian Chevy Chase has said he now believes that "socialism works" and that Castro, apparently, has pulled off this grand trick in Cuba. Other Hollywood notables who have visited this island country and have come back singing hallelujah: Robert Redford, Spike Lee, Danny Glover, Shirley MacLaine, Leonardo DiCaprio, and Kevin Costner.

"Costner," writes Morano, "visited Cuba in 2001 for the premiere of his film on the Cuban Missile Crisis, *Thirteen Days*, and attended a private screening with Castro.... Costner was clearly impressed," remarking at a Havana press conference, "'It was an experience of a lifetime to sit only a few feet away from him and with him relive an experience he lived as a very young man.'"[1] (At the time he actually *was* living this experience, the young Fidel urged the Soviet Union *to strike America with nuclear weapons*.)

One must also mention *Fidel*, an Estela Bravo "documentary" glorifying the Cuban dictator and featuring such gushingly pro-Castro personalities as Harry Belafonte and Ted Turner. Even the *New York Times* movie critic A. O. Scott called it "an exercise not in biography but in hero worship."

There are, of course, a flock of Hollywood folk who are also moonstruck by Fidel's longtime sidekick Ernesto "Che" Guevara, celebrated in Steven Soderbergh's movie *Che*. Actor Benicio Del Toro, who played this hard-core revolutionary, compared him to Jesus Christ. Director Steven Soderbergh praised his dream of a classless society, largely indifferent to his homicidal methods and totalitarian ideology.

What is it about Fidel and his compatriots that Hollywood stars find so thrilling? Thoughtful observers have to wonder whether it's the same thing that initially attracted so many Hollywood figures to Stalin: the aura of a powerful anti-American personality who has imposed a totalitarian socialist government on his people.

Cuba, like Soviet Russia when Stalin was in command, became a harsh dictatorship under Fidel. He and his men confiscated private wealth, shut down small businessmen, demolished Christian churches, executed thousands, and imprisoned and brutalized peaceful opponents.

Consider, for instance, how the very liberal organization Human Rights Watch described Cuba the day Fidel resigned as president. "Even if Castro no longer calls the shots, the repressive machinery he constructed over almost half a century remains fully intact," remarked José Miguel Vivanco, director of the

Americas Division of Human Rights Watch. For nearly five decades, the human rights organization stated , "Cuba has restricted nearly all avenues of political dissent. Cuban citizens have been systematically deprived of their fundamental rights to free expression, privacy, association, assembly, movement and due process of law." The 2014 Human Rights Watch report made virtually the same assessment.[2]

Amnesty International, another liberal human rights group, had these things to say about Cuba in 2007, after many of Hollywood's celebrities had paid homage to Fidel:

- Severe restrictions on freedom of expression and association affect thousands of people across Cuba.
- In Cuba, all print and broadcast media are under state control....
- Dissidents and critics of the regime, including journalists, are frequently arrested and detained, some of them on charges of "pre-criminal dangerousness."
- ...prisoners of conscience—people such as teachers, journalists and human rights defenders detained for their peaceful activities—are currently held in prisons across Cuba, following unfair trials that failed to uphold international standards....
- Amnesty International receives almost daily reports of political dissidents, independent journalists and critics being arrested for carrying out dissident activities or reporting on the human rights situation in Cuba and sent to prison where they await trial. In some cases they wait for months or even years....[3]

The U.S. State Department, not exactly a right-wing organization, released a similar evaluation in 2009. "Cuba, with a population of approximately 11.2 million, is a totalitarian state," and the government, even after Raul Castro succeeded his brother, Fidel, as president in 2006, "continued to deny its citizens their basic human rights."

Among other human rights abuses listed by the State Department: "beatings and abuse of detainees and prisoners, including human rights activists, carried out with impunity; harsh and life-threatening prison conditions, including denial of medical care; harassment; beatings and threats against political opponents by government-recruited mobs, police, and State Security officials...."

According to State, political prisoner Tomás Ramos Rodriguez, released in 2008 after eighteen years in Castro's jails, "stated that in the Combinado del Este prison in Havana Province, prison authorities beat prisoners with truncheons on a near daily basis."[4]

What's so difficult to comprehend is why scores of Hollywood liberals, who insist they have been profoundly shattered by the fact that Americans may have "abused" a bona fide terrorist bent on our annihilation—in the case, for example, of the successful waterboarding of Khalid Sheikh Mohammed—appear to reconcile themselves so effortlessly to the brutality of the oppressive Cuban regime. Various Hollywood types are also drawn to Fidel's loyal ally Hugo Chavez in Venezuela, including Sean Penn, Danny Glover, and Kevin Spacey. The 2008 U.S. State Department report on Chavez's country is hardly flattering: "Politicization of the judiciary and official harassment of the political opposition and the media characterized the human rights situation during the year." Among the reported human rights "problems": "unlawful killings; harsh prison conditions; arbitrary arrests and detentions;" and "a corrupt, inefficient and politicized judicial system characterized by trial delays, impunity and violations of due process." More abuses abounded, according to State, including "official intimidation and attacks on the independent media; discrimination based on political grounds; widespread corruption at all levels of government; violence against women; trafficking in persons; and restrictions on workers' right of association."[5]

RED TRUMBO: STILL A HOLLYWOOD HERO

The Hollywood tilt toward Marxist totalitarians explains why its inhabitants are still drawn to Dalton Trumbo, a high-profile member of the Ten, who remains one of the town's most revered icons. In his later years, both Trumbo and his admirers portrayed him as a virtual libertarian, a crusader for individual rights, bucking the crushing power of the state, persecuted by Joe McCarthy and the House Un-American Activities Committee.

McCarthy, despite liberal propaganda to the contrary, never set his sights on Trumbo or, for that matter, Hollywood. And HUAC proved, beyond question, that Trumbo was a rip-roaring Red whose allegiance was to an enemy nation bent on our destruction. Here was a man who allied himself with Stalin and Hitler and produced a manuscript giving a glowing account of Kim Il-sung's totalitarian North Korean regime. Yet he is still seen in Hollywood and in many other liberal precincts as a magnificent defender of the First Amendment.

America should have been viewed by liberals and even Soviet sympathizers as a beneficent nation for most of the 1940s. The United States rescued much of the world from Nazi Germany during World War II, including the USSR, with FDR lavishing Moscow with substantial aid and major territorial concessions at Yalta. In the postwar period, we transformed Germany, a historical foe of Russia, into a non-threatening democracy. Nor were we unsympathetic to the Soviets, even during the Cold War. Under the Marshall Plan, when we offered billions of dollars in American largesse to war-ravaged Europe, we also offered, in the Christian tradition of forgiving your enemies, critical assistance to Russia and the nations it dominated in Eastern and Central Europe (though Stalin rejected our offer). Nor was the Marshall Plan the first time we had sought to aid our Soviet enemy. When Lenin's Russia was suffering a massive famine in the early 1920s, Herbert Hoover headed a relief mission that prompted the famous Russian author Maxim Gorky to write the future president that he would "long remain in the memory of millions of Russians whom you have saved from death."

One would have thought Trumbo and his Red friends might, at least grudgingly, have tipped their hats to America's generosity, especially since it was Stalin who rejected our aid and a hand of friendship. Instead, they unleashed ferocious attacks designed to undermine our very existence. And what was the Hollywood Communists' precious Soviet Union doing during the same postwar period? Conquering one hundred million people in Eastern and Central Europe, imposing totalitarian regimes in North Korea and North Vietnam, providing crucial assistance to Mao in his successful effort to establish brutal, genocidal rule over six hundred million Chinese, initiating a terrible war against South Korea, and plotting to overthrow America. Not to mention, of course, imposing one of the cruelest regimes in the twentieth century on its own people.

Stalin's American screenwriters, along with their innumerable apologists, have wrapped their years of subversion in the American flag and the First Amendment. Yet for most of their adult lives, these men and women worked hard to undermine our country and eliminate the freedoms that we cherish and which they so loudly pretended to champion. They paid a price for sleeping with our Soviet enemy, but I believe most Americans would judge it a certain rough justice.

THE COMMUNIST CARDS OF THE HOLLYWOOD TEN

L ouis J. Russell, who had previously served with the FBI for a decade, was a staff investigator for HUAC during the famous 1947 Hollywood hearings. Reading from photostatic copies, he entered into the hearing record testimony on either the Communist Party cards or the Communist Political Association cards, or both, of each of the Hollywood Ten members. (The Political Association was the name of the Party for about fourteen months during WWII.) Below is a summary of Russell's testimony in each case.[1] The names are given in the order of their appearance before HUAC.

John Howard Lawson: Russell said that for the year 1944, Lawson's Party card, which Russell sometimes referred to as a "Party registration" card, "bears the number 47275 and is made out in the name of John Howard Lawson, 4542 Coldwater Canyon; city, Los Angeles; county, Los Angeles; state, California."

Dalton Trumbo: Russell testified that a copy of Trumbo's Party card for 1944 "bears the number 47187" and that "the name 'Dalt T'" was the name used on the card. This card also "reflects that 'Dalt T' resided at 620 Beverly Drive; city Beverly Hills; county Los Angeles; state, California."

Albert Maltz: Russell noted that Maltz's 1944 Party card "bears the number 47196. The address of Albert M [name on the card] is given as 8526 Linden Hurst; city, Los Angeles; county, Los Angeles; state, California."

Alvah Bessie: Russell said Bessie's 1944 Party card number "bears the number 47279." It also "contains the name Alvah Bessie. His address is given as 4653 Coldwater Canyon; city, Hollywood; county, Los Angeles; state, California."

Samuel Ornitz: Russell noted that the 1944 Party card "bears the number 47181." The name on the card, Sam O, "is given as 1044 South Redondo; city, Los Angeles; county, Los Angeles; state, California."

Herbert Biberman: Russell testified that Biberman's 1944 card bears his name, Herbert Biberman, and "bears the number 47267." The address "is given as 3259 Deronda Drive; city, Los Angeles; county, Los Angeles; state, California."

Edward Dmytryk: Russell said that Dmytryk was recruited into the Party in the spring of 1944 by Biberman, who was "reported to have been a member of the Party for approximately 18 years." Dmytryk, he went on, "was issued Communist Party book No. 84961 for the year 1944...." When the Party changed its name to the Communist Political Association in the summer of 1944, Dmytryk "was issued 1944 Communist Political Association membership card No. 46859 and for 1945 the Communist Political Association membership card No. 47238."

Adrian Scott: Russell stated that in the fall of 1944, Scott "was issued 1945 Communist Political Association Card No. 47200.... In the fall of the year 1945, Scott was issued Communist Party...card No. 35394 for the Year 1946." (The Communist Political Association became the Communist Party again in 1945.)

Ring Lardner Jr.: Russell said that Lardner's Party card number for the year 1944 "bears the number 47180. It is made out in the name of Ring L."

Lester Cole: Russell testified that Cole's 1944 Party card "bears the number 47226" and was "made out in the name Lester Cole."

APPENDIX B

SELECTED FILMOGRAPHY

elow is a condensed filmography for a few of the well-known radicals (many of them overt Communists) who populated the movie industry in the 1930s and '40s and many of whom were blacklisted in the 1950s.

Members of the Hollywood Ten are identified by asterisks (*), a dagger (†) indicates an Academy Award nomination, and a double dagger (††) indicates an Academy Award.

Alvah Bessie* (1904–1985) was a screenwriter with screenplay credit on five films released between 1943 and 1948, including:

- 1943 *Northern Pursuit* (starring Errol Flynn)
- 1945 *Hotel Berlin* (all-star cast including Raymond Massey and Peter Lorre)
- 1945 *Objective, Burma!*† (cowritten with Lester Cole; starring Errol Flynn)

Herbert Biberman* (1900–1971), writer, director, and producer, was credited on eight Hollywood films between 1935 and 1946. He also directed the black-listed documentary *Salt of the Earth*, produced by **Paul Jarrico**, in 1954. Among his credits:

- 1944 *Action in Arabia* (starring George Sanders)
- 1944 *The Master Race* (starring George Coulouris)
- 1947 *New Orleans* (all-star cast including Louis Armstrong and Billie Holiday)
- 1969 *Slaves* (starring Ossie Davis)

Michael Blankfort (1907–1982) contributed to seventeen films as a screenwriter between 1935 and 1966. He also fronted for the blacklisted **Albert Maltz** on the Academy Award–nominated screenplay of *Broken Arrow*† in 1950. His own work includes:

- 1939 *Blind Alley* (starring Chester Morris) and its 1948 remake, *The Dark Past* (with William Holden)
- 1950 *Halls of Montezuma* (starring Richard Widmark and Jack Palance)
- 1953 *The Juggler* (directed by **Edward Dmytryk**; starring Kirk Douglas)
- 1956 *Tribute to a Bad Man* (starring James Cagney)

John Bright (1908–1989), one of the ten cofounders of the Screen Writers Guild in 1933, created the gangster movie genre and was credited with contributing to twenty-four films between 1931 and 1951. Among the best-known:

- 1931 *The Public Enemy* (starring James Cagney)
- 1932 *Three on a Match* (starring Bette Davis, Joan Blondell, and Humphrey Bogart)
- 1933 *She Done Him Wrong* (starring Mae West and Cary Grant)

Sidney Buchman (1902–1975), screenwriter, contributed to thirty-five films between 1927 and 1946 but did not receive credit for his work on *The Awful Truth* (1937), *Lost Horizon* (1937), or *The Jolson Story* (1947). His credits include:

- 1938 *Holiday* (cowritten with **Donald Ogden Stewart**; starring Katharine Hepburn and Cary Grant)

- 1939 *Mr. Smith Goes to Washington* (starring Jimmy Stewart)
- 1941 *Here Comes Mr. Jordan* (starring Robert Montgomery)

Hugo Butler (1914–1968), Academy Award–winning screenwriter, contributed to thirty-one films between 1936 and 1968, at least five under pseudonyms and one without credit. His credits include:

- 1938 *A Christmas Carol* (starring Reginald Owen and Gene Lockhart)
- 1939 *Huckleberry Finn* (starring Mickey Rooney)
- 1940 *Edison, the Man*†† (starring Spencer Tracy)
- 1943 *Lassie, Come Home* (starring Roddy McDowall and Elizabeth Taylor)

Lester Cole* (1904–1985) contributed to thirty-seven films as a screenwriter between 1929 and 1947, including (covert and uncredited) *Chain Lightning* (1950). His credits include:

- 1941 *Among the Living* (starring Albert Dekker and Susan Hayward)
- 1945 *Blood on the Sun* (starring James Cagney and Sylvia Sidney)
- 1945 *Objective, Burma!*† (cowritten with **Alvah Bessie**; starring Errol Flynn)
- 1966 *Born Free* (credit restored; starring Virginia McKenna)

Richard Collins (1914–2013) contributed to nineteen known screenplays between 1937 and 1968, with unknown scripts black-marketed between 1947 and 1951. From the 1960s through the 1990s, he produced two popular television series, *Bonanza* and *Matlock*. Among his screenplay credits:

- 1943 *Song of Russia* (cowritten with **Paul Jarrico**; starring Robert Taylor)
- 1943 *Thousands Cheer* (cowritten with **Paul Jarrico**; starring Kathryn Grayson and Gene Kelly)
- 1954 *Riot in Cell Block 11* (starring Neville Brand)
- 1957 *My Gun Is Quick* (starring Robert Bray as Mickey Spillane's Mike Hammer)

Edward Dmytryk* (1908–1999), director, had more than fifty films to his credit between 1935 and 1976, including:

- 1947 *Crossfire*[†] (with Robert Mitchum, Robert Ryan, and Gloria Graham; nominated for Best Picture)
- 1953 *The Juggler* (written by **Michael Blankfort**; starring Kirk Douglas)
- 1954 *The Caine Mutiny* (starring Humphrey Bogart)
- 1957 *Raintree County* (starring Montgomery Clift and Elizabeth Taylor)
- 1958 *The Young Lions* (starring Marlon Brando and Montgomery Clift)

Dashiell Hammett (1894–1961) was the novelist who created the "hardboiled" detective genre. His novels provided the story lines for classic films, but when he was hired as a Hollywood screenwriter in the 1930s, he was assigned only a couple of minor features. He was, however, later credited with the Academy Award–winning adaptation of *Watch on the Rhine*[††] based on the play by his longtime lover, **Lillian Hellman**. His credits include:

- 1934–1941 *The Thin Man* series, seven films in all (starring William Powell and Myrna Loy)
- 1941 *The Maltese Falcon* (starring Humphrey Bogart)
- 1942 *The Glass Key* (starring Alan Ladd)
- 1943 *Watch on the Rhine*[††] (starring Paul Lukas and Bette Davis)

Lillian Hellman (1905–1984), playwright, Academy Award–nominated screenwriter, and memoirist, was credited with nine screenplays between 1934 and 1965, two of them based on her own Broadway plays. Her filmography includes:

- 1936 *These Three* (from her play *The Children's Hour*; with Miriam Hopkins and Merle Oberon)
- 1937 *Dead End* (starring Humphrey Bogart and the Dead End Kids)
- 1941 *The Little Foxes*[†] (adapted from her play; starring Bette Davis and Herbert Marshall)
- 1943 *The North Star*[†] (starring Dana Andrews and Walter Huston)

Paul Jarrico (1915–1997), Academy Award–nominated screenwriter, was credited with at least thirteen films between 1937 and 1950 and several more between 1969 and 1988. He sued for the right to screen credit for *The Las Vegas Story* in 1951 but lost the case and continued to write—either without credit or as "Devery Freeman" and "Peter Achilles." His credits include:

- 1939 *Beauty for the Asking* (starring Lucille Ball)
- 1941 *Tom, Dick and Harry*† (starring Ginger Rogers)
- 1950 *The White Tower* (starring Glenn Ford)

Gordon Kahn (1902–1962), screenwriter, contributed to about thirty films released between 1931 and 1950. As far as is known, he sold nothing for the screen after 1950 but wrote magazine articles under the pseudonym "Hugh G. Foster" and a 1948 book, *Hollywood on Trial*. His screen credits include:

- 1942 *Tarzan's New York Adventure* (starring Johnny Weiss-muller and Maureen O'Sullivan)
- 1944 *Lights of Old Santa Fe* (starring Roy Rogers and Dale Evans)
- 1948 *Whiplash* (starring Dane Clark and Alexis Smith)
- 1948 *Ruthless* (starring Zachary Scott)

Elia Kazan (1909–2003), director for stage and screen, producer, writer, and actor, directed twenty films between 1945 and 1976 (eight of which he also produced), netting five Academy Award nominations for direction and two wins. Those five films are:

- 1947 *Gentleman's Agreement*†† (starring Gregory Peck)
- 1951 *A Streetcar Named Desire*† (starring Marlon Brando and Vivian Leigh)
- 1954 *On the Waterfront*†† (starring Marlon Brando)
- 1955 *East of Eden*† (starring James Dean)
- 1963 *America, America*† (starring Stathis Giallelis)

Howard Koch (1902–1995), screenwriter, was nominated twice for the Academy Award and won once. He was credited on thirteen Hollywood films between 1940 and 1951 and on four films made in England in the 1960s. His American credits include:

- 1940 *The Sea Hawk* (starring Errol Flynn)

- 1941 *Sergeant York*[†] (starring Gary Cooper)
- 1942 *Casablanca*[††] (starring Humphrey Bogart and Ingrid Bergman)
- 1943 *Mission to Moscow* (starring Walter Huston and Ann Harding)
- 1948 *Letter from an Unknown Woman* (starring Joan Fontaine and Louis Jourdan)

Ring Lardner Jr.* (1915–2000), two-time Academy Award–winning screenwriter, contributed to fifteen known films between 1937 and 1951 but did not receive credit for his work on *A Star Is Born* (1937) or *Laura* (1944). Blacklisted, he continued writing as "Philip Rush" and "Oliver Skeyne." He returned to Hollywood in the mid-'60s, writing four more screenplays under his own name. His work includes:

- 1942 *Woman of the Year*[††] (starring Katharine Hepburn and Spencer Tracy)
- 1947 *Forever Amber* (starring Linda Darnell and Cornel Wilde)
- 1965 *The Cincinnati Kid* (starring Steve McQueen)
- 1970 *M*A*S*H*[††] (starring Donald Sutherland and Elliott Gould)

John Howard Lawson* (1894–1977), Academy Award–nominated screenwriter, had nineteen screen credits between 1928 and 1947 and at least one known black market script in 1952, with credit restored in 1998. His work includes:

- 1938 *Blockade*[†] (starring Henry Fonda)
- 1943 *Action in the North Atlantic* (starring Humphrey Bogart)
- 1943 *Sahara* (starring Humphrey Bogart)
- 1945 *Counter-Attack* (starring Paul Muni)
- 1952 *Cry, the Beloved Country* (credit restored; starring Sidney Poitier and Canada Lee)

Albert Maltz* (1908–1985), screenwriter with two Academy Award nominations, contributed to at least thirteen known films between 1932 and 1973, including the Russian propaganda film *Moscow Strikes Back* in 1942 and the ten-minute short *The House I Live In* (1945), which used Frank Sinatra to preach religious tolerance. His career as a credited writer was on furlough between 1948 and 1970. His films include:

- 1942 *This Gun for Hire* (starring Alan Ladd)
- 1945 *Pride of the Marines*† (starring John Garfield)
- 1950 *Broken Arrow*† (credited to **Michael Blankfort**; starring Jimmy Stewart and Jeff Chandler)
- 1953 *The Robe* (uncredited; starring Richard Burton)
- 1970 *Two Mules for Sister Sara* (starring Clint Eastwood and Shirley MacLaine)

Arthur Miller (1915–2005), the Pulitzer Prize–winning author of more than thirty Broadway plays, many of which were adapted for the screen, and one original screenplay, is also noted for his marriage to film star Marilyn Monroe, which lasted from 1956 to 1961. His plays-into-movies include:

- 1947 *All My Sons*, filmed in 1948 (starring Edward G. Robinson)
- 1949 *Death of a Salesman*, filmed in 1951 (starring Fredric March)
- 1953 *The Crucible*, filmed in 1996 (starring Daniel Day-Lewis and Winona Ryder)
- 1961 *The Misfits* (original screenplay; starring Clark Gable and Marilyn Monroe)

Clifford Odets (1906–1963) was a playwright, screenwriter, director, and founding member of the Group Theatre in 1931. Between his first play, *Waiting for Lefty* in 1935, and 1961, he wrote eleven more plays and seven screenplays, some of which he also directed. His plays provided story lines for the films *Clash by Night*, *Golden Boy*, *The Big Knife*, and *The Country Girl*. His screenplays include:

- 1936 *The General Died at Dawn* (starring Gary Cooper)
- 1944 *None but the Lonely Heart* (starring Cary Grant)
- 1957 *The Sweet Smell of Success* (starring Burt Lancaster and Tony Curtis)
- 1959 *The Story on Page One* (starring Rita Hayworth and Anthony Franciosa)

Samuel Ornitz* (1891–1957), screenwriter and novelist, was credited with contributing to twenty-five films between 1929 and 1945. Among them:

- 1932 *Hell's Highway* (starring Richard Dix)
- 1934 *The Man Who Reclaimed His Head* (starring Claude Rains and Joan Bennett)
- 1937 *The Hit Parade* (featuring the Duke Ellington and Eddie Duchin bands)
- 1940 *Three Faces West* (starring John Wayne)

Abraham Polonsky (1910–1999), screenwriter and director, was credited with four screenplays and was nominated for one Academy Award between 1947 and 1951. Blacklisted, he wrote pseudonymous television scripts for Edward R. Murrow's *You Are There* series and worked on uncredited screenplays, emerging from the underground in 1968 to contribute to seven more films. His work includes:

- 1947 *Body and Soul†* (produced and directed by **Robert Rossen**; starring John Garfield)
- 1948 *Force of Evil* (starring John Garfield)
- 1959 *Odds against Tomorrow* (credit restored; starring Harry Belafonte)
- 1969 *Tell Them Willie Boy Is Here* (starring Robert Redford)

Robert Rossen (1908–1966), screenwriter, director, and producer, was credited on twenty-six films between 1934 and 1964. He was twice nominated for triple Academy Awards, as writer, director, and producer. His work includes *Body and Soul†* (see **Abraham Polonsky**) and also:

- 1946 *The Strange Love of Martha Ivers* (starring Barbara Stanwyck and Van Heflin)
- 1949 *All the King's Men††* (starring Broderick Crawford)
- 1959 *They Came to Cordura* (starring Gary Cooper and Rita Hayworth)
- 1961 *The Hustler†* (starring Paul Newman)

Waldo Salt (1914–1987), screenwriter with three Academy Award nominations and one win, contributed to twenty films between 1937 and 1978. During the 1950s he wrote unknown, uncredited screenplays, returning to write for Hollywood under his own name in the early 1960s. His best-known scripts include:

- 1948 *Rachel and the Stranger* (starring Loretta Young, William Holden, and Robert Mitchum)
- 1969 *Midnight Cowboy*†† (starring Dustin Hoffman and Jon Voight)
- 1973 *Serpico*† (starring Al Pacino)
- 1978 *Coming Home*†† (starring Jon Voight and Jane Fonda)

Adrian Scott* (1912–1973), producer and screenwriter credited on eleven films between 1941 and 1947, in the 1950s wrote pseudonymous television scripts and collaborated with an also pseudonymous **Dalton Trumbo** on the screenplay for the 1960 film *Conspiracy of Hearts*. His credits include:

- 1943 *Mr. Lucky* (starring Cary Grant)
- 1944 *Murder, My Sweet* (directed by **Edward Dmytryk**; starring Dick Powell)
- 1946 *Deadline at Dawn* (written by **Clifford Odets**; starring Paul Lukas)
- 1947 *Crossfire* (directed by **Edward Dmytryk**; starring Robert Mitchum and Robert Ryan)

Donald Ogden Stewart (1894–1980), playwright, screenwriter, novelist, and actor, contributed to at least thirty-five films between 1926 and 1962, winning one Academy Award and receiving a second nomination. A member of the Algonquin Round Table in the 1920s, he later joined Dorothy Parker in founding the Hollywood Anti-Nazi League. Among his screen credits are *Holiday*, cowritten with **Sidney Buchman**, plus:

- 1940 *The Philadelphia Story*†† (starring Katharine Hepburn and Cary Grant)
- 1940 *Kitty Foyle*† (cowritten with **Dalton Trumbo**; starring Ginger Rogers)
- 1942 *Keeper of the Flame* (starring Spencer Tracy and Katharine Hepburn)
- 1949 *Edward, My Son* (starring Spencer Tracy and Deborah Kerr)

- 1957 *An Affair to Remember* (credit restored; starring Deborah Kerr and Cary Grant)

Dalton Trumbo* (1905–1976), screenwriter, contributed to more than fifty films between 1936 and 1973 and received two Academy Award nominations and one win. Once "the highest-paid writer in Hollywood," he wrote at least fifteen scripts under a range of pseudonyms or fronted by other writers during the blacklist. In 1960, he became the first to break the blacklist, writing two major films (*Exodus* and *Spartacus*) under his own name. His work includes:

- 1940 *Kitty Foyle*† (cowritten with **Donald Ogden Stewart**; starring Ginger Rogers)
- 1944 *Thirty Seconds over Tokyo* (starring Spencer Tracy)
- 1945 *Our Vines Have Tender Grapes* (starring Edward G. Robinson and Margaret O'Brien)
- 1956 *The Brave One*†† (written as "Robert Rich"; starring Michael Ray and Rudolfo Hoyos)
- 1960 *Exodus* (starring Paul Newman)
- 1960 *Spartacus* (starring Kirk Douglas and Peter Ustinov)
- 1962 *Lonely Are the Brave* (starring Kirk Douglas)

SCRUBBING ROBERT TAYLOR'S NAME

O n November 15, 1989, Lorimar Studios stripped the name of Robert Taylor, the star of *Magnificent Obsession*, *A Yank at Oxford*, and *Bataan*, from its Robert Taylor Building in Los Angeles after some fifty producers and screenwriters who worked in the building petitioned for the name change. "They gathered signatures," Lorimar Studios spokesman Barry Stagg informed *Human Events* shortly thereafter, "and included copies of testimony that Robert Taylor was alleged to have given" to the House Committee on Un-American Activities in 1947. "Concurrent with that, Lorimar Studios was looking for a way to honor [director] George Cukor, who made so many pictures for MGM...."[1]

Taylor did "name names pretty seriously" and "destroyed careers," Stan Zimmerman, who led the petition drive, told the *Los Angeles Times* on January

1, 1990. "In the age of [the late conservative senator] Jesse Helms and other right-wing noise makers, we decided to take action."[2]

Zimmerman's claims were untrue. Taylor, a major Hollywood star, was clearly opposed to having Communists work in the industry and told how he initially balked at starring in *Song of Russia*, a 1944 movie written by two Communists, Richard Collins and Paul Jarrico, which gave a rosy view of the Soviet Union. But he didn't ruin any careers, nor did he name names "pretty seriously." He mentioned only three people in an unflattering light—Howard Da Silva, Karen Morley, and Lester Cole—and wouldn't even say whether they were Communist Party members. He said of Da Silva and Morley that "I don't know" whether they are Communists, but he did accuse them of disrupting Screen Actors Guild meetings and appearing to follow the Communist Party line. Screenwriter Cole, he said, "is reputedly a Communist. I wouldn't know personally."[3]

That was the supposedly scurrilous "naming of names" that Zimmerman says Taylor indulged in. As it turned out, Taylor had severely understated the case against the three, since several former Communist Party members identified each of these individuals as having been CP members, and each of them refused to answer questions about their Party activities before the House Un-American Activities Committee (HUAC). As we have seen, Lester Cole eventually wrote a memoir in which he bragged he was a Communist.[4]

So far as ruining careers went, Karen Morley, the only person Taylor named who was alive at the time of Lorimar Studios' actions, told the *Los Angeles Times* that dozens—the word used by the *Times*, but not placed in quotes—labeled her a Communist. And she did not deny the charge. The *Times* also reported that Morley herself "said Taylor's testimony had not specifically damaged her career. 'He had no effect....'"[5]

In short, the Hollywood Left lied about Taylor as an excuse to dishonor him, making it appear as if he had engaged in reckless mud-slinging and had tarnished reputations unfairly. His real "crime," it seems, was to have expressed his intense opposition to Communism and those who wished to impose it on this country.

ACKNOWLEDGEMENTS

The following people were instrumental in helping me complete this book, on which I worked in occasional spurts for over a decade. Special thanks go to Tom Winter, my longtime colleague and editor emeritus at *Human Events*, who insisted this was a story that needed to be told. My great friend Stan Evans, who also encouraged me to write this work, kindly furnished me a cubbyhole at the Education and Research Institute (ERI), where I did much of the writing. I am also greatly indebted to the encyclopedic knowledge of the late Herbert Romerstein, one of the foremost experts on the subject of Communism in the world. Mark LaRochelle, the webmaster at ERI, provided me invaluable assistance, as did Larry Cott, a well-known writer on Communist intrigue.

Others deserve mention as well, including Keith Costa, Ellen Delage, Cliff Kincaid, and John Meroney, whose own book on Hollywood is going to be a must-read for scholars on this subject. I owe a special debt of gratitude to the folks at Regnery, of course, including Marji Ross, Harry Crocker, Alex Novak, my editor, Elizabeth Kantor, and my copyeditor, Katharine Spence. I must also single out for special mention Greg Mueller, who proved instrumental in selling the book idea to Regnery's editorial board. And I am indebted to the Art Department, with special thanks to Jason Sunde, who helped produce the initial draft, and to Amber Colleran.

I must, of course, thank my wife, Jaime Ryskind, for her assistance and patience and putting up with the amazing clutter that comes with amassing documents, congressional hearings, old newspapers, and historical works that are needed for any journalistic effort of this kind. Four other Ryskind relatives (cousin, sister, son, and grandson) need to be mentioned for their splendid assistance: Linda Stewart, Ruth Ohman, Sam Ryskind, and John Paul Teti.

NOTES

CHAPTER 1: THE STALINIST TEN

1.   Michael Kilian, "Recalling a Time of National Shame," *Chicago Tribune*, October 29, 1997, http://articles.chicagotribune.com/1997-10-29/features/9710290301_1_ blacklist-directors-guild-writers-guild.

2.   Bernard F. Dick, *Radical Innocence* (Lexington, KY: The University Press of Kentucky, 1989), 80. (I retrieved a copy of the screenplay from the Wisconsin State Historical Society.)

3.   Philip Dunne, *Take Two* (New York: McGraw Hill Book Company, 1980), 10.

4.   Larry Ceplair and Steven Englund, *The Inquisition in Hollywood: Politics in the Film Community, 1930–60* (New York: Doubleday, 1980), 283.

5. Note one easily demonstrable error of fact that has crept into the standard history of the Hollywood hearings. The late Jack Valenti, who represented the motion picture industry for nearly half a century, writes in his 2007 memoir, *This Time, This Place*, that the anti-Communist producers had been "frightened" into blacklisting writers and others because of the "witch hunt in Washington conducted by the House Un-American Activities Committee [HUAC] headed by Sen. Joe McCarthy."

   This "fact" has been almost baked into the historical cake, as it has been restated countless places as diverse as the *New York Times* crossword puzzle (the clue for 23 DOWN in the August 10, 1999, puzzle [Will Shortz, ed., E8] was "Sen. McCarthy's grp," and the answer published the next day [Will Shortz, ed., E8] was "HUAC"); a blurb decorating the CD cover of a Dalton Trumbo documentary written by his son, Christopher; and even *The O'Reilly Factor* (August 11, 2003)—though the staunchly conservative O'Reilly's heart is clearly in the right place. Joe McCarthy, however, was never a member of the House of Representatives, so he never headed HUAC. Nor did he ever investigate Hollywood. The blacklist was inaugurated in 1947, and McCarthy did not begin his anti-Communist crusade until 1950.

6. In 1940 the American Civil Liberties Union kicked out Communist Elizabeth Gurley Flynn and barred all Communists from leadership and staff positions. In January 1947, the cream of the liberal leaders in America formed the Americans for Democratic Action, which barred "Communists or sympathizers" from becoming members—a blacklist that prominent liberals did not quarrel with at the time.

7. In *The Inquisition in Hollywood*, Ceplair and Englund state, inexplicably, "There is reason to believe that the ten Communist cards introduced into the hearing record were fabrications. The Communists with whom we talked claimed they were not issued cards, precisely to avoid this exposé."

   The bizarre view that the cards are "fabrications" has to be false. None of the Ten ever challenged the Committee on that score, nor did they ever come forth with a scrap of evidence to show this to be the case in the years after the hearings. Several of them later admitted to Communist Party membership.

8. Ring Lardner Jr., *The Lardners* (New York: Harper & Row, 1976), 255–56.

9. Ceplair and Englund, *The Inquisition in Hollywood*, 239–41.

CHAPTER 2: BIRTH OF THE SCREEN WRITERS GUILD

1. Nancy Lynn Schwartz, *The Hollywood Writers' Wars* (New York: Alfred A. Knopf, 1982), 18.

2. Ibid., 45.

3. Ibid., 24.

4. John Howard Lawson, "Straight from the Shoulder," *New Theatre*, November 1934, p. 11.

5. "Smut Wire Splits Writers Guild: Smite Lawson's Testimony in House Group," *Daily Variety*, March 28, 1936, p. 4.

6. Schwartz, *The Hollywood Writers' Wars*, 58.

7. Ernest Pascal, "One Organization for All American Writers," *Screen Guilds' Magazine*, April 1936.

8. Schwartz, *The Hollywood Writers' Wars*, 59.

9. John Cogley, *Report on Blacklisting I: Movies* (Washington, DC: Fund for the Republic, 1956), 58.

10. "New Writers Group Ups Its Aims," *Daily Variety*, May 12, 1936.

11. Schwartz, *The Hollywood Writers' Wars*, 78–79.

12. Richard Collins testimony, April 12, 1951, *Communist Infiltration of Hollywood Motion-Picture Industry: Hearings before the Committee on Un-American Activities, House of Representatives* (Washington, DC: Government Printing Office, 1951), 221–22.

13. Schwartz, *The Hollywood Writers' Wars*, 157.

14. Ibid.

CHAPTER 3: "COMMUNISM...MUST BE FOUGHT FOR"

1. Max Eastman, *Artists in Uniform: A Study of Literature and Bureaucratism* (New York: Alfred A. Knopf, 1934), 3–12.

2. Eugene Lyons, *The Red Decade: The Stalinist Penetration of America* (Indianapolis: Bobbs-Merrill, 1941), 130–31.

3. Henry Hart, ed., *American Writers' Congress* (International Publishers, 1935), 10–11.

4. Ibid., 11–12.

5. Langston Hughes, "One More 'S' in the USA," *Daily Worker*, April 2, 1934, p. 7.

6. Hart, ed., *American Writers' Congress*, 9–13.

7. Granville Hicks, *Part of the Truth* (New York: Harcourt, Brace & World, 1965), 128–29.

8. Hart, ed., *American Writers' Congress*, 13.

9. Ibid., 24.

10. Ibid., 47, 51.

11. Ibid., 44.

12. Ibid., 69.

13. Ibid., 70.

14. Ibid., 71.

15. Ibid., 188.

16. Ibid., 192.

17. Unpublished chapters of Lawson's autobiography, John Howard Lawson papers, Southern Illinois University in Carbondale, Illinois.

CHAPTER 4: ANTI-FASCIST, OR PRO-STALIN?

1. Henry Hart, ed., *The Writer in a Changing World* (New York: Equinox Cooperative Press, 1937), 195–96.
2. Ibid., 197.
3. Ibid., 205.
4. Ibid., 64–67.
5. Ibid., 62.
6. Ibid., 49–54.
7. Donald Ogden Stewart, *By a Stroke of Luck!* (New York: Paddington Press, 1975), 240.
8. Hart, ed., *The Writer in a Changing World*, 119–32.
9. Stewart, *By a Stroke of Luck!*, 247.
10. Eugene Lyons, *The Red Decade: The Stalinist Penetration of America* (Indianapolis: Bobbs-Merrill, 1941), 320.
11. Donald Ogden Stewart, ed., *Fighting Words* (New York: Harcourt, Brace, 1940), 154.
12. "Writers Congress Backs New Deal, Firm Peace Policy," *Daily Worker*, June 5, 1939, p. 2.
13. Beth McHenry, "Thomas Mann Elected Honorary President of Writers Congress; Fight on Fascism Stressed," *Daily Worker*, June 6, 1939, p. 5.
14. Lyons, *The Red Decade*, 321.

CHAPTER 5: THE HOLLYWOOD ANTI-NAZI LEAGUE

1. John Cogley, *Report on Blacklisting I: Movies* (Washington, DC: Fund for the Republic, 1956), 35–39; and Larry Ceplair and Steven Englund, *The Inquisition in Hollywood: Politics in the Film Community, 1930–60* (New York: Doubleday, 1980), 104–11.
2. Cogley, *Report on Blacklisting I*, 37.
3. "Hollywood Answers Dies," *People's Daily World*, August 26, 1938, p. 1.
4. Ceplair and Englund, *The Inquisition in Hollywood*, 110–11.
5. Donald Ogden Stewart, *By a Stroke of Luck!* (New York: Paddington Press, 1975), 247.
6. *Investigation of Un-American Propaganda Activities in the United States: Appendix Part IX, Communist Front Organizations, with Special Reference to the National Citizens Political Action Committee* (Washington, DC: Government Printing Office, 1944), 779–84; and *Fourth Report of the Senate Fact-Finding Committee on Un-American Activities in California, 1948: Communist Front Organizations* (Sacramento, CA: California State Senate, 1948), 249–56.
7. Hy Kraft, *On My Way to the Theater* (New York: Macmillan, 1971), 153–54.
8. Leo C. Rosten, *Hollywood: The Movie Colony, the Movie Makers* (New York: Arno Press and *New York Times*, 1970), 140–43.

9. Cogley, *Report on Blacklisting I*, 35–36.

10. Salka Viertel, *The Kindness of Strangers* (New York: Holt, Rinehart and Winston, 1969), 211.

11. Ceplair and Englund, *The Inquisition in Hollywood*, 105–6.

12. Kraft, *On My Way to the Theater*, 148.

13. Ibid., 145.

14. *Fourth Report of the Senate Fact-Finding Committee on Un-American Activities in California, 1948: Communist Front Organizations*, 250.

15. Cogley, *Report on Blacklisting I*, 38.

16. Eugene Lyons, *The Red Decade: The Stalinist Penetration of America* (Indianapolis: Bobbs-Merrill, 1941), 293–94.

17. Cogley, *Report on Blacklisting I*, 38–39.

18. *Hollywood Now*, January 12, 1940, pp. 1–4, including editorial titled, "Tell It to Congress."

19. Ibid.

20. Lyons, *The Red Decade*, 295.

CHAPTER 6: THE PRO-HITLER CONGRESS

1. Eugene Lyons, *The Red Decade: The Stalinist Penetration of America* (Indianapolis: Bobbs-Merrill, 1941), 197–98.

2. Philip Jaffe, *The Rise and Fall of American Communism* (New York: Horizon Press, 1975), 40.

3. Ibid., 44–45.

4. Ibid., 46–47.

5. Malcolm Cowley, "In Memoriam," *New Republic*, August 12, 1940, pp. 219–20.

6. Larry Ceplair and Steven Englund, *The Inquisition in Hollywood: Politics in the Film Community, 1930–60* (New York: Doubleday, 1980), 165–68.

7. William L. Shirer, *The Rise and Fall of the Third Reich* (New York: Touchstone, 1990), 233.

8. Ibid., 431.

9. Art Shields, "Writers Congress Scores War Drive; Theodore Dreiser Gets Peace Award," *Sunday Worker* (Sunday edition of the *Daily Worker*), June 8, 1941, p. 3.

10. Ibid.

11. "Theodore Dreiser Gets Peace Award: Honored by Writers for His 'Service to Cause of Culture,'" *New York Times*, June 7, 1941, p. 5.

12. Richard Wright, "Not My People's War," *New Masses*, June 17, 1941, p. 8.

13. "Writers Congress Adopts Firm Anti-War Program," *Daily Worker*, June 9, 1941, p. 1.

14. Ibid.

15.   Ibid.

16.   Russell B. Porter, "Reds Here Shift in Stand on War," *New York Times*, July 27, 1944, pp. 16ff; and *Congressional Record*, 77th Congress, vol. 88, part 6, 1942, p. 7445.

CHAPTER 7: RED AND BROWN SABOTAGE

1.   "Communist-Inspired Strikes," *New York Times*, June 10, 1941, p. C22.

2.   Elmer Freitag testimony, May 29, 1941, *Investigation of Un-American Propaganda Activities in the United States: Hearings before a Special House Un-American Activities Committee, House of Representatives, Volume 14* (Washington, DC: Government Printing Office, 1941), 8594–95.

3.   Benjamin Stolberg, "Inside Labor," *American Mercury* 53, no. 212 (August 1941), 180.

4.   *Investigation of Un-American Propaganda Activities in the United States: Report of the Special Committee on Un-American Activities; Report on the CIO Political Action Committee* (Washington, DC: Government Printing Office, 1944), 134ff.

5.   Louis Stark, "CIO Split Widens: Communist-Line Groups Threaten Bolt, Murray Defies Them to Go: Showdown Believed Near: CIO President Appeals in Vain to California Union to Return to Work," *New York Times*, June 9, 1941, p. 1.

6.   Stolberg, "Inside Labor," 177.

7.   Richard T. Frankensteen, "Text of Frankensteen's Declaration on Aviation Strike," *New York Times*, June 8, 1941, p. 37.

8.   Stolberg, "Inside Labor," 180.

9.   Hugh Ben Inzer testimony, May 29, 1941, *Investigation of Un-American Propaganda Activities in the United States: Hearings before a Special Committee on House Un-American Activities, House of Representatives, Volume 14* (Washington, DC: Government Printing Office, 1941), 8532–58.

10.   *Investigation of Un-American Propaganda Activities in the United States: Appendix Part IX, Communist Front Organizations, with Special Reference to the National Citizens Political Action Committee* (Washington, DC: Government Printing Office, 1944), 971.

11.   Max Kampelman, *The Communist Party vs. the CIO* (New York: Frederick A. Praeger, 1957), 25–26.

12.   Ibid., 26–27.

13.   Stolberg, "Inside Labor," 178.

14.   House Committee on Education and Labor, Report No. 1508, 1948, p. 24.

CHAPTER 8: THE AMERICAN PEACE MOBILIZATION GOES TO WAR

1.   J. B. Matthews, *Odyssey of a Fellow Traveler* (New York: Mount Vernon, 1938), 135–39, 154–56; and *Investigation of Un-American Propaganda Activities in the United States: Appendix Part IX, Communist Front Organizations, with Special Reference to the National Citizens Political Action Committee* (Washington, DC: Government

Printing Office, 1944), 412–28. The World Congress against War, which was held in Amsterdam in August 1932 and led to the formation of the American League against War and Fascism, was formed on the instructions of the Communist International and was presided over by Henri Barbusse, the noted French Communist. Of the 2,196 delegates at the gathering, 830 were avowed Communists, with the remainder unavowed Reds or fellow travelers. The Congress's manifesto, written in Moscow, declared that "all capitalist powers" were intent on undermining the Soviet Union and called for "a program of struggle against the growing threat to Soviet Russia." To protect the USSR against capitalism and imperialism, the Congress set up the World Committee against War—with Barbusse as chairman—the major purpose of which was to establish "peace" organizations in capitalist countries. The American League against War and Fascism, also known as the League against War and Fascism, traced its direct descent from the Amsterdam Congress in its organizational handbook.

2.   Ibid., 172.

3.   FBI report on American Peace Mobilization, no. 100-32736.

4.   Frederick Vanderbilt Field, *From Right to Left* (Westport, CT: Lawrence Hill, 1983), 186–87, 169.

5.   Ibid., 187.

6.   My copy of Eugene Dennis's letter comes from the files of Herbert Romerstein.

7.   Ibid.

8.   *Investigation of Un-American Propaganda Activities in the United States: Appendix Part IX, Communist Front Organizations, with Special Reference to the National Citizens Political Action Committee*, 431.

9.   Field, *From Right to Left*, 191.

10.   Ibid., 194.

11.   Theodore Dreiser, *America Is Worth Saving* (New York: Modern Age Books, 1941), 223, 134.

12.   Ibid.

13.   Bruce Cook, *Dalton Trumbo* (New York: Charles Scribner's Sons, 1977), 137.

14.   FBI report on the American Peace Mobilization, January 13, 1941, no. 61-10478-324.

15.   FBI report on the American Peace Mobilization, August 6, 1941, no. 100-24499-5, pp. 76–77.

16.   FBI report on the American Peace Mobilization.

17.   Minutes from the Executive Board meeting of the Hollywood chapter of the League of American Writers, February 29, 1940, and May 8, 1941.

18.   Leaflet titled "Songs of APM," including such parodies as "Franklin, Oh, Franklin," "Jim Crow," and "Billy Boy."

19.   Eugene Lyons, *The Red Decade: The Stalinist Penetration of America* (Indianapolis: Bobbs-Merrill, 1941), 391.

20. Special Agent B. E. Sackett in a letter from New York to FBI director J. Edgar Hoover. The date it was mailed is unclear, but it was probably sent in March of 1941.

21. "For Full and Immediate Aid to the USSR," *Daily Worker*, June 25, 1941, p. 6.

22. Copy of the June 30, 1941, "Recommendations of the National Board of the American Peace Mobilization" to the APM's national council. The recommendations were adopted.

CHAPTER 9: RED PROPAGANDA IN FILMS

1. John Howard Lawson, "Straight from the Shoulder," *New Theatre*, November 1934, p. 11.

2. John Charles Moffitt testimony, October 21, 1947, *Hearings regarding the Communist Infiltration of the Motion Picture Industry: Hearings before the Committee on Un-American Activities, House of Representatives* (Washington, DC: Government Printing Office, 1947), 112.

3. John Cogley, *Report on Blacklisting I: Movies* (Washington, DC: Fund for the Republic, 1956), 42.

4. Ibid., 225.

5. Dorothy B. Jones, "Communism and the Movies: A Study of Film Content," prepared for Cogley, *Report on Blacklisting I*, Seeley G. Mudd Manuscript Library, Princeton University, 36–39.

6. Cogley, *Report on Blacklisting I*, 229.

7. Jones, "Communism and the Movies," 136–58.

8. Cogley, *Report on Blacklisting I*, 223.

9. Lester Cole, *Hollywood Red* (Palo Alto, CA: Ramparts Press, 1981), 159.

10. Ibid., 138.

11. Ibid., 14.

12. Ibid., 147.

13. Ibid., 149.

14. Ibid., 172–73.

15. Ibid., 164–65.

16. Jones, "Communism and the Movies," 102–35.

17. Cole, *Hollywood Red*, 203–4.

18. David Lang testimony, March 24, 1953, *Investigation of Communist Activities in the Los Angeles Area, Part 1: Hearings before the Committee on Un-American Activities, House of Representatives* (Washington, DC: Government Printing Office, 1953), 341.

CHAPTER 10: *BLOCKADE*: THE PARTY TARGETS SPAIN

1. Unpublished chapters of Lawson autobiography, collection 16, box 98, folder 3, part VI, 468–471A, John Howard Lawson papers, Southern Illinois University in Carbondale, Illinois.

2. Ibid.

3. Ibid.

4. Ibid.

5. Dorothy B. Jones, "Communism and the Movies: A Study of Film Content," 1956, prepared for John Cogley, *Report on Blacklisting I: Movies*, Seeley G. Mudd Manuscript Library, Princeton University, 102–35.

6. Ibid.

7. Ibid.

8. Ibid.

9. Ibid.

10. Ibid.

11. Ibid.

12. Ibid.

13. Ibid.

14. Hugh Thomas, *The Spanish Civil War* (New York: Harper & Brothers, 1961), 80.

15. Ibid., 84.

16. Ibid., 107.

17. David Cattell, *Communism and the Spanish Civil War* (Berkeley: University of California Press, 1955), 17.

18. Ibid.

19. Winston S. Churchill, *The Second World War*, vol. 1, *The Gathering Storm* (New York: Bantam Books, 1961), 191.

20. Eugene Lyons, *The Red Decade: The Stalinist Penetration of America* (Indianapolis: Bobbs-Merrill, 1941), 268.

21. Walter Krivitsky, *In Stalin's Secret Service* (New York: Harper & Brothers, 1939), 75, 91.

22. Thomas, *The Spanish Civil War*, 214–17.

23. Ibid., 217.

24. Cattell, *Communism and the Spanish Civil War*, 116–17.

25. Thomas, *The Spanish Civil War*, 294–306.

26. Alvah Bessie testimony, October 28, 1947, *Hearings regarding the Communist Infiltration of the Motion Picture Industry: Hearings before the Committee on Un-American Activities, House of Representatives* (Washington, DC: Government Printing Office, 1947), 383–84.

27. Ring Lardner Jr., *The Lardners* (New York: Harper & Row, 1976), 267–75.

28. "Spain never entered the war by the side of Hitler, who was moved to declare 'that all his aid to Franco was an absolute gift....' Even his worst enemies would not deny that Franco's achievement in keeping Spain out of the war was a remarkable one. This is the most obvious way in which Franco differs from the popular, expansionist Fascist dictator." Thomas, *The Spanish Civil War*, 618–19.

29. "All we wanted was the neutrality of Spain. We wanted to trade with Spain. We wanted her ports to be denied to German and Italian submarines. We wanted not only an unmolested Gibraltar, but the use of the anchorage of Algeciras for our ships and the use of the ground which joins the Rock to the mainland for our ever-expanding air base. On these facilities depended in large measure our access to the Mediterranean. Nothing was easier than for the Spaniards to mount or allow to be mounted a dozen heavy guns in the hills behind Algeciras. They had a right to do so at any time, and, once mounted, they could at any moment be fired and our naval and airbases would become unusable.... Spain held the key to all British enterprises in the Mediterranean, and never in the darkest hours did she turn the lock against us." Churchill, *The Second World War*, vol. 2, *Their Finest Hour*, rev. ed. (New York: Houghton Mifflin Company, 1986), 459–60.

CHAPTER 11: *NINOTCHKA* SLIPS THROUGH A RED FILTER

1. Jack Warner testimony, October 20, 1947, *Hearings regarding the Communist Infiltration of the Motion Picture Industry: Hearings before the Committee on Un-American Activities, House of Representatives* (Washington, DC: Government Printing Office, 1947), 28.

2. Maurice Zolotow, *Billy Wilder in Hollywood* (New York: Proscenium Publishers, Limelight Editions, 1987), 79.

3. Ernst Lubitsch, born January 28, 1892, in Berlin, wanted to become an actor from the age of six. He joined a theater company run by Max Reinhardt, the driving force behind contemporary German theater, and later became a director, moved to America in the early 1930s, and directed such well-known movies as *Heaven Can Wait, To Be or Not to Be*, and *The Shop around the Corner*.

4. Billy Wilder was an amazing presence in Hollywood. He would direct, write, and/or produce such films as *Bluebeard's Eighth Wife, Double Indemnity, The Lost Weekend, Stalag 17, Sabrina, The Spirit of St. Louis, Witness for the Prosecution*, and *Some Like It Hot*. In 1960, he won three Oscars—as a writer, director, and producer—for *The Apartment*, named the Best Picture of the Year.

5. Scott Eyman, *Ernst Lubitsch: Laughter in Paradise* (New York: Simon & Schuster, 1993), 233.

6. Salka Viertel, *The Kindness of Strangers* (New York: Holt, Rinehart and Winston, 1969), 211.

7. Henry G. Weinberg, *The Lubitsch Touch* (Mineola, NY: Dover Publications, 1977). All quotations of *Ninotchka* are from pages 190 to 222.

8. Zolotow, *Billy Wilder in Hollywood*, 84–85.

CHAPTER 12: RED HEYDAY IN HOLLYWOOD

1. Alvah Bessie, *Inquisition in Eden* (New York: Macmillan, 1965), 67–68.

2. David Lang testimony, March 24, 1953, *Investigation of Communist Activities in the Los Angeles Area, Part 1: Hearings before the Committee on Un-American Activities, House of Representatives* (Washington, DC: Government Printing Office, 1953), 336–55.

3. Bernard Dick, *The Star-Spangled Screen: The American World War II Film* (Lexington, KY: University Press of Kentucky, 1985), 21–22.

4. *The Fallen Sparrow*, Richard Wallace, director (Los Angeles: RKO Radio Pictures, 1943).

5. Dick, *The Star-Spangled Screen*, 22.

6. Ibid., 22

7. Ibid., 271, note 17.

8. Ibid., 211.

9. In the April 12, 1951, HUAC hearings, Collins testified that both he and Jarrico were Party members. See Richard Collins testimony, April 12, 1951, *Communist Infiltration of Hollywood Motion-Picture Industry, Part I: Hearings before the Committee on Un-American Activities, House of Representatives* (Washington, DC: Government Printing Office, 1951), 236.

10. *Thousands Cheer*, George Sidney, director (Los Angeles: MGM, 1943).

11. Dick, *The Star-Spangled Screen*, 212.

12. Lillian Hellman, *The North Star* (New York: Viking Press: 1943). A copy of Viking's "master script" of the movie, which was sold in bookstores, is in my possession.

13. Ibid., 9.

14. Ibid., 26–27.

15. Ibid., 27–32.

16. "Stenographic Report" of "Meeting of the Cinema Section to Discuss the Film *North Star*," April 13, 1944 (presumably held in Moscow), chairman, Vsevolod Pudovkin, in the Lawson collection at Southern Illinois University.

17. Carl Rollyson, *Lillian Hellman: Her Legend and Her Legacy* (New York: St. Martin's Press, 1988), 203.

18. Ibid.

19. Clayton R. Koppes and Gregory D. Black, *Hollywood Goes to War: Patriotism, Movies, and the Second World War, from "Ninotchka" to "Mrs. Miniver"* (Berkeley: University of California, 1990), 211.

20. Louis B. Mayer testimony, October 20, 1947, *Hearings regarding the Communist Infiltration of the Motion Picture Industry: Hearings before the Committee on Un-American Activities, House of Representatives* (Washington, DC: Government Printing Office, 1947), 71.

21. Ibid.

22.   Ibid.; and Robert Taylor testimony, October 22, 1947, *Hearings regarding the Com-
      munist Infiltration of the Motion Picture Industry: Hearings before the Committee on
      Un-American Activities, House of Representatives*, 166.

23.   Dick, *The Star-Spangled Screen*, 211.

24.   Quoted in ibid., 212.

25.   Garry Wills, introduction to *Scoundrel Time* by Lillian Hellman (Boston: Little,
      Brown, 1977), 2.

26.   Ayn Rand testimony, October 20, 1947, *Hearings regarding the Communist Infiltration
      of the Motion Picture Industry: Hearings before the Committee on Un-American
      Activities, House of Representatives*, 82–90.

27.   Collins testimony, *Communist Infiltration of Hollywood Motion-Picture Industry:
      Hearings before the Committee on Un-American Activities, House of Representatives*,
      217–58.

28.   Howard Rushmore testimony, October 22, 1947, *Hearings regarding the Communist
      Infiltration of the Motion Picture Industry: Hearings before the Committee on Un-
      American Activities, House of Representatives*, 171–81.

29.   Bernard Dick, *Radical Innocence* (Lexington, KY: University Press of Kentucky, 1989),
      58.

30.   Ibid., 59.

31.   Bessie, *Inquisition in Eden*, 65–68.

CHAPTER 13: MISSION FOR STALIN

1.   Mike Gold, "Change the World: 'Mission to Moscow', the 'Uncle Tom's Cabin' of the
      Present Era," *Daily Worker*, May 3, 1943, p. 7; David Platt, "Critics Laud *Mission to
      Moscow*," *Daily Worker*, May 2, 1943, p. 7; Platt, "*Mission to Moscow*—A Great Win-
      the-War Film," *Daily Worker*, April 30, 1943, p. 7; Platt, "*Mission* Is the Talk of the
      Town," *Daily Worker*, May 10, 1943, p. 7; and "Hollywood's First Realistic Film about
      the Soviet Union," *Daily Worker*.

2.   Jack Warner testimony, October 20, 1947, *Hearings regarding the Communist Infiltra-
      tion of the Motion Picture Industry: Hearings before the Committee on Un-American
      Activities, House of Representatives* (Washington, DC: Government Printing Office,
      1947), 32–39.

3.   Davies's views as portrayed in *Mission to Moscow*, Michael Curtiz, director (Los
      Angeles: Warner Brothers, 1943).

4.   George F. Kennan, *Memoirs, 1925–1950* (Boston: Little, Brown, 1967), 82–84.

5.   Nancy Rubin, *American Empress: The Life and Times of Marjorie Merriweather Post*
      (Lincoln, NE: iUniverse, 2004), 231–32.

6.   David Culbert, *Mission to Moscow* (Madison: University of Wisconsin Press, 1980),
      17. Culbert dug deep into the archival history of *Mission to Moscow* and interviewed
      major players, including author Howard Koch and members of the diplomatic corps

who served with Joseph Davies when he was ambassador to Moscow. While the book is excellent in many ways, and I have relied on many of his findings, I also believe Culbert takes a tendentious view of the House Un-American Activities Committee and is fundamentally incorrect about the political leanings of those who worked on *Mission*, including the scriptwriter, Howard Koch.

7.   Ibid., 26.

8.   Ibid., 25.

9.   Larry Ceplair and Steven Englund, *The Inquisition in Hollywood: Politics in the Film Community, 1930–1960* (New York: Doubleday, 1980), 132.

10.   Howard Koch affidavit to HUAC in my possession.

11.   Howard Koch, *As Time Goes By: Memoirs of a Writer* (New York: Harcourt Brace Jovanovich, 1979), 98, 102, 116, 117.

12.   Eugene Lyons, *The Red Decade: The Stalinist Penetration of America* (Indianapolis: Bobbs-Merrill, 1941), 139.

13.   Koch, *As Time Goes By*, 117.

14.   Copy of FBI memoranda in Si-Lan Chen Leyda Papers at the Tamiment Library at the Elmer Holmes Bobst Library in New York City.

15.   Si-Lan Chen's papers at the Tamiment Library show that after studying dance in London, she joined her father in China in 1926. Then the Chen family fled to Moscow in 1927 when Chiang Kai-shek pulled off a coup against the Communists. She gave her first important dance recital in 1930 at the Moscow Conservatory, adapting her style to "reflect a proletarian ideology." Thirteen FBI memos also reveal that her close friends were frequently Communists and that she performed for or was affiliated with a score of Soviet fronts.

16.   Koch, *As Time Goes By*, 122.

17.   Leopold Atlas testimony, March 12, 1953, *Investigation of Communist Activities in the Los Angeles Area, Part 5: Hearings before the Committee on Un-American Activities, House of Representatives* (Washington, DC: Government Printing Office, 1953), 941.

18.   Koch, *As Time Goes By*, 105.

19.   Ibid., 122.

20.   Ibid., 125.

21.   The Davieses were hardly unaware of the Soviet famine and the ongoing food shortage in the early 1930s, despite the movie's determination to put a happy face upon this Stalin-made catastrophe. When Davies was appointed ambassador, his wife caused a mini-scandal by having twelve food lockers stuffed with Bird's Eye frozen food and two thousand pints of frozen cream shipped to Russia aboard the *Sea Cloud*, a "350-foot refrigerator ship," for her family's personal use. See Rubin, *American Empress*, 223–24.

22.   All quotations attributed to the principals in *Mission to Moscow* come from a copy of the film in my possession.

23. Culbert, *Mission to Moscow*, 30.

24. Ibid., 38.

25. Excerpt of Quentin Reynolds, *The Curtain Rises* (New York: Random House, 1944), in Warner testimony, October 20, 1947, *Hearings regarding the Communist Infiltration of the Motion Picture Industry: Hearings before the Committee on Un-American Activities, House of Representatives*, 37–38.

26. Charles E. Bohlen, *Witness to History, 1929–1969* (New York: W. W. Norton, 1973), 44–45, 123.

27. John Dewey and Suzanne La Follette (letter to the editor dated May 6, 1943), "Several Faults Are Found in 'Mission to Moscow' Film," *New York Times*, section 4, p. 8.

28. Ibid.

29. Joseph E. Davies, *Mission to Moscow* (Simon & Schuster, 1941), 302–3.

30. Ibid., 52–53.

31. Ibid., 389–90.

32. Culbert, *Mission to Moscow*, 257–59.

33. Koch, *As Time Goes By*, 129.

34. Bosley Crowther, "Mission to Moscow, Based on Ex-Ambassador Davies's Book, Stars Walter Huston, Ann Harding at Hollywood," *New York Times*, April 30, 1943, p. 25.

35. James Agee, "Films," *Nation*, May 22, 1943, p. 749.

36. "Why the Whitewash?," *Nation*, May 8, 1943, p. 87.

37. Koch, *As Time Goes By*, 129.

38. Quoted in Culbert, *Mission to Moscow*, 257–59.

CHAPTER 14: THE GREAT ESCAPE

1. *Sunday Worker* (Sunday edition of the *Daily Worker*), April 14, 1946, p. 4

2. Ibid.; Clifton Brock, *Americans for Democratic Action: Its Role in National Politics* (Westport, CT: Greenwood Press, 1985), 46.

3. James Loeb Jr., "Progressives and Communists," *New Republic*, May 13, 1946, p. 699.

4. Ibid.

5. Ibid.

6. Quoted in Brock, *Americans for Democratic Action*, 52.

7. Wilson Wyatt's April 8, 1947, broadcast, reprinted in *ADA World*, April 12, 1947, p. 2.

8. William A. Donohue, *The Politics of the American Civil Liberties Union* (Piscataway, NJ: Transaction Books, 1985), 145–47.

9. "Mrs. Roosevelt Defeats Her Own Aims," *Daily Worker*, April 8, 1946, p. 6.

10. Ibid.

11. Max Kampelman, *The Communist Party vs. the CIO: A Study in Power Politics* (New York: Frederick A. Praeger, 1957), 47.

12. Ibid., 49.

13. Ibid., 54–57.

14. Quoted in ibid., 56.

15. Quoted in ibid., 85.

CHAPTER 15: THE ANTI-COMMUNISTS WEIGH IN

1. James Kevin McGuinness, "Double Cross in Hollywood," *New Leader*, July 15, 1944, p. 119.

2. "Motion Picture Alliance States Its Principles," *Daily Variety*, February 7, 1944, p. 5.

3. Ibid., 3.

4. "An Announcement by Emergency Committee of Hollywood Guilds and Unions," *Hollywood Reporter*, June 23, 1944, p. 7.

5. Elmer Rice, "The MPA and American Ideals," *Saturday Review of Literature*, November 11, 1944, p. 18.

6. Morrie Ryskind, "A Reply to Elmer Rice about the MPAPAL," *Saturday Review of Literature*, December 23, 1944, pp. 9–10.

7. Elmer Rice, "A Reply to Morrie Ryskind," *Saturday Review of Literature*, December 23, 1944, p. 10.

8. McGuinness, "Double Cross in Hollywood."

9. "MPA Exposed at Meeting of 950 Guild, Union Delegates," *Guild Bulletin*, August 1, 1944, p. 1.

10. Larry Ceplair and Steven Englund, *The Inquisition in Hollywood: Politics in the Film Community, 1930–60* (New York: Doubleday, 1980), 171–72.

11. *The Screen Writer*, June and October 1945.

CHAPTER 16: THE COLD WAR BEGINS

1. *The Front*, Martin Ritt, director (Los Angeles: Columbia Pictures, 1976).

2. Jacques Duclos, "On the Dissolution of the Communist Party of the United States," *Daily Worker*, May 24, 1945, p. 7. There is some dispute as to whether Duclos was the real author, and some historians believe the letter was actually written in the winter of 1944 in Moscow.

3. William Henry Chamberlin, *America's Second Crusade* (Chicago: Henry Regnery, 1950), 197–205.

4. Quoted in Philip J. Jaffe, *The Rise and Fall of American Communism* (New York: Horizon Press, 1975), 207.

5. Quoted in ibid.

6. Quoted in ibid.

7. Ibid., 69–71. According to Jaffe, language experts consider "seizure" a more accurate translation from the French than "conquest," but the word "conquest" appears in the English-language translation published in the May 24, 1945, edition of the *Daily Worker*.

8. Richard Collins testimony, April 12, 1951, *Communist Infiltration of Hollywood Motion-Picture Industry: Hearings before the Committee on Un-American Activities, House of Representatives* (Washington, DC: Government Printing Office, 1951), 251.

9. Quoted in Bruce Cook, *Dalton Trumbo* (New York: Charles Scribner's & Sons, 1977), 163.

10. Norma Barzman, *The Red and the Blacklist: The Intimate Memoir of a Hollywood Expatriate* (New York: Thunder's Mouth/Nation, 2003), 63.

11. The Bessie interview was conducted by Patrick McGilligan and Paul Buhle and published in their *Tender Comrades: A Backstory of the Hollywood Blacklist* (New York: St. Martin's Press, 1997), 101–2.

12. Ring Lardner Jr., *The Lardners* (New York: Harper & Row, 1976), 317.

13. Jaffe, *The Rise and Fall of American Communism*, 206–10.

14. Ibid.

CHAPTER 17: SCREENWRITERS EMBRACE A COMINTERN AGENT

1. "Help Defend Civil Liberties," Civil Rights Congress advertisement, *People's Daily World*, May 2, 1947, section II, p. 3.

2. Louis Budenz testimony, November 22, 1946, *Investigation of Un-American Propaganda in the United States: Louis F. Budenz; Hearings before the Committee on Un-American Activities, House of Representatives* (Washington, DC: Government Printing Office, 1946), 2ff.

3. Gerhart Eisler testimony, February 6, 1947, *Hearings on Gerhart Eisler: Investigation of Un-American Propaganda in the United States, Transcript of Proceedings, Committee on Un-American Activities, House of Representatives* (Washington, DC: Government Printing Office, 1947), 2–3; and "Communist Chief in U.S. Is Accused of Revolution Plot; House Un-American Committee Holds Eisler in Contempt as He Balks at Taking Oath," *New York Times*, February 7, 1947, pp. 1, 3.

4. Ruth Fischer testimony, February 6, 1947, *Hearings on Gerhart Eisler: Investigation of Un-American Propaganda in the United States, Transcript of Proceedings, Committee on Un-American Activities, House of Representatives*, 29–35.

5. William Nowell testimony, February 6, 1947, *Hearings on Gerhart Eisler: Investigation of Un-American Propaganda in the United States, Transcript of Proceedings, Committee on Un-American Activities, House of Representatives*, 14–29.

6. Ibid., 17–19; and Fischer testimony, *Hearings on Gerhart Eisler: Investigation of Un-American Propaganda in the United States, Transcript of Proceedings, Committee on Un-American Activities, House of Representatives*, 35–38.

7. Nowell testimony, February 6, 1947, *Hearings on Gerhart Eisler: Investigation of Un-American Propaganda in the United States, Transcript of Proceedings, Committee on Un-American Activities, House of Representatives*, 5–9; and *Congressional Record*, 80th Congress, 1947, pp. 1129–30.

8.   February 6, 1947, *Hearings on Gerhart Eisler: Investigation of Un-American Propaganda in the United States, Transcript of Proceedings, Committee on Un-American Activities, House of Representatives*, 11–12. The FBI report on Hanns Eisler is number 100-195220. FBI agent Robert Lamphere played a key role in the Eisler matter. Toward the end of World War II, the FBI assigned him to Soviet espionage matters, and from then until 1955 he was a specialist in counterintelligence. Lamphere monitored Eisler's moves in the United States along with other FBI agents, prepared a lengthy report on him for FBI chief J. Edgar Hoover, and proved a key witness in Eisler's 1946 trial on passport fraud. He discusses the Eisler case in his book, *The FBI-KGB War*, originally published in 1986 by Random House. Robert J. Lamphere, *The FBI-KGB War* (Macon, GA: Mercer University Press, 1995).

9.   "Film Notables Urge End to Un-Americans at Rally Here," *Daily Worker*, November 3, 1947, p. 6; and "19 Movie Figures to Fight Charges: To Urge Unions to Put Pressure on Congress to Vote Down Contempt Citations," *New York Times*, November 3, 1947, p. 19.

10.   Ibid.

11.   Lamphere, *The FBI-KGB War*, 64–65.

CHAPTER 18: HUAC

1.   Jack Warner testimony, October 20, 1947, *Hearings regarding the Communist Infiltration of the Motion Picture Industry: Hearings before the Committee on Un-American Activities, House of Representatives* (Washington, DC: Government Printing Office, 1947), 9–54.

2.   Gordon Kahn, *Hollywood on Trial* (New York: Boni & Gaer, 1948), 12. Herbert Biberman, one of the Hollywood Ten, is named as the copyright holder on the book's copyright page.

3.   Larry Ceplair and Steven Englund, *The Inquisition in Hollywood: Politics in the Film Community, 1930–60* (New York: Doubleday, 1980), 132.

4.   Samuel Grosvenor Wood testimony, October 20, 1947, *Hearings regarding the Communist Infiltration of the Motion Picture Industry: Hearings before the Committee on Un-American Activities, House of Representatives*, 54–69.

5.   Louis B. Mayer testimony, October 20, 1947, *Hearings regarding the Communist Infiltration of the Motion Picture Industry: Hearings before the Committee on Un-American Activities, House of Representatives*, 69–82.

6.   Ayn Rand testimony, October 20, 1947, *Hearings regarding the Communist Infiltration of the Motion Picture Industry: Hearings before the Committee on Un-American Activities, House of Representatives*, 82–90.

7.   John Moffitt testimony, October 21, 1947, *Hearings regarding the Communist Infiltration of the Motion Picture Industry: Hearings before the Committee on Un-American Activities, House of Representatives*, 108–28.

8. Jack Warner testimony, October 20, 1947, *Hearings regarding the Communist Infiltration of the Motion Picture Industry: Hearings before the Committee on Un-American Activities, House of Representatives*, 52.

9. Howard Rushmore testimony, October 22, 1947, *Hearings regarding the Communist Infiltration of the Motion Picture Industry: Hearings before the Committee on Un-American Activities, House of Representatives*, 171–81.

CHAPTER 19: MORE FRIENDLY WITNESSES

1. Morrie Ryskind testimony, October 22, 1947, *Hearings regarding the Communist Infiltration of the Motion Picture Industry: Hearings before the Committee on Un-American Activities, House of Representatives* (Washington, DC: Government Printing Office, 1947), 181–88.

2. Fred Niblo testimony, October 23, 1947, *Hearings regarding the Communist Infiltration of the Motion Picture Industry: Hearings before the Committee on Un-American Activities, House of Representatives*, 189–96.

3. Richard Macaulay testimony, October 23, 1947, *Hearings regarding the Communist Infiltration of the Motion Picture Industry: Hearings before the Committee on Un-American Activities, House of Representatives*, 197–203.

4. Oliver Carlson testimony, October 24, 1947, *Hearings regarding the Communist Infiltration of the Motion Picture Industry: Hearings before the Committee on Un-American Activities, House of Representatives*, 238–80.

5. Robert Montgomery, George Murphy, and Ronald Reagan testimonies, October 23, 1947, *Hearings regarding the Communist Infiltration of the Motion Picture Industry: Hearings before the Committee on Un-American Activities, House of Representatives*, 203–18.

CHAPTER 20: PHIL DUNNE'S STRANGE CRUSADE

1. Philip Dunne, *Take Two* (New York: McGraw-Hill, 1980), 109–10.

2. Ibid., 119.

3. Ibid., 127–28.

4. Each of the nineteen was either an active Communist Party member, a very recent CP member, or an undeviating CP supporter. None had publicly voiced any opposition to Communism or CP activities.

5. In *Bogart* (New York: William Morrow, 1997), A. M. Sperber and Eric Lax tell the story of how for a while Dunne used his neighbor's phone to organize his Committee for the First Amendment. Dunne and his wife, Amanda Duff, had just moved to Malibu, and their phone wasn't yet installed. So Dunne used the phone of his neighbor, Isobel Lennart, who was in New York, while he was putting the CFA together. When Dunne told her of the calls when she returned, her face turned ashen. Dunne thought it was because of the price of the calls. The truth was that Lennart, who was

a Communist at the time, was afraid that Dunne's crusade might be undermined by association with a CP member. See Isobel Lennart testimony, May 20, 1952, *Communist Infiltration of the Hollywood Motion-Picture Industry, Part 8: Hearings before the Committee on Un-American activities House of Representatives* (Washington, DC: Government Printing Office, 1952), 3512–29.

6.   Quoted in Larry Ceplair and Steven Englund, *The Inquisition in Hollywood: Politics in the Film Community, 1930–60* (New York: Doubleday, 1980), 277.

7.   Dunne, *Take Two*, 193–94.

8.   Abraham Polonsky testimony, April 25, 1951, *Communist Infiltration of Hollywood Motion-Picture Industry, Part 2: Hearings before the Committee on Un-American Activities, House of Representatives* (Washington, DC: Government Printing Office, 1951), 395–408.

9.   Ceplair and Englund, *The Inquisition in Hollywood*, 275.

10. Ibid., 277.

11. Dunne, *Take Two*, 197.

12. Advertisement or advertisements including statements from the Committee for the First Amendment and the "Hollywood Nineteen," *Washington Post*, October 27, 1947, p. 14.

13. A. M. Sperber and Eric Lax, *Bogart* (New York: William Morrow, 1997), 354–88; Frank Wilder, "26 Film Folk Fly Here for Probe Protest," *Washington Post*, October 27, 1947, p. 1; and "Communists Probe Denounced on Broadcast," *Daily Variety*, October 27, 1947, p. 7.

14. Wilder, "26 Film Folk," 1.

15. Ibid.

16. Ring Lardner Jr., *The Lardners* (New York: Harper & Row, 1976), 320. Not only were virtually all of the nineteen unfriendly witnesses Communist Party members, but two of the key lawyers that advised them, Ben Margolis and Charles Katz, were CP members as well. Both attorneys would take the Fifth Amendment in hearings before HUAC on September 30, 1952. The Communist influence in the legal profession in the Golden State is attested by the fact that the National Lawyers Guild, named as a Communist front in various government sources, had as its vice president Robert Kenny, a former California attorney general.

17. Ibid., 321.

CHAPTER 21: THE WRITERS SELF-DESTRUCT

1.   Ring Lardner Jr., *The Lardners* (New York: Harper & Row, 1976), 320.

2.   Eric Johnston, "The Citizen before Congress," *Washington Post*, October 27, 1947, p. 8.

3.   Quoted in Gordon Kahn, *Hollywood on Trial* (New York: Boni & Gaer, 1948), 72–77.

4. John Howard Lawson testimony, October 27, 1947, *Hearings regarding the Communist Infiltration of the Motion Picture Industry: Hearings before the Committee on Un-American Activities, House of Representatives* (Washington, DC: Government Printing Office, 1947), 287–304.

5. Quoted in Kahn, *Hollywood on Trial*, 72–77.

6. Dalton Trumbo testimony, October 28, 1947, *Hearings regarding the Communist Infiltration of the Motion Picture Industry: Hearings before the Committee on Un-American Activities, House of Representatives*, 329–42.

7. Albert Maltz testimony, October 28, 1947, *Hearings regarding the Communist Infiltration of the Motion Picture Industry: Hearings before the Committee on Un-American Activities, House of Representatives*, 363–82.

8. Ring Lardner Jr. testimony, October 30, 1947, *Hearings regarding the Communist Infiltration of the Motion Picture Industry: Hearings before the Committee on Un-American Activities, House of Representatives*, 479–86.

CHAPTER 22: PORTENTS OF DISASTER

1. Quoted in Larry Ceplair and Steven Englund, *The Inquisition in Hollywood: Politics in the Film Community, 1930–60* (New York: Doubleday, 1980), 284.

2. Edward Dmytryk, *Odd Man Out: A Memoir of the Hollywood Ten* (Carbondale: Southern Illinois University Press, 1996), 72–76.

3. Philip Dunne, *Take Two: A Life in Movies and Politics* (New York: McGraw-Hill, 1980), 190–208.

4. Eric Johnston testimony, October 28, 1947, *Hearings regarding the Communist Infiltration of the Motion Picture Industry: Hearings before the Committee on Un-American Activities, House of Representatives* (Washington, DC: Government Printing Office, 1947), 305–28.

5. Emmet Lavery testimony, October 29, 1947, *Hearings regarding the Communist Infiltration of the Motion Picture Industry: Hearings before the Committee on Un-American Activities, House of Representatives*, 419–59.

6. Bertolt Brecht testimony, October 30, 1947, *Hearings regarding the Communist Infiltration of the Motion Picture Industry: Hearings before the Committee on Un-American Activities, House of Representatives*, 491–504.

CHAPTER 23: *THE SCREEN WRITER*: RED AS A ROSE

1. Kahn was actually called to testify about his Communist Party membership in 1947 but was spared the ordeal when the Committee cut the hearings short.

2. Richard Collins, "Shooting the Conference," *The Screen Writer*, July 1945, pp. 1ff.

3. Alvah Bessie, "Blockade," *The Screen Writer*, January 1946, pp. 16ff.

4. Howard Koch, "The Historical Film: Fact and Fantasy," *The Screen Writer*, January 1946, pp. 1ff.

5. Larry Ceplair and Steven Englund, *The Inquisition in Hollywood: Politics in the Film Community, 1930–60* (New York: Doubleday, 1980), 250.

6. "Record of Herbert K. Sorrell," *IATSE Informational Bulletin*, November 13, 1945; and John Cogley, *Report on Blacklisting I: Movies* (Washington, DC: Fund for the Republic, 1956), 50–55, 60–68.

7. Cogley, *Report on Blacklisting I*, 60.

8. John Howard Lawson, "Theodore Dreiser Joins Communist Party," *Daily Worker*, July 30, 1945, p. 5.

9. Oliver Carlson testimony, October 24, 1947, *Hearings regarding the Communist Infiltration of the Motion Picture Industry: Hearings before the Committee on Un-American Activities, House of Representatives* (Washington, DC: Government Printing Office, 1947), 242.

10. Ceplair and England, *The Inquisition in Hollywood*, 250.

11. Alfred Hayes, "Lyons Tale: A Report," *The Screen Writer*, April 1947, pp. 18ff.

12. See the coverage of the Motion Picture Alliance founding statement and Sam Wood's press conference in *Daily Variety*, February 7, 1944, pp. 1–5, and Dalton Trumbo, "Samuel Grosvenor Wood: A Footnote," in the June 1945 *Screen Writer*, pp. 22ff. The MPA, Trumbo argued sarcastically, was "promoting morale among the armed forces by forthright opposition to every government agency which sought…to convince the men in uniform that their sacrifices might conceivably result in a better world for themselves and their children." But Trumbo to the contrary, the MPA did *not* trash "Hollywood's war effort by proclaiming it the work of Communists, crackpots and radicals." What the MPA's founding statement *did* say was that "*we resent the growing impression* that this industry [emphasis added]" is made up of such folks. In the news conference launching the MPA, Wood had proclaimed, "We intend to correct that impression immediately." There was nothing in the MPA statement that came anywhere close to denouncing the entire Hollywood war effort.

13. Dalton Trumbo, "Notes on a Summer Vacation," *The Screen Writer*, September 1945, pp. 17–41. See also Eugene Lyons, *The Red Decade: The Stalinist Penetration of America* (Indianapolis: Bobbs-Merrill, 1941), 313. George Seldes, editor of *In Fact*, had once been anti-Soviet, but around 1937 was "far inside the Communist orbit, a regular contributor to Stalin's American press," as Lyons informs readers in *The Red Decade*. *In Fact* proved a vigorous Stalin ally during the war, criticizing virtually any publication or newsman who defended Finland and Poland against their Soviet conquerors. The very popular commentator Lowell Thomas, for instance, was condemned by Seldes in his March 13, 1944, front-page piece as a "reactionary radio newscaster who has always plumped for Finland and smeared Russia."

14. Drew Pearson, one of the most powerful journalists in the country in the 1940s and 1950s, was considered sympathetic toward the Soviet Union during World War II and in the immediate postwar period. He frequently targeted anti-Communist public

figures in his widely read column. Two of his most important legmen, David Karr and Andy Older, were exposed as having been Communists. In diaries that Pearson kept for a decade (1949–59) and that were published after his death, he forgives Karr for what he says were youthful indiscretions and insists he fired Older once he found out he was a Communist Party member. Drew Pearson, *Drew Pearson Diaries, 1949–1959* (New York: Holt, Rinehart and Winston, 1974), 75, 173.

15. Konstantin Simonov, "The Soviet Film Industry: An Analysis by Konstantin Simonov," *The Screen Writer*, June 1946, 17ff.

16. Lyons, *The Red Decade*, 132.

17. Mikhail Heller and Alexander Negric, *Utopia in Power: The History of the Soviet Union from 1917 to the Present* (New York: Summit Books, 1986), 274–76.

18. Mark Kramer, ed., *The Black Book of Communism* (Cambridge: Harvard University Press, 1999), 199–200.

19. John Cogley, *Report on Blacklisting I: Movies* (Washington, DC: Fund for the Republic, 1956), 40–41.

20. Robert Rossen testimony, May 7, 1953, *Investigation of Communist Activities in the New York City Area: Hearings before the Committee on Un-American Activities in the New York City Area* (Washington, DC: Government Printing Office, 1953), 1472–80.

21. Ceplair and Englund, *The Inquisition in Hollywood*, 190–91.

22. *Fourth Report of the Senate Fact-Finding Committee on Un-American Activities in California, 1948: Communist Front Organizations* (Sacramento, CA: California State Senate, 1948), 23–26.

23. Ceplair and Englund, *The Inquisition in Hollywood*, 72.

24. Dorothy Jones, "The Hollywood War Film: 1942–44," *Hollywood Quarterly*, October 1945, p. 15.

25. *Communiqué*, December 1, 1944; March 1945; July 1945.

26. Cogley, *Report on Blacklisting I*, 41.

27. Nancy Lynn Schwarz, *The Hollywood Writers' Wars* (New York: Alfred A. Knopf, 1982), 323.

28. William Pomerance testimony, February 5, 1952, *Communist Infiltration of Hollywood Motion Picture Industry, Part 7: Hearings before the Committee on Un-American Activities, House of Representatives* (Washington, DC: Government Printing Office, 1952), 2377–78.

29. Quoted in Ceplair and Englund, *The Inquisition in Hollywood*, 295.

CHAPTER 24: EMMET LAVERY'S CRITICAL TURNAROUND

1. "Red Beach-Head!," *Hollywood Reporter*, August 20, 1946, pp. 1,4; "Hywd's Red Commisars!," *Hollywood Reporter*, August 21, 1946, pp. 1, 4; "More Red Commisars!," *Hollywood Reporter*, August 22, 1946, pp. 1, 4; W. R. Wilkerson, "My Dear Mr.

Lavery;," *Hollywood Reporter*, September 11, 1946, pp. 1, 4; Wilkerson, "My Dear Mr. Lavery;," *Hollywood Reporter*, September 12, 1946, pp. 1, 4, 6.

2.   Emmet Lavery, "Emmet Lavery's Answer: Screen Writers Guild President Replies to the Reporter's Editor," *Hollywood Reporter*, August 29, 1946, pp. 10–11.

3.   Rupert Hughes testimony, October 21, 1947, *Hearings regarding the Communist Infiltration of the Motion Picture Industry: Hearings before the Committee on Un-American Activities, House of Representatives* (Washington, DC: Government Printing Office, 1947), 129.

4.   Lavery won $30,000 from Rogers and six other defendants in 1951 on the grounds that her remark had irreparably damaged the play in the eye of prospective attendees. When the play debuted on December 9, 1947, *Variety* said it wasn't Red but amounted to nothing more than a "stream of wild mouthings by its central character." The trade publication also predicted it would be "short-lived." "Lavery's Loquacious 'Gentleman' Doesn't Talk B'Way B.O. Lingo," December 10, 1947, p. 1.

5.   Lavery's response (1949), 7–8, to Dalton Trumbo's pamphlet *The Time of the Toad: A Study of Inquisition in America,* in the Trumbo collection at the Wisconsin Historical Society.

6.   Lavery's role in preventing the SWG from backing Sorrell's violent strike against the studios in 1945 was described in the Fund for the Republic's report on blacklisting (John Cogley, *Report on Blacklisting I: Movies* [Washington, DC: Fund for the Republic, 1956], 65). In the Screen Writers Guild, notes the Fund study, "Emmet Lavery, then president, supported by a number of others, had successfully resisted the attempts of certain members of the Board of Directors to involve the union in the strike.... On two occasions, Lavery himself stepped down to break a seven-to-seven tie. At membership meetings, the all-out Sorrell supporters were more decisively beaten. Oliver Garrett denounced a resolution that the Guild support the strike. He traced the resolution to the Communist party line and received general endorsement."

7.   The Guild's Executive Board had been funding the HWM to the tune of $2,500 a year but by mid-1945 was becoming wary of the Mobilization's left-wing direction, explains the Fund for the Republic study (Cogley, *Report on Blacklisting I*). "Lawson and the SWG radicals," note Ceplair and Englund, "vocally defended the HWM, while Lavery and Allen Rivkin believed it was becoming a serious liability to the SWG" and persuaded the Guild to cut off its subsidy. Larry Ceplair and Steven Englund, *The Inquisition in Hollywood: Politics in the Film Community, 1930–60* (New York: Doubleday, 1980), 230.

8.   Lavery's response, 7–8.

9.   Lavery's unpublished article for *The Screen Writer*, circa late October 1947, circulated to SWG members by the All-Guild Committee, in the Trumbo collection at the Wisconsin Historical Society.

10.   Ibid.

11. Ibid.

12. Emmet Lavery testimony, October 29, 1947, *Hearings regarding the Communist Infiltration of the Motion Picture Industry: Hearings before the Committee on Un-American Activities, House of Representatives*, 420, 442.

13. Ibid., 444.

14. Lavery hardly considered his anti-Red activities a "betrayal." He readily admitted in his 1949 response to Dalton Trumbo's *Time of the Toad* that "in the fall of 1947, I most certainly was opposing some of the 'unfriendly writers' in the guild elections." He seemed delighted with the fact that his appearance before HUAC "made conspicuous... the unwillingness of other screen writers to testify" and took pride in showing that there was more than a choice between "the shouting of Congressman J. Parnell Thomas, on the one hand, and the shouting of non-responsive witnesses from Hollywood on the other."

    Even more stunning for one with his liberal credentials, Lavery would also strongly back the Guild "for having consistently refused to take any part of the contempt cases," insisting the Ten's conviction for "contempt"—i.e., not answering—was *not* the same thing as punishing "free speech." The Guild, he noted, was just not prepared to defend "non-responsive" witnesses "on the contempt issue: either on the point of Guild membership or on the question as to alleged membership in the Communist party."

15. All-Guild slate advertisement, *The Screen Writer*, November 1947.

16. "Communist Issue Splits SWG," *Hollywood Reporter*, November 4, 1947, pp. 1ff.

17. "SWG Elects Anti-Red Officers: Gibney Chosen President; All-Guild Slate Sweeps 5 Other Tops into Office," *Hollywood Reporter*, November 20, 1947, pp. 1, 4; "Anti-Reds Sweep 20 of 21 Offices in SWG Election," *Hollywood Reporter*, November 21, 1947, pp. 1-2.

CHAPTER 25: THE BLACKLIST BEGINS

1. *Congressional Record*, 80th Congress, November 24, 1947, pp. 10769–71.

2. Ibid., 10775–76.

3. Ibid., 10778–79.

4. Ibid., 10782.

5. Ibid., 10782–83.

6. Ibid., 10793.

7. "Johnston Blasts '10': Says Industry Must Act on Reds," *Hollywood Reporter*, November 20, 1947, pp. 1, 15. Johnston's speech was also reported in *Daily Variety* ("Johnston Hits Cited Ten; Censor Idea of Hearst Is Condemned," November 20, 1947, pp. 1, 14) and the *Los Angeles Times* ("Johnston Scores Refusal to Testify: Ten Hollywood Figures Did Film Industry Disservice, Executive Says," November 20, 1947, p. 2).

8. "Studios Will Fire 'Hostile 10,'" *Hollywood Reporter*, November 26, 1947, p. 1.

9.   Ibid.

CHAPTER 26: GAME, SET, MATCH

1.   A. M. Sperber and Eric Lax, *Bogart* (New York: William Morrow, 1997), 356–403.
2.   Larry Ceplair and Steven Englund, *The Inquisition in Hollywood: Politics in the Film Community, 1930–60* (New York: Doubleday, 1980), 339–40.
3.   *Lawson v. United States* and *Trumbo v. United States,* decided together on June 13, 1949, by the U.S. Court of Appeals, District of Columbia.

CHAPTER 27: HERB SORRELL AND THE CSU STRIKE

1.   John Cogley, *Report on Blacklisting I: Movies* (Washington, DC: Fund for the Republic, 1956), 61.
2.   Ibid., 61.
3.   Ibid., 63–64.
4.   John Earl Haynes and Harvey Klehr, two widely renowned scholars of American Communism, discovered in the Soviet Comintern archives a crucial document that proved conclusively that Bridges was a secret member of the American Communist Party. He served on the CPUSA National Central Committee under a pseudonym. See John Earl Haynes and Harvey Klehr, "Communists and the CIO: From the Soviet Archives," *Labor History* 35 (Summer 1994), 3
5.   Record of Herbert K. Sorrell, *IATSE Informational Bulletin,* November 13, 1945.
6.   *Third Report, Un-American Activities in California: Report of Joint Fact-Finding Committee to the 57th California Legislature* (Sacramento, CA: California State Senate, 1947), 169–72.
7.   Roy Brewer testimony, October 28, 1947, *Hearings regarding the Communist Infiltration of the Motion Picture Industry: Hearings before the Committee on Un-American Activities, House of Representatives* (Washington, DC: Government Printing Office, 1947), 348–49.
8.   Cogley, *Report on Blacklisting I,* 54.
9.   Ibid., 55.
10.   Ibid., 62.
11.   The Screen Writers Guild, "This Strike Can Be Settled" (advertisement with the Screen Directors Guild), *Daily Variety,* March 16, 1945, pp. 48–49.
12.   Cogley, *Report on Blacklisting I,* 62.
13.   "Support the Strike of the Film Unions!," *People's Daily World,* July 24, 1945, p. 1.
14.   Larry Ceplair and Steven Englund, *The Inquisition in Hollywood: Politics in the Film Community, 1930–60* (New York: Doubleday, 1980), 220–21. Both liberals and conservatives opposed the motion.
15.   Ibid., 221.
16.   "Film Strike Riot Ended by Police," *Los Angeles Times,* October 6, 1945, p. 1.

17.   "Unionists Defy Court on Film Picket Limit," *Los Angeles Times*, October 7, 1945, p. 2.

18.   "Film Strike Riot," 1.

19.   "Unionists Defy Court," 2.

20.   "Film Strike Riot," 1.

21.   "New Strike Crisis Feared: Curb Bands, Order from Biscailuz," *Daily Variety*, October 10, 1945, p. 9.

22.   "Sorrell Defi to Green's Orders: Dozen Injured in Melee at Warner's Entrance: Union Leader Arrested," *Daily Variety*, March 19, 1945, p. 6. The Left loves to portray the Sorrell-led strike as a valiant fight for the workingman against a corrupt IA and the intransigent studios. But several facts are customarily omitted from the Left's retelling of the tale. For one thing, as we have seen, Sorrell called the strike when the dispute was still under consideration by both the War Labor Board and the National Labor Relations Board. He also prodded his members to engage in massive unlawful picketing, resulting in scores of injuries, many of them serious, and the blocking of legal entry to the workplace by willing workers. He was called to task by numerous authorities, including judges, federal officials, newspapers, and the head of the AFL, the labor organization that had chartered the unions belonging to Sorrell's CSU. The War Labor Board chairman, George Taylor, in a wire to Sorrell in March, referred to the work stoppage as "a flagrant disregard of the no-strike pledge to the President and of the procedures established for peaceful settlement of labor disputes in time of war."

Variety reported AFL president William Green's harsh condemnation of Sorrell, including his complete wire to the labor leader:

> I regard strike of workers employed at motion picture studios in Hollywood, which press reports state you have sponsored, as a violation of the no-strike pledge made by the American Federation of Labor to the President of the United States for duration of the war.
>
> It should never have occurred and ought to be terminated at once. Millions of members affiliated with the American Federation of Labor have upheld the honor, integrity, standing and good name of the American Federation of Labor by adhering strictly to its no-strike pledge. You ought to join them by doing likewise.
>
> I officially disavow your strike and call upon you and your associates to cease and desist from using name of American Federation of Labor in any way in connection with your strike, particularly by banners carried by pickets or in advertisements or public statements.
>
> I also call upon you and those on strike whom you represent to exercise good judgment and terminate immediately the unjustified strike

in which you are engaged and take up grievances for adjustment through agency set up for settlement of grievances during existing war emergency.

CHAPTER 28: REAGAN OUTWITS THE REDS

1.   John Cogley, *Report on Blacklisting I: Movies* (Washington, DC: Fund for the Republic, 1956), 67.

2.   Ronald Reagan, *Where's the Rest of Me?* (New York: Duell, Sloan and Pearce, 1965), 167.

3.   Ibid., 169.

4.   The Board of Directors of the Screen Actors Guild took out an ad in the September 19, 1946, *Hollywood Reporter* (p. 7), which read, in part,

> Your Officers and Board of Directors have investigated fully all aspects of the present dispute between the IATSE and the Carpenters Union and have examined the official A.F. of L. position therein. We have made every possible effort to aid in a settlement of this dispute but to no avail.
>
> We find that the present dispute is a jurisdictional one and is so designated by the American Federation of Labor.
>
> No A.F. of L. union is required to take sides and respect picket lines in a jurisdictional dispute between either A.F. of L. unions.
>
> In the best interest of all actors, you are instructed as follows:
>
> IF PICKET LINES ARE ESTABLISHED IN THIS CONTROVERSY, MEMBERS OF THE SCREEN ACTORS GUILD WILL PASS THROUGH THE PICKET LINES AND LIVE UP TO THEIR CONTRACT.

5.   "Actors Urged to Cross Lines: Scores of Stars at Legion Stadium Rally Applaud SAG Board's Recommendation," *Hollywood Reporter*, October 3, 1946, p. 1.

6.   Sterling Hayden testimony, April 10, 1951, *Communist Infiltration of Hollywood Motion-Picture Industry, Part 1: Hearings before the Committee on Un-American Activities, House of Representatives* (Washington, DC: Government Printing Office, 1951), 161.

7.   Ibid., 162.

8.   Cogley, *Report on Blacklisting I*, 73.

9.   *Tenth Report of the Senate Fact-Finding Committee on Un-American Activities, 1959* (Sacramento: California State Senate, 1959), 115.

CHAPTER 29: THE SILENCING OF ALBERT MALTZ

1.   Paul Jarrico testimony, April 13, 1951, *Communist Infiltration of Hollywood Motion-Picture Industry, Part 1: Hearings before the Committee on Un-American Activities,*

House of Representatives (Washington, DC: Government Printing Office, 1951), 274–83.

2. Allan Ryskind, "The Truth about the Hollywood Ten," *Human Events* 54, no. 1, January 2, 1998.

3. American writers in the '30s were told that Soviet writers were not being suppressed. But Schulberg later discovered that scores of literary figures—many of whom he had known—had been murdered or imprisoned under Stalin.

4. Budd Schulberg testimony, May 23, 1951, *Communist Infiltration of Hollywood Motion-Picture Industry, Part 3: Hearings before the Committee on Un-American Activities, House of Representatives* (Washington, DC: Government Printing Office, 1951), 581–624.

5. Edward Dmytryk, *Odd Man Out* (Carbondale: Southern Illinois University Press, 1996), 18–23.

6. Edward Dmytryk testimony, April 25, 1951, *Communist Infiltration of Hollywood Motion-Picture Industry, Part 2: Hearings before the Committee on Un-American Activities, House of Representatives* (Washington, DC: Government Printing Office, 1951), 408–40.

7. Mike Gold, "Change the World: The Road to Retreat," *Daily Worker*, February 12, 1946, p. 6; and Samuel Sillen, "Art and Politics," February 12, 1946, p. 6.

8. John Howard Lawson, "Art Is a Weapon," *New Masses*, March 19, 1946, p. 18.

9. Leopold Atlas testimony, March 12, 1953, *Investigation of Communist Activities in the Los Angeles Area, Part 5: Hearings before the Committee on Un-American Activities, House of Representatives* (Washington, DC: Government Printing Office, 1953), 935–52.

10. Albert Maltz, "Moving Forward," *New Masses*, April 9, 1946, p. 8.

CHAPTER 30: DALTON TRUMBO, COMMUNIST CONFORMIST

1. Bruce Cook, *Dalton Trumbo* (New York: Charles Scribner's Sons, 1977), 230–32, 259–61, and postscripts.

2. Ibid., 268–78.

3. Christopher Trumbo interview with Michele Volansky in Philadelphia Theatre Company's "Playwise Excerpts," undated.

4. Edward Guthman, *San Francisco Chronicle*, March 3, 2005, pp. E1–E2.

5. Dalton Trumbo Papers, Wisconsin Historical Society, box 41, folder 7.

6. Ibid., box 44, folder 2.

7. Ibid., box 40, unnumbered folder.

8. Cook, *Dalton Trumbo*, 148.

9. Trumbo Papers, box 40, folder 9.

10. Larry Ceplair and Steven Englund, *The Inquisition in Hollywood: Politics in the Film Community, 1930–60* (New York: Doubleday, 1980), 59.

11.   Cook, *Dalton Trumbo*, 148.

12.   Dorothy B. Jones, "Communism and the Movies: A Study of Film Content," prepared for John Cogley, *Report on Blacklisting I: Movies*, Seeley G. Mudd Manuscript Library, Princeton University, 136–58.

13.   Trumbo says he began writing *Johnny* in 1938, when pacifism was an "anathema to the American left," suggesting the views it expressed were sincerely held convictions, not Communist propaganda. The facts are, however, that it was published ten days after the Soviet-Nazi Pact and that Trumbo allowed only the Communist Party and the Left to use it for propaganda purposes.

14.   The first excerpt in the series appeared on March 17, 1940, in the *Daily Worker*.

15.   Dalton Trumbo, *Johnny Got His Gun* (New York: Bantam Books, March 1970), 240–43.

16.   Trumbo, *The Remarkable Andrew* (Philadelphia: J. P. Lippincott, 1941), chapters 9 and 10.

17.   As we have seen, the North American Aviation strike in June of 1940, believed to have been instigated and fostered by Communist labor leaders, was ended when President Roosevelt seized the company with federal troops.

18.   This information comes from the FBI files on Trumbo.

19.   On June 30, 1941—eight days after Hitler invaded the USSR—the American Peace Mobilization's National Board submitted to its National Council several recommendations, including the following: "Aid to the people of Great Britain and the Soviet Union and to all people in their fight against Nazi Germany."

The board explained, "Prior to the attack on the Soviet Union, APM faced a world situation in which the principal elements were . . . an imperialist conflict between the British Empire on the one hand and Nazi Germany and Fascist Italy on the other. . . ." With Hitler's attack against the Soviet Union, however, the APM must now "represent the people's interests" and thus calls "for active support of the Soviet Union as well as of all other forces fighting Nazi Germany."

Because the American Peace Mobilization was so identified with the anti-interventionist foreign policy of the Hitler-Stalin Pact period, it changed its name to the American People's Mobilization, demanded American aid to all nations fighting fascism, and called for an economic embargo on Japan. The new APM's executive secretary was the same as the old: Communist Frederick Vanderbilt Field.

CHAPTER 31: FROM PACIFIST TO HOLY WARRIOR

1.   Bruce Cook, *Dalton Trumbo* (New York: Charles Scribner's Sons, 1977), 137.

2.   FBI interview with Trumbo, January 8, 1944.

3.   Edith Anderson, "Great Man Who Calls Himself a Little Man," *Daily Worker*, October 19, 1942, p. 7.

4.   Ibid.

5.   Dalton Trumbo, "Notes on a Summer Vacation," *The Screen Writer*, September 1945, pp. 17–41.

6.   Cook, *Dalton Trumbo*, 163.

7.   Dalton Trumbo, *An American Story*, Dalton Trumbo Papers, Wisconsin Historical Society.

8.   Trumbo Papers, Wisconsin Historical Society, box 40, unnumbered folder.

CHAPTER 32: LILLIAN HELLMAN: SCARLET WOMAN, SCARLET LIES

1.   Lillian Hellman testimony, May 21, 1952, *Communist Infiltration of the Hollywood Motion-Picture Industry, Part 8: Hearings before the Committee on Un-American Activities, House of Representatives* (Washington, DC: Government Printing Office, 1952), 3545–46.

2.   Ibid., 3544.

3.   Ibid., 3546–48.

4.   Joseph Rauh's papers in Manuscript Division of the Library of Congress.

5.   Lillian Hellman, *Scoundrel Time* (New York: Little, Brown, 1976), 45–46.

6.   Ibid.

7.   Rauh's papers.

8.   "Actors Widen Split on Finn Benefits: Special Meeting Expected in Controversy Over Presenting Performances for Fund: Dulzell Criticizes Idea: Too Many Extra Shows Are on Calendar Already, He Says—TMAT Backs Plan," *New York Times*, January 20, 1940, p. 11.

9.   Margaret Case Harriman, "Miss Lily of New Orleans," *New Yorker*, November 8, 1941, pp. 22–33.

10. Hellman's account in *Pentimento* of her stand on Finland "is one of her more disingenuous efforts," writes Carl Rollyson in *Lillian Hellman: Her Legend and Her Legacy* (New York: St. Martin's Press, 1988), 149. She insists she had been in Helsinki for two weeks in 1937, where she observed "giant posters of Hitler pasted to the side wall" of her hotel and attended a "large rally of Hitler sympathizers." Somehow, that point never made it into the American press at the time of the controversy. In fact, there is good reason to believe that she was not even in Helsinki when she claimed to be, as William Wright points out in his biography, *Lillian Hellman* (New York: Simon & Schuster, 1984).

11. Rollyson, *Lillian Hellman*, 146–48.

12. "In Defense of Culture: Call to 4th Congress of League of American Writers," *Daily Worker*, April 5, 1941, p. 7.

13. League of American Writers document, cited in FBI file, LA 100-22366, p. 9; and *Congressional Record*, 80th Congress, 1947, p. 7445.

14. "Russia Acclaimed by Miss Hellman," *New York Times*, March 2, 1945, p. 5 (copy in FBI file on Hellman, 100-28760-A); and Rollyson, *Lillian Hellman*, 235.

15. United Press, "Lillian Hellman, after USSR Trip, Hits Soviet-Baiters," *Daily Worker*, February 2, 1945, p. 8.

16. Richard H. Parke, "Our Way Defended to 2,000 Opening 'Culture' Meeting: Americans against Reds, Not against Peace, Says Norman Cousins at Waldorf Session: But Russian Sets Theme: Atlantic Pact and Atomic Program Attacked by Fadeyev—Briton Warns of War Apathy," *New York Times*, March 26, 1949, p. 1; and Richard H. Park, "Global Unity Call, Cheered by 18,000, Ends Peace Rally: Declaring Soviets Seek Only Friendship, Fadeyev Wins Most Applause at Garden: 2,000 Pickets Boo Outside: Permanent Body for World Amity Links Is Set Up at Earlier Plenary Session," *New York Times*, March 28, 1949, pp. 1, 3.

17. Rollyson, *Lillian Hellman*, 373.

CHAPTER 33: DONALD OGDEN STEWART: HOLLYWOOD REVOLUTIONARY

1. Donald Ogden Stewart, *By a Stroke of Luck!* (New York: Paddington Press, 1975), 213.

2. Ibid., 216.

3. Ibid.

4. Ibid., 222–23.

5. Larry Ceplair and Steven Englund, *The Inquisition in Hollywood: Politics in the Film Community, 1930–60* (New York: Doubleday, 1980), 103.

6. Ibid.

7. Stewart, *By a Stroke of Luck!*, 240.

8. Quoted in Henry Hart, ed., *The Writer in a Changing World* (New York: Equinox Cooperative Press, 1937), 128.

9. Ibid., 124.

10. Stewart, *By a Stroke of Luck!*, 247.

11. Ibid., 276.

12. Ibid., 249.

13. Ibid., 256.

14. Ibid.

15. Ibid., 263.

16. Ibid., 262.

17. Ibid., 276.

18. Ibid., 278.

CHAPTER 34: JOHN HOWARD LAWSON: THE CP'S "GRAND POOH-BAH"

1. Larry Ceplair and Steven Englund, "Lawson's Tumult in Blacklist Era," *Los Angeles Times*, August 21, 1977, p. N46.

2. Gary Carr, *The Left Side of Paradise: The Screenwriting of John Howard Lawson* (Ann Arbor: UMI Research, 1984), 8.

3. Mike Gold, "A Bourgeois Hamlet of Our Time," *New Masses* 11 (April 10, 1934), 29.

4. John Howard Lawson, "Inner Conflict and Proletarian Art: A Reply to Michael Gold," *New Masses* 11 (April 17, 1934), 29–30.

5. John Howard Lawson Papers, Morris Library, Southern Illinois University, collection 16, box 98, folder 7.

6. Martin Berkeley testimony, September 19, 1951, *Communist Infiltration of Hollywood Motion-Picture Industry, Part 4: Hearings before the Committee on Un-American Activities, House of Representatives* (Washington, DC: Government Printing Office, 1951), 1580.

7. Lawson Papers, collection 16, box 98, folder 7.

8. Carr, *The Left Side of Paradise*, 62.

9. John Howard Lawson, "Sec'y Perkins Vague on Terror; B'mingham Cops Jail 'Daily' Correspondent," *Daily Worker*, May 18, 1934, p. 1.

10. Ibid.

11. Berkeley testimony, September 19, 1951, *Communist Infiltration of Hollywood Motion-Picture Industry, Part 4: Hearings before the Committee on Un-American Activities, House of Representatives*, 1590.

12. John Howard Lawson, "Towards a Revolutionary Theatre," *New Theatre*, June 1, 1934, pp. 6–7.

13. Lawson Papers, collection 16, box 98, folder 7.

14. See the sworn affidavit of Rena Vale, *Report, Joint Fact-Finding Committee on Un-American Activities in California to the California Legislature* (Sacramento, CA: California State Printing Office, 1943), 122–75.

15. Berkeley testimony, September 19, 1951, *Communist Infiltration of Hollywood Motion-Picture Industry, Part 4: Hearings before the Committee on Un-American Activities, House of Representatives*, 1590.

16. Rena Vale testimony, July 22, 1940, *Investigation of Un-American Propaganda Activities in the United States, Volume 3, Executive Hearings: Hearings before a Special Committee on Un-American Activities, House of Representatives* (Washington, DC: Government Printing Office, 1941), 1222–23.

17. John Howard Lawson, *Theory and Technique of Playwriting and Screenwriting* (New York: Garland Publishing, 1985), 47.

18. Lawson Papers, collection 16, box 98, folder 7.

19. *Tocsin*, June 1963.

CHAPTER 35: ELIA KAZAN DESERVED HIS OSCAR

1. Elia Kazan, "A Statement," a paid advertisement in the *New York Times*, April 12, 1952, p. 7.

2. Elia Kazan, *Elia Kazan: A Life* (New York: Doubleday, 1989), 453–55.

3. Samuel Sillen, "Elia Kazan Urges Intellectuals in U.S. to Betray Themselves," *Daily Worker*, April 17, 1952, p. 8.

4. Kazan, *Elia Kazan*, 468.

5. Ibid., 500.

6. Ibid., 469.

7. Ibid., 458.

8. Allan H. Ryskind, "Elia Kazan Deserves His Oscar," *Human Events* 55, no. 11 (March 19, 1999), 1.

9. Maureen Dowd, "Streetcar Named Betrayal," *New York Times*, February 24, 1999, p. A21.

10. Robert Koehler, "Stage Light," *Los Angeles Times* (Valley Edition), February 25, 1999, p. 50.

11. Sharon Waxman, "Honor for Elia Kazan Stirs Up Those Blacklisted in McCarthy Era," *Washington Post*, February 25, 1999, p. C1.

12. Elia Kazan written and amended testimony, April 10, 1952, *Communist Infiltration of Hollywood Motion-Picture Industry, Part 7: Hearings before the Committee on Un-American Activities, House of Representatives* (Washington, DC: Government Printing Office, 1952), 2407–14.

13. Kazan came under fire from the bulk of the Hollywood community for naming these eight names. He did also name a few other Communists from the entertainment world, including a late actor, four men connected with Frontier Films (a Communist organization), and four people with the League of Workers Theatres, which Kazan bluntly described as "unquestionably a Communist-controlled group." Kazan's mention of these individuals, however, never became a part of the controversy.

14. Kazan testimony, April 10, 1952, *Communist Infiltration of Hollywood Motion-Picture Industry, Part 7: Hearings before the Committee on Un-American Activities, House of Representatives*, 2407–14.

15. Interview with Gordon reported in Ryskind, "Elia Kazan Deserves His Oscar."

16. Patrick McGilligan and Paul Buhle, *Tender Comrades: A Backstory of the Hollywood Blacklist* (New York: St. Martin's Press, 1997), 2–28.

17. Abraham Polonsky testimony, April 25, 1951, *Communist Infiltration of Hollywood Motion-Picture Industry, Part 2: Hearings before the Committee on Un-American Activities, House of Representatives* (Washington, DC: Government Printing Office, 1952), 405.

18. Ryskind, "Elia Kazan Deserves His Oscar."

19. Ibid.

20. McGilligan and Buhle, *Tender Comrades*, 646.

CHAPTER 36: ARTHUR MILLER—WAS HE OR WASN'T HE?

1. Radio Hanoi, August 22, 1972.

2. Arthur Miller testimony, June 21, 1956, *Investigation of the Unauthorized Use of United States Passports, Parts 3 and 4: Hearings before the Committee of Un-American Activities, House of Representatives* (Washington, DC: Government Printing Office, 1956), 4686.

3. Ibid., 4664.

4. Ibid., 4665.

5. Ibid., 4665–66.

6. Ibid., 4672–75.

7. Ibid., 4684.

8. Arthur Miller, *Timebends: A Life* (New York: Penguin Books, 1995), 407.

9. Elia Kazan, *Elia Kazan: A Life* (New York: Anchor Books, 1989), 414.

10. Miller testimony, June 21, 1956, *Investigation of the Unauthorized Use of United States Passports, Parts 3 and 4: Hearings before the Committee of Un-American Activities, House of Representatives*, 4685.

11. Ibid., 4687.

12. Kazan, *Elia Kazan*, 472.

13. Victor Navasky, *Naming Names* (New York: Viking Press, 1980), 199.

14. Miller, *Timebends*, 329.

15. Ibid., 408.

16. Ibid., 347.

CHAPTER 37: THE CURIOUS CASE OF MICHAEL BLANKFORT

1. Louis Budenz testimony, January 15, 1952, *The Role of the Communist Press in the Communist Conspiracy: Hearings before the Committee on Un-American Activities, House of Representatives* (Washington, DC: Government Printing Office, 1952), 2242–44.

2. Michael Blankfort testimony, January 28, 1952, *Communist Infiltration of Hollywood Motion-Picture Industry, Part 7: Hearings before the Committee on Un-American Activities, House of Representatives* (Washington, DC: Government Printing Office, 1952), 2327–32.

3. Ibid., 2340–41.

4. Ibid., 2341.

5. Ibid., 2348–49.

6. Ibid., 2343.

7. Ibid., 2343, 2363.

8. Ibid., 2345.

9. Ibid., 2347.

10. Ibid., 2348.

11. *Wikipedia*, s.v. "Mother Bloor," http://en.wikipedia.org/wiki/Mother_Bloor.

12. Blankfort testimony, January 28, 1952, *Communist Infiltration of Hollywood Motion-Picture Industry, Part 7: Hearings before the Committee on Un-American Activities, House of Representatives*, 2348.

13. Ibid., 2350.

14. Larry Ceplair and Steven Englund, *The Inquisition in Hollywood: Politics in the Film Community, 1930–60* (New York: Doubleday, 1980), 167–68.

15. "Help Defend Civil Liberties," Civil Rights Congress advertisement, *People's Daily World*, May 2, 1947, section II, p. 3.

16. Evans Carlson, *Twin Stars of China* (New York: Dodd, Mead, 1940), 318.

17. Michael Blankfort, *The Big Yankee* (New York: Little, Brown, 1947), 272.

18. Ibid., 372.

19. Ibid.

20. Victor Navasky, *Naming Names* (New York: Viking Press, 1980), 199.

21. Representative Francis Walter's statement on Blankfort's testimony, January 28, 1952, *Communist Infiltration of Hollywood Motion-Picture Industry, Part 7: Hearings before the Committee on Un-American Activities, House of Representatives*, 2365.

22. Navasky, *Naming Names*, 377.

23. *Wikipedia*, s.v. "Michael Blankfort," http://en.wikipedia.org/wiki/Michael_blankfort.

24. Navasky, *Naming Names*, 378.

CHAPTER 38: REDS ON THE BLACKLIST

1. Larry Ceplair and Steven Englund, *The Inquisition in Hollywood: Politics in the Film Community, 1930–60* (New York: Doubleday, 1980), 366.

2. Ibid., 387.

3. Ibid., 371–72.

4. John Cogley, *Report on Blacklisting I: Movies* (Washington, DC: Fund for the Republic, 1956), 106–7.

5. Howard Da Silva testimony, March 21, 1951, *Communist Infiltration of Hollywood Motion-Picture Industry, Part 1: Hearings before the Committee on Un-American Activities, House of Representatives* (Washington, DC: Government Printing Office, 1951), 119.

6. Cogley, *Report on Blacklisting I*, 107–9.

7. Richard Collins testimony, April 12, 1951, *Communist Infiltration of Hollywood Motion-Picture Industry, Part 1: Hearings before the Committee on Un-American Activities, House of Representatives*, 119.

8. Paul Jarrico testimony, April 13, 1951, *Communist Infiltration of Hollywood Motion-Picture Industry, Part 1: Hearings before the Committee on Un-American Activities, House of Representatives*, 275–77. Apparently Jarrico never chose to say where Collins had committed perjury or to refute the charge that he could not support the United States in a war with Russia. In his interview in *Tender Comrades*, Jarrico devotes just

nineteen words to Collins, insisting that the "most painful betrayal was that of Collins," but never challenges a bit of Collins's account before HUAC.

9. Ibid., 283.

10. Ibid., 269–70.

11. Michael Wilson testimony, September 20, 1951, *Communist Infiltration of Hollywood Motion-Picture Industry, Part 5: Hearings before the Committee on Un-American Activities, House of Representatives* (Washington, DC: Government Printing Office, 1951), 1677.

12. Abraham Polonsky testimony, April 25, 1951, *Communist Infiltration of Hollywood Motion-Picture Industry, Part 2: Hearings before the Committee on Un-American Activities, House of Representatives* (Washington, DC: Government Printing Office, 1951), 405.

13. Cogley, *Report on Blacklisting I*, 137–39.

14. Ibid., 139–41.

CHAPTER 39: REHABILITATING EX-REDS

1. John Cogley, *Report on Blacklisting I: Movies* (Washington, DC: Fund for the Republic, 1956), 112.

2. Ibid., 84–85; and Victor Navasky, *Naming Names* (New York: Viking Press, 1980), 232–38.

3. Cogley, *Report on Blacklisting I*, 85.

4. Ibid., 85–87.

5. Sterling Hayden testimony, April 10, 1951, *Communist Infiltration of Hollywood Motion-Picture Industry, Part 1: Hearings before the Committee on Un-American Activities, House of Representatives* (Washington, DC: Government Printing Office, 1951), 139–44.

6. Ibid., 152.

7. Sterling Hayden, *Wanderer* (New York: Alfred A. Knopf, 1963), 390.

8. Cogley, *Report on Blacklisting I*, 85–88.

9. Navasky, *Naming Names*, 99.

10. Ibid., 91.

11. Phil Dunne, *Take Two: A Life in Movies and Politics* (New York: McGraw-Hill, 1980), 214.

12. Ibid., 215.

CHAPTER 40: RED REMINISCENCES

1. Patrick McGilligan and Paul Buhle, *Tender Comrades: A Backstory of the Hollywood Blacklist* (New York: St. Martin's Press, 1997), 325–50. According to McGilligan, Andrei Zhdanov "intellectually justified and administratively guided the purges of intellectual and cultural figures in the post–World War II era." After a series of

speeches in 1946 and 1947 denouncing cosmopolitanism and worship of things foreign (code words for Jews), Zhdanov arranged expulsions from the Union of Writers in Russia.

> Not long afterward, arrests began, in the end destroying the Soviet Union's Yiddish literature and theater. So great did his influence grow that Stalin himself became jealous and "retired" the theorist-apparatchik, later blaming Zhdanov's early death on a "Jewish doctor's plot." Elsewhere in the world, "Zhdanovism" became synonymous with listing logic-chopping on intellectuals to force them to toe the Party line carefully or face defamation.
>
> Ding Ling, Red China's most famous writer and feminist, resisted Mao's doctrinaire view of "art as a weapon" and became a victim of the Cultural Revolution (pp. 343–44).

2.   Ibid., 199–224.

3.   Ibid., 128–54.

4.   Ibid., 495–539.

5.   Norma Barzman, *The Red and the Blacklist: The Intimate Memoir of a Hollywood Expatriate* (New York: Thunder's Mouth/Nation, 2003), 3–7.

6.   McGilligan and Buhle, *Tender Comrades*, 1–28.

7.   Barzman, *The Red and the Blacklist*, 418.

8.   Ibid., 419.

9.   Ibid., 420.

10.   Ibid., 422.

CHAPTER 41: HOLLYWOOD TODAY

1.   Marc Morano, "Critics Assail Fidel Castro's 'Sickening' Grip on Hollywood Celebs," CNS News, July 7, 2008, http://cnsnews.com/news/article/critics-assail-fidel-castros-sickening-grip-hollywood-celebs.

2.   Human Rights Watch, "Cuba: Fidel Castro's Abusive Machinery Remains Intact: Major Obstacles Remain for Human Rights," February 19, 2008, http://www.hrw.org/news/2008/02/18/cuba-fidel-castro-s-abusive-machinery-remains-intact; and Human Rights Watch, "Cuba," *Human Rights Watch World Report 2014*, January 21, 2014, http://www.hrw.org/world-report/2014/country-chapters/cuba.

3.   Amnesty International, "Cuba: Amnesty International's Human Rights Concerns" (AI Index: AMR 25/003/2007), January 29, 2007, http://www.amnesty.org/en/library/asset/AMR25/003/2007/en/e4deb925-a5fd-4217-85df-1b091cfd5efa/amr250032007en.html.

4.   Bureau of Democracy, Human Rights, and Labor, "2008 Human Rights Report: Cuba," U.S. Department of State, 2008 Country Reports on Human Rights Practices, February 25, 2009, http://www.state.gov/j/drl/rls/hrrpt/2008/wha/119155.htm.

5.   Bureau of Democracy, Human Rights, and Labor, "2008 Human Rights Report: Venezuela," U.S. Department of State, 2008 Country Reports on Human Rights Practices, February 25, 2009, http://www.state.gov/j/drl/rls/hrrpt/2008/wha/119177.htm.

APPENDIX A: THE COMMUNIST PARTY CARDS OF THE HOLLYWOOD TEN

1.   Louis J. Russell testimony, October 27, 1947, *Hearings regarding the Communist Infiltration of the Motion Picture Industry: Hearings before the Committee on Un-American Activities, House of Representatives* (Washington, DC: Government Printing Office, 1947), 296–305.

APPENDIX C: SCRUBBING ROBERT TAYLOR'S NAME

1.   "Dishonors Robert Taylor: Hollywood Powerhouse Besmirches a Patriot," *Human Events*, January 13, 1990, p. 5.

2.   Shawn Pogatchnik, "4 Decades Later, Blacklist Furor Is Rekindled," *Los Angeles Times*, January 1, 1990, p. 6.

3.   Robert Taylor testimony, October 22, 1947, *Hearings regarding the Communist Infiltration of the Motion Picture Industry: Hearings before the Committee on Un-American Activities, House of Representatives* (Washington, DC: Government Printing Office, 1947), 164–71.

4.   Lester Cole, *Hollywood Red* (Palo Alto, CA: Ramparts Press, 1981), 159.

5.   Pogatchnik, "4 Decades Later."

INDEX